# THE
# ROMAN CATHOLIC CHURCH
# IN IRELAND

and the

# FALL OF PARNELL,

1888–1891

The Most Reverend Dr. William J. Walsh
*Photograph by William Lawrence, Dublin*
*Reprinted by permission of the National Library of Ireland*

# THE
# ROMAN CATHOLIC CHURCH
# IN IRELAND

## and the
# FALL OF PARNELL,
## 1888–1891

by
Emmet Larkin

The University of North Carolina Press
Chapel Hill

*Library of Congress Cataloging in Publication Data*

Larkin, Emmet      1927–
    The Roman Catholic Church in Ireland and the fall of
Parnell, 1888–1891.

    Includes bibliographical references and index.
    1. Ireland—Politics and government—1837–1901.
2. Irish question.   3. Parnell, Charles Stewart,
1846–1891.   4. Catholic Church in Ireland—History.
I. Title
DA957.9.L37          322'.1'09415          78-22056
ISBN 0-8078-1352-4

To
MAY McDONAGH

# CONTENTS

# PREFACE

In the first published volume of this work I explained how and why I embarked on writing a history of the Roman Catholic Church in Ireland in the nineteenth century;[1] I will not, therefore, burden the reader again on that score. I have once again adopted techniques of style and scholarly apparatus that are not quite orthodox, and I think it would be helpful to repeat to some extent what I said in my earlier volumes about technique. The richness in the quality and quantity of both the general archival materials and the personal papers of the principal characters in this study is still very impressive. In presenting the evidence, therefore, I have again used a technique that I call "mosaic." The many varied and colored bits and pieces of evidence have been selected and arranged to create a portrait of the Church between 1886 and 1888. There are, I believe, a number of advantages in using the mosaic technique when the materials are appropriate. Because the writing of history can never result in more than a representation of what was "true," a historical portrait in mosaic is perhaps more "realistic" than might at first be supposed. The technique of mosaic allows for the inclusion of a great deal more of the evidence in its original form and contributes, therefore, not only to the immediacy of the actual experience but to the authority of the representation, thereby enhancing the reality of the portrait. In all representations, and perhaps even more so in a mosaic, appreciation has a great deal to do with the proper relationship of the elements to the mind's eye—in a word, the achievement of perspective. If I have been successful, then, in constructing my

1. *The Roman Catholic Church and the Creation of the Modern Irish State, 1878–1886* (Philadelphia, 1975).

[ix]

mosaic, the numerous details should integrate and the various parts should harmonize when the volume is read as a whole.

Because the system of footnoting in this volume is also somewhat unorthodox, I think an explanation to the reader is again in order. Most of the ecclesiastical as well as the lay correspondence quoted here has not been catalogued in any more systematic way than by date. This correspondence, therefore, has been noted in the text simply as K (Kirby), W (Walsh), C (Croke), and so forth, with the dates and correspondents also indicated in the text. The problem of showing a break or omission in any particular letter quoted has been resolved by using the word "then" in parenthetical interpolation: for example, "This Parnell scandal," Walsh informed Croke on November 17, "is a supreme disaster" (C). "If he insists on continuing as Leader," Walsh *then* added, "I apprehend a very ugly struggle," indicates that between the last quotation and the previous one there has been a break in the original text. Sometimes the letter used for the quotation was a copy rather than the original, as is revealed in the designation. For example, if Walsh wrote Croke and the designation is W rather than C, the letter quoted is obviously a copy. If there has been any variation from this procedure, it has been noted. The various abbreviations used for the correspondence quoted are listed on page xv.

In turning to the many obligations I have incurred in the researching and writing of this volume, I must note that there is still no one to whom I am more indebted than the Most Reverend Dr. Donal Herlihy, Bishop of Ferns and formerly Rector of the Irish College in Rome. I also sincerely thank the Most Reverend Dr. Dominic Conway, Bishop of Elphin and formerly Spiritual Director and then Rector of the Irish College in Rome, for all his help and kindness. I am under considerable obligation to the present and late Archbishops of Dublin, the Most Reverend Doctors Dermot Ryan and John Charles McQuaid, respectively, for granting me permission to research in the archdiocesan archives. I once again thank the Most Reverend Dr. Thomas Morris, Archbishop of Cashel, for his permission to read the Croke correspondence on microfilm in the National Library of Ireland. I am also under obligation to the late Bishop of Elphin, the Most Reverend Dr. Vincent J. Hanly, for his permission to read the Gillooly correspondence on microfilm. Both

Dom Mark Tierney, O.S.B., who has arranged and cataloged the Croke papers in the Cashel archives, and Father Kevin Kennedy, archivist of the archdiocese of Dublin, gave me very considerable help, and the late Professor Myles Dillon, of the Dublin Institute for Advanced Studies, kindly allowed me to research in his father's papers. I am still under considerable debt to the late Mina Carney, for all her help and encouragement in the process of researching and writing. To the staff of the National Library, and particularly to its Director, Mr. Ailfred MacLochlainn, I again offer my thanks for their unvarying patience, kindness, and generosity. The late May McDonagh of Hollybank Road, Drumcondra, Dublin, and her family provided me for many years with a home away from home; Mrs. "Mac" was a rare human being, whom one could not help but love, and I have dedicated this book to her.

I acknowledge with gratitude the generosity of The American Irish Foundation in support of this publication.

In conclusion, I must also take this opportunity, inadequate as it is, to thank all those who have had hand or part in the making of this book, and especially the Marquess of Salisbury and the Trustees of the British Museum for their respective permissions to quote from the Salisbury and Balfour papers. I am grateful to the editor of the *Review of Politics*, as well as to *Victorian Studies* and the Trustees of Indiana University, for permission to reproduce portions of articles that appeared originally in their journals. Finally, no one but myself is responsible for the errors that may yet be found in this volume.

# ROMAN CATHOLIC ARCHBISHOPS AND BISHOPS IN IRELAND, 1888–1891

[xiii]

BISHOPS OF THE PROVINCE OF CASHEL

Cork: T. A. O'Callaghan, O.P., 1886–1916
Cloyne: James McCarthy, 1874–93
Kerry: Andrew Higgins, 1881–89
        John Coffey, 1889–1904
Killaloe: Michael Flannery, 1858–91
        James Ryan (Coadjutor), 1872–89
        Thomas McRedmond (Coadjutor), 1890–1904
Limerick: Edward Thomas O'Dwyer, 1886–1917
Ross: William Fitzgerald, 1877–97
Waterford: Pierce Power, 1886–89 .
        John Egan, 1889–91

BISHOPS OF THE PROVINCE OF TUAM

Achonry: John Lyster, 1888–1911
Clonfert: Patrick Duggan, 1872–96
        John Healy (Coadjutor), 1884–1903
Elphin: Laurence Gillooly, C.M., 1858–95
Galway: Francis MacCormack, 1887–1908
Killala: Hugh Conway, 1873–93

# ABBREVIATIONS

| | |
|---|---|
| B | Balfour Papers |
| C | Croke Papers |
| D | Dillon Papers |
| F.O. | Foreign Office Papers |
| G | Gillooly Papers |
| K | Kirby Papers |
| M | Manning Papers |
| O'B | O'Brien Papers |
| S | Smith Papers |
| SY | Salisbury Papers |
| W | Walsh Papers |

# PROLOGUE

This is the story of the second and final phase of the consolidation of the modern Irish state. In creating that state between 1878 and 1886, Charles Stewart Parnell structured two political alliances of crucial importance. The first, the Clerical-Nationalist alliance, was basic to the stability of Parnell's state. This informal concordat between Parnell's Irish Parliamentary Party and the Bishops as a body was arranged in October 1884. The terms of the alliance assured the Bishops that the initiative and control in all educational matters would rest with them, and the Party and its Leader were recognized by the Bishops as the bona fide political medium for decisions on an acceptable solution to the land and Home Rule questions. The second of Parnell's political arrangements, the Liberal-Nationalist alliance, was fundamental to making the Parnellite de facto state as legal as it was real. That alliance was prefigured as early as May 1882 in the so-called Kilmainham Compact, when the then prime minister, William Gladstone, agreed to release Parnell and his followers from jail in return for their political cooperation in Parliament and Ireland. When Gladstone finally opted for Home Rule in 1886 and committed the Liberal Party to that course, the seal was set on an arrangement that was to endure until both the Liberal and Nationalist parties were destroyed in the general election of 1918.

Because the Clerical-Nationalist alliance was as basic to the stability of Parnell's de facto state as the Liberal-Nationalist alliance was necessary to the making of that state de jure by constitutional means, the Conservative government, which succeeded upon Gladstone's failure to pass Home Rule in 1886, made every effort to destroy both alliances. Because those alliances were a function of something even more fundamental, Parnell's de facto state, the Conservative prime minister, Lord Salisbury, in concert with his nephew and chief secretary for Ireland, Arthur Balfour, also attempted to break up Parnellite power by the relentless and systematic application of coercion to Ireland. Parnell, for his part, attempted to protect his alliances, while at the same time maintaining that iron grip on the country on which his de facto control so much depended.

The issue on which the combined conservative assault was joined was the Plan of Campaign. The Plan, which was prompted by two successive bad harvests and a very serious worldwide decline in agricultural prices, was launched by John Dillon and William O'Brien, two of the more prominent members of the Party, in October 1886. Because the Irish tenant farmers as a class would not be able to meet their usual rents and still maintain their current standard of living, the tenants on each estate were advised by Dillon and O'Brien to combine and offer the landlord what they considered a fair rent. If the landlord refused to come to terms, the tenants were to place the proffered rent in the hands of trustees, chosen by themselves, and if the landlord proceeded to evict for nonpayment of rent, the money in trust would be then used to fight the evictions and support those who might be eventually evicted. The Plan further guaranteed that if the tenants' "campaign fund" were not sufficient, the resources of the National League, the Irish Party's political machine in the country, would be used to support the tenants until the landlord came to terms. Finally, the proponents of the Plan warned that anyone who should dare to take the farm of an evicted tenant would be boycotted. Shortly after the launching of the Plan by Dillon and O'Brien, the leader among the Irish Bishops, the archbishop of Dublin, William J. Walsh, publicly declared the Plan to be morally within the Pale. Walsh maintained that because of the unique situation created by the Land Act of 1881, which legalized a system of "dual ownership" between landlord and tenant, the terms "contract" and "private property" had taken on new meanings in Ireland.

The Conservative government naturally viewed the Plan as fundamentally subversive of all society and government and succeeded in

passing a very severe Coercion Act to combat it. While the Plan
initially caused some consternation in the ranks of the Liberals, they
were in the end even more outraged at the coerciveness of the
proposed Conservative remedy, and the result was a strengthening
rather than a weakening of the Liberal-Nationalist alliance. The
effect of the Plan on the Clerical-Nationalist alliance, however,
was both more prolonged and more serious. Lord Salisbury and
his nephew attempted to persuade Pope Leo XIII to condemn the
developing agrarian agitation in Ireland in the light of the doubtful
moral implications of the Plan and Boycotting. They enlisted the aid
of the duke of Norfolk, the premier English Roman Catholic peer,
and his good friend Major John Ross of Bladensburg, an Irish
landlord who was also a Catholic and a Conservative in his politics,
to represent the views of the government at Rome. The pope became
so concerned about the conflicting reports he was receiving on the
state of Ireland that he finally decided, in the late spring of 1887, to
send an apostolic visitor to find out exactly what was happening and
to report directly to Mariano Cardinal Rampolla, his secretary of
state. The pope chose as his visitor one of the most able men in his
service, Monsignor Ignatius Persico,[1] who was fluent in English
and also knew the English-speaking world well. Monsignor Persico,
who arrived in Ireland in early July 1887, spent some six months
touring the country gathering information for his report to Rome.
When Rome did finally condemn the Plan and Boycotting in its
famous Decree of April 1888, the Irish people not only felt that they
had been betrayed by Persico but were outraged at Rome.

The Irish Bishops, cruelly caught between their duty to the pope

1. *Ignatius Persico* (1823–95), missionary and diplomat: Born in Naples; educated by the Jesuits and entered the Capuchin Order, 1839; ordained, 1846; served
as missionary in India, 1846–60; appointed coadjutor to the bishop of Bombay,
1854; returned to Italy because of ill health, 1860; appointed administrator of the
diocese of Charleston, U.S.A., 1867; attended Plenary Synod of Baltimore, 1869,
and Vatican Council, 1870; appointed bishop of Savannah, 1870, and resigned
1872 because of ill health; served on various diplomatic missions, 1873–78; appointed consulting prelate to Propaganda, 1878; appointed bishop of the United
Dioceses of Aquino, Pontecorvo, and Sora, 1879, and resigned 1886 because of ill
health; appointed titular archbishop of Damietta, 1886; appointed papal envoy to
Ireland, 1887; secretary for the affairs of the oriental rite at Propaganda, 1889; secretary of Propaganda, 1891; created cardinal, 1893; appointed prefect of the Congregation of Indulgences and Rites, 1893.

and their loyalty to their people, opted not to enforce the Roman condemnation when it came. They told the pope plainly, in fact, in a joint letter signed by twenty-eight of the thirty Irish Bishops, that they knew more about the Irish situation than either he or his advisers and that the price to be paid for making his will effective in Ireland would be the loss not only of their own power and influence but of millions of Irish Catholics at home and abroad. By refusing to enforce the Roman Decree, the Bishops, in effect, had chosen allegiance to the Clerical-Nationalist alliance rather than to Rome.

By the end of 1888, then, not only were the Liberal and Clerical-Nationalist alliances intact, but, even more significantly, a giant step had also been taken in the consolidating of Parnell's de facto Irish state, for Irish power had been strengthened in relation to the British presence and, furthermore, in the crisis precipitated by the Plan, there had also emerged a genuine constitutional arrangement between the constituent parts of the governing Irish consensus— Leader, Party, and Bishops. In that crisis, the working agreement between the constituent parts was actually transformed into a constitutional system still fundamental to any understanding of the modern Irish political system.

The constitutional system was to be further tested between the end of 1888 and the end of 1890, and it was not to be found wanting. During this period the Conservative government continued its effort to break up Parnellite power in the country by an even more strenuous and rigorous application of coercion. The result, however, was only a further hardening in the temper of the Irish people and a further strengthening of Parnell's de facto control. By proposing, in the summer of 1889, measures for the higher education of Irish Catholics, the government hoped at least to weaken, if not to disrupt, both the Clerical- and Liberal-Nationalist alliances. After the experiences of the Decree, for example, a considerable number of the members of the Irish Party, and particularly the agrarian wing, were very much concerned that the Bishops might be forced, on orders from Rome, to forsake their nationalist allegiance for a government-subsidized college or university for Irish Catholics. Archbishop Walsh, however, quickly spiked all suspicions and fears by declaring that no bargain on the education question could be struck with the Irish Bishops if it involved any abridgment of the aspirations of the Irish people with regard to either the land question or Home Rule.

Between 1888 and 1890, then, the Conservative government's attempts to drive wedges at home and at Rome in the Clerical- and Liberal-Nationalist alliances, as well as its efforts at coercion, were all successfully thwarted. In England, continuing Liberal victories at by-election after by-election were eroding the government's majority, as well as its morale, both in the House of Commons and in the country. The Conservative government was, in fact, staggering toward its end in the summer and fall of 1890, and the prospects for a Liberal victory at the polls in the inevitable general election were never more promising.

At this most auspicious moment in modern Irish history, in November 1890, the consolidated de facto Irish state, the emergent constitutional system, and the Liberal-Nationalist alliance were all suddenly placed in jeopardy by the now well-known revelations in the London divorce court concerning Parnell's relationship with Mrs. O'Shea. In what was certainly the supreme crisis in modern Irish political history, the de facto state, the constitutional system, and the Liberal-Nationalist alliance, all survived the fall and death of Parnell. The governing consensus of Leader, Party, and Bishops, though severely shaken, emerged intact from the crisis. Parnell was deposed and replaced as Leader. The Party effectively limited and eventually contained that large minority in the Party who had sided with Parnell in the crisis. The Bishops were virtually unanimous in declaring against Parnell and succeeded in carrying the great majority of the clergy with them in helping the Party to break Parnellite power in the country. Indeed, of all the many cruel ironies in Irish history, perhaps the cruelest was that the survival of the Irish political system in the Parnell crisis was no small tribute to the man who had done most to create and consolidate it: his system transcended him not only in life but in death.

# I

# THE CLERICAL-NATIONALIST
# ALLIANCE

Provinces and Dioceses of Ireland

# I

# THE CLERICAL-NATIONALIST ALLIANCE
## December 1888–December 1889

The year following the publication of the celebrated Roman Decree condemning the Plan of Campaign and Boycotting was perhaps the worst period in the whole history of Irish relations with the Holy See. The Decree, issued in April 1888, was followed by a letter from the pope to the Irish Bishops in late June, complaining that his Irish children had not received his admonition with that respect and submission due his office as father of the faithful, and further exhorting the Bishops to do their duty in making the Decree effective. The Bishops, however, given the excited and angry state of Irish public opinion, did not dare to attempt to enforce the pope's will as expressed in the Decree. When, in early September, the Bishops received yet another letter from the pope's secretary of state, Cardinal Rampolla,[1] charging that they were wanting both in loyalty and in dutifulness, they had indeed had enough. At their annual general meeting in early October 1888, they decided to send a collective letter to the pope. The letter, which was finally sent

1. *Mariano Rampolla del Tindaro* (1843–1913), diplomat and statesman: Born in Polizzi, Sicily, and educated at Rome; ordained, 1866; Doctor *in utroque jure*, 1870; served in congregation for extraordinary ecclesiastical affairs, 1870–75; appointed counselor in nunciature in Spain, 1875, and chargé d'affaires there, 1876; appointed secretary for the affairs of the oriental rite at Propaganda, 1877; appointed secretary for extraordinary ecclesiastical affairs, 1880; appointed nuncio to Spain, 1882; appointed titular archbishop of Heraclea, 1882; created cardinal, 1887; appointed secretary of state, 1887; appointed secretary of the Holy Office, 1903.

3

off in early December, signed by twenty-eight of the thirty Irish Bishops, was exceedingly strong. In effect they told the pope that they knew more about the situation in Ireland than he did and that they could "not enforce the 'Decree' without jeopardizing both his and their own authority in Ireland." This collective letter obviously had the necessary and intended effect on the pope and his advisers, for they ceased to insist that the Bishops take a strong line on the Plan and Boycotting.

The Bishops, of course, did not immediately realize that their letter had been successful. They continued very wary and suspicious of Rome's intentions, and relations between them and the pope were actually going to grow worse before they became better. Nearly everything that issued from Rome in this period, however innocuous or even well intentioned, was greeted with a jaundiced eye by the Bishops, and even the most absurd rumors, which in other days would have been simply dismissed as ridiculous, were given unusual credence by them. Shortly after William J. Walsh, the archbishop of Dublin and leader among the Irish Bishops, sent off the collective letter, a report was circulated in the press that the pope was so annoyed with the Irish that he had actually refused to bless medals and beads for distribution in Ireland. Archbishop Walsh, who had in recent months been under very great pressure, overreacted and immediately wrote Tobias Kirby, archbishop of Ephesus and rector of the Irish College in Rome.[2] "I have only just time," he reported to Kirby, who also served as the official representative of the Irish Bishops in Rome, "to send Y. G. the enclosed."[3] "It is really very hard on our poor people to have to submit to all this," he went on to complain. "All the Protestant papers to-day print it as you can see in the most prominent type. No one here can venture to contradict it, for with our knowledge of things that have actually occurred, we should shrink from saying that anything is impossible. If *the*

2. *Tobias Kirby* (1804–95), educator and administrator: Born in Waterford, Ireland; entered Roman Seminary of Sant'Appollinare; ordained, 1833; appointed vice-rector of Irish College, Rome, 1836, and rector, 1850; official agent of Paul Cullen, archbishop of Armagh (1849–52) and Dublin (1852–78) in Rome; monsignor, 1860; titular bishop of Lita, 1882; titular archbishop of Ephesus and official agent of Irish hierarchy, 1885; lifelong friend of Leo XIII, with whom he had been a student at the Appollinare.

3. Kirby Papers (K), Archives of the Irish College, Rome.

*authorities* at Rome do not think the matter of sufficient importance to contradict it as most insulting to the Holy See as well as the most obedient and devoted Catholic people in the Church, we cannot help them. Y. G. would I assure you, be *frightened* if you only heard the comments that are now most freely made." "I have often said to Y. G.," he reminded Kirby once again, "that what I most dread is having this country forced into the position now occupied—and apparently without much reluctance—by countries that were once almost as Catholic. Now just imagine what I heard to-day!" " 'If our people showed the Pope,' " he quoted his anonymous observer for Kirby, " 'that they cared as little for his views on politics as his own people have shown him long ago, he would think twice before insulting us in this way. We don't hear of his refusing to bless medals for distribution in Italy.' What is most alarming is that the truth of even the most insulting statements is freely believed." "It is well," Walsh noted soberly in conclusion, "Y. G. should know all this."

Kirby telegraphed Walsh that there was no foundation in the report, adding that it would be contradicted in the *Osservatore Romano*. "I am doing the best I can," Walsh replied on December 22, "in reference to the Roman news. As yet the *Osservatore* with the contradiction has not come to hand" (K). "In the meantime," Walsh then explained, "acting on the telegrams, I arranged for the insertion of an article that, I dare say, will be useful, in the Freeman a few days ago. I assume that Y. G. saw it. It would be well if it appeared in the Roman Papers. I enclose a cutting from the *Catholic Times* of Liverpool. Y. G. will see from it the real state of public feeling." Walsh paraphrased and quoted the article for Kirby: "If the Pope does not openly insult the Irish Catholic race, it is because 'he has *too much prudence*' to speak out in that way!" Walsh then went on to complain not only that the editor of the influential *Moniteur de Rome* was the Roman correspondent of the London *Daily Chronicle*, which was one of the worst offenders in the rumor-mongering about the blessing of the beads, but that the pope knew that he was the London correspondent of that paper. Walsh also charged that the editor of the *Moniteur* was in intimate contact with Abbot Bernard Smith, an Irish Benedictine long resident in Rome, who was influential both there and in high Conservative government circles in London,[4] and that Smith was promoted by the pope "to a most honorable and confidential post since it became fully known at the Vatican that he was the medium through which the press reports defamatory to Ireland got circulation." Walsh declared in conclusion, "The more plainly all this is kept in view, and the more openly and directly it is dealt with, the better it will be for the recovery of the old feeling of our people towards the Holy See."

In an obvious attempt both to calm and to mollify Walsh, Kirby again wrote and telegraphed him that the pope was preparing an "act of Kindness for the Irish Church, and that the Papal communication was on its way." "The newspapers are still at work," Walsh observed cautiously in reply to Kirby on December 28, "so we must hope that this communication will be of a kind to check their proceedings effectually. It will not be easy to do so" (K). He added, thereby explaining what was currently upsetting him,

This constant succession of telegrams and communications all pointing in one direction is doing immense harm. We found, for instance, that it could do no possible good, and might do great harm, if we published the text of the paragraph in the *Osservatore*. There is not one word of sympathy in it from beginning to end—not that mere expressions of sympathy would now go for much—but the *absence* of them, as they cost so little is noticed by all. The tone of the *Osservatore* paragraph was that this gross insult had not been offered to Ireland, and that the people should know that the Pope would not act so to *any* of his children—that is to say, richly as they might deserve it, he would not speak of them so.

"However," Walsh continued pointedly, "God grant that this latest communication may give some indication that the Pope knows that there are two sides to the Irish Question, and that he recognises his duty of speaking out the truth about the rich Catholic oppressors of the poor, as well as about the excesses into which those humble victims of oppression may be led in defending themselves against it.

4. *Bernard Smith* (1812–92), theologian and administrator: Born in county Cavan, Ireland; entered Irish College, Rome, 1834; attended Collegio Romano and ordained, 1839; Doctor of Theology, 1840; entered Benedictine Order and was professed, 1847; was secularized and appointed vice-rector of the Irish College, Rome, 1850; rejoined Benedictines, 1856; professor of theology, College of Propaganda in Rome; rector of San Anselmo, 1868; consultor to various congregations of the Curia (Propaganda, Holy Office, etc.), and official agent of various members of the Irish, American, English, and Australian hierarchies, as well as numerous religious communities, 1856–92; titular abbot of San Calisto in Trastevere, Rome, 1885.

Until *this* is done in some plain and unmistakable way, our poor people will remain in their present firm conviction that the Holy Father is now one of the strongest supporters of their oppressors." "P. S.," Walsh added, "I posted yesterday a strong collective letter on the subject of the Encyclical De Libertate &c &c."

The pope had indeed written a cordial, if ambiguous, letter to his Irish children, but the furthest he would go in reassuring them was to say, "Such is Our affection for you that it does not suffer Us to allow the cause for which Ireland is struggling to be weakened by the introduction of anything that could be justly brought in reproach against it."[5] In the course of his letter he also referred, somewhat indelicately, to those who had purposefully misconstrued his advice to the Irish people in the hope of uprooting their renowned attachment to the Holy See. In a letter covering the pope's, Kirby explained that His Holiness had also promised to send the Irish Church a portion of those gifts he had received from the faithful in honor of his recent jubilee. "The most welcome letter of His Holiness," Walsh reported more enthusiastically on December 30, forgetting for the moment his own sine qua non, "came this morning. It occurs to me that I ought to read it from the pulpit at the thanksgiving devotion in the Cathedral to-morrow, saying a few words to explain its full significance. It is a happy coincidence that the letter which I was able to send a few days ago conveying the dutiful adhesion of our Irish Episcopate to the Encyclical *De Libertate* should have arrived this morning in Rome" (K). "I sent Yr. Grace yesterday," Walsh then reported, in reference to the prayers ordered by Propaganda to offset recent provocative acts directed by the Italian government against the Holy See, "an unrevised copy of a letter I sent out to be read in the Churches to-day explaining the recent decree of the Sacred Congregation about tomorrow's devotions, and also making as plain as I could, the present deplorable position of the Holy See and the Holy Father."

Walsh did, in fact, read the pope's letter at the thanksgiving devotion in his procathedral. He then forwarded the letter from Kirby that had covered the pope's to his colleague Thomas W. Croke, archbishop of Cashel and second only to himself in influence

5. *Irish Catholic* (Dublin), January 5, 1889.

among the Irish bishops, asking him to forward it in turn to their archepiscopal brethren of Armagh and Tuam. In acknowledging to Walsh on January 7, 1889, that he had sent on the letter, Croke observed that Walsh had certainly "made the most" of it.[6] "Indeed," he added candidly, "I think you made too much of it. To be sure, it was, in some respects, friendly and even fervid, and showed as you say some 'heart': but to my mind it was not kind of him, nor diplomatic, nor even true, to say that a false construction was put upon his counsels 'in the *hope* of uprooting that renowned' attachment." "Still," Croke then confessed, "I am not sorry that you glossed it over and glossed over it so adroitly, though I have good reason to know that people generally have taken it 'cum grano salis.' "

"As to the 'munera,' " Croke noted, referring to the pope's promised presents, "he could scarcely have failed to send some, as he had already presented them to other less deserving Churches. And I notice in Dr. Kirby's letter, at first, he meant nothing better for us than beads and medals, and that the more valuable 'munera' were an afterthought, consequent on the explosion of the *beads* incident." "Apropos of that," he added, "I may say, 'en passant,' without venturing an opinion one way or another, that one of the most respectable priests in Munster told me, within the last ten days, that a young priest lately returned from Rome assured him that the Pope refused to bless *his* crosses and beads in the manner and in the words complained of." Turning to another question raised by Walsh in an obvious effort to prevent relations with Rome from growing worse, Croke commented: "An annual deputation of two Bishops to Rome would, I think, give rise to complications, and ultimately do more harm than good. Cardinal Howard proposed it to me some six or seven years ago. In what rotation would they go? Would they go in the order of seniority or would it be a senior and junior together?" "The truth is," Croke declared, "that, in my estimation, our Bishops, as a body, are not staunch enough to stand the test of Roman diplomacy, and to state their case from a thoroughly Irish standpoint and with a view solely to Irish interests and

6. Walsh Papers (W), Archives of the Archdiocese of Dublin, Dublin.

Irish aspirations, regardless of Roman views and Roman tendencies. The envoys—that is some of them—would be apt to ascertain first what was pleasing to the authorities, and then to act and speak accordingly." "God forgive me," he confided, "anyhow, I believe that the only effective weapon against Roman intrigue and Roman political interference in Irish affairs is *fear*, and I believe it has had something to do with latter day developments." In a postscript he then added, more goodhumoredly, "No need to publish this Epistle."

Walsh's letter and his discourse on the recent provocations of the Italian government in the procathedral in Dublin obviously did not give full satisfaction to the Roman authorities. After some thought, Kirby wrote Walsh to complain. Walsh's reply was reminiscent of Croke at his best, nearly ten years before during the Land League crisis. "I am afraid from Y.G.'s letter," he informed Kirby on February 4, "that you have in no way realised the state of feeling in this country about Roman and Italian affairs" (K). "In the letter that I wrote and in my discourse in the Cathedral," he explained patiently, "I went to the very extremity of what is possible. It may be a bad state of things, but it is the truth that just now (since the Persico intrigue with the landlords, and the issuing of the Decree on one-sided and confessedly false information) our people have no sympathy with H.H. in regard to his *temporal* difficulties. It is perfectly plain to us all here that they were originally brought on by downright mismanagement. It is equally plain that by the exercise of the most ordinary tact, they could have been put an end to long ago." "The Irish people did their part and more than their part," Walsh declared, in a bitter reference to the "illegal" recruiting on Irish soil of a brigade to defend the temporal power of the pope in the 1860s. "They were encouraged to do so, although in doing it they were obliged to proceed in direct violation of the law—we heard very little about 'verecundia legum' then—it is thrown in our faces now in the form of an open and public insult at our pilgrimage to the Vatican for the Pope's Jubilee." "But not withstanding every insult of the kind," Walsh added stoically, "our people will do their duty. They will not, however, be moved to go one inch beyond it. What they say, and say with perfect and obvious truth is, that until the Italians themselves, priests and Bishops as well as laymen, make some sort of move in response, as it were, to all that has already been done *ab extra*, we can do no more.''

"As to joint letters," Walsh informed Kirby firmly, "I do not intend to have anything more to do with them except in case of absolute necessity. If the Pope addresses us collectively, we must, I suppose, send him a formal collective reply. When he writes to me individually, I will reply to him individually, and in no other way. Our recent joint letter of protest about his present position, and of adherence to his Encyclical *De Libertate* has been treated in a way that cannot but be regarded as scandalous. Although I sent it by registered letter, I had to write weeks afterwards to know if it had been received!"[7] "Letters from the Bishops of every country in the world, great and small," he complained to Kirby, "are paraded in the *Osservatore Romano*. Our letter sent on the 27th of December, has not up to this been even mentioned in it! So you can see, my dear Lord, that the chances of our taking the trouble of collecting signatures and sending another joint letter just now are not very good ones. All the same, we have to do what we can to keep our poor people in the best respect we can towards the Holy See."

Meanwhile, Denis Pettit, Archbishop Walsh's chaplain and one of Kirby's former students in Rome, had also written his old mentor. "We are all in great excitement," Pettit assured Kirby on January 30, "over the Papal presents on their way here. The Archbishop intends to have them on exhibition for a week or ten days at the College at Clonliffe so that the whole of Dublin may have the opportunity of seeing them" (K). "This most generous act of his Holiness," Pettit concluded rather naively, "has had a most favourable effect on the people and will it is hoped bring them back to the old state of cordial attachment and devotion to the Holy See." Some

7. See Gillooly Papers (G), Archives of the Diocese of Elphin, Sligo, for Walsh to Gillooly, January 26, 1889:

As regards the Papal question, it is really deplorable that we were treated in such a way. I could not, of course, take the Letter in hand until the former document [the collective letter] was sent off. I then got what time I could to put together a general resume of the encyclical *De Libertate*, and threw it into the form of a letter of adhesion with a strong and suitable reference to the existing state of things in Rome. I signed for all, as I was authorised. The letter went registered to Card. Simeoni on the 27th Dec[r]. This day week having lost all patience I telegraphed. On Monday [January 21] came reply "accepi letteras per gratas Pontifici: scribum quam-primum." Nothing since!

two weeks later, however, a much less naive Croke wrote Walsh reporting the news he had just received from Rome. Dr. O'Connell, the rector of the American College in Rome, had seen the *munera* intended for Ireland, Croke warned Walsh on February 15, and had told his informant that "they were worth nothing. The Italians had their pick and choice: we got the refuse" (W). When the presents did finally begin to arrive at the end of the month, Walsh wrote to Kirby on February 29 to explain that they had been delayed at customs because of the duty due on them (K). Between the duty and the shipping charges, Walsh further complained, the cost came to considerably more than a hundred pounds. He expected, however, that though many of the Bishops would grumble a good deal, most of them would reimburse him for their share in the end.

"Six of the cases from Rome," a chastened and enlightened Pettit informed Kirby on March 3, "were opened yesterday at Clonliffe College by order of the Archbishop and the contents arranged in the exhibition hall" (K). "Everyone was struck by the number of the Gifts," Pettit explained, attempting to put the best face on what was simply an embarrassment, "and the fact that they came from the Holy Father made them precious; but I confess that there was general disappointment expressed at the small intrinsic value of the Gifts individually and the exceedingly poor display they made when laid out in the hall. Some of them are disgracefully shabby. There is one set of vestments amongst those allotted to Dr. Croke, which I fear will give him great displeasure. Worst of all it is a green set and is patched all over." "There are two boxes yet unopened," Pettit observed hopefully, "which may retrieve those already opened. The Archbishop is congratulating himself in his good fortune in not having publicly announced his intention to exhibit them. He could not think of doing so now." "My dear Lord Archbishop," Pettit finally confessed sorrowfully to his old rector, "I cannot tell you how much pained I am to write such an account to you. I would not think of doing so if you had not asked me. As much as possible will be made of them in the papers in a general vague way without entering into details."

Nearly a week later, a very sober and much disappointed Archbishop Walsh also wrote Kirby. "As Fr. Pettit has already written to Y.G.," Walsh explained on March 9, "the gifts have arrived. He wrote, it seems, before the last two boxes were opened. At that time, we had decided simply to send them quietly to the various Bishops. As, however, it had got out through a paper called the Irish Catholic that they were to be seen here in Dublin, I thought it better to run the risk of showing them" (K). "So we had them laid out," he added, noting delicately that the collection was not large enough for the exhibition hall, "in the Church of the Diocesan Seminary. There is great dissatisfaction felt by the priests at the shabbiness of the entire collection. What will it be in each diocese when they have not even the advantage of numbers to set them off!" "I am afraid Y.G.," he complained, "when you consented to send them over at all must have had strange notions of the condition of our Irish Church. In the City of Dublin alone we could in 24 hours bring together from the city churches a really fine show of vestments and of altar plate—far exceeding in every respect the whole of this collection taken all together. Still of course, we must do our best. I have induced Canon Daniel, *but only with considerable difficulty* to give a fair account of them in the Freeman." "I had been strongly pressed by a number of our priests," he confided, "to put in a few dozen really good vestments, chalices, &c of our own so as to try in this way to save the Holy Father's reputation. But I feared this could not be kept secret, and then the remedy would be worse than the original evil. One difficulty pressed very much upon me is, that if we act in any way seeming to indicate that we regard them as at all respectable we shall thereby defame this poor Church of ours at Rome. I am afraid that many of the Bishops will be very much annoyed. Still, as I have said, we must make the best of it."

Kirby must have been, indeed, sorely tried in this developing estrangement between the Irish Church and Rome. Some sixty years in the service of Rome and his deep personal attachment to Leo XIII, however, left little doubt where his ultimate loyalty would lie. Furthermore, other information from Ireland was not nearly as one-sided as that presented to him by Walsh. Not only were those bishops who supported and agreed with Walsh more prudent in their letters to Kirby, in that they left most of the home truths to their archepiscopal brother in Dublin, but they were also more discreet in the way they phrased the truth they had to tell. Moreover, those bishops who were opposed to the way in which the agrarian agitation was being conducted, such as Edward Thomas O'Dwyer of Limerick and Pierce Power of Waterford, were more encouraging in their letters to Kirby about the beneficent results of recent action by Rome.[8] Kirby's Roman attachments, as well as his conservative predilections, therefore, must have caused him to give greater weight to the less credible part of his Irish correspondence at this time. His confidence in Walsh's prudence, for example, must have been considerably shaken by a letter he received in late January from the bishop of Cork. "I wish to tell your Lordship an event that happened at the last meeting of the Bishops," T. A. O'Callaghan wrote on January 21, "which I have left pass by and for peace sake have said nothing about it but I may tell you" (K). "Dr. Walsh charged me before all the Bishops," he complained, referring to the October meeting, "that while I was in Rome last year and professing to act with him that underhand I acted against him. He quoted as his authority Cardinal Rampolla. As such [it] is *absolutely false*. I cannot understand why Card. Rampolla should have made such an impression on him or that he should have turned on me so bitterly. I have not said anything about it, nor shall I do so but it will be a lesson to me for the future."

A short time later, Mary A. Carbery, wife of a cousin of Croke's, wrote Kirby a scathing account of the fruits of the Clerical-Nationalist alliance in Queenstown. The occasion for Mrs. Carbery's letter was the recent arrest of William O'Brien[9] by the government, which had precipitated widespread excitement and great indignation among all classes of Nationalists in the country. "On Sunday last," Mrs.

8. See K, January 16 and 30, respectively, for letters from Power and O'Dwyer.

9. *William O'Brien* (1852–1928), Irish Nationalist and politician: Educated at Cloyne Diocesan School; reporter, Cork *Daily Herald*, 1868–76; attended Queen's College, Cork; special correspondent, Dublin *Freeman's Journal*, 1876–81; editor, *United Ireland*, 1881; imprisoned for Land League activities, 1881–82; M.P., Mallow, 1883–85, South Tyrone, 1886, North-east Cork, 1887–92; launched Plan of Campaign with John Dillon, 1886; imprisoned, 1889; rearrested but fled to America, 1890; declared against Parnell's leadership, 1890; returned to Ireland with John Dillon and imprisoned, 1891; M.P., Cork City, 1892–95; founded United Irish League, 1898; joined with Dillon and Redmond in reuniting Irish Party, 1900; M.P., Cork City, 1900–1918; policy of conciliation resulted in Wyndham Land Act of 1903; resigned from Irish Party, 1903, and founded All for Ireland League, 1910; refused to oppose Sinn Fein in the general election of 1918 and retired from public life.

Carbery reported to Kirby on Tuesday, February 5, ''I was one of the congregation at nine o'clock Mass, and to my astonishment heard the officiating clergyman calling on the Congregation to all assemble in the afternoon and denounce the treatment by the Government of Mr. William O'Brien, whom he eulogised in the highest degree'' (K). ''Yesterday the shops were closed,'' she continued;

I went into one to make a purchase, enquired the reason for closed shutters. The young girl informed me they were forced to do it for three days. That was what had been ordered by the Speakers on the previous day (Sunday). She had been present and heard the speakers who were a ''Mr. Healy and Father Barry (the Administrator here) and Father Murphy.'' Now as Mr. William O'Brien has since the recent ''Papal Decree'' showed his contempt for ''our Most Holy Father'' by propagating the ''Plan of Campaign,'' despite every law humane and Divine what are Catholics who love their religion, and whose forefathers have suffered so much in its defence to do? Are we to submit quietly to see those men who by the power derived from Rome—have been ordained priests proclaim in the temples dedicated to Roman Catholic worship that we are to honour those whose glory is that they are the propagators of what the Head of the Church condemns. To my mind, it amounts to practically a ''schism,'' as well as compelling people under the abused name of liberty to submit to a most odious form of tyranny. Our Bishop of Cloyne Dr. MacCarthy (one of the best of men) is I regret to say deaf, and on that account is prevented from knowing much that takes place in his diocese.

Less than two weeks later, the venerable rector of the Irish College in Paris also wrote Kirby a long lament, marked ''*Private*,'' on the Irish Bishops' apparent lack of enthusiasm for their Roman allegiance. ''Is it not sad,'' Thomas McNamara pointed out on February 17, ''that Ireland is not sending like other Churches all over the world addresses under existing circumstances to his Holiness?'' (K). ''I have written to some Bishops with whom I could take the liberty of doing so,'' he reported, ''and in their replies they expressed their regret, but explained that the *people* are so fretted on account of the decrees about the plan of campaign and boycotting that it would be untimely if not worse to make a manifestation of feeling which otherwise they may be credited to cherish. The excuse of going so much with the prevailing agitation was to keep the people in their hands that they might guide and restrain them. It is to be seen now, if instead of doing so they have not allowed themselves to be dragged down the precipice." "Alas," he concluded appropriately, "*facilis descensus Averni.*"

Several days later, Kirby was certainly apprised of the ease of the descent into Hell, when he received on February 23 an undated, anonymous letter from Dublin, expressing a point of view he had not yet heard. "My Lord," his anonymous correspondent wrote, "I suppose you are aware that the Pope and the Vatican Gang have dished themselves in Ireland. No amount of second hand plate will undo the mischief. Stoles and Chalices are good enough in their way but men who are the living temples of the Holy Ghost are much better" (K). "Now you as an Irishman," he charged Kirby, "must know that the homes and bodies of the Irish people have been doomed to fire and sword by an alien unsympathetic Gov$^t$ and its trusty agents the Landlords. When the Irish people asked for protection in their sufferings, they were derided and finally when they resolved to fight for their own and to defend themselves and their wives and helpless little children, the Vatican Gang to propitiate the British Gov$^t$ declare that it is contrary to the true Religion for the Irish people to protect themselves." "The Irish People," he declared—and Kirby must have been scandalised—"told the Pope to go to H—ll and wiped their boots in his lying Rescript and determined to follow their Priests who have never sold them. Little doctor Walsh of this city went over from Ireland with his usual self sufficiency to settle the question. He returned to Ireland after six months without settling anything and with his tail between his legs where it remains still." "It strikes me as curious," he concluded, "that you have never raised your voice when your country was being traduced by the Vatican Gang the paid agents of the British Government. A dog that wont bark is gen'rally hanged or drowned. You can have your choice." "I am," he finally signed himself, "IRELAND FOR THE IRISH AND NO ITALIAN ORGAN GRINDERS."

There is little doubt that the Irish Bishops were correct in their assessment of the temper of the Irish people and that their decision not to enforce the Decree, therefore, was both prudent and wise. The Bishops, however, and especially Walsh and Croke, were so angry at Rome's continued insistence on enforcing the Decree that they did not seem to notice the very subtle change in Roman policy that took place soon after their collective letter reached the pope in early December. This change had two main causes. First of all, Rome was concerned, if not frightened, by the solid phalanx of episcopal and clerical opinion mobilized by Walsh and Croke in their considered refusal to give the Decree any practical effect in Ireland. After their collective letter, for example, Rampolla wrote no more letters in either the pope's or his own name to the Irish Bishops. Instead, the pope wrote a friendly if innocuous letter in late December—at which an oversensitive Croke took unnecessary umbrage—as well as sending the *munera*, which, whatever their intrinsic value, were hardly *intended* as an insult. The second reason for Rome's reconsideration of its policy in Ireland was that the pope and his advisers were sorely disappointed in Lord Salisbury's diplomatic withdrawal after the Decree. The pope had hoped that Rome's demonstration of good will in Ireland would result in the reestablishment of diplomatic relations between the Vatican and the Court of St. James. Given the British coolness, especially after he had risked so much, the pope could hardly be expected to do the British government any more favors, especially in Ireland, where Roman power now appeared to be in as much jeopardy as British.

The pope was, in fact, in an even more awkward position than the one in which he had found himself after his condemnation in 1883 of the Parnell Testimonial Fund. The difference, of course, was that this time he did not have to disengage from the British government, for Salisbury had left him diplomatically in the lurch; but, of even greater importance, the reconstructing of his power and influence in Ireland would in 1889 be much more difficult than it had been in 1883, because by 1889 the Irish Church was resolutely led and strongly united behind Walsh and Croke. Because his gestures in word and deed had not resulted in effecting very much good will in Ireland, the pope wisely decided that the best policy for the time being would be to do nothing. In biding his time, the pope could either look forward to a more favorable opportunity for reconstructing his power and influence in the Irish Church or wait until Walsh and Croke should have proved so difficult for the British government to manage that Salisbury would be forced to seek Rome's aid and counsel once more in the good government of Ireland.

The result of Walsh's and Croke's continuing difficulties with Rome was that they proceeded to commit themselves even more wholeheartedly to the strengthening and maintaining of the Clerical-Nationalist alliance. The greatest danger to that alliance was the agrarian agitation, and their most serious problem, therefore, was how to use their enormous moral and political influence to keep the agitation within legal and constitutional bounds, while at the same time preventing that influence from being further diminished by the new lay leadership that had emerged in the crisis after the Decree. Their double task was eased somewhat at this time by two important considerations. First, Parnell was even more determined than they were, and for his own very good reasons, that the agrarian agitation would remain subordinate to the political side of the movement. Second, the agrarian agitation was very expensive, and the lay leadership simply could not finance it without the support or, at the least, the tacit approval of the clergy.

On January 12, therefore, Archbishop Croke wrote another of those famous letters that over the preceding ten years had made him the idol of the Irish people at home and abroad. The letter, in which he enclosed fifty pounds for the evicted tenants of Donegal, went to Patrick O'Donnell, the bishop of Raphoe; it deserves to be quoted in full:

> The Palace, Thurles
> January 12, 1889
>
> My dear Lord,
>
> The Secretary of the Young Ireland Society, Belfast, sent me, yesterday, a copy of Resolutions passed by that association on the 10th inst in reference to the doings of Messrs Balfour and company in Donegal. The first Resolution affirms that "the scenes enacted in Donegal, under Tory rule, are a shocking violation of the commonest rights of man, and merit the condemnation and censure of the civilized world." The second Resolution expresses, "satisfaction at the manly defence of their homes made by the brave peasants of that historic County against the cruel assaults of felonious Landlordism."
>
> I accept the above Resolutions as a fair if not full embodiment of my views in reference to the poor and unprotected people to whom they refer, and I shall add, moreover, that as far as I know, and I know a good deal about savage as well as civilized countries, there is no land on the face of the habital globe except unhappy Ireland in which such scandalous, heart-rending, and unchristian scenes could take place with any approach to

impunity or without much fierce contention and even bloodshed. Sending the armed forces of the Crown to tear down the rafters and demolish the humble dwellings of the poor, for the benefit of a pampered few appears to me to be sin that cries to heaven for vengeance and surely if Holy Writ has justly consigned to everlasting perdition the heartless creatures who refuse shelter to those that need it, to the homeless stranger whom they could not "take in," what must be thought of our present moralizing Rulers who, far from being content with the negative attitude of non-intervention, bring all the weight of their authority, such as it is, to sanction such guilty excesses, and hold in hand a gang of ruthless desperadoes to carry them into effect?

The sympathies of all good men are with your Lordship and your heroic people in the deadly struggle in which you are engaged, and I pray you to accept from me the enclosed cheque for £50 towards relief of the recently evicted tenants in dauntless Donegal.

I remain my dear Lord—your faithful and devoted servant

+T. W. Croke
Archbishop of Cashel[10]

This letter of Croke's is not only a very good indication of how far that able and courageous man was willing to go in putting heart and fibre into the agrarian agitation; it also shows that he, for one, was fully and openly prepared to continue to uphold the clerical end of the Clerical-Nationalist alliance. Walsh, though substantially and publicly at one with his brother in Cashel, had a more cautious and prudent temperament. The difference is well illustrated by his correspondence with one of the most able, if most conservative, members of the episcopal body, Laurence Gillooly, the bishop of Elphin. About the middle of January, Gillooly wrote Walsh asking his advice on a quarrel that had developed concerning the present year's rent on the French Park estate of Lord de Freyne in his diocese.[11] Gillooly also wrote that he was very upset at a recent provocative speech at French Park by William O'Brien and was thinking seriously of interfering pastorally by publicly instructing his clergy and flock.[12]

In a long reply of January 15, marked "*Confidential*," Walsh admitted that it was hard to say what he would do and then proceeded to explain that, first, he would send for the local representatives of the tenants, individually or collectively, depending on the

10. *Freeman's Journal* (Dublin), January 15, 1889.
11. G, draft, no date [January 14, 1889].
12. See *Irish Catholic*, January 5, 1889, for O'Brien at French Park.

circumstances, and reason the matter out with them in a friendly way (G). He would then point out to the tenants that, whatever the merits of their case, their mode of action made it impossible for the priests to continue in any active participation in the local movement for their protection. Gillooly then should ask them, Walsh advised, "to consider the land and National movements generally, and how much they have been helped by 'the active sympathy and support of priests and Bishops' ''; he should also impress on the local political leaders the gravity of continuing without the clergy.

The tenants would then ask, Walsh warned Gillooly in anticipation, for an alternative policy. "I would earnestly press upon them," Walsh suggested, "the adoption of the course advocated by Mr. Wm. O'Brien in the case of the 'Kenmare' tenantry," that is, arbitration by Scottish or English M.P.'s, two or three chosen from each side, with an impartial umpire; whoever refused to live with the decision would be placed hopelessly in the wrong. Walsh further suggested that the local leaders be asked to consider the case in its purely political or secular aspect. "Dealing with this," he explained to Gillooly most interestingly, "I would, as far as possible, avoid urging the *authority* of the *decree*. (I say this for several reasons, mainly because I see certain difficulties that could be pressed against it, which I certainly should find myself unable to answer; I would therefore keep as clear as possible of any argument from mere authority.)'' It should be argued instead, Walsh maintained, that there was no excuse for exacting a general reduction in rents that was not justified by the merits of the individual cases, for this demand was only the rule of force; and the landlord, moreover, could not be expected to cut the rents of tenants who were fairly well-to-do.

"Now from the way the De Freyne tenants acted last year," Walsh observed, "it is clear that this justification is altogether absent in their case. The net result was that Lord De Freyne had to give in a number of cases the larger reduction he promised to give and, on the other hand, he did not get from the other tenants the rents which they formally undertook to pay. Worked in this way the Plan of Campaign is not far removed from a swindling transaction." He added ironically, "The depositing of rents in the hands of trustees— which though it is a point singled out by Cardinal Monaco, in his unfortunate letter, as one of the grounds of condemnation, is really one of the redeeming points of the system—turned out in their case to be little better than a show. In such a case, I do not see how there can be any second opinion as to the truth of the decision of the Holy Office." "Of course," he reminded Gillooly, "your Lordship recollects that it keeps quite clear of the abstract question. It deals only with the 'Plan' etc *as worked in practice.* I would keep then to this view of the case, waiving, as much as possible, all reference to the consideration of ecclesiastical authority." Walsh further advised Gillooly to make notes of all that he proposed to say and to speak from them as from a brief. Finally, he suggested that Gillooly have these notes published and circulated among the tenants by the priests, but not in the churches if it could be avoided.

Some ten days later Walsh again wrote Gillooly about the situation on the De Freyne estate. "Of course you will understand," Walsh explained on January 26, "this is exclusively for yourself and for your personal guidance merely" (G). "Jn. Dillon,[13] as it happened," he reported, "called here yesterday evening, to see me before his departure for Australia. I am very glad he did so as we had, I think, a very useful conversation on things in general. I had not received your Lordship's letter at the time but I spoke to him about the De Freyne case." "He thinks," Walsh observed, referring undoubtedly to De Freyne's action against his French Park tenants in Bankruptcy Court, "that the recent proceeding of invoking the aid of the 'Star Chamber' procedure puts things beyond all possibility of a settlement. It seems he had written to Mr. John French after he had heard from me about the proceedings being taken

13. *John Dillon* (1851–1927), Irish Nationalist and politician: Educated at Catholic University, Dublin, 1866–74; qualified in medicine, 1875; active in politics, 1876–80; joined Parnell on his American tour, 1880; M.P., Tipperary, 1880; imprisoned for Land League activities, 1881; retired to America for reasons of health, 1883–85; M.P., East Mayo, 1885–1918; launched Plan of Campaign with William O'Brien, 1886; imprisoned, 1888; rearrested but fled to America, 1890; declared against Parnell's leadership, 1890; returned to Ireland and imprisoned, 1891; chairman of Irish Parliamentary Party, 1896–1900; joined with John Redmond in reuniting Irish Party, 1900; prominent in helping to establish the National University in Dublin, 1908; succeeded Redmond as chairman of Irish Party, 1918; defeated in East Mayo in general election of 1918 and retired from public life after the Party was destroyed by Sinn Fein in that election.

merely for the recovery of what was agreed to under last year's settlement. He informed Mr. French that in the circumstances he considered it a case in which the costs should be paid out of the funds of the organization, and that he would see to this if a fair settlement were made for the present year." "I do not know," Walsh confessed, "whether it was to Mr. French or otherwise he then made known his view that the settlement [for the present year] should not be obstructed on the score of the reduction of only 15 per cent to the tenants over £50 valuation. Beyond this, he could not undertake to go. He says to me that he does not believe the tenants below £50 valuation are really able to pay on the terms offered by the landlord. This being so, he cannot advise them to settle on those terms, or in any way dissuade them from combining on their own terms."

Walsh's correspondence with Gillooly illustrates two things— that he would not invoke the authority of the papal Decree but would consider each case instead on its merits, and that Dillon was a free agent whom he both respected and believed was amenable to reason. The cause of Dillon's trip to Australia was, of course, the serious financial difficulties confronting the Plan of Campaign. Dillon had written Parnell on January 14, asking him for £10,000 to carry on the Plan until the receipts from his proposed Australian tour began to come in.[14] He explained that in the previous June the cost of the Plan was £750 per month, but after the papal Decree, evictions were increased and the cost went up to £1,200 per month. Though the expenses had been crushing, Dillon added, the influence of the Decree was no longer felt and he expected expenses would fall. Parnell replied on January 26 that he was expecting a check from Cecil Rhodes and would try to scrape together the £10,000, including some £2,000 recently received from America (D). "But," Parnell warned Dillon, referring to the securities under his control deposited with Messrs. Munroe and Company, an investment banking house in Paris, "I must again remind you that I do not feel justified in selling any more Bonds." "I will carry out your wishes re Sidney & Melbourne," Parnell then promised (Dillon had requested an announcement that he was traveling in Parnell's and

14. Dillon Papers (D), Trinity College, Dublin.

the Party's name), "& if O'Brien starts will also cable America if he desires it."

O'Brien, however, was arrested a few days later and lodged in Clonmel Gaol, where he fiercely resisted the attempt of the authorities to force him to wear prison garb. Dillon feared that, with O'Brien in jail and in delicate health, his own absence just then might precipitate the collapse of the agrarian agitation by leaving it leaderless; and he decided to postpone his departure for Australia. O'Brien managed to smuggle out a short penciled note on February 4 or 5, however, assuring Dillon that he was well and that there was no need for worry about his health. "I beg of you," he pleaded with Dillon, "to go at once. Want of money alone could beat us."[15] Within the week Dillon had set out for Australia, where he remained until the end of the year, collecting some thirty thousand pounds for the Plan of Campaign. Before he left, however, he took the added precaution of calling a meeting of the agrarian wing of the Party in order to ensure that the Plan would not collapse through lack of leadership in his absence. Besides Dillon, ten M.P.'s were present, as well as the indomitable Plan organizer Matt Harris; Dillon had the direct or indirect assurance of support from eleven more M.P.'s and from Alderman Hooper and Thomas Maguire.

"I was in Clonmel, yesterday," Croke reported to Walsh on Monday morning, February 4, from Cashel, "to get authentic information about poor O'Brien. The newspaper accounts are mainly correct. He was treated barbarously, but he is getting on well now in bed, fairly provided with covering, and dreading nothing but another attempt to force the prison clothes on him—which [he] is determined to resist to the death" (W). "Clonmel," Croke then noted, "was full of troops. Of course I did not see O'Brien. I had asked for no such permission as I know it would be refused. But I met the Chaplain and *all* the Catholic Visiting Justices and learned all about the situation that I desired to know." Earlier in the letter, Croke commented on his and Walsh's decision to get up a protest, to be signed by the Bishops, against O'Brien's treatment in prison: "I agree with you fully and had no sooner taken to think over the whole matter, on my way here on Saturday, than I began to see your

15. D, no date, but the envelope containing the note was dated February 5, 1889.

undertaking to send out the *protest* would entail certain inconveniences." Walsh had, in fact, circumspectly arranged that the Lord Mayor of Dublin, Thomas Sexton, should be the initiator, if not the author, of the "protest." "I have not seen this day's *Freeman* yet," Croke then added, "but Sexton wired me the form of *protest*. It was well and judiciously worded, and I cannot conceive how any Irish Bp. could refuse to sign it. I anticipate that *all* signatures will not be to it, as it may not have reached several of their Lordships, for various reasons, such as absence from home &c—It would be well, I think, when all will have had time to have answered—say on Wednesday next—to have it reissued with all signatures to it of those who accepted it." "Then the Non-Signatories," he observed sardonically, "would be duly cornered." "P.S.," Croke then noted, "Have just seen *Freeman*, Protest splendid."

Several days later Croke again wrote Walsh about the need for the clergy to maintain as united a front as possible. Croke's concern on this occasion, however, was not how to keep their episcopal brethren up to the mark, but rather what to do about that most difficult member of the second order of the clergy, Canon Arthur S. Griffin, parish priest of Millstreet, county Cork, in the diocese of Kerry. Griffin, in apologizing for being unable to attend a banquet in honor of the chief secretary, Arthur Balfour, had denounced the agrarian agitation, which he maintained had no regard for life or property. "On consideration," Croke explained to Walsh on February 8, "I think Canon Griffin's letter to the Balfour banquetter should be brought under the notice of the Propaganda" (W). "The Bps and priests," he then declared, "generally sustain this agitation, and believe it to be useful and morally unassailable; and surely a Kerry cleric like Griffin should not be allowed to arraign it, and denounce it, as he has done in the teeth of the Irish Bishops and priests." "*Quid Dicis*?" he asked Walsh, who could hardly have been anxious at this time either to call attention to or to invoke Rome's aid concerning the canon. Walsh undoubtedly suggested to Croke that they should wait a little to see if the canon represented any real threat. Croke replied firmly on February 15, obviously missing Walsh's point completely: "The iron should be struck while hot in Griffin's case. If we wait for a month more, we might as well hold our tongues. *Ten* lines would do" (W). "Things *are* lively in

Paris," he observed, indicating the constitutional crisis threatened by the fall of the Floquet ministry the day before; he added, more significantly as far as Ireland was concerned, "and begin to look so in the London Commission Court."

What Croke was referring to in London was, of course, the special commission set up by act of Parliament the previous summer to inquire into the charges made by the London *Times* in its series of articles entitled "Parnellism and Crime," published in the spring of 1887, and the further charges that subsequently emanated from them. The most notorious of these articles had printed, on April 18, 1887, a "facsimile" letter purportedly written by Parnell, con-doning the murder of T. H. Burke in the Phoenix Park some five years before. When Frank Hugh O'Donnell, journalist and former M.P., sued the *Times* for libel for some references to him in the "P rnellism and Crime" series, the *Times* produced more facsimile letters allegedly written by Parnell, even more damaging than the first. The decision went againt O'Donnell, and the next day, June 6, 1888, Parnell asked in the House for a select committee to inquire into the whole matter of the facsimile letters. For political and tactical reasons, the government was unwilling to grant a select committee but offered eventually a special commission. The commission, with Sir James Hannen as president, assisted by two colleagues, began sitting on October 22, 1888. By February 1889 the *Times*'s counsel, who was also a member of the government in the person of the English attorney general, was completing a review of ten years of Irish crime and disorder; finally on February 20, 1889, he put Richard Pigott, a shady Dublin journalist, in the witness box.

Archbishop Walsh, who had had some correspondence with Pigott immediately before and during the publication of the "Parnellism" series in the *Times*, decided to allow Sir Charles Russell, Parnell's counsel in the commission hearings, to use the correspondence in his cross-examination of Pigott. What the letters proved was that, despite his denial, Pigott had certainly known about the "Par-nellism" series before its publication and that he undoubtedly had some knowledge of the origin of the facsimile letters as well. Under a very skillful cross-examination by Russell, Pigott misspelled the word "hesitancy," which was also misspelled in one of the facsimile letters. When confronted with his correspondence with Walsh, Pigott went completely to pieces in the witness box. The following day, Friday, February 22, Russell completed his melancholy cross-examination by securing Pigott's admission that he had indeed procured the letters for the secretary of the Irish Loyal and Patriotic Union, Edward Caulfield Houston, who had sold them to the *Times*. Russell then destroyed Pigott's credibility as a witness by confronting him with the doubts he had expressed in his correspondence with Walsh about the authenticity of the first facsimile letter published in the *Times*, condoning the murder of Burke. The following day, Pigott signed a full confession, admitting that he had forged the facsimile letters, and then fled the country. Several days later he committed suicide in Madrid.

"I am very glad," Croke congratulated Walsh on Tuesday, February 26, before the news of Pigott's confession or escape had broken, "the *Freeman* has published your correspondence with Piggott [*sic*] in a clear and consecutive shape. It was not easy to see our way through it, and note exactly its significance, as it was presented in the cross-examination of the Arch traitor himself. It has done immense good. I had heaps of letters from him and telegrams, but destroyed them all. Things are beginning to look more cheerful. To-day's Cross Examination of Pigott will I dare say shed additional light on the vile and wicked ways of the *Times* and its supporters" (W). "We have a big ceremony here today, at the Ursulines," Croke apologized in conclusion, "and I can only therefore drop you this hurried line to congratulate you on the important part played by you in the historic drama."

With Pigott's flight and suicide, the full impact of the recent events in the special commission court in London and their significance was finally grasped by the public. "I am sure your Grace was delighted," Denis Pettit wrote Kirby on March 3, at the end of his letter about the arrival of the *munera*, "at the ignominious defeat of the 'Times' and indeed of the enemies of Ireland generally within the last fortnight. The people have great hope that a new era is dawning for the country" (K). "I hope," he concluded, "an era of prosperity will do as little harm to the faith of our poor people as many centuries of poverty & persecution." The following day, the pious bishop of Ardagh, Bartholomew Woodlock, on hearing of

Pigott's suicide, also wrote Kirby. "What an awful tragedy," he noted on March 4, "has this unhappy Commission ended in!! Truly, *'Deus non irridetur: quae omni seminaverit homo, haec et metet.'* That wretched man has been trading all his life on Secret Societies: Fenians &c &c. What a lesson his end ought to teach the dupes of those Societies in Ireland and elsewhere!!''

Another moral, however, was drawn from the Pigott episode by Sir George Errington, an Irish landlord and staunch Unionist,[16] in writing to his old friend and contact in Rome, Abbot Bernard Smith. "All these Pigott affairs," Errington assured Smith on March 6, from the Reform Club in London, "have caused a great sensation. The 'Times' people have behaved in a most foolish & disastrous manner and they will suffer."[17] "The Govt. of course," he observed shrewdly, "is indirectly shaken, but not I think seriously. The misfortune is that these letters have raised a false issue: to us who know the facts concerning Ireland, there is no doubt of the complicity of the Parnellite leaders in the crimes of the agitation, but the question has been confused by the letters & the Pigott forgeries, & the truth thereby obscured."

Although Errington was correct in his observation that the government in London was not seriously shaken by the Pigott episode, the same cannot be said for the Irish administration in Dublin. As the drama began to unfold, the chief secretary for Ireland, Arthur Balfour, did his best to bolster the sagging morale of his subordinates in Dublin. "To a person of cynical mind," Balfour superciliously confided from London to his undersecretary, Sir Joseph West Ridgeway,[18] on February 22, "there is something extremely

16. *Sir George Errington* (1839–1920), Irish politician: Educated at Ushaw and Catholic University, Dublin; nephew of George Errington, titular archbishop of Trebizond; M.P., county Longford, 1874–85; unofficial British representative at the Vatican, 1880–85; baronet, 1885; Gladstonian Home Ruler, 1886–88; joined Liberal Unionists, 1888.

17. Smith Papers (S), Archives of St. Paul Outside the Walls, Rome.

18. *Sir Joseph West Ridgeway* (1844–1930), soldier and administrator: Joined Bengal Infantry, 1860; political secretary to Lord Roberts, 1879; distinguished himself on English commission sent to determine, with Russian commission, the ill-defined northern boundary of Afghanistan, 1884–86; sent to St. Petersburg to continue negotiations, which were successful, 1887; undersecretary for Ireland, 1887–92; governor of the Isle of Man, 1893–95, of Ceylon, 1896–1903; chairman of committee that reported in favor of granting responsible government to Transvaal

entertaining in the present posture of affairs with regard to the Parnell Commission. That the 'Times' has been stupid beyond all that history tells us of stupidity is surprising enough. It is perhaps even more surprising that the results of their stupidity should have spread such dismay among our own people."[19] "The A.G., as you know," Balfour explained, referring to Peter O'Brien, the Irish attorney general, who had lost his nerve, "has been telegraphed for. I shall do my best to cheer him up, and of whatever else he may convince himself, I think I shall make it tolerably clear that the Government are not going out of Office on Piggott [sic] which appears at present to be his settled conviction." Within a week, however, Balfour had to report to Ridgeway that the news of Pigott's flight and suicide had affected Conservative morale even on his side of the Irish sea. "I am very sorry to see," Ridgeway noted on March 2 from Dublin, "that the demoralization here has extended to England. It is a boom which will soon pass away. But while it lasts it is very unpleasant. Here (in the Castle) speculation is keen as to who will be the new Lord Lieutenant. All seem certain that Parnell will be Chief Secretary. If a general election were at hand this might be."[20] "What a state of things," he exclaimed in exasperation, "when the fate of an Empire depends on a Cass or a Pigott! I am sure that if the Parnellites get rope enough, they will spoil their case, they *always* do. They have," he observed urbanely, "no taste." "Luckily," he concluded consolingly, "they have not all the wisdom & self-control of Parnell."

Since the *Times*'s case had been either destroyed or confused in the public mind, depending on the point of view, by the Pigott disclosures, it might have been better from the Parnellite view to allow the whole case to rest there and withdraw from the proceedings in the London commission court. Sir Charles Russell, however, decided not to allow the case to drop and proceeded, instead, to present a rebuttal. Whether this move was really advantageous to his client was then and is now open to serious doubt, because in presenting his rebuttal Russell was admitting, at least implicitly, that

and Orange River Colony, 1906; president, British North Borneo Company, 1910; K.C.S.I., 1886.

19. Balfour Papers (B), British Museum, Add. MS 49827.

20. B, 49809.

the case against "Parnellism" was indeed more, as the supporters of the *Times* had argued and would continue to argue, than the simple question whether the letters published by the *Times* were genuine. Whatever the merits of continuing or not continuing the case, however, Russell opened his rebuttal with a truly magnificent effort. His argument was essentially that, instead of being the authors and instigators of crime in Ireland, Parnell and his Party had, by staunchly defending the right against both the might of irresponsible government and the outrages of "Captain Moonlight" for the past ten years, contributed fundamentally to the peace and good order of that unfortunately oppressed country.

The impact of all this on the Irish clergy was perhaps best summed up by W. H. Murphy, another of Kirby's former students, in a long and very able letter to his old mentor. Murphy, who was then serving as Walsh's private secretary, had been asked by the archbishop to forward the usual dividend for the Irish College funds invested in Dublin. "Having this occasion to write," Murphy explained to Kirby on April 13, "it naturally occurs to me to give your Grace any information that might interest you, and to say that it might be a relief to myself to communicate" (K). "In this latter connection," he confessed, "I will say at once to your Grace—trusting to you to understand the liberty I take—that the whole tenor of events here is calculated to grieve one brought up in Rome, who would most ardently desire to see his own affection for, and confidence in, the Holy See justified to the whole world by facts. But for some time past, by some unhappy fatality, facts have pointed in the contrary direction, and pointed so unambiguously that a person devoted to the Holy See knows not what to say when confronted with them."

"If I refer," Murphy continued, citing the pope's condemnation of some six years before "to the unfortunate letter in the Parnell Testimonial, it is only because the proceedings last week before the Commission in London have reviewed it in the public mind. Your Grace will remember that one of the statements in that ill-omened letter was that crime and outrage were never denounced by the Parnellite Party." "Well, last week, in an English Court," Murphy reported, referring to Russell's opening statement, "before the whole world, there was produced a continuous and relentless denunciation of crime on the part of that same Parnellite Party from its inception down to the present hour. Your Grace will easily understand how painful it must be to hear the Holy See charged with acting on one-sided information; even more, of sacrificing justice to political expediency,—and to be confronted with a fact like the above which makes reply impossible.''

He added:

Then there is another matter which, if I may, I should like to communicate to your Grace.

On the 23rd [*sic*] of last Dec., the Irish Bishops addressed a joint letter to the Holy Father, congratulating him on the service done to the Church by the Encyclical ''De Libertate,'' and protesting against the new penal code [Italian]. The ''Osservatore'' has published similar protests from the Hierarchies of the various countries of the world: the protest from the English, and I believe the Scotch Bishops, have appeared in its columns; latterly it has begun to publish similar documents from individual dioceses —but no notice whatever of the Irish Hierarchy. Your Grace will, I am sure, feel with me that this is a most unfortunate state of things. In the face of it, how is one to reply to the taunt that Rome takes our service, takes our Peter's Pence and other pledges of devotion, but cares nothing for us, and makes it Plain to the whole world how little account she makes of us? I suppose the incident I speak of is due to the oversight of some official, but of course that explanation would be laughed at here. Perhaps at the eleventh hour the mistake might be rectified.

I fear it will be some time before the Irish Bishops address a similar letter to the Holy Father. Again, I should like to say a word about the gifts, as I think it well that your Grace should know what exactly the feeling is. Just after they were sent to the various dioceses, there was a meeting of the Bishops here, and I heard most of the remarks they made concerning the presents. These remarks were uniformly three, and they will strike your Grace as sufficiently significant: blank disappointment, and astonishment that anything so poor should come to the country as a Papal gift; mis-givings as to the effect on the people; the determination when thanking the Pope to say not one word which would imply that the gifts ''in se'' deserved any gratitude. Your Grace will easily imagine how painful all this must be to those who have the feelings uniformly left by education in Rome.

''Your Grace,'' Murphy then apologized, ''will I trust pardon me for writing at such length, and will take what I say in the sense intended. Apart from the relief it is to me to speak thus freely, there may be some hope of doing good by acquainting you exactly with the state of things here. It would be infinitely agreeable to me to give a different account, and I should never be so frank writing to anyone but your Grace, or one thoroughly saturated with the Roman spirit.''

Kirby replied that he certainly took Murphy's letter as it was intended and asked him to forward a copy of the letter written by the Irish Bishops to the pope the previous December. He also obviously gave Murphy an account of Padre Agostino, a preacher who was then making quite an impression at Rome, for in his response to Kirby, Murphy politely found his old mentor's report ''most consoling'' (K). ''The Archbishop,'' Murphy noted of Walsh in his response of April 30, ''is in London at present—in connection with the proceedings of the Commission. The business of the Commission possesses in reality a deep religious interest,—as your Grace has doubtless observed. The character of a Catholic people, the character of a movement in which the Bishops and priests of a country are mixed up, are at stake and the efforts made to show that the Catholic Church here only acted in the spirit of sympathy with the poor and the downtrodden in blessing the movement, is a service rendered to religion.'' In preparing his rebuttal, Sir Charles Russell had asked a number of Irish bishops and prominent priests to appear as witnesses. Among the bishops, Walsh, John MacEvilly, the archbishop of Tuam, and Francis MacCormack, the bishop of Galway, agreed to testify.[21] Croke, however, in spite of an initial request from Parnell and two further requests from Russell, refused to testify, pleading unconvincingly the soreness of the affliction caused by the recent deaths of his brother and sister.[22] Parnell was the first witness called by Russell, beginning his testimony on April 30 and concluding it on May 8, when Walsh was called as the second witness.

''Your note, dated yesterday,'' Croke reported to Walsh on May 2, ''reached me a while ago, and afforded me much pleasure. To begin with, I am delighted to see you at Parnell's side, as your presence must give him courage, and show the enemy besides, that the Irish Church is with him and the Party. I have fairly read over Parnell's evidence. It is good: but I suppose the Attorney General will have a *go* at it, with more or less of success'' (W). ''The truth is,

21. K, MacEvilly to Kirby, May 5, 1889.
22. Croke Papers (C), Archives of the Archdiocese of Cashel, Parnell to Croke, March 12, 1889; Croke to Russell, April 13 and 16, 1889.

so far as I am a judge," he confessed, giving some insight into his real reasons for refusing to testify, "having in view all *I know* of the doings of the party, for the last 10 years, that there is a great deal that Parnell will find it difficult to explain away." "This is but natural," he admitted, "a man fighting a constitutional battle would be more than human if he openly repudiated assistance from other quarters not quite so Constitutionally disposed, especially if he had no valid reason to think, that all his proceedings would be reviewed before a Royal [*sic*] Commission."

"Hence," Croke added, "had I a voice in the matter, after Pigott's flight, I should have thrown up the sponge, and simply challenged the *Times* to connect the Members of the Irish Party with the commission of crime and outrage—65 members are, I believe, supposed to be on trial." "Of these," he enumerated, "40 have had nothing said against them in the course of the investigation, thus reducing the number of incriminated M.P.'s to 25. Harrington and Kenny alone, and, perhaps, Matt Harris have been *directly* and pointedly incriminated—So, I do not well understand what all this fuss is about, seeing that it is now individuals, and not an organisation, that are on their trial." "However," he admitted, "this is all talk. I have not studied the case, and am unfit to give judgment on it." "What Bishops," he asked, "are to give evidence besides yourself?" "I am very much upset," Croke then noted, referring to the bishop of Kerry, "by poor Dr. Higgins' death. I had a great regard for him personally. He was a very honest man, and an excellent Ecclesiastic."

"Welcome home," Croke wrote Walsh again on May 10: "I have read over your evidence in this day's *Freeman*, and congratulate you on it. There are a few points on which I do not fully agree with your expressed opinions. But, on the main, you expressed the orthodox view of things, and did admirably. I still think it would have been better to have no witnesses called, except to exculpate the incriminated M.P.'s and that no attempt should have been made to clear up, justify, or even palliate, much of the sayings and doings of witnesses, or orators, in connection with Land League meetings, or Land League-organs" (W). "O'Brien," Croke maintained, "should answer for United Ireland; T. D. [Sullivan] for Nation *et sic de caeteris*. However, I am but ill informed as to the whole bearing of the case, and would be unwilling to press my peculiar views accordingly. I am very glad you attended the Court so regularly. It must have inspirited poor Parnell, who, making allowances for his very peculiar position, shuffled himself out of difficulties with much cleverness and fair success. Nothing hurtful was brought against him personally anyhow." Croke added, referring to the bishop of Galway, "I see Dr. MacCormac [sic] is on the sod. Is he to be brought forward as a witness?" "Poor Dr. Higgins," Croke then noted again of the late bishop of Kerry, "was swept off very suddenly. We buried him in state. No news here."

Several days later, on May 13, Murphy again wrote Kirby to explain that Walsh had returned from London and was reading Padre Agostino's sermons, which Kirby had sent him, undoubtedly to provide spiritual refreshment after his recent political ordeal. Walsh's statement, Murphy commented, "that he found nothing in the League calling on him to discourage his clergy from joining it made a great impression on the judges" (K). "Your Grace has heard," Murphy then noted, "of the unexpected death of the Bishop of Kerry." "Much interest will attach to the appointment of a successor," he added, alluding to the fact that the late bishop was no warm friend of either the Party or the agrarian agitation, "owing to the bad prominence Kerry has gained, and the connection popularly established between this and the policy of the late Bishop." "I am sure it is not wrong," Murphy boldly maintained, "to say frankly that to appoint a Bishop who should perpetuate the policy of Dr. Higgins would be a grievous injury to religion."

The continuing and increasing committment of Walsh and Croke to the Clerical-Nationalist alliance on the political side was obvious, and, on that side, there was no apparent diminution in their or the Irish clergy's influence. On the agrarian side, however, despite Walsh and Croke's efforts, the clergy in general began to find its influence decreasing. This was nowhere more evident than in the critical policy decisions that had to be made about the conduct and support of the land agitation. Until the early part of 1889 and up to Dillon's departure for Australia, Walsh had been able, as evidenced in his correspondence with Gillooly about the De Freyne estate, to hold his own with the lay Nationalist leadership. After March 1889, however, the tide turned slowly against clerical influence in the land agitation. The turn was not caused by any conspiracy among the laity to dominate the land agitation but was the result mainly of the laity's being forced to take the initiative in organization and fund-raising, because the clergy, high and low, appeared reluctant to take a lead after the Decree was issued.

This new crisis for the clergy in the land agitation was precipitated not by Rome but by Arthur Balfour, in his efforts to break the Plan of Campaign in the spring of 1889. In spite of the demoralization following the Pigott disaster and the consequent shakiness of the government, Balfour continued his policy of supporting landlords in their efforts at eviction, especially on Plan of Campaign estates. Earlier in the year, he had secretly structured a landlord syndicate, to pool the combined resources of a dozen or so wealthy English and Irish landlords and thereby prevent the collapse of those Irish land-lords who were in pecuniary difficulties because of fighting the Plan. The syndicate, with Balfour's secret blessing, launched its operations by taking over financial responsibility for the Ponsonby estate near Youghal in County Cork, because Ponsonby, who had been fighting the Plan for two years, was virtually bankrupt. The syndicate put new heart into the landlords, and those who desired to clear the tenants, especially those on the Plan estates, were given the full support of the Irish administration by Balfour.

"The Colonisation by Protestants of the Masserene Estate," Ridgeway reported to Balfour from Dublin on April 30, adding a new twist to the procedure, "is a serious matter. It is a good thing 'pour encourager les autres' but I would be very reluctant to see the experiment recklessly extended. It might end in a religious war and it certainly would rouse very bitter sectarian feeling, and enrage the Priests. I would hold it over them as a rod in pickle. Louth is a good County wherein to try the experiment—there are so many protestants."[23] "I have sent a special officer," Ridgeway noted in conclusion, "to report on the whole affair, so you will have an opportunity of forming an opinion."

"I am not quite happy," Balfour confessed to Ridgeway by return of post the following day from London, "about our eviction policy.

23. B, 49809.

If we were to remain in office forever, I think your suggestion for making Clanricarde"—the most unreasonable and stubborn of the Irish landlords—"pay for protection unless he behaved like a reasonable being would be most sound, but it is a precedent capable of grave abuse and I am unwilling to set it except after the most careful consideration."[24] He concluded, "Again, though I entirely feel the force of all you say with regard to the difficulties that may arise in cases where Protestant tenants are planted down on the evicted farms of Plan of Campaign estates, I am so keenly alive to the disastrous consequences of allowing the Plan to spread, that I am not sure whether I ought not to encourage this and other such heroic measures as pulling down houses on those estates where the Plan has actually taken hold."

Therefore, when O'Brien was released from jail in early May, the cause of the tenants did not look very bright, and he once again began to press for arbitration on the Plan estates. This was a very clever tactic, especially in view of English public opinion, as the odium of having refused could only fall on the landlords. In general, it is the party that thinks it is winning in a dispute, labor or agrarian, that refuses to arbitrate; and, with the syndicate's resources and the government's new-found resolution, the landlords were now more inclined to fight than to arbitrate. "I had a long conversation yesterday," Balfour informed Ridgeway from London on May 15, "with Robert Olphert, Mr. Kettlewell, Mr. T. W. Russell, and the Solicitor General."[25] "The question to be determined," Balfour explained, with a reference to an English Liberal M.P., "was the answer to be given to a letter of Lefevre's on the subject of Arbitration. Arbitration is a matter which requires delicate handling. It has only been seriously started during the last few weeks by the Nationalists, and obviously for the purpose of securing a colourable victory to the Plan of Campaign, which, at this moment, is not in a flourishing position." "The priests," Balfour summed up shrewdly, "are frightened of the Colonisation scheme—the politicians are nervous about funds." In thus discouraging arbitration, the government proceeded to support evictions on two of the most notorious of the Plan estates—Luggacurren in Queen's County, owned by

24. B, 49827.
25. Ibid.

Lord Lansdowne, and Falcarragh in Donegal, which belonged to Wybrants Olphert.

Dr. J. E. Kenny, M.P., a militant member of the agrarian wing of the Party, reported to Dillon on Tuesday, June 4, from Dublin: "A good fight was made at Luggacurren on the last day of the Evictions, but not on the two previous days, but on the Olphert Estate the fight was first rate, & in one day a dozen or so of the police got ugly cuts etc" (D). "I hope you got a good report," Kenny then noted most significantly, in reference to a motion by O'Brien in the House of Commons: "of Parnell's speech on Willies motion for adjournment re Luggacurren on last Monday week 27 May. It was first rate and amounted practically to an unsaying of his 80 Club speech as far as the 'Plan' is concerned. He wound up by saying that he sent a message that night to every Tenant threatened with unjust eviction that whether under the 'Plan of Campaign' or not under the 'Plan' he promised them all the support in his power to the last farthing of our resources. It created a great impression, and the Tories looked exceedingly glum when they heard him. He seems not perfectly alive to the fact that the 'Plan' is & has been [the] saving of the situation." "I regard his speech," Kenny observed more warmly, "as good as £10,000 to us." "The people," he assured Dillon in conclusion, "are very firm & confident, and don't seem to care a rap for the prosecutions."

Meanwhile, shortly after this speech of Parnell's, Balfour wrote Ridgeway. "I saw Fisher for a moment last night," he reported on May 30, "and he told me that in ten cases out of a total of nineteen the tenants of Luggacurren settled on their landord's terms. This is a most remarkable fact after Parnell's and Wm O'Brien's speeches on Monday night. There is a curious lull in politics both here and in Ireland. I hope it is not a lull that precedes a storm. But there are rumours about (more or less well authenticated) that if the Judges find against the Parnellites"—the many Campaigners and Irish M.P.'s then being tried under the Crimes Act—"they will give up, during the remainder of Parliament, the Constitutional game altogether, and will retire to Ireland and promote a recrudescence of crime and outrage. If there is any truth whatever in these rumours, they are partly satisfactory and partly disquieting. They are satisfactory because they imply the Parnellites are beaten on their present field of battle; they are also disquieting because if the whole strength of the Parliamentary Party is diverted we may have considerable trouble there."[26]

"I am quite sure," Ridgeway replied from Dublin on May 31, "the present lull is artificial but it must last at least until the Commission report which I suppose will not be for 3 or 4 months. Meantime, a good harvest and the rustiness of their machinery, ought to be useful. I do not, however, see how the Parnellites can revive outrages so long as they play the Constitutional game, and they will scarcely give that up unless (1) they are deserted by the Gladstonians or (2) are forced to do so by the Extremists."[27] "Of (1) there is I suppose no chance," he confessed disconsolately, "and (2) will take some time to develop. So I hope that the present lull may *last* for some time." "Have you observed," he then asked Balfour, "how the Co. Court Judges have combined to reduce sentences? Of all that is contemptible in this Country, the Irish Judge is not the least contemptible. There is not one who does not fear the newspapers more than he fears God."

O'Brien, meanwhile, was determined to have no settlements except by arbitration. "The settlement offered to my tenantcy," the Earl of Kenmare explained to Balfour on June 16, "has been rejected in an ultimatum signed by 3 Parish Priests at the dictation of William O'Brien himself & which concluded with these words, 'we now repeat the offer of Arbitration made in behalf of the tenants before Judge Curran on March 26th at Killarney & declared by his Honor to be just & reasonable.'"[28] "The mischievous action of Judge Curran on that occasion," Kenmare complained, naming one of those county court judges complained of by Ridgeway, "has greatly contributed to the lamentable state of things. I have the best reasons for knowing that the tenantcy would gladly have accepted the very liberal terms offered to them had they been able to act as free men. I send you in confidence a letter (which I should be glad to have returned). The writer is thoroughly well informed, & you may rely implicitly upon what he says." "My Lord," L. T. Griffin, who is not to be confused with his namesake, Canon Griffin, had written

26. B, 49828.
27. B, 48909.
28. B, 49845.

Kenmare from the Priory, Killarney, on June 13, "I have ascertained that the refusal to accept the settlement offered to your tenants & the ultimatum in the document & signed by the three Priests that 'only the arbitration originally proposed' would be accepted was dictated by Wm O'Brien himself. At the same time, if the Priests had had the courage to vote for the acceptance of the settlement offered the M.P.'s who sat in council with them here would have given no very strenuous opposition as it is believed by the majority of their party that W. O'Brien made a great mistake in choosing your estate as his weapon for attacking Mr. Balfour."[29] "The action of the Priests in the matter," Griffin then reported, "is explained by the great pressure brought to bear on them by the Moonlighting section of the tenants who do not seem to think the all round abatement of 25 per cent would meet their needs or who have *orders* from *head* quarters not to settle and are underpaying. I think my Lord, you may rely on the correctness of the information about W. O'Brien tho I am precluded from disclosing the source from which I have it."

In early July, O'Brien scored yet another personal triumph when it was formally announced that a new Tenants' Defence League would be formed to meet the challenge of the landlords' combination. On July 15, the Party resolved "That the members of the Irish parliamentary party declare that it is imperatively necessary that the tenant farmers of Ireland should be invited to combine themselves against their attempted extermination by the landlord conspiracy."[30] A Party Committee was then appointed to draw up, under Parnell's guidance, a draft constitution for the new league. "We are in the thick of a big fight here now," Croke had reported to Kirby on July 13, "against the combined Landlords who wish to replant the country with Orangemen, and to chase away our Catholic tenants, on the ground of their unwillingness (that is inability) to pay exorbitant rents. The fight will be a stiff one, but, with God's help, and by keeping within strictly legal lines, we hope to be victorious" (K).

Several days later, Kenny again wrote Dillon, explaining that

29. Ibid.
30. Minutes of Irish Parliamentary Party, July 15, 1889; quoted in Conor Cruise O'Brien, *Parnell and His Party, 1880–1890* (Oxford, 1957), pp. 229–30.

O'Brien was in Portumna, county Galway, putting some back-bone into the local parish priest and the Campaigners on Lord Clanricarde's Woodford estate, who were wobbling on the Plan. Kenny enclosed a very interesting clipping from the *Ballymena Observer*, a provincial newspaper of Tory persuasion. "The Irish question," the *Observer* reported on July 19, "has once more taken a new turn. Mr. Parnell, driven from corner to corner, has at last been forced into the open and his announcement that a Tenants' Defence League will shortly be formed to take the place of all other organisations has created a certain amount of interest."[31] "It is a noteworthy fact," the *Observer* shrewdly pointed out, "that Mr. Parnell has not himself been the medium through which the new departure has been made public. It was only by persistent pressure of the O'Brien wing of the Nationalist party that the silent Leader was forced into giving his consent to what everyone must feel is 'a strategic retreat to the rear.'"

A week later, O'Brien wrote Dillon himself, explaining that the situation in Woodford had indeed been deplorable and that the situation in general was not much better. "The position," he complained on July 24, "was simply untenable unless we could secure money help. I told P[arnell] plainly that he had but two alternatives. If he would take the responsibility of surrender, I would take all the odium on myself & so manage that the tenants would get good terms. But if he wanted the fight to go on, he must openly help us & initiate a fund that would give us £30,000 in addition to the £30,000 we count upon you for" (D). "He appeared to be rather helpless," O'Brien reported, "as to suggestions himself, but said surrender would be fatal & that he was willing to give any help that would not pin him to the Plan. I then proposed to him that while we carried on our Plan as before he should aid us by a non-committal performance pledging him only to fight landlord combinations on all estates where the tenants were willing to accept arbitration. My idea was that he himself should begin the ball by attending a Convention at Thurles or Cork & this he has all but promised to do. The country was never riper for a great Defense Fund, if properly appealed to."

31. D, July 18, 1889. Kenny must have begun his letter on July 18 and kept it open until the following day, when he enclosed the clipping from the *Observer*.

O'Brien reported to Dillon again three weeks later, on August 14, in a long letter marked "CONFIDENTIAL": "Things have reached a crisis between Parnell and myself. Having started the new Tenants Defence League with the assurance that it would be used in supporting the Plan, he now flatly refuses to take any effective steps to put life into it. He first allows me to announce that he will throw himself into the fight and now says he cannot see his way to starting any new movement & will not do anything himself" (D). "I am aware this will not surprise you," O'Brien added, "but I confess that until last night I did not believe him capable of taking advantage of our difficulties to deliberately make the situation intolerable." "I have told you that for several months the weight of undivided responsibility on my shoulders was becoming utterly unbearable. I had absolutely no one except Tom Gill to consult with, all our good men were in jail or disabled." "Those who remained," O'Brien noted interestingly, "were not influential enough to bear up against the constant intrigues for settlements set on foot by the priests. It was only by dint of rushing here and there, & taking people by the throat that I was able to prevent an ignominious surrender on the Clanricarde estate. In my absence, and notwithstanding the exertions of Jack Redmond & Gilhooly, the priests on the Kenmare estate succeeded in making their own terms with Leonard parish by parish." "The Glensharold men," O'Brien maintained, referring to another Plan estate, "were prevented by desperate measures from doing the same." "The Smith Barry [sic] men," he declared, naming the leading spirit in the new landlord syndicate, "were willing to do anything, but they were kept . . . without any hint of what they were [to] do while P. was making up his mind."

"I told him," O'Brien then reported, "I had considered the matter carefully & no longer felt equal to the undivided task of carrying on the new movement in face of his attitude—that it was plain that instead of relieving us, the new League would simply be an additional burden which we were expected to work, while he continued to look on in an attitude of cold apathy. I told him plainly that the moment I could communicate with you, he would have to consider whether we could any longer remain in so intolerable a position. He said with the most brutal frankness that we could not get out of it—that we had got ourselves into it, adding 'you forced me to say that.' '' ''I said,'' O'Brien noted, '' 'I am glad that I forced you to be frank, but I think you will find you are mistaken in supposing that you have us tied to the stake & that you can leave all the responsibility on our heads while you take all the advantages & none of the labour.' '' ''After thrashing the matter fully out,'' O'Brien continued, with a reference to Thomas Sexton, lord mayor of Dublin and one of Parnell's chief lieutenants, ''he would go no further than offering to send Sexton to Tip [to the convention that would inaugurate the new Tenants' League in the country], apparently thinking it was my business to explain why he was not doing anything himself to carry out the programs he deliberately put forward. I told him I should have to consider what my own course should be, & so we parted.''

O'Brien, who was scheduled to be tried again under the Coercion Act the following week and was certain to receive another sentence of two or three months, also explained to Dillon in this long letter that he was determined to play Parnell's silent game by going to jail without appealing or saying anything. He argued that this procedure would at least maintain the status quo until Dillon returned. ''P.S.'' O'Brien added, more optimistically, and unconsciously acknowledging the truth in Parnell's brutal frankness, ''Don't be afraid that there will be any collapse pending your advice. *Our boys will hold the fort.*''

Because a letter to and a response from Australia took almost three months, O'Brien did not receive Dillon's reply, written September 23, until November 11.[32] By that time, the whole situation had been transformed by the launching at the Mansion House, in Dublin on October 25, of a new Tenants' Defence Association.[33] Earlier in October, Parnell had written to the lord mayor of Dublin an open letter that defined the objects of the new association as being protection of the tenants against the landlord conspiracy, upholding of civil liberties, and assertion of the basic trade union right of combination; his letter at the same time very carefully limited, as

32. O'Brien replied to Dillon on November 11, 1889: ''Had he [Parnell] continued to thwart, or was there any reasonable danger of breakdown, I should not have hesitated to give him the definite notice you suggested, but I dare say you are already aware that the situation has so changed for the better that it would be mid summer madness to precipitate an open *esclandre*'' (D).

33. C.C. O'Brien, *Parnell*, pp. 229–30 ff.

the *Irish Catholic* noted approvingly on October 12, "the sphere of action of the new League. It was, we believe, a wise proceeding on the part of Mr. Parnell to circumscribe the sphere of operations of the new League as he has done."[34] "In no way," the *Catholic* added, "will its operations clash with those of the National League, which will continue to discharge its proper functions as the principal political organisation in this country." The Mansion House meeting proceeded to ratify the constitution drafted under Parnell's guidance by the committee of the Party appointed the previous July, which provided for an elected council of fifteen to govern the association. The council, which was elected at the Mansion House meeting, included, significantly enough, fourteen members of the Party and Michael Davitt.

The professed objects and the constitution, however, were all very much democratic window dressing, for the real purpose of the association was to raise funds at home and abroad for the evicted tenants and those threatened with eviction. A series of conventions were, therefore, launched in various parts of the country, beginning in Thurles on October 28 and continuing well into January, to mobilize and to sustain public opinion, while providing the necessary local organization and machinery for the levying of three pence in the pound on the Poor Law valuation of each member of the association. Parnell, it appears, would have nothing to do with the new association, beyond giving it his very nominal blessing in his letter to Sexton and making sure it did not trench on the political side of the National movement. What finally forced him to go as far as he did was the increasing militancy of both the leadership and the rank-and-file of the agrarian wing of the Party, which was given a particular focus in the action in September and October of A. H. Smith-Barry's tenants in the town of Tipperary. Smith-Barry, a director of the landlord syndicate and the man chiefly responsible for saving the Ponsonby estate from surrendering to the Plan, was finally attacked. His tenants, the shopkeepers of Tipperary town, were organized by Plan leaders and became determined enough to decide that, if necessary, they would forsake the old town and build a New Tipperary, rather than pay the rent demanded by Smith-

34. *Irish Catholic*, October 12, 1889.

Barry. In a note from Galway gaol, four days before the Mansion House meeting, O'Brien explained to Dillon, who was still in Australia, why the movement had suddenly taken fire. "P. wd. not budge himself," O'Brien noted on October 21, "but the magnificent action of the Tip Fellows & the resolute pressure of our own best men forced him to go ahead with the Conventions" (D).

Shortly after the first of the conventions was held in Thurles, Walsh wrote Croke asking him what indeed the new association was all about. "Like yourself," Croke replied on October 31, "I have been left completely in the dark as regards the aims and object of the new Association" (W). "The 'patriots' came down here," he noted tartly, "apparently with a one article programme, that, namely, of putting a tax on the Country of $3^d$ in the pound, raising simultaneously the wind in towns and cities. It was close on three o'clock, the day of the Convention, when Father Fennelly, my administrator here, came to me with a slip of paper handed to him by Mr. T. P. Gill, and on which it was written the question as to whether *I* thought Nov 10' or 17' would be a suitable day for holding a general collection throughout the Diocese of Cashel for the new defence League." "I had never heard a word," Croke confided, "about such [a] thing before, though I had spent an hour, or more in conversation with the Lord Mayor, Dr. Kenny, '*et hoc genus omne.*' I directed Father Fennelly to tell Gill & Co. that I could hold no Collection for them in this Diocese, as I had Diocesan Collections on, in November, which I could not displace or postpone. So I believe the Collection has been put off till December." "I can not understand at all," he confessed, "what they are at, or how they mean to carry on the war in future, as contradistinguished for [*sic*] past strategy."

"Tipperary town," Croke went on, "is in a dreadful state of confusion." "S. Barry will ruin the Shopkeepers, and these latter are *going ahead*, daily foolishly imagining that this new Association will bear them indemnified, no matter what may befall them. I had an interview with a few of the ringleaders, about ten days ago, and found them impervious to reason. Sexton begged of me to address a letter to the Convention 'by way of giving it tone.' But I declined to do so." "Still," Croke posed the dilemma for Walsh, "if you and I hold back and do not subscribe to the new League, it will languish and, perhaps, die ignominiously; and it would be thrown in our face that in a critical moment we had abandoned the people and, by our silence, wrecked a project that was designed for their protection and relief. So what is to be done? The thing seems to have hung fire already, as is shown by this day's list in *Freeman*. Write me, again by return.'' If indeed Walsh replied by return post, he was obviously of no mind to come to terms with the new association, at least immediately, especially as the Dublin convention was not scheduled until the middle of December. Croke, however, was in a more awkward position; all eyes were on him because the inaugural convention had taken place in Thurles, and every day's delay was proving more strange. ''I have just posted a letter to *Freeman* on the New Association,'' he explained half apologetically to Walsh over two weeks later, on November 16. ''I could not well have kept from doing so longer. Besides, I am greatly afraid there will be bad work in Tipperary, and I have sounded a note of warning'' (W). ''I subscribe,'' he added, '' £50.''

Sir George Errington alerted Abbot Smith about a week later, on November 24, from London:

You may have seen by the papers that there is a great row going on in Tipperary about Mr. Smith Barry's property. The League has compelled his tenants to refuse him their rents *not because they cannot pay* or that the rents are unfair, but because Smith Barry is [a] Member of a landlord Society which is trying to make the Tenants of a Mr. Ponsonby, in a totally different part of the Country, pay *their* rents!!!! What has this to do with the rents of Smith Barry's tenants? The latter is very rich & means to fight to the death; the tenants are in despair, for they are very well off, and wish to pay their rents, but the league will not allow them. My property is in that neighbourhood, and I fear the example *''cum proximus ordit.''* Dr. Croke, Canon Cahill, & other prominent anti-landlord & anti-rent leaders during these years have now got frightened and tried to restrain the people but they are scouted; in the last few days I heard they have *again* decided to *swim with the stream*!! We always said the Clergy were sowing the Wind and would reap the whirlwind, but I did not think it would come so soon. [S]

At this point the bishop of Limerick, Edward Thomas O'Dwyer, further complicated matters by demanding from the organizers of the Tenants' Defence Association assurances regarding the papal Decree, before he would consent to allow his clergy to attend the convention scheduled for Limerick in early December. The bishop's secretary, Andrew Murphy, wrote on November 29 to John Redmond, who was to chair the Limerick convention: "In reference to the letter addressed to Rev. R. J. Ambrose, and forwarded to the Lord Bishop, I am directed by his lordship to inquire whether he is to understand by the assurance, 'that proceedings at the Limerick Convention will be carried out on the lines of Mr. Parnell's letter to the Lord Mayor,' that there will be no open or covert advocacy of the 'Plan of Campaign,' as it is only on this express condition that he can allow the clergy of the diocese to be present at the Convention."[35]

"In reply to your letter of yesterday," Redmond responded on November 30, "I beg to enclose for the information of his Lordship the Bishop of Limerick a copy of the constitution of the Irish Tenants' Defence Association, from which his lordship will perceive that the Association does not involve or contemplate the advocacy of any particular combination amongst the Irish tenant farmers, but is intended to protect them against attack by combinations of landlords, or by any landlords engaged in any such combinations. As the council," Redmond concluded coolly, "have done me the honour to nominate me as chairman of the Limerick Convention, it will be my duty to secure that the proceedings are conducted in accordance with the constitution."[36]

"I am directed by his lordship the Bishop," Father Murphy replied on Sunday, December 1, "to express his regret that you have not given him the assurance which, as I stated unequivocally in my letter of the 29th ult., was the condition on which the clergy of this diocese can be allowed to attend the Convention on Tuesday next.[37] His lordship," Murphy assured Redmond, "is already familiar with the constitution of the Tenants' Defence Association; but as he presumes that its principles are the same everywhere, he cannot accept them as a guarantee against the open disrespect and disobedience to the supreme authority of the Church teaching of a question of morals, of which members of Parliament and others, at least as reported in the *Freeman's Journal*, have been guilty at several

35. *Freeman's Journal*, December 6, 1889.
36. Ibid.
37. Ibid.

Conventions throughout the country. The 'Plan of Campaign' has been condemned as sinful. That decree beyond yea or nay binds the conscience of every Catholic in Ireland under pain of mortal sin.'' ''If you doubt this,'' Murphy advised, ''take this letter to the Archbishop of Dublin and ask him is it not so. You cannot then think the bishop is going beyond his clear duty when he asks as a condition of allowing his clergy to take part in a Convention, an undertaking on the part of its chairman that he will not allow the 'Plan of Campaign' to be referred to in terms that are inconsistent with the loyal and obedient submission due to the teaching authority of the Church.'' ''His lordship is most anxious that he and his clergy should be able to join the Tenants' Defence Association,'' Murphy added, appearing to soften a little, but really offering Redmond a deadly way out of the dilemma, ''and he will take it as a personal favour on your part if you give him the assurance that he conscientiously requires. In that case, the Convention will pass off smoothly and successfully, and no reference need be made in public to this correspondence. If, then, you desire the attendance of the clergy on these terms, kindly send me as early as possible to-morrow, by telegraph, the one word 'Yes,' and I shall then have the necessary permission sent at once to the clergy.''

''Your letter,'' Redmond telegraphed on Monday, December 2, at six P.M., ''just received. I infer from it that the meaning of my letter of the 30th November has not been fully apprehended.''[38] ''I pointed out therein,'' he noted, ''that the constitution does not include or contemplate the advocacy of any particular plan of combination amongst tenants, and I undertook to use my authority as chairman to keep the proceedings within the lines of the constitution; but you will perceive that it is impracticable for me as a layman to undertake in advance to prevent such references in speeches as might afterward be construed by more competent judges to be inconsistent with the due submission to the teaching authority.'' ''I have undertaken what substantially meets the case,'' Redmond cleverly assured Murphy in conclusion, ''and I cannot undertake what is impossible, namely—the function of determining matters which I am neither authorised nor competent to decide.'' ''Thanks for the telegram,''

38. Ibid.

Murphy replied some three hours later, "which is entirely satisfactory and sufficient."[39]

This correspondence is, of course, extremely important in what it tells about the Clerical-National alliance and the growing sophistication and self-assurance of the lay politicians in their ability to deal with even so able and shrewd a prelate as the bishop of Limerick. While the hand was the hand of the bishop's secretary, the voice was the authentic voice of O'Dwyer himself. He shrewdly attempted to lure Redmond into a "personal favour," which would have secured for him the precedent of dealing with the Irish Party as an individual bishop and would, in turn, have further threatened the unity of the episcopal body, so jealously guarded by Walsh and Croke in their contest with Rome. The self-assurance and sophistication of the lay politicians was made public when the *Freeman's Journal* provoked O'Dwyer, in a leading article on the Limerick convention, into making a public reference to the correspondence, which then allowed Redmond to publish it. "Under all the circumstances," the *Freeman's Journal* noted archly on December 6, "we cannot help congratulating Mr. Redmond on his part in the correspondence. He had a difficult and delicate task. He had to refuse the request of a Bishop, who stands alone among the members of the Hierarchy in his active hostility to the agrarian and National movement, and he had to do so without giving offence. He had to remember that if he offended Dr. O'Dwyer's susceptibilities he endangered the opportunity of priests of the diocese to be with their people at the Convention. This difficulty was most successfully overcome by Mr. Redmond's skill and adroitness."[40]

Walsh, meanwhile, was faced with the problem of dealing with Dublin's forthcoming convention of the new association, scheduled for early December. He considered whether indeed the boldest course might not prove to be the safest: perhaps he should address the delegates in person, rather than simply send his customary assurances and greetings. What appeared to concern him the most was whether his clergy would follow suit if he took the lead. A poor attendance of the Dublin clergy at the convention, with their archbishop on the platform, would be nothing less than a disaster for the

39. Ibid.
40. Ibid.

Clerical-Nationalist alliance. Walsh, therefore, wrote Croke asking advice. "Your appearance at the Dublin Convention," Croke assured him on December 7, "would do a great deal of good, and form a new departure. If it were known amongst the Dublin priests, dignitaries included, it would have the effect of bringing a swarm of them around you. Anyhow, I'm quite sure there will be a fair muster of the cloth" (W). With Croke's encouragement, Walsh did appear in person at the Dublin Convention on December 11 and, in the presence of a large number of clergy, addressed the delegates on the land question.[41] In a very able presentation, he emphasized that the principle of "dual ownership" of landed property in Ireland had been established by Gladstone's Land Act of 1881, so that the terms "property" and "contract" no longer had the same meaning in Ireland as in England or elsewhere. Given the uniqueness of the Irish situation, therefore, the ordinary norms and laws were not necessarily applicable.

No one was more aware at this time just how true Walsh's words were than the redoubtable archbishop of Cashel. "The Tipperary trouble," Croke had added in his letter of December 7 to Walsh, "is daily growing greater. It forms a phenomenal chapter in Irish history. I was not at all prepared for such self abnegation and heroic defiance as the people are showing there. It is refreshing, though in a sense to be deplored. The fine old town may disappear, but a new one is sure to rise beside its ruins" (W). "Such," he concluded soberly, "is the project."

Two weeks later, however, one of Croke's priests, James J. Ryan, of St. Patrick's College in Thurles, was a good deal more pessimistic about the trouble in Tipperary. "Here at home," he confessed, in writing Kirby for Christmas on December 21, "we are still in a state of unrest and anxiety. This country which throughout the period of agitation was singularly free from disturbance, is now the battleground of a fierce struggle between the Landlord eviction syndicate & the people. Already the once flourishing town of Tipperary is, by half, reduced to ruins. The Ponsonby property, as you know, [is] depopulated. Evictions are of daily occurrence throughout the County, even now, during this time of 'peace & good will,' and

41. Ibid., December 14, 1889.

many families are living, from hour to hour, in the fear of seeing roof top torn from over them before Christmas day'' (K). ''Such are our surroundings,'' Ryan concluded sadly, ''on the eve of the Nativity.''

Croke, meanwhile, had astutely invited O'Brien, who was to be released from jail shortly before Christmas, to come and spend the feast of the Nativity with him.[42] ''I gave O'Brien your message,'' Croke reported to Walsh on December 27. ''He is looking fairly, and his health is excellent. He is in good spirits too. He is in Tipperary by this time, having left me for Tip this morning. I laid out a program for him to which he is solemnly pledged to adhere. It will not expose him to any risks''(W). ''We do not want him,'' Croke observed—significantly, in the light of what happened in Tipperary when O'Brien was in jail—''to be 'run in' again. He has had enough of prison life, and any more of it would cause people to think he preferred it to anything else.'' ''The Tipperary imbroglio,'' he confessed more seriously, ''is at its height. O'Brien and Co. are sure, *they say*, of victory. I'm afraid they are too ardent. The nuns paid their rent and nothing but my personal influence could have prevented them from being *boycotted*. The Christian brothers also are in a bit of a fix on the same score. But I believe we will be able to steer through. I had the Ponsonby case on hand, but I have retired from it. I think I could have settled it, but complications arose, and my interference is at an end.'' ''They (the Ponsonby people),'' he complained, indicating the tenants, ''would make no settlement in which the Tipperary men were not included. So the thing fell through.''

The archbishop of Tuam, John MacEvilly, summed up the situation in Ireland for Kirby and Roman consumption on December 29: ''We are engaged in a new Association for the *defense* of our poor tenants. It is a matter of absolute necessity for the preservation of our Catholic people. There is a *manifest* determination of landlords to get rid of them and plant the country with Godless emergency men, and Protestants of the worst type'' (K). ''I regard it,'' he declared most formally, ''as a sacred and solemn duty, as a Catholic

42. C, O'Brien to Croke, December 5, 1889, accepting the invitation.

Bishop, and in view of future judgment, to give it every encouragement and support *intra limites juris*, in every constitutional strictly legal form. Anything else would be madness and criminal, as it would only throw us back for years, and destroy our people. I never fail to repeat O'Connell's golden maxim 'the man who commits a crime gives strength to the enemy.'" "I must confess," he then confided to Kirby, "I have very little hopes of practical sympathy from an English government. They will *use* Ecc[l] powers as long as they are useful and throw them aside at will. The *'no popery'* savagery of the English people, let men pretend what they like, *would* suppress and *will* suppress every expression of sympathy with the H. Father and the recovery of his inheritance, the temporal power, so necessary for the freedom of the Father of the faithful."

In thus committing themselves to the Tenants' Defence Association at the end of 1889, the Bishops were once again attempting to stabilize their own deteriorating political power and influence. The year before, they had only checked the rapid erosion of their strength by refusing to enforce the Roman Decree. The founding of the landlord syndicate, however, backed by a more aggressive coercionist government policy, had precipitated another change in the balance of power within the governing consensus. The Bishops had continued to lose ground to the Leader and the Party throughout the summer and fall of 1889; and with the founding of the Tenants' Defence Association they finally came to realize that, as far as the agrarian side of the Nationalist movement was concerned, they had been reduced from equals to auxiliaries. What made the Bishops' position even more difficult over this whole period was their continual fear that Rome, in the interest of diplomatic relations, would further embarrass them with the Irish people by again accommodating the British government in its Irish difficulties. Indeed, the British government was extremely active at Rome during this period, attempting at least to impair, if not actually break up, the Clerical-Nationalist alliance. Just the appearance of Roman cooperation with the British government not only weakened the Bishops in their attempt to hold their own with the Leader and the Party in the governing consensus but further contributed to the diminution of their power and influence in the country. In spite of all the efforts of the British government both at home and at Rome, however, the Bishops loyally continued to support the alliance; in doing so, they not only helped to consolidate the de facto Parnellite state but preserved their own power and influence, in the long run, in that state.

# 2

# ROMAN POWER

## August 1888–January 1890

Rome indeed sacrificed a great deal of her power and influence in
Ireland by insisting that the Irish Bishops enforce her will over the
Decree. But why did Rome persist in pursuing a policy so patently
at odds with her own real interests in Ireland? Rome's motives
were, of course, mixed, but only a confirmed cynic could maintain
that they were entirely discreditable. Part of the answer is certainly
that the pope and his advisers were genuinely concerned about the
moral welfare of the Irish people and that they had become convinced that both the Plan of Campaign and Boycotting were not fit
instruments for a Catholic people, no matter how noble or exalted
the ends for which those means were to be used. There were, however, several other reasons why Rome pursued the policy she did in
Ireland, and though these were not perhaps discreditable to her good
intentions, they were certainly unflattering to her judgment.

First of all, Leo XIII, ever since he had succeeded Pius IX in
1878, had had his heart set on establishing diplomatic relations
with all the non-Catholic, European great powers. By 1888 he had
brought the Russian and German empires within his diplomatic
orbit, and only the British remained outside. Leo XIII believed, in
fact, that he had been called by God to fulfill a twofold mission:
both teaching, which required him to speak to the modern world
through his encyclical letters, and diplomacy, by which he would
reconstruct the temporal power of the papacy in a new and imaginative way. Only when the vicar of Christ on earth was placed on a
level of diplomatic equality with the other sovereign princes of the

51

world would his words be received with that respect due his holy office, and only then would his acts carry the weight that would make his power and influence real once again in the modern world. Whatever may be said about Leo XIII's good intentions toward Ireland, there is little doubt that, in his dealings with the British government over Ireland, his ability to distinguish between appearance and reality was seriously impaired by his diplomatic needs.

The other reason why the pope pursued his chosen Irish policy is more understandable but in the last analysis not very creditable to him. He allowed Lord Salisbury to take advantage of him because of his intense desire to establish diplomatic relations with England. Lord Salisbury, in concert with his nephew, Arthur Balfour, in fact played a very dexterous diplomatic game after the pope issued the Decree in late April 1888. Salisbury immediately began a diplomatic withdrawal, plausibly pleading that any reciprocal action on his part just then would have the semblance of a quid pro quo, which would be ruinous not only to him in England but also to the pope in Ireland. At the same time, Balfour was skillfully keeping alive Roman hopes for some reciprocal action by initiating a very discreet set of negotiations concerning the prospects of Catholic higher education for Ireland. The negotiations, begun in early June, were conducted by Balfour and an Alsatian Jesuit, Dr. Baynard Klein, who was also a professor of natural philosophy at the Royal University in Dublin. Klein was a close friend of the earl of Denbigh, an English Catholic peer influential in Conservative political circles and also an old personal friend of Leo XIII.

To encourage Roman hopes, Balfour asked Klein to draw up a scheme for Catholic higher education that would be acceptable both to Rome and to Irish Catholics. "With this note," Klein informed Balfour on August 8, 1888, "I beg to send you the scheme which you kindly asked me to supply. This scheme of course does not go into details, yet I hope it will suffice to indicate the main features of the measure."[1] "Some points in it will probably seem obscure," Klein apologized in conclusion, "but when they are explained, I think you will agree that they are—really adapted to the supreme end in view." Whatever the supreme end in view may have been,

1. B, 49841.

Klein's plan for "St. Patrick's University," as Balfour must have realized immediately, was politically impossible. After setting up a chancellor, general council, and faculties of arts, science, law, and medicine, Klein proposed that the new university have a faculty of Catholic theology, which would include philosophy.[2] "The reference to the Theological Faculty in the Act & the Royal Charter," Klein then explained rather naively, "may be made only in general terms; but as soon as the Chancellor and the 32 Councillors have been appointed, the said Chancellor acting in the name of the Council would apply to the Holy See for a Bull granting the necessary powers for a faculty of Catholic Theology." "Thus," he added, even more naively, "at the time of the laying of the foundation-stone of the New University, the Pope's Bull might be published granting the necessary powers & taking the Catholic teaching of the University under his own exalted patronage as a pledge of his paternal affection for Ireland; whilst the Sovereign Pontiff would also formally invite the Irish people to avail themselves fully of these means of learning which they have so long and so justly asked for." "As regards the Professors of the Faculty of Theology," Klein then observed, "the General Council shall frame a rule by which no appointment to a Professorship is to be held valid until it has received the approbation of the Holy See (acting through the Sacred Congregation of the Propaganda). Appointments in this Faculty are *always* to be made on testimonials." Balfour, who would have had to face a House of Commons with these proposals, could not have taken them very seriously, but he continued to keep Klein on hand for obvious reasons.

It appears, however, that Father Klein, who was also in the confidence of Cardinal Rampolla, the pope's secretary of state, was commissioned by him to report on the situation in Ireland for the benefit of Rome. When Patrick Cardinal Moran, archbishop of Sydney and former bishop of Ossory in Ireland, arrived in Ireland in early August, rumors were rife that the cardinal had a mission from Rome. Klein wrote Balfour that it was necessary to contradict the rumors, and he then wrote Rome for the authority to do so. "You

2. Ibid., "Scheme of an Act to provide for Higher Education of Irish Catholics," August 7, 1888.

may have noticed in Saturday's Times," Klein finally reported to Balfour on 24 September,

a paragraph on Cardinal Moran, to the effect that "it is proper and necessary to state in the plainest manner and on the highest authority, that his Eminence has received from the Holy See no mission whatever . . . and that it is the understanding of the Holy See that he is in Ireland only in the interest of his Australian diocese." This paragraph was communicated by me on reception of a letter from the Cardinal Secretary of State in answer to a letter of mine. I strongly felt, as I had the honour to write to you some time ago . . . that the rumours not quite unreasonably circulated of late concerning the Cardinal's dealings in Ireland must be met and resolutely put down, and I said so much to the Cardinal-Secretary at Rome. He has answered me by a letter as plain and as straight forward as I could wish for, and I thought you would like to see such publicity given to the statement as would suffice to remove all possible doubt. I never believed myself that the Cardinal had any mission from Rome, but could not help seeing that certain appearances were doing much harm, and that it was high time that the Holy See should realize how matters stood in respect to this visit. I should be glad to have an opportunity of putting before you the letter of the Secretary of State to me, as well as another private letter received from the same source some days before. I also wish to inform you that I start for Ireland again on the 30th of this month and shall be kept there for several weeks. I should like so much to submit to you my present ideas as to my work there. I believe they would meet with your approval.[3]

Klein obviously had a double commission from Rome. Not only was he empowered by Cardinal Rampolla to find out and then report directly to him about the situation in Ireland concerning enforcement of the Decree, but he was also to explore with the government the possibilities of effecting a scheme for Catholic higher education in Ireland. When Balfour crossed over to Dublin from London in mid-October, therefore, Klein took occasion to write him again to remind him that they had arranged a tentative appointment. "Previous to my coming to Dublin," Klein explained to Balfour on October 20, "I have been travelling in the Country and have gathered important information which I have duly forwarded to Rome. I also have much from there which I am anxious to mention to you whenever you can spare me a moment. I am sure you will forgive me when I say how delighted I have been by reading your

3. Ibid.

speeches lately (including the paper before the Church Congress which of course touched me more specifically). Some of the speeches (Glasgow & Haddington) I have partly translated & sent on to Rome, thinking that would do more good than any words of mine."[4]

Meanwhile, the premier English Roman Catholic peer, the duke of Norfolk,[5] who had recently been employed by Salisbury on several delicate diplomatic missions to Rome and who looked upon himself therefore as the official medium through which any British-Roman negotiations should be conducted, was very upset to learn of Balfour's negotiations with Klein. The duke obviously came to the conclusion during the summer or fall that he was being trifled with, because in early December he finally decided to have the whole matter out with Balfour. "My dear Uncle Robert," Balfour complained to Salisbury on December 11, "Norfolk has just been here in a most unreasonable frame of mind. He wanted me to tell Klein and Denbigh, that I would have nothing to do with them, and that their visits to me led to a misrepresentation of their relations to the Government, which might produce unfortunate complications at Rome, and might leave it in doubt who was the accredited agent of the Go$^{vt}$. This course I refused to take. But I have given him a letter, a copy of which I enclose, which I told him he might use as his credentials in the proper quarter."[6] The letter enclosed read:

My dear Duke,
    In reference to our conversation of Sunday last in which I communicated to you confidentially the intentions of the Go$^t$. with regard to Higher Catholic Education in Ireland, let me just add that as soon as our proposals are in shape I will submit them to you. *As you will be the only person outside the Government to whom these proposals will be shown* by me I trust to your discretion to make only such use of them as will further the final success of the scheme.[7]

---

4. B, 49842.
5. *Henry Fitzalan-Howard*, fifteenth duke of Norfolk (1847–1917), English Roman Catholic politician. Succeeded father, 1860; educated at Oratory School, Edgebaston; headed mission to Rome, 1887–88; continued close relations with Vatican; postmaster-general in Salisbury's third ministry, 1895–1900; as Earl Marshall largely responsible for coronation ceremonies of Edward VII (1903) and George V (1910); noted builder of Gothic churches.
6. B, 49821.
7. Balfour's copy of this letter to Norfolk is undated.

What had undoubtedly contributed to the duke's decision to force the issue at this particular moment was that Salisbury had decided to start yet another diplomatic horse with regard to Rome, and the duke did not wish to find himself replaced by the earl of Denbigh in the new arrangement. Because of Salisbury's disappointing diplomatic withdrawal after the Decree, the pope naturally began to temporize about assurances he had made at the end of June concerning removal of Monsignor Antonio Buhagiar, the episcopal administrator of the bishop of Malta, and his replacement by Monsignor Peter Pace, bishop of Gozo and persona grata to the British government. In November, therefore, Salisbury authorized Gerald Strickland,[8] an important British official in the Maltese government, to open negotiations with the Holy See about the ecclesiastical situation in Malta. The pope had learned his diplomatic lesson from Salisbury, however, and was in no mood for trifling. Although he assured Strickland that he would remove Buhagiar before a certain fixed date, he insisted on his quid pro quo before appointing Pace coadjutor with the right of succession to the bishopric of Malta. Strickland reported, in a memorandum drawn up at a later date for Salisbury, that "His Holiness the Pope desired him to convey to Her Majesty's Government the request of the Holy See that diplomatic relations should be re-established, and that His Holiness was now willing to accept an 'officious Representative' from England if Lord Salisbury was not able to countenance a regular Mission."[9]

Salisbury was obviously unprepared for so direct and undip-

8. *Gerald Strickland* (1861–1940), colonial administrator and politician: Born in Malta; succeeded as sixth count della Catena, 1875; educated at Oscott and Trinity College, Cambridge; called to the bar (Inner Temple) and president of union, 1887; helped to frame Maltese Constitution, 1887; chief secretary, Malta, 1889–1902; governor, Leeward Islands, 1902–04; Tasmania, 1904–09, Western Australia, 1909–13, New South Wales, 1913–17; M.P., Lancaster Division, 1924–28; helped draft Maltese Constitution, 1921; member Maltese legislative assembly, 1921–30; formed Anglo-Maltese party; prime minister and minister for justice of Maltese coalition government with labor, 1927–30; leader of elected members, Council of Government, 1939–40; unceasing in opposing Italian influence in Malta; founded *Times of Malta*; K.C.M.G., 1897; baron, 1928.

9. Salisbury Papers (SY), Hatfield House, Hatfield, Herts., "Memorandum to the Secretary of State for Foreign Affairs with Reference to Diplomatic Relations with the Holy See and to Ecclesiastical Questions in Malta," January 30, 1889.

lomatic an approach from the pope and decided to play for time
by recalling Strickland to London. Eric Barrington, Salisbury's
secretary, telegraphed J. G. Kennedy, the British ambassador at
Rome, on December 20: "Count Strickland asks me to send you the
following—'Let Rampolla be inf^d that I have seen Lord Salisbury
and that a friendly answer will shortly be sent to the Pope's message.
For your own guidance the policy to be followed is to temporize' "
(SY). "Count Strickland," Barrington reported to Salisbury that
same day, "left with me this draft of a letter to Cardinal Rampolla
for your approval. He suggested that he should show it to the Duke
of Norfolk, and also asked whether the Duke might see Kennedy's
dispatch about the question of reopening diplomatic relations with
the Pope. Something on the subject appeared through a newspaper
agency two days ago, which looks as if the Vatican were communicating with the Press" (SY). "Strickland," Barrington explained,
"is therefore eager to be allowed to put the 'Times' on the right scent
as to what is taking place, but I fear his keeness might induce him to
tell more than was actually true. He had better leave that to you."

Salisbury did not, in fact, approve the draft of Strickland's letter
to Rampolla for another ten days, and when he did allow the letter to
be sent it was, in effect, only another polite postponement, in that a
further reply was deferred until Strickland should return to Malta
through Rome. The letter was interesting, however, for its outline of
the formal reasons why Her Majesty's government was hesitant
about making a move in the direction desired by Rome. "IN compliance with the duty," Strickland reported to Rampolla finally on
December 30, "with which I had the honour to be intrusted in
Rome, the desire of His Holiness, that diplomatic relations should
be resumed in a more formal manner between the Holy See and this
country, has been duly submitted to Her Majesty's Government."[10]
The letter went on:

2. His Holiness will learn with pleasure that the best feeling exists with
reference to this proposal, and that it is the earnest wish of the statesmen of
this Empire to see the accomplishment of some arrangement which would
be no less pleasing to the Holy See than beneficial to Her Majesty's
subjects.

10. SY, quoted in the appendix to Strickland's "Memorandum."

3. It will also give satisfaction to His Holiness to be informed that the efforts which have been made to overcome the difficulties in English politics, of which His Holiness is aware, have tended considerably towards improving the position of affairs.

4. Being strongly animated with these views, Her Majesty's Government seem disposed to the opinion that a hasty step at this moment might ultimately delay the satisfactory arrangement which they desire most heartily.

5. The warlike conditions and state of tension in Europe present diplomatic considerations, which, as your Eminence will easily understand, do not admit of any important step being taken just at present.

6. Nevertheless, Her Majesty's Government would gladly welcome any opportunity which, without incurring the dangers alluded to, would enable them to forward the reestablishment of diplomatic relations with the Holy See.

7. I trust that this early communication will convince His Holiness of the attention which the question is receiving, and pray that the postponement of a further reply will be granted by His Holiness until my return to Rome.

This was really a very skillful and clever performance by Salisbury: he began by raising the hopes of the Holy See by pointing out that the internal political difficulties leading to his diplomatic withdrawal the previous July were now on the mend; but he ended by dashing those hopes, invoking the dangerous international situation in which, as far as British strategic thinking was concerned, the security of Malta played a vital role. What Salisbury was telling the pope, therefore, was that His Holiness would have to honor the assurances he had made about Malta the previous June before the British government could again consider diplomatic relations and, moreover, that he had until Strickland returned to Rome to make up his mind.

Salisbury's real view—if anyone could ever be sure of it— appears to have been revealed in a letter he wrote to the marquis of Dufferin in Rome, two days before he "approved" Strickland's letter to Rampolla. Salisbury regretted that Dufferin, who had just resigned as viceroy of India, had not arrived in Rome sooner, because the Italian prime minister, Francesco Crispi, had been stirring up all sorts of trouble with France and thereby endangering world peace. British policy now, Salisbury explained in his December 28 letter, was to give Crispi a much wider berth than before (SY). "One other point should be mentioned," he added. "For many reasons—among them on account of Ireland—we are anxious to put an end to the absurd practice which prevents us from accrediting an Envoy to the Vatican. At one time I thought we should be able to do it—but I found our Liberal Unionist friends were so nervous about it that I did not venture. Just now, the friction between Italy and the Vatican is more strained than usual. For the present, therefore, I have abandoned the idea. I have told Catalani''—the Italian foreign minister—''that we think relations ought to exist—but that for the present we contemplate no move in that direction.''

In approving Strickland's letter to Rampolla, however, Salisbury had decided to sugar that rather large pill for the pope by expressing his wish ''that in future all communications with the Vatican which might have the approval of Her Majesty's Government should be made through the Duke of Norfolk, or with his knowledge and sanction.''[11] ''This would establish,'' as Strickland in his Memorandum later noted, ''that certainty and continuity of action which was so conspicuously absent in the various kinds of agencies hitherto made use of. The protection of the [Foreign] Office bag was also granted to such correspondence as had the Duke of Norfolk's approval.'' In this great game of diplomatic chess, the pope had, in fact, once again allowed his appetite to get the better of his judgment, in juxtaposing two very unequal pieces—diplomatic relations as against bishopric—and Salisbury quickly taught the pope that among the masters untraditional gambits were seldom profitable. In any case, not only did the pope give up his piece with very good grace, but, to his credit, he did it quickly and with a certain élan. On January 11, Monsignor Buhagiar was recalled from Malta, and on January 17, the governor of Malta received official notification from Cardinal Rampolla that Monsignor Pace had been nominated by the pope to the see of Malta. As a further result of Pace's translation to Malta, the pope proposed Father Camilleri, a persona grata to Her Majesty's government, for the vacated see of Gozo.

Balfour, meanwhile, was having a very difficult time of it in Ireland, between evictions and such irresponsible landlords as the earl of Clanricarde. On January 15, Balfour wrote his uncle to complain about the letter of January 12 from Croke to Patrick

11. Ibid.

O'Donnell, the bishop of Raphoe, in which Croke had enclosed £50 for the relief of the evicted tenants of Donegal. "I enclose a letter," Balfour, who was very much annoyed, advised Salisbury, "that appeared this morning from Archbishop Croke. I am turning over in my mind the policy of prosecuting him. Our decision must of course partly depend on the legal aspect of the case—the possibility of proving that he wrote it, and so forth. But if all these preliminary difficulties can be smoothed away, the more serious question of policy remains. The best thing would be that Rome should act decisively."[12] "Croke's action," he argued, making more of a case than actually existed, "is a direct defiance of the Pope:—for the tenants had joined the Plan, and the Archbishop condemns, in language verging on impiety, the only method by which the Plan can be met. In the event of Rome declining to act or postponing action, ought we to remain quiescent? We shall have a good many evictions soon on 'Campaign' estates: and it is with a view to these no doubt that Croke has written the letter. Turn the matter over in your mind, but do not bother to answer this until you hear from me again."

Salisbury, however, chose to write his nephew the next day. "I send back Croke's letter," he replied on January 16, in an attempt to prevent his diplomatic lines from being fouled, "in order to suggest that you should send it to whoever has been your Roman advisor— Norfolk or (I should prefer Norfolk) Klein. I would do so with a letter civilly indicating that you fear the Pope is throwing us over. I suggest this only diplomatically—to place me in a better position in dealing with R.C. educational demands. Of course, as to the main point—the prosecution—I reserve my opinion until I hear what the lawyers say."[13] Two days later, on January 18, Balfour dutifully reported to his uncle: "I communicated Croke's letter at once to Norfolk, but without comment. If he—or those with whom he acts,

12. B, 49834. See also B, 49827, Balfour to Ross, January 15, 1889: "In case you should not otherwise see it, I enclose a letter which appeared in this morning's 'Freeman's Journal' from Archbishop Croke. When we recollect that the tenants who were evicted were evicted for non-payment of rent which they were perfectly able to pay but which being engaged in the Plan of Campaign conspiracy they refused to pay, I think you will agree with me that the letter is one of the most monstrous that was ever penned by an ecclesiastic."
13. B, 49689.

—do nothing I will write again in the sense you suggest. I gather that the legal difficulties in the way of prosecution are sufficiently grave to make it inexpedient.''[14]

At that moment, however, Salisbury was not particularly anxious to ask Rome to do any more. He was undoubtedly thinking, instead, how he could as gracefully as possible temper the hopes he had raised in Rome about diplomatic relations. The situation was all the more awkward for Salisbury because his emissary, Count Strickland, was still under the impression that, as the pope had responded so nobly about Malta, Salisbury would authorise him on his return to Malta via Rome to offer something more substantial than the sincere thanks of Her Majesty's government for all that His Holiness had done.

Strickland's ideas on the subject were, in fact, not only interesting but most imaginative. "I have just seen Balfour," he reported to Barrington on January 22, from Dublin, "who discussed the past correspondence & present prospects with much interest. He is very well pleased with the idea of starting diplomatic relations as a Maltese question on the subject of a 'Concordat' for the ecclesiastical affairs of that Island, & then making use of that standpoint for any other convenient purpose for further development. He desired me to tell Lord Salisbury that this proposal appeared to him to be for the best that had yet been brought forward, & that he hoped it would have the best consideration''(SY). "I also discussed with him," Strickland added, with a reference to the ancient Statute of Praemunire, "the Legal difficulties (which are only vague doubts), & the political difficulties. He thinks that as we *must* have diplomatic relations with reference to Malta where the Canon Law is solemnly recognized by the Crown, nobody could seriously object to our doing so openly. We also discussed a way of getting over the Crispi difficulty which is not great after all.'' "You will have heard that the nomination of Pace to the See of Malta," Strickland observed proudly, if innocently, "& the official notification of the fact by Rampolla to the Malta Gov$^t$, has established the complete success of the recent mission. I shall now prepare the Memorandum for Lord Salisbury.''

14. B, 49834.

"As I understand that you have directed," Norfolk informed Salisbury, somewhat self-importantly, about a week later, "that all matters relating to questions connected with the Holy See should pass through my hands I now beg to enclose a Memorandum drawn up by Count Strickland the suggestions contained in which I very earnestly commend to your attention as an opportune and favourable way of forwarding an object the immense importance of which we are all agreed upon as also the desirability of attaining it by some practical method without indefinite delay."[15] Strickland's memorandum was a very long, comprehensive, and generally able document, which argued in a partisan fashion for the Maltese gambit in establishing diplomatic relations with the Vatican. The weakest part of the memorandum and the part that must have interested Salisbury the most was the section concerning the effect the proposed diplomatic relations might have on the Italian government.

"As regards the *diplomatic* difficulties," Strickland pointed out, "it may be observed that friendship and real good-will to Italy and its dynasty is very different to acquiescence to Signor Crispi"(SY). "The present Premier of Italy," the count explained, and Salisbury must have smiled, "has few real friends, and for social and other reasons cannot have many." "He and his party," Strickland argued a little naively, "are more feared than respected, and are dominant because they show ability and a strong hand, but day by day they can less afford to make enemies. The German Mission to the Vatican or the Russian unofficial Mission on Polish affairs, have not resulted in consequences which are to be regretted by their Governments, and they have proved that such diplomatic difficulties may be ignored." "Further," he noted, returning to his original theme, "Signor Crispi's impulsive temper may be met by informing him that the delay in sending such a Mission was out of deference to him, but that England cannot any longer remain in a worse position than Russia as to Colonial questions. He might even be asked what form of unofficial representation would be least distasteful to him, and an Italian would hardly fail to give a civil answer to a question so put." "As to the *political* difficulties," Strickland then observed, in the final section of his memorandum, "they appear to be so

15. SY, no date.

doubtful that perhaps they are excessively feared, and it is submitted that the course suggested would bring them to the surface, and place them under control without giving rise to any danger. Unless public opinion is thus tested, the Pope and his advisers may soon come to the conclusion that a possible Mission on a grand scale in the distant future is only kept within sight for the avoiding of something more practical.''

In the course of his memorandum, Strickland noted that the governor of Malta desired his return not later than February 24, and he asked, therefore, to be advised what he might tell the pope when he stopped over in Rome, as he had promised in his letter of December 30 to Rampolla. When he was finally instructed to proceed instead directly to Malta, and write Rampolla a note of apology from there, Strickland must have realised that the world of diplomatic realpolitik often required a strong stomach as well as a not very tender conscience. "In accordance with your suggestion," a sadder but wiser Strickland informed Barrington on February 25 from Malta, "I have on my return sent a polite explanation to Card. Rampolla for my non-appearance in Rome to give him further light as to the question which he has so much at heart" (SY). "I send you a copy for your information," he added dryly, "& hope it succeeds in not containing much more than what was said before. I have also endeavoured to keep him from jumping too quickly to the conclusion, that having got our cake (Pace) we are quite unmindful of past favours or insensible to the probable necessity of having to reckon with favours to come, should they have to be asked for before a 'quid pro quo' is more substantially held out."

"This letter," Barrington noted, in passing Strickland's copy along to Salisbury, "seems quite harmless, but in any case it c^d not have committed H.M.G." (SY). "As he had promised to go back," Barrington added half apologetically, "it was necessary that he sh^d write some excuse for not doing so." This correspondence was simply initialed by Salisbury in red ink, without any comment.

In facing up not only to the sad fact that his Decree was unenforceable in Ireland but also to the realization that he had been diplomatically hoodwinked once again by Salisbury, the pope decided that his wisest course for the time being was to do nothing. In late February 1889, however, Salisbury decided that the Maltese gambit was politically inopportune, if not dangerous; shortly thereafter an intimate personal friend and confidant of the duke of Norfolk, John Ross of Bladensburg,[16] industriously began to prepare a long "Memorandum on the Pope's action in Ireland" for Arthur Balfour. Ross, who, in concert with the duke, had done more in recent years than perhaps anyone else to promote British-Roman relations in the hope of checking the progress of the National movement in Ireland, was an Irishman, a Catholic, an extreme Tory, and a major in the Coldstream Guards. He was, moreover, a close personal friend of Abbot Bernard Smith and Domenico Jacobini, the secretary of Propaganda, and was therefore well connected in influential Roman circles. Ross's long memorandum, dated March 19, was a persuasive attempt to explain why, in the light of recent events in Ireland, some sort of diplomatic relations with Rome were now more necessary than ever. He began his memorandum with the interesting assertion that Rome had issued the Decree in April 1888 because of the information supplied by Monsignor Persico, who had been commissioned by the pope in late June 1887 to proceed to Ireland as his apostolic visitor. Persico spent some six months in Ireland between July 1887 and January 1888, traveling about, collecting information, and forwarding interim reports directly to the cardinal secretary of state. Whether the issuing of the Decree was more the result of Monsignor Persico's final report or of Ross and Norfolk's own strenuous efforts at Rome at the same time is, however, a very moot point. In any case, after this brief, if questionable, introduction, Ross proceeded to the matter at hand.

"It is needless," he assured Balfour, "to recapitulate how the Decree has been treated by the Irish Episcopate, Clergy, and Nationalist Party. The history of the past few months is fresh in the minds of all. It is sufficient to say, whatever private effect the Pope's

16. *John Foster Ross* of Bladensburg (1848–1926), soldier, diplomat, and administrator: A.D.C. to Lords Spencer and Carnarvon, lord lieutenants of Ireland, 1884–86; secretary to British Missions to the Holy See, 1887 (Norfolk), 1889–90 (Lintorn Simmons); lieutenant colonel, Coldstream Guards, 1896; chief commissioner, Dublin Metropolitan Police, 1901–14; K.C.B., 1903; K.C.V.O., 1911.

action may have had, publicly it is a dead letter."[17] "Now it must be remembered," Ross then maintained,

that the Bishops are the only accredited Agents of the Holy See in a Cath^c country, where no other means of communication exist between the Govt. of that country & the Pope. This is the case in Ireland.

The Bishops have told his Holiness that the present grievances of the Irish people are crushing and exasperating. The Bishops do not appear to criticise the conclusions arrived at by the Decree; They profess in theory to agree with it, but they add that the position of the Country is wholly abnormal, that their people are the victims of cruelty and tyranny, and that these facts render it extremely difficult for them promptly to execute the decision of the Holy See upon the methods employed in the agitation. The Land Question is an example. An Episcopal Declaration upon that matter, dated last July purported to give a catalogue of the present woes of the Irish tenants. These woes were painted in very lively colours, & according to this document the cultivators of the soil are still being treated with great and unnecessary harshness. Nor should it be forgotten that this Declaration was not adhered to only by those Bishops who by silence or active means are thwarting the Decree; its importance was considerably enhanced by the fact that it was also signed by those who may be regarded as Papal Bishops —Ecclesiastics who have exerted themselves to make known and to enforce the condemnation against immoral practices.

The Declaration seemed to many to be misleading and indeed fallacious. They considered that all material grievances had been swept away and that the position of the Irish tenant was anything but unfavourable and contrasted well with that of other occupiers in modern Europe. A reply to the Declaration was sent to Rome. Previous efforts however had been made to explain the nature of the Agrarian system as at present developed in Ireland. These papers have no doubt received attention. But never should it be forgotten that these private efforts, undertaken by private individuals, though useful up to a certain point, cannot overcome the prejudice that must be produced by the far more official statement signed by the whole & united Hierarchy of Ireland.

"If the Pope," Ross then argued, "were to appreciate the exact truth with regard to Irish grievances, their hollowness & the fictitious grounds upon which they are constructed, he would then be able to take stronger measures than heretofore to put down the revolt against authority. And if this is so, is there any valid or sufficient

17. B, 49821.

reason why he should not have this truth put before him in the only way in which he can listen to it?''

"Unionists often dwell (and justly so)," Ross then admitted, "upon the improvement which has been effected in Ireland, by the results of firm & impartial Gov$^t$ & by the accident of a revival in trade. This improvement is of course considered exceedingly satisfactory; but it does not and cannot go to the root of the evil, & should present circumstances alter, it is to be feared that disorder would not be slow to reassert itself. In other words anarchy has been checked and put down, but the seeds from which it springs have not been destroyed.'' "There is," Ross then noted, saving the most valid reason for last, "but one point more. Some fear may exist that the Unionist cause would be weakened by relations with the Holy See; since one or more of the political groups that now sustain Gov$^t$ in power might be alienated from their present allegiance by such a policy. Any grave defection of this nature would be a very serious catastrophe, & none for a moment would urge or tolerate a scheme which would be suicidal to the best interests of Church & State. The question arises whether the fear is well founded or not exaggerated in the reverse." "Are there no means," he inquired, "of making the attempt with caution, to open up negotiations on a particular point & let them develop themselves, according as they are found to be useful and unprejudicial to the Unionist position in the Country." "It is unnecessary to suggest," Ross added, in an obvious reference to the Maltese gambit, "any proposal in detail. If the matter has any real importance, some small & perhaps remote risk may have to be incurred, but means can be taken to test its value, & if the principle be adopted, gradually to bring it about."

Exactly what effect Ross's memorandum had it is, of course, difficult to gauge, but two weeks later the colonial secretary, Lord Knutsford, with Salisbury's concurrence, initiated the Maltese gambit. The governor of Malta, Sir H. Torrens, replied on April 18 to Knutsford's "Secret" dispatch of April 2, in his best diplomatic jargon: "In compliance with your Lordship's instructions, I have the honour to report that I entirely concur in the opinion expressed by Lord Salisbury and in which your Lordship agrees as to the desirability of some clear understanding being arrived at with the Vatican in reference to the residence of higher Ecclesiastics in Malta and generally with reference to various points on which the influence of the Pope may affect the security and tranquility of Her Majesty's subjects in Malta."[18] Meanwhile, Rampolla had written Norfolk asking him, obviously, to promote the Maltese gambit, for the duke wrote Salisbury on April 20 to ask for an interview (SY). He spoke to Salisbury during the following week about opening diplomatic relations with Rome on the Maltese question, and Salisbury must have informed him that he had already written asking the opinion of the new governor of Malta. "I conclude," the duke reminded Salisbury on Saturday, May 4, "you have now received a dispatch from Malta on the matter we have discussed and which dispatch was shown to me at the Colonial office two days ago. If this is so, I should be glad if you would let me see you on Tuesday or Thursday" (SY).

A month later the project of the Maltese mission had progressed to the point where Salisbury and Norfolk were discussing who should head it.[19] Then suddenly Salisbury decided to postpone the mission until the following autumn. "There is one disadvantage," Norfolk worried Salisbury on June 13, "in the delay of the Mission to Rome to the Autumn" (SY). "This is," he explained, in a reference to Kerry, Waterford and Killaloe, "that two Irish Sees are at this moment vacant and another likely to be so any day." "As the mission is now I suppose certain to be sent," he suggested, shrewdly trying to pin Salisbury down, "I want to know if I may write to Rampolla saying that it will be sent in the autumn and will be before long announced in Parliament and also that the Government would be very glad if the appointments of any Bishops to vacant Sees could be put off until its arrival as there were no doubt points connected with such nominations on which the Holy See might be glad to receive official information." "I need not dwell on the extreme importance of these appointments," he emphasized in conclusion, "not only as regards the point of whether or not the new Bishops are to be instruments of Walsh or opponents of his policy, but also as showing to the Clergy in Ireland on which side the Pope's sympathies really are."

18. Foreign Office Papers (F.O.), Public Record Office, London, 358/6.
19. SY, Norfolk to Salisbury, June 9, 1889.

"I enclose you," Norfolk informed Salisbury some six weeks later, on August 1, "a translation made by Ross of a letter from Cardinal Rampolla in response to mine telling him of the advent of the Mission and at the intention on the part of the Government of announcing it in Parliament" (SY). "We thought the letter an important one," the duke explained, "and I tried with Ross at the F.O. to see if it was possible to show it to you. As this was not possible, we saw Balfour who thought nothing could be done to deal with the frame of mind the letter represents until Ross gets to Rome when he ought to do all he can to open the eyes of the Vatican to the false views put before them and evidently not without success. I hope very much the mission will be worked in such a way as to allow him time for this and that its chief will be thoroughly impressed by the Irish Office with the importance of the Irish part of the affair." "I should be glad," he noted in conclusion, "if I might see you before you [sic] the announcement is made in Parliament."

"Referring to my former letter of the 4th April," Rampolla had written Norfolk on July 20, "I am glad to inform you in reply to your private and confidential communication of the 8th Inst., that on the part of the Holy See there is no difficulty, and that Government can carry out next autumn their intention, of which you have told me, of sending an official Mission to His Holiness to negotiate questions which refer to Malta" (SY). Rampolla went on, in Ross's very awkward translation, with a reference to Sir John Lintorn Simmons:[20] "Nor is it necessary that you should give special assurances relating to the happy relation of the person who is proposed by Ld Salisbury for this business. As this gentleman is fully accepted by His Holiness, he will be received at the Vatican with all the consideration due both to the official character with which he is

20. *Sir John Lintorn Arabin Simmons* (1821–1903), soldier and administrator: Joined Royal Engineers, 1837; served in Canada, 1839–45; employed under Railway Commissioners, 1846–54; British commissioner with Omar Pasha's Turkish army on the Danube, 1855; took part with Turkish army in the siege of Sevastopol; C.B., 1855; British consul at Warsaw, 1858–60; commanding Royal Engineers at Aldershot, 1860–65; director Royal Engineers' Establishment at Chatham, 1865–68; lieutenant-governor of Royal Military Academy at Woolich, and K.C.B., 1869; governor, 1870–75; inspector-general of fortifications at War Office, 1875–80; military delegate at Congress of Berlin, 1878; general, 1877, G.C.B., 1878; governor of Malta, 1884–88; G.C.M.G., 1887; field marshal, 1890.

invested, and to the individual qualities which distinguish him. I would however ask you if you could let me have confidentially before hand, at least in general terms the points, more or less explicitly, which are to form the object of the negotiations, so that I may inform the Holy Father and be able to know H. H.'s views thereon."

The cardinal continued, turning to what was the real purpose of the mission: "In your letter of the 8th, you also make some allusion to Irish affairs. As I wish to be entirely frank with you, I think it opportune to say that with reference to this delicate and grave question, that as the Holy See has already done of its own initiative that which was due to its office, now all the circumstances considered, the Holy See is not in a position to intervene." "And this because," the translation went on, "such intervention would become confused with political questions which have become more and more acute and difficult, and also because the Holy See, according to its own view of the matter, believes that the true and complete pacification of that Island is not to be hoped for, until certain obstacles are completely removed,—obstacles which arise from internal legislation." "However this may be," Rampolla concluded politely, keeping the opportunity to negotiate alive, "there is no intention to exclude information given as mere information, which the British Government may wish to lay before the Holy See, and this if communicated through their non official Envoy, or through yourself will always be received with pleasure."

The pope and his advisers had obviously finally come to realize that, whatever else Walsh and Croke had done, they had once again placed the papacy in an excellent position to bargain with the British government. When Rampolla wrote Norfolk on July 20, three episcopal appointments were still pending, and the actuality of Rome's power, however limited, in the good governance of the Irish Church could be easily demonstrated. The real question at issue, however, was whether it was really in Rome's own interest, either in maintaining her own power and influence in Ireland or in attempting to consummate diplomatic relations with Britain, to exercise her power in Britain's favor. Rome had to realize, in fact, that the only reason the British government was willing to think about diplomatic relations was that there was an Irish problem. Furthermore, even if

Rome could solve that problem—and on this point Rampolla's letter suggested very serious doubts—the attempt to solve it could easily wreck what was left of her power and influence in Ireland and remove, thereby, the raison d'être for official British-Vatican relations. In the next six months, therefore, while she attempted to conserve and reassert her power and influence in Ireland and simultaneously to keep alive British hopes that she would use that power and influence in England's interest, Rome had a very delicate diplomatic game to play.

The death of the bishop of Kerry on May 1 had provided Rome with an opportunity to begin the restructuring of her power in the Irish Church. By the first week in June, moreover, two other Irish sees were vacant: the bishop of Waterford, Pierce Power, died unexpectedly at the end of May, and the infirm coadjutor of the bishop of Killaloe, James Ryan, finally decided to retire. Three bishoprics in the province of the troublesome archbishop of Cashel, therefore, were suddenly at the disposition of Rome; and two of them, Kerry and Killaloe (Clare), were undoubtedly among the most difficult to govern, politically and ecclesiastically, in Ireland. The Killaloe case had, in fact, been under consideration since the previous November, when Cardinal Simeoni, the cardinal prefect of Propaganda,[21] had written Croke asking what he thought should be done about the diocese: the bishop was mentally ill and living in seclusion in Paris and his coadjutor had become physically incapacitated. Croke immediately took counsel with Walsh,[22] and the upshot of all the various conversations, letters, and negotiations over the next six months was that the coadjutor was finally persuaded to retire. On June 5, 1889, Simeoni instructed Croke to convene the priests of the diocese of Killaloe so that they might commend a *terna* for the appointment of a new coadjutor *cum jure successionis* (C).

21. *Giovanni Simeoni* (1816–92), diplomat and statesman: Born in Paliano, near Rome; family dependent on Colonnas, who assisted in his education; taught philosophy and theology at Roman College of Propaganda; appointed auditor at nunciature in Spain; appointed titular archbishop of Chalcedon and secretary of Propaganda, 1868; appointed nuncio to Spain, 1875; created cardinal, 1875; appointed secretary of state, 1876; appointed prefect of Propaganda, 1878.

22. W, November 13, 1888. See two letters to Walsh from Croke on that day.

The same day that the cardinal was thus writing Croke, the clergy of Kerry assembled to commend their three names to Rome. The results of a very brisk month of canvassing and caucusing were that Thomas Canon Lawler, a former Kerry priest who was then on the mission in the English diocese of Southwark, emerged as *dignissimus*, with twenty-two votes; John Coffey, dean of the chapter and a favorite of the late bishop, was *dignior*, with fifteen votes; and Rev. Michael O'Sullivan rounded out the *terna* as *dignus*, with five votes.[23] "Kerry did fairly," Croke, who had presided, reported to Walsh on June 9. "I do not know Lawler personally; but all I hear of him is to his credit, both as regards character and capacity" (W). Of Coffey he commented, "The *Dean* is a rank Tory." "I cannot possibly be at the Maynooth Meeting," he continued, "as the election of Bishop is to take place in Waterford on the 24th inst. I do not know who will come to the front there. Dr. Cleary"—the bishop of Kingston in Canada and a former Waterford priest—"will get votes; But I fancy will hardly lead the van. Fr. Joe Phelan will also be supported. The Killaloe case is just on the point of being brought to a close. I had a letter, yesterday, from Cardinal Simeoni to that effect."

The events in Kerry were quickly reported to Balfour by Arthur Canon Griffin, parish priest of Millstreet and friend and correspondent of Ross and Norfolk. "I think it right to tell you," Griffin explained to Balfour on June 12, "that a large section of the priests of Kerry are working to get a Nationalist appointed as successor to the late Bishop Dr. Higgins. I enclose a copy of a letter which was sent to several Parish Priests before the election took place by Rev[d] P. O'Connor, P. P. of Molahiffe, who is closely related to Canon Lawler, mentioned in it."[24] "This Rev[d] Gentleman," Griffin added, meaning O'Connor, "is at this moment heading the 'Plan of Campaign' on Lord Kenmare's estate, and is the man who treated Mrs. Curtin so badly after the murder of her husband. I know Canon Lawler intimately as he commenced his studies with me in France but you can understand from the letter that he is an extreme Nationalist and in touch with the Parnellites of the Diocese. The original of one of the letters came into my hands, and I shall find means of

23. *Kerry Sentinel* (Tralee), June 8, 1889.
24. B, 49844.

sending it to the Holy See." "In such cases," he remarked regretfully, "it is deplorable that the English Government has not diplomatic relations with the Vatican. Yet Lord Salisbury may find some way of representing to His Holiness the great danger of appointing such men to Bishoprics. Dean Coffey, P.P. of Tralee, is the only man in the Diocese fit, in the present circumstances, to be raised to the Episcopacy."

Father O'Connor's letter, enclosed by Griffin for Balfour, illustrates the intensity of feeling among the majority of the second order of clergy in Kerry:

> Farranfore
> Co. Kerry
> June 1, 1889

My dear Fr. Molyneaux,

Of course you are aware that the election of Candidates for the vacant Mitre of Kerry will come off at Killarney on Wednesday next.

A very considerable number of the P.P.s of the diocese are strongly persuaded that Thomas Canon Lawler of Southwark, England who perhaps you know, would be the best selection for the office. He made a brilliant display of talent and knowledge when he stood for the Chair in Maynooth with O'Rourke, and the very best Judges pronounced him to be the most competent to fill the place.

He also acquitted himself with credit as President of the Killarney Seminary and was elected by a majority of the Chapter of Southwark to be their Provost.

If he get a strong support from the P.P.s with these high recommendations he will most probably be appointed at Rome.

The priests think they have had quite enough of Antinational Rule which is likely to be continued by Dean Coffey and his clique and would desire to have a Bishop of National principles and in harmony with their own political feelings.

I just put these things before you for your consideration and leave you to reflect upon them for your guidance in the matter of the election. I remain my Dear Fr

> Very faithfully yours,
> P. O'Connor[25]

Griffin did not have to wait very long to find his means of sending O'Connor's letter to Rome. Abbot Smith, with Ross and Norfolk in partial diplomatic eclipse after the British-Vatican standoff in late

25. Ibid.

February over Malta, wrote his old friend Sir George Errington, asking him to send immediately what information he could supply about Kerry. "The following facts," Errington assured Smith from London on June 19, "I can absolutely vouch for, but I hope in a few days to send you letters & other confirmatory documents" (S). "Dean Coffey P.P. of Tralee & V.G. of the Diocese," Errington reported, "is an able & strong man, obedient to the Holy See & the Decrees of the Holy Father, at the same time wise & prudent. His position as Dean of the Chapter & V.G. showing [sic] the high opinion entertained of him by the late Bishop. (The late Bishop was one of the only 3 Bishops in Ireland who had the courage to refuse to sign the resolution in favour of Mr. O'Brien, which emanated from the Lord Mayor of Dublin, one of Parnell's most trusted lieutenants)." "No. 1 Canon Lalor [sic] of Southwark," he continued, "was at one time President of the Seminary at Killarney, in diocese of Kerry of which he is a native. *He is* related to the Rev. P. O'Connor P.P. of Firies in Kerry, & it is mainly through his exertions that Canon Lalor is *1st on* the list sent to Rome. (I shall send you in a day or two a remarkable letter about this.)"

Errington continued:

*Father O'Connor* is the leading Priest in Kerry of the party who oppose the Pope's decrees, & in his *Parish openly advocates the Plan of Campaign* & sets the Holy See at defiance.

It was he who took such active part in the scandalous Curtin case in his parish. Curtin the father of the family, was murdered in his house, & his daughters were so boycotted and insulted by the people that the late Bishop put the Church under an interdict & would not allow Father O'Connor to officiate in it. Father O'C. took the most active part in the persecution of this unhappy family.

I mention this to show the nature of the party who are endeavouring to promote the Election of Canon Lalor. I may add that Dr. Croke is working hard for him, and it is believed that Cardinal Manning who is strongly in favour of the Nationalist party is aiding.

You may rely on this, and it shows what an unfortunate thing it would be to appoint Canon Lalor. To do so would leave the Bishop of Limerick (Dr. O'Dwyer) without anyone to support him in his wise & moderate policy, against Dr. Croke & the other Bishops of the Province. This would be very hard for Dr. O'Dwyer is courageously standing alone in favour of Charity and Justice & showing deference to the Decrees of the Holy Office.

"The Rev. M. O'Sullivan," Errington then noted, rounding out his comments on the *terna*, "is a worthy & much respected Parish Priest, a good man but not at all equal to Dean Coffey." "Do you think," he then asked, "it would be useful to get Lord Kenmare to write a moderate letter in this sense. You know well his position in Kerry, his high rank & position as a Catholic, & his enormous property." "Such a letter," Errington then explained, "would I think be most valuable in the *Ponenza*. What would be the best way of sending it? Would it be well to send it *officially* to you, or should it be sent direct to Mgr. Jacobini, or what do you advise?"

"I now send you," Errington wrote Smith on June 22, "an *important Circular letter* addressed to all the P.P.'s of Kerry by *Father O'Connor of Firies* the priest of whom I spoke in my last. This bears out my statement that Canon Lalor's [sic] choice on the 'Terna' is the result of an intrigue. I call your attention to the expressions in the letter about 'Antinational Rule' & 'Dean Coffey.' Dean Coffey as I told you was the trusted friend of the late Bishop. Pray remember what I said in my last about Father O'Connor's character (writer of the enclosed letter)" (S). "In furtherance of this," he reported, "I send you 'The Times' in which I have marked the report of his Examination before the Commission, which took place yesterday & the day before. Could there be anything more unworthy? I call your attention to the answer from him 'I am not a walking Almanac,' and to the public reproof of the Presiding Judge. *This is the man* who is organising the *support to Canon Lalor*, hence you may judge what the results of Canon Lalor's Election would be.

"I had a long conversation," Errington further reported, "with Lord Kenmare yesterday. He fully confirms all I wrote: He says that Canon Lalor's Election would produce a blaze over the diocese, & would cruelly weaken in the Province the only moderate bishop Dr. O'Dwyer." "Lord Kenmare says," Errington then noted, "Dean Coffey would be far the best man who could be chosen in the diocese: & that though he is returned as having only *17* votes, he lost two votes by *merely formal errors*; Dr. Croke presided at the Election & struck off two votes; virtually therefore he had *19* against Canon Lalor's *22*." "I have asked Lord Kenmare," he informed Smith, "to write a letter for the information of Propaganda on these subjects, and I cannot help thinking that coming from a Catholic of his exceptional position & character it ought to have weight; & should be printed in the *Ponenza*! I send however my letter to-day with the papers & enclosures without delay: perhaps you will inform me how Lord K's letter had best be sent, I suppose there is no pressing hurry about it. My suggestion to him was that he should write a formal letter, which Dease should give to me for transmission to you." "Lord K's name," he cautioned Smith, "should in this case be kept an ABSOLUTE SECRET! I am sure we can rely on Mgr. Jacobini for this."

"I send you now," Errington reported to Smith some six days later, on June 28, "Lord Kenmare's letter."[26] "I think," he then suggested, "you should see it is properly translated, for I have not much confidence in the linguists of Propaganda. It is I think a good & weighty letter. If you think however, that a letter from Lord K. *direct* to Mgr. Jacobini would be much better, I might arrange it. Lord Kenmare was unwilling in the first instance to write direct, fearing that they might think him intruding or officious." Turning his attention once again to Canon Lawler, Errington went on: "Last year some remarkably strong letters appeared signed *Clericus* in the *Tablet*, against the *Papal decrees*; they were I am told of a very antipapal tone and I am informed on the best authority that they were written by the *Canon Lalor* in question. It would be difficult to get the letters now, but if you think it *very important* I would try & do so: they gave much scandal at the time I am told. I write in haste for post, I hope you will let me hear SOON how things go & what further information you want; I can get you anything you wish." "Pray let me know SOON," Errington then emphasized in a postscript, "whether you think Lord Kenmare had better write directly to Mgr. Jacobini." He added, referring undoubtedly, in part, to the new low water mark in the quest for diplomatic relations with England, "What you tell me of Vatican affairs is very sad."

Meanwhile, on June 24, the clergy of Waterford had met to commend their *terna* to Rome. The *dignissimus*, James V. Cleary, bishop of Kingston in Canada, received fifteen of the thirty-one votes cast; Father Joseph A. Phelan, parish priest of Saints Peter and Paul in Clonmel, emerged as *dignior*, with eight votes, and Father

26 S. See also S, Kenmare to Edmund Dease, June 23, 1889.

Patrick McCarthy, former professor at All Hallows Seminary in Dublin, was *dignus*, with six. The other two votes went to Father Peter Casey, parish priest of Dungarvan, and Dr. James Murray, bishop of Maitland in Australia. "Back home from Waterford," Croke reported to Walsh on June 25, "where I found everything in the greatest confusion. 'Kingston,' having been communicated with by a *friend*, wrote back to said friend saying, that he would not come home, if voted for, and that, if he willed it, he would not come, as the Roman authorities need his services where he is. This threw his friends into confusion. It was not easy to rally them after that. But, the rally was made, and he came well to the front" (W). "Father Joe Phelan's ranks," Croke noted, "were mercilessly and unmeaningly, broken into by one McCarthy, sometime, I believe professor in All Hallows, but now some sort of pensioner, and living without employment in Tramore. I had never heard of him: but through the EXERTIONS of his cousin, Rev^d McCarthy, P.P. Tramore, Six Sogarths were induced to vote for him, and thus poor Joe was left in the lurch." "P.S.," Croke then added, referring to the deceased bishop of Waterford, "only think of Dr. Pierce Power but dead with 8 or 10-000 pounds every penny of which he left to his relatives brothers, sisters, nieces, and two nephews students Queens College, Cork. He did leave a penny for his soul: and only 30 pounds for his funeral. Priests refused to bury him til relatives gave a guarantee for expenses. Great scandal!"[27]

Croke reported again to Walsh on July 17, the day after the bishops of the province of Cashel met to report on the commendation of the clergy to Propaganda: "The Munster Bishops were unanimous in the support of Dr. Cleary for the See of Waterford. The question now is, will the Roman authorities allow him to come home. We spoke highly of him" (W). Because of Cleary's own predilections, however, and because Rome was then in the process of elevating the diocese of Kingston to the dignity of a metropolitan see, the authorities thought it best that he should remain where he was and wanted to be. Cardinal Simeoni, therefore, wrote Croke on

27. See also K, M. Mooney, parish priest of Cahir, Tipperary, in the diocese of Waterford, to Kirby, July 23, 1889. In referring to Phelan, for example, Mooney wrote, "*good man* i.e., 'Melchisedeck' *no nephews or relatives, to encumber him!*"

July 28, ordering a new *terna* for Waterford and informing him at the same time that Dean Coffey had been appointed bishop of Kerry (C). To complicate matters in the province of Cashel even further, the ailing coadjutor to the bishop of Killaloe died on July 20. On August 1, therefore, only a week after the funeral, the clergy of Killaloe also met to select three names to be commended to Rome. The Killaloe clergy, Croke reported to Simeoni that same day, overwhelmingly named Father Thomas McRedmond *dignissimus*, with thirty-eight votes; the *dignior*, Father Michael Culligan, and the *dignus*, Father Denis Kelly, received only six and five votes, respectively (C).

Walsh and Croke were both furious about the Kerry appointment. "The news about Kerry," Walsh informed Kirby on August 5, "is indeed deplorable. It fully confirms the worst suspicions that were entertained about the political intriguing that has been going on for the last two years or so" (K). "Even the 'Veto,'" he maintained, speaking of the quid pro quo demanded by the British government early in the century, in return for Catholic Emancipation, which should be exercised with [*sic*] more or less publicly, and under some sense of responsibility, would be preferable to the System under which affairs are managed now. Bad as the influence of the British Government is, we should prefer it to the influence of broken down landlords. It is indeed a deplorable thing to find these men openly boasting that the nomination to the Episcopacy in Ireland lies for the future in their hands. No doubt it does, but this cannot last forever." "The worst feature of the case," Walsh explained, in an allusion to the advanced age and delicate health of the pope, "is that our people now openly express their anxiety for the change which they trust will put an end to the reign of intrigue at headquarters. It is, I suppose, the first time in our history when the Irish people hoped for relief in such a way. Perhaps, however, even this is better than the open disregard of what any Pope may say or do which is so painfully exhibited now in so many ways in countries that still call themselves Catholic." Croke's reaction to the Kerry appointment, which, surprisingly enough, was more restrained than Walsh's, was nevertheless characteristic. "The appointment to Kerry took everyone by surprise," he confessed to Kirby on August 10, "though it was well known that Lord Kenmare and his friends were plotting against Fr.

Lalor [*sic*]. It will do a great deal of mischief in more ways than one. The 'situation' is a strange one, indeed, when the unanimous voice of the Bishops of Munster is held, in Rome, to be of no account against the representatives of titled laymen and calumniators. That's all I'll say now.''[28]

Croke, meanwhile, presided once again when the Waterford clergy assembled on August 8 to commend a new *terna*. On this occasion, however, the clergy's inability to focus on any candidate resulted in confusion compounded, as some thirty-one votes were distributed among eleven candidates. Croke did not help matters by giving his opinion that a *nova terna* rendered the previous three names ineligible. At last, however, as Croke reported to Simeoni on August 8, Father Phelan was returned as *dignissimus*, with nine votes; Father Peter Casey of Dungarvan received seven votes as *dignior*, and Father William Walsh rounded out the *terna* as *dignus*, with five (C). The remaining ten votes were divided among some eight others. "A remarkable thing," Errington informed Smith from Ireland on August 15, "has taken place about the 2nd Election for bishoprick of Waterford; the votes have been scattered in a most unusual way, showing that there is no strong feeling among the Clergy for any individual. The 3 first only received 9 · 7 · 5 votes, and no less than six others received one vote each" (S). "Among the latter," Errington added significantly, naming one of the two bishops who refused to sign the collective letter to the pope the previous December, "are Dr. Healy Coadjutor of Clonfert. He is you know one of the best as well as one of the few learned Irish Bishops. If he could be chosen for Waterford, it would be an immense thing, and it seems to me that this scattering of votes gives the Holy See a good opportunity for doing this." "I believe the Archbishop of the Province," he explained hesitantly and incorrectly, "is obliged to return to Rome not only the 3 first names, but the names of *all* who received any votes; is this so? For it is important Propaganda should know Dr. Healy was voted for. Mr. Dease (Lord Kenmare's Cousin),

28. K. Croke may have been indulging in hyperbole in maintaining that the Munster bishops were "unanimous" in their report to Rome on the Kerry *terna*. The bishop of Limerick appears to have asked Croke in writing to give his vote to Dean Coffey. See C, O'Dwyer to Croke, June 16, 1889. This letter is misplaced in the Croke Papers and is located among the 1884 letters.

with whom I am staying, agrees strongly with me about this, & is going to send me an interesting statement about it which I will send to you.''

Errington fulfilled his promise to Smith four days later, on August 19: "I enclose you an interesting letter from Mr. Dease, about Waterford Bishoprick'' (S). "I hope you will agree with our views,'' Errington added; "you can make use of Mr. Dease's letter. I hear Dr. Croke is trying to get his friend Dr. Fitzgerald Bishop of Ross translated to Waterford. But Dr. Fitzgerald has not been named in the voting, and his translation would simply mean an acceptance of Dr. Croke's nomination, and a direct strengthening of the *Anti-papal* party.'' In urging the translation of Healy to Waterford, Dease, in the course of his long letter to Errington of August 17, had argued that the reappointment of the coadjutor to Clonfert

would be a direct mark of approval, by the Holy See, of those brave Bishops, who have the courage to speak out & stand firm, by the Pope & the teachings of the Church. It would give courage to the *weak-kneed*— who *feel* with the minority— but who are *afraid* to speak out—in fact who know what is right—but fear the *abuse* of the *vile*, and *revolutionary press*—& it would have immence [*sic*] importance in showing the majority that "he who is not for me is against me" & that they must take courage, & teach, & obey the decrees of the Holy See. The division amongst the Waterford Priests, the fact of Dr. Healy's having received a vote, & the knowledge that he is one of the most able of the Bishops would make his appointment to the See of Waterford, the most important, & far reaching for good, in its consequences that has been made for years. (S)

A week later, Errington wrote Smith again, enclosing another letter from Dease, written August 18, which invoked the third-party opinions of Patrick Canon O'Neill (S). "Canon O'Neill whom he speaks of,'' Errington informed Smith on August 25, "is a well known priest of Dublin Diocese, an old friend of my mother's'' (S). Errington then concluded, after promising to come to Rome for Christmas, "Pray let me know about what further information would be useful to you respecting Waterford.''

Kirby, meanwhile, had written Croke, explaining that if the bishops sent more "ample'' reports to Rome, their wishes concerning vacant sees might receive more attention. Kirby also suggested to Croke, as indeed he had suggested to a number of the other Irish bishops at this time, that the pope's recent letter to the faithful, which protested the insult intended by the Italian government in erecting a statue to Giordano Bruno in Rome, should be acknowledged collectively by the Irish hierarchy. Croke, who was on his way to the Continent for a holiday, wasted little sympathy or time in his reply to Kirby from London. "The Bishops cannot give 'ample' reports about the Candidates for Vacant Sees," he explained on August 28, "for the best reason possible, namely, that, for the most part, they know next to nothing of them having never heard of some of them until their names appeared on the list of three. As regards Killaloe and Waterford, we entered fully into particulars, and, I am sure, Cardinal Simeoni will find our report satisfactory" (K). "If there is anything to be written about Bruno," Croke noted further, "of whom nobody in Ireland ever heard a tittle until the Pope's letter was read for them in the Churches, the Primate is, I should think, the person who should initiate the matter, and have the Bishops collectively take it up. Such publications do not suit us here at all. Our people are in blissful ignorance of Continental depravity and mischief making, and the less said about fellows like the Apostate Bruno the better. This, I feel certain, is the view of the case, likely to be taken by the Irish Bishops." "The Bp. Elect of Kerry," Croke pointed out tartly in conclusion, "is an excellent Ecclesiastic; but unfortunately, his politics are not those of his people."

The following day, August 29, the archbishop of Armagh, Michael Logue, also replied to Kirby, assuring him that while no one felt the insult offered his Holiness by the Bruno celebration in Rome more than the Irish bishops, it was impossible just then to get them together, and the next general meeting was not until October. Logue then confided to Kirby "that most of this apparent want of zeal on the part of the Irish Bishops arises from the fact that the Papal documents are hardly ever forwarded to them till after they have gone the round of the whole Catholic world" (K). "Very often I have these documents," he explained, "from New York published in the 'Catholic Review,' long before we receive authentic copies from Rome." By that time, Logue added, he was too embarrassed to publish them.

The archbishop of Tuam replied to Kirby two days later, on September 1: "Be assured there is no other people subject to his

Superior pastoral sway, who felt more keenly or more intensely the atrocious outrage offered to him in the erection of a statue under his own eyes to that great villain Bruno, the enemy of God and Man'' (K). But, MacEvilly went on to explain, as he and many of his brother prelates were on their visitations, could not the joint protest wait until their October meeting? ''I know little of the history of Jordano Bruno,'' one Irish bishop confessed to Kirby on September 6, ''but we all feel that honor paid to him is an insult to the H. Father & to religion. The bishops may send a protest from our October meeting'' (K). ''In the meantime,'' he suggested, ''I would gladly send one in the name of this diocese. Perhaps your Grace would kindly send us a draft of what you know would suit.''

On September 1, meanwhile, another Irish see became vacant when the venerable bishop of Derry, Francis Kelly, died. When Logue met Walsh and MacEvilly, as well as the other bishops of the province of Armagh, at Kelly's funeral, all agreed that a joint letter about the Bruno affair had better wait until the October meeting. ''I may tell your Grace *in confidence*,'' Logue reported on September 10 to Kirby, ''that there is a special reason why I should hesitate to act without a commission in the matter'' (K). ''There is a good deal of soreness,'' he explained, referring to the collective letter sent concerning *De Libertate* the previous December, ''about the last document forwarded by the Irish Bishops.'' ''By the way,'' Logue then noted in conclusion, ''there is a general feeling here among Bishops and priests that it is far from prudent to familiarize our simple people with the character of Giordano Bruno or the doings of his followers.''

When he had finished his visitations some two weeks later, MacEvilly also wrote Kirby again. He reported darkly from Tuam on September 23: ''There is a great deal of dissatisfaction throughout the Country among all classes, Bishops, Priests &c, most devoted to the H. See about the Kerry appointment. A latent comment, very general '*the Veto revived*' '' (K). In reference to the refusal of the bishops of the province of Cashel in their report to Propaganda, to recommend any of the three names in the second *terna* for Waterford, MacEvilly continued: ''There is a general hope that the Bishop of Ross, Dr. Fitzgerald, a magnificent prelate, would be promoted to a See in the South in wh you naturally feel interested.[29] The late admin[n] there has been talked of very freely even outside the Province. However, as this is in the Province of our brother of Cashel, it would [be] indelicate of me to say a word." "Pardon me," he apologised in conclusion, "If I have spoken too freely."

The Irish Bishops' determination to do as little as possible to give Rome moral support in its difficulties with the Italian government had been intensified in early August by the announcement of the appointment to Kerry; that determination had also been much stiffened by an early July letter from Propaganda to the Irish bishops, commanding them to hold a collection in their respective dioceses on the first Sunday in October for the new "National" Church of Saint Patrick in Rome. The bishops resented not only being asked to provide a church for the Augustinians in Rome, over which they would have no control or say, but also being ordered to hold a collection, and at the most inconvenient season of the year. They generally held their own important diocesan collections then, because money was usually more plentiful immediately after the harvest.[30] On July 23, MacEvilly had written Kirby plaintively, explaining in a paragraph marked "*Private*" that he had received a pressing letter from Propaganda but that holding a collection on the first Sunday in October would interfere with the Peter's Pence collection held on the first Sunday in November (K). He further noted that his parish priests, to a man, were opposed to collecting for the Augustinians. He then concluded by asking Kirby what he should do.

Kirby must have advised MacEvilly to ask for a postponement, but apparently MacEvilly's appeal was in vain. Instead, he received

29. MacEvilly referred to Kirby's interest in Waterford because Kirby was a native of that diocese. See also K, James McCarthy, bishop of Cloyne, to Kirby, August 23, 1889: "You have heard I dare say that the Munster Bishops declined to recommend to The Holy See any of the candidates elected by the Priests for the Diocese of Waterford." McCarthy went on to recommend that Fitzgerald be translated to Waterford from Ross.

30. See G, Walsh to Gillooly, July 28, 1889. Walsh's inclination, he told Gillooly, was to answer Propaganda that, because the collection was at the express direction of the Holy See, he took it that he had no option, but he added that he did not think this was a wise course of action at the moment and that it would probably interfere with future requests.

yet another letter from the secretary of Propaganda, requesting some financial support for one of his own Roman good works. "I send a trifle," MacEvilly explained to Kirby on December 29, "to Monsignor Archbishop Jacobini, Secretary of Propaganda for his Association of Roman Workmen etc. Our truly zealous Mgr is and [*sic*] deserving of all support" (K). "The numberless collections made," he advised Kirby, "are felt by our people and they are not disposed to respond. I sent Father Glynn"—the prior of the Augustinian convent in Rome—"£500 for his Church. But the priests and people declared they would not have a second. So the collection of Peter's Pence for *this* year—(and [I] never omitted it for a single year from the beginning) is put aside. I must tell you, I would sooner make it than the one for Father Glynn, but Propaganda on the part of the Pope, made Father Glynn's mandatory. I suspect that in many other places also, the same occurs." "We can't do everything," he pointed out to Kirby in conclusion; "our people have to be managed."

Croke, who had been on his way to the Continent for a holiday, had in the meantime been delayed in London for another week. "I was not prepared," he explained to Walsh on September 3, "for Dr. Kelly's death. I thought he was on the mending line. He was an honest man" (W). "I attended the Hyde Park meeting on Sunday," Croke then reported, referring to the London docker's strike. "The speaking was good: but the crowd was small, and there was little or no enthusiasm amongst them. The strike will do good, and tis supposed, the strikers will, before long, get all they are asking for." He advised Walsh: "You ought to manage, by hook or by crook, to get away. It does not do to be chained down always to the 'grinding stone.' " "The Killaloe and Waterford cases," he noted in conclusion, "will be settled in the next 'Congregation'—whenever that may be. Sic Simeoni."

A month later Croke was again in London, after having spent some three weeks in France and Belgium. There he received another letter, dated September 27, from Cardinal Simeoni.[31] The prefect of Propaganda had informed him, Croke reported to Kirby on October 2, that Thomas McRedmond, the *dignissimus* on the Killaloe

31. See K, Croke to Kirby, November 17, 1889, for the date.

*terna*, had been appointed coadjutor. Simeoni had stated, moreover, "that, on learning the state of the case from [the] Secretary of Propaganda, the Holy Father has taken the Waterford Business into his own hands '—hanc sibi omnino reservavit.' I would ask you then to see his Holiness, as soon as you can, and suggest to him the claims and suitability of Dr. Fitzgerald for the post in question. You know the Bishop of Ross. He is an excellent and energetic man, and has done wonders in his small Diocese" (K). "Do not," he then warned Kirby, realizing that any recommendation from him at Rome would be the kiss of death, "mix me up in the matter at all. Other Bishops have, I hear, interested themselves in it." "Their testimony," Croke suggested shrewdly, obviously thinking of MacEvilly, "should not be overlooked. There is not [a] fit man in the Diocese of Waterford itself. There is question, now, of an 'outsider'—and Dr. Fitzgerald has superior claims."

That same day, October 2, immediately after the customary month's mind, the clergy of Derry assembled to elect their *terna*. Their commendation was very similar to the second Waterford *terna*, in that the votes were scattered among a great many candidates. The *dignissimus*, John Keys O'Doherty, and the *dignior*, Bernard McLaughlin, received only nine and eight votes respectively, and Father John Kearney and the Reverend Professor Edward O'Brien tied for *dignus* with four votes each.[32] The remaining four votes were distributed among three other candidates.

James Hasson, a Derry priest and vice-rector of the Irish College, who was in Ireland attempting to raise money and find students, wrote Kirby on October 7: "In my last letter I gave you no news about the election for the Bishopric of Derry. Well, I was not by any means edified with all I saw and heard on that subject" (K). "I am afraid," he confessed, somewhat naively, "the Old P.P.'s don't allow the Holy Spirit much scope in the matter. The man whom I considered as the most eligible person—in fact he was the only eligible person—got only three votes [*sic*]. The '*dignissimus*' indeed had only nine votes, and out of such a large Diocese that is very poor support. I was perfectly indifferent as to the result, but the action of the priests would almost change me." "I would be very

32. *Londonderry Sentinel*, October 3, 1889.

sorry,'' Hasson noted sadly, "to see the Diocese divided into factions and parties as seems to be the inevitable result. No fewer than seven names have been returned by the Primate to the Propaganda, my own among the number. I must put a lot of strange facts before your Grace when I go out.''

Shortly after Kirby received this disquieting news about the diocese of Derry, he received the even more disturbing information that the pope had announced the appointment of John Egan as bishop of Waterford. Originally a priest of the Killaloe diocese and one-time president of the diocesan seminary in Ennis, Egan had been living for many years in Dublin, holding a teaching fellowship in the Royal University. If Kirby wrote to break the news to Croke, the archbishop of Cashel does not appear to have trusted himself to reply. Kirby did, however, write Walsh of Egan's appointment. "I am very glad that the matter about which Y. G. has kindly written to me,'' Walsh replied in measured terms on October 20, "is one in which I have no responsibility, official or otherwise. It raises one of the gravest questions that could be raised in reference to our Irish Church'' (K). "The Bishop is, personally,'' Walsh admitted of Egan, "a most amiable ecclesiastic. But, as the only trustworthy way in which the Holy See can obtain information as to the qualifications of any Irish Priest for an Irish Bishopric is the way for many years recognised and followed by the Holy See in its dealings with us in such matters, I cannot but feel most strongly that, this way having now been abandoned, a grave and most perilous crisis has been reached in the relations between the Holy See and Ireland.'' "The recommendation of ecclesiastics for the office of Bishop,'' Walsh maintained, "has now, beyond question, been raised out of the hands of the Irish Bishops. We must only hope that this new system may work as well as the old one has worked for many years. A right of nomination, or even of recommendation, independently of all reference to the Bishops, is in many ways more perilous than a right of exclusion by way of a veto. And again, a power of any kind exercised by irresponsible and unknown individuals, whether ecclesiastics or laymen, is in many ways more perilous than a power exercised in the light of day by a responsible Government.'' "P.S.,'' Walsh then added grimly, "I hope it is *distinctly* understood that the omission of all reference to me, as Bishop of the Diocese in which the priest in question has now resided for many years, relieves me of any responsibility that would otherwise exist.''

"No news about Dr. Egan,'' Croke reported to Walsh nearly a month later, on November 16. "I have not heard from Rome, nor have I written to Rome, since I saw you. It is passing strange. We must make out how Dr. E's name got under the notice of the Pope'' (W). "Dr. Coffey's consecration,'' Croke then reported, "was a success. He will do well.'' After a second thought, Croke added, "At any rate, he will be passive.'' The following day, Croke, as good as his word, wrote Kirby, attempting to find out how Egan had come to the attention of the pope. "I have received,'' Croke explained to Kirby on November 17, "no official account of the appointment of Dr. Egan to the See of Waterford, though, in a letter dated from Propaganda 27 of September, Cardinal Semeoni [sic] told me that, as soon as the appointment would be made, he would give me notice thereof—'quam primum tibi significandum curabo.' But the puzzle is who recommended Dr. E. or who brought his name before the Pope?'' (K). "Dr. E. is a sort of 'letterateur,' '' Croke noted, entering on a brief character sketch. "He has been for years off the mission, engaged exclusively in secular affairs, and by all accounts has no taste for anything else. He weighs at least 20 stone, is extremely delicate and, of course, unwieldy; and report says something else of him also that I do not care to put on paper.'' "But, as I have said,'' Croke again inquired discreetly, "the puzzle is who recommended him to his Holiness for the See of Waterford. Lord Emly and his gang are friends; and he has a brother high up in the Constabulary in touch with the Castle. But, any how, his appointment opens up a very wide and important question which sooner or later will have to be dealt with by the Irish Bishops.'' "Dr. Coffey's Consecration,'' he added, "passed off well. There was a fine gathering of priests and Bishops; and in the course of the after-dinner speeches he was spoken very highly of for his prudence, energy, and attainments. Dr. McRedmond will be a great acquisition. He is a rock of sense.''

Walsh's as distinguished from the general attitude of the Irish Bishops—and Croke's own private misgivings—about Rome's plans for filling Irish episcopal appointments, were certainly deepened during the autumn by the action of a number of English Tory Catholics. In August, these Catholic Tories had decided to initiate a vote of thanks to the duke of Norfolk for his recent efforts on behalf of British-Vatican relations. The architect, if not the author, of the presentation, W. Hussey Walsh, included a brief historical sketch that attributed to the influence of the duke the securing of the Persico mission for Ireland. When the presentation was being circulated, a copy of it fell into the hands of Archbishop Walsh. "I think it right," Walsh immediately informed Kirby, on August 30, "to let Y.G. know AT ONCE that absolutely conclusive evidence has been discovered of the origin of the unfortunate Persico mission. I have now in my possession a letter from a leading English Catholic to certain associates of his. The Duke of Norfolk was the agent of communication with Rome!" (K). "A presentation is to be made to his Grace," Walsh explained, "ostensibly for his services in receiving Mgr. Ruffo-Scilla on the occasion of the Jubilee mission to the English Court, but really for his services in procuring the Persico mission to Ireland! A private circular has been issued. It will infallibly come to light. So it is well to be prepared for it."

Walsh warned Kirby: "The effect of the revelation here will be disastrous. It is not for me to suggest a course to the authorities of the Holy See. But if they wish to avert a grave calamity, they will take some means of forestalling the effect of publication." "I have myself abstained from mentioning the matter to anyone," Walsh assured Kirby, "even to the Vicars General, or Dr. Murphy, or Fr. Pettit. Viewing as I do, the awful results of the revelation, if it comes to be made, I must secure myself against all self-reproach on the score of having by any possible imprudence, however unwittingly, contributed to the scandal that may result. It is, I know, anticipated that other important discoveries may soon be made. I do not, however, know, in what direction." "I understand," he concluded, indicating what strides rumor and fear were making, "that some clues were found among the papers of the unfortunate Pigott!"

Shortly after writing this letter to Kirby, Walsh decided to follow Croke's advice and take a holiday. He spent most of September in southern Germany and Switzerland, and because his going and coming coincided with Croke's in London, they undoubtedly had full conversations together, and with Cardinal Manning, the arch-bishop of Westminster,[33] as well, about the policy they should pursue toward Rome. "I have from Rome," Walsh reported to Cardinal Manning from Bâle on October 2, while on his return to London, "a communication of great importance. It is the result of a very strong letter of mine to Dr. Kirby. I wrote, insisting on the necessity of contradicting Hussey Walsh's statements. The docu-ment has been drawn up by the Pope's direction and was sent by Card. Rampolla to Dr. Kirby. The substance of it is that Hussey Walsh's letter is 'o *mendace* o *apocrifa*!' "[34] "Cardinal R.," Walsh added, "in a conversation with Dr. Kirby said he supposed it was 'apocrifa,' the work of some wicked people trying to sow dissen-sions between the Pope and Ireland, 'just,' he said, 'as Pigott forged the letters against Mr. Parnell.' I shall ask for your Eminence's advice also as to the use you think I should make of this."

"I enclose the Vatican document," Walsh wrote the cardinal two days later, on October 4, from the Charing Cross Hotel in London. "Your Eminence will kindly send it to me in Dublin as I leave London this afternoon" (M). He referred to the origin of the Persico mission: "Observe that there is no denial of *representations* or even of *suggestions* having been made in favour of the course which is described as taken by the purely personal decision of H.H. I believe as a matter of fact such suggestions were made. Hussey Walsh, stupid as he may be, would not refer to the action taken by his friends, as a matter so well known that it would be superfluous to describe it in detail, if no such action had been taken. Still, the document is of very high importance." "What strikes me as most important about it," he concluded very significantly, "is the evidence it gives of the present anxiety of the Holy Father to repudiate the

33. *Henry Edward Manning* (1808–92), ecclesiastical politician and statesman: Born in Hertfordshire, England; educated at Harrow, 1827, and Balliol College, Oxford, 1830; fellow, Merton College, Oxford, 1832; curate, Lavington-with-Graffham, 1833–40; married Caroline Sargent, who died in 1837; archdeacon of Chichester, 1840–51; joined Roman Catholic Church, 1851; ordained, 1851; studied at Accademia dei Nobili Ecclesiastici, 1851–54; founder and superior of the Oblates of St. Charles, 1857–65; appointed monsignor and pronotary apostolic, 1860; archbishop of Westminster, 1865; created cardinal, 1875.
34. Manning Papers (M), Archives of the Church of St. Mary of the Angels, Bayswater, London.

connection which some of our 'Unionist' Catholics are so anxious to boast of.''

''Your Grace's letter containing the document sent to you from the Vatican,'' Walsh finally replied to Kirby in the course of a letter of October 20, ''came here during my absence. I have taken the best and wisest council available as to the prudence of making any public use of it'' (K). ''The result was,'' Walsh explained, emphasising that he had waited to see if indeed the pope was anxious to repudiate the Unionist Catholic connection, ''that I delayed until the appointment should be made to Waterford, in reference to which very strange rumours were afloat. Those rumours, as we now see, most fully confirm the boasts of those whose views are expressed by Mr. H. W. in his own famous letter. Any publication of the document now would only expose the Holy See to insult. The technical contradiction so carefully worded would be received with open incredulity. It flatly contradicts a most formal statement of Mgr. Persicos!''

Some three weeks later, at the conclusion of a very long letter of November 11 in which he explained to Cardinal Manning his efforts to coordinate the temperance movement in Ireland, Walsh again referred to the delicate subject of Rome's intentions and recent episcopal appointments in Ireland. ''Some circumstances connected with recent''—he crossed out ''political''—''episcopal appointments here have given rise to a very uneasy feeling'' (M). ''The publication of Mr. Stead's conversation,'' Walsh went on, naming the editor of the *Pall Mall Gazette*, who was then doing a series of articles on the Church, ''with (unmistakably) Abbot Smith, has simply established, beyond all possibility of displacing it, the view taken by many political leaders that everything is tending to the establishment of a veto in its most objectionable form (that is, a veto exercised not by a responsible government, but a political party working underground).'' Walsh continued, with a reference to the fact that Stead and Smith had met on the journey from Paris, where the abbot had been taking his holidays, to Rome, where Stead was to collect material for his articles: ''The Abbot, speaking to this chance fellow traveller, an English Protestant, has actually mentioned me by name as one of the evil results of the absence of formal Government interference. He has done this in a conversation in which he boasts of the high official position (!) which he holds in

Rome.'' ''Is it not a case,'' Walsh half asked and half suggested in conclusion, ''in which I should write to the Holy Father, telling him of the difficulties in which we are placed by such proceedings?''

''My fellow-traveller,'' Stead had reported of this interview with Abbot Smith, which had taken place toward the end of October, ''was a man of powerful intelligence, with a range of acquaintance extending far beyond ecclesiastical circles. There were few of our English ambassadors whom he did not know personally. He knew Mr. Gladstone, Lord Salisbury, and Lord Hartington, and although, as he repeatedly reminded me, he was only an outsider who took a distant view of English politics, all the more prominent incidents in our recent history were focused in his mind with remarkable clearness and precision.''[35] ''He spoke,'' Stead observed, ''with great freedom and intelligence upon the prospects of our Ministry and the significance of the recent by-elections, and we were soon in the depths of a discussion as to the establishment of diplomatic relations between the Vatican and the English Government.''

Stead quoted Abbot Smith:

''The Pope is very displeased with England, because of its refusal to enter into relations with him. There is not any day in which we do not come into contact with England at some part of the world. To-day it is in Ireland, yesterday it was in India, to-morrow it may be in Canada. But wherever it happens, there is no one with whom the Pope can speak who stands for England. It is a perpetual irritation, a constant inconvenience. Nearly every English statesman to whom I have spoken admits that it would be advantageous to have some one to represent your country at the Vatican, but as one of them said to me after admitting that it was desirable, 'English Governments can never forget that they are living practically under a regime of universal suffrage.' The fact is, I suppose there is no party strong enough to dare to make a change which all admit to be advantageous, for fear of a popular out cry.''

''I explained to him,'' Stead added, ''that the objection that weighed with us was not so much the Protestant prejudice to which he attached too much importance, as the political objection to anything that seemed likely to give substance to the dream of re-establishing the temporal power and the religious objection taken by the Irish Bishops, and therefore by the Irish members, to anything that in-

35. *Freeman's Journal*, November 7, 1889.

creased the power of the English Government over the head of the Church.'' '' 'But,' was the instant retort of my Roman doctor''— Stead again quoted Smith—'' 'do you not see what an enormous advantage it would be for England to enter into such relations with the Pope as would enable you to prevent the appointment of any Irish Bishops who were hostile to the Government? Do you think that if you had had a fully accredited representative at the Vatican you would ever have had Dr. Walsh as Archbishop of Dublin?' ''

"I felt rather sick, I confess," Stead remarked, "with this cynical way of putting it. 'What?' 'Had it come to this, that anyone in Rome, which in her early prime had defied all the Powers and principalities of this world in order to preserve in [sic] intact and unimpaired the exclusive right of selecting as bishops of the flock the men whom she considered most faithful, was now ready even to press upon a heretical Government the right of veto in exchange for this poisonous mess of diplomatic pottage?' '' "I sincerely hope," Stead then observed of Smith, "that he does not really represent Rome. If he does, Heaven help Rome! It was difficult to imagine that such a man should feel himself at home in a Church which has a Manning and Moran and Gibbons among its Cardinals and Walsh and Croke among its Archbishops, and much more difficult to think that he could enjoy the confidence of the Holy See." "It was a good thing, no doubt," Stead explained to his readers, "for me at the very inception of my inquiries to be brought into close contact with a spirit so absolutely opposed to the mind that is in Cardinal Manning. Of course, in himself my travelling companion proves nothing. He may be a white blackbird, or rather a black swan, among the ecclesiastics of the Curia." "But," Stead then confessed somberly, "it would be idle to deny that among those outside the Church with whom I have spoken there is a general concurrence of opinion that I shall find he is much more in accord with the prevailing spirit at the Vatican than is Cardinal Manning. A fervid and conscientious Catholic layman said to me, 'It is Bishop Vaughan[36]

36. *Herbert Alfred Vaughan* (1832–1903), ecclesiastical politician, publisher, and administrator: Educated at Stonyhurst, Belgium, Downside, and Rome; ordained, 1854; joined congregation of Oblates of St. Charles, 1857; missionary in Caribbean and Central and South America, 1863–65; built St. Joseph's College for missionary students, 1866; bought and edited the *Tablet*, 1868–71; appointed

rather than Cardinal Manning who represents the temper of the Papal Court. The views which shocked you so much on the part of your travelling companion are held and pressed with diplomatic modifications by the highest personages around the Pope.' " " 'Captain Ross of Bladensburg,' " Stead then concluded, still quoting his anonymous Catholic layman, " 'an Irish landlord born in Italy, to whom the Duke of Norfolk was a mere figurehead, has more influence with the Pope than all the Irish bishops put together.' "

What Walsh and Croke and Manning and Stead all failed to understand, however, was that Rome was acting not in the British but rather in her own interest, in attempting to reassert her authority in the Irish Church. In accepting that the Decree could not be enforced in Ireland, Rome had, by December 1888, ceased to insist that the Irish Bishops exert themselves to maintain her authority. In the summer of 1889, when Rome began once again to bring pressure to bear on the Irish bishops—by commanding a special collection for Saint Patrick's Church, by appointing John Coffey bishop of Kerry, and by suggesting a collective letter to support the pope in his difficulties with the Italian government—the Irish clergy, high and low, misunderstood Rome's motives. Their suspicions were certainly not allayed by the curious appointment in early October of John Egan as bishop of Waterford. When the government, moreover, finally announced at the end of October an intention to send a special mission to Rome, ostensibly concerning Malta, the Irish Bishops seemed confirmed in their worst doubts; their suspicions increased when John Ross of Bladensburg was announced as secretary to the mission. When *all* the episcopal appointments made during this period are reviewed in detail, however, and the special mission of Sir John Lintorn Simmons is carefully examined, it becomes evident that British influence at the Vatican during 1889 was minimal and that the various machinations of the Unionist Catholics, who were active at Rome and about whom Walsh and Croke and Manning were so much concerned, actually counted for very little, if, indeed, for anything at all.

---

bishop of Salford, 1872; took leading part in attempting to solve Manchester's social problems, 1872–92; appointed archbishop of Westminster, 1892; created cardinal, 1893.

When Salisbury decided once again in late August, just before Parliament recessed for the autumn session, to postpone the announcement of the special mission to Rome, Norfolk and Ross were naturally perturbed. In an interview in London, Ross not only asked Balfour for information about the vacant Irish bishoprics and the disposition of the Irish government toward the various candidates, but also raised the question why Salisbury had neglected to have the Roman mission announced as he had promised in June. "I spoke to Lord Salisbury," Balfour informed Ross on September 4, from Scotland, "as I promised in respect of the non-announcement of the Malta mission in the House of Commons."[37] "I gather from him," Balfour explained without giving much satisfaction, "that the omission was by design." "With regard to the vacant Bishoprics," he reported, abruptly changing the subject, "I hear varying accounts of Redmond who has been nominated *Dignissimus* for Killaloe. Healy would, of course, be good anywhere.[38] Killaloe if Redmond is not selected or Waterford. I am told that Casey, third on the list for Waterford, is a fair man." "P.S.," Balfour noted hurriedly, "I have just received information which would appear to indicate that Redmond would not be satisfactory." "What I should really like," he concluded, somewhat indiscreetly, "would be to get Healy appointed to Killaloe should that be possible or Casey for Waterford."

Ross wrote Balfour from London on September 10: "I received your letter of the 4th today. It reached Rostrevor on the 8th and was forwarded. I am sorry that I did not tell you I was staying in town for the present. I will do all I can regarding the matter you wrote about. Speaking off hand, it strikes me that there may be difficulty in getting Healy put where he got no votes."[39] "This difficulty would be lessened," he suggested, adroitly referring to the hitch in the Malta mission, "were it possible to speak instead of writing to the authorities. I may take it, I suppose, that the chance of getting Dr. Healy in one of the Sees should not be lost." Balfour replied the following day, September 11, but omitting the usual "My dear

37. B, 49828.
38. See B, 49810, Ridgeway to Balfour, September 3, 1889: "Dr. Healy *can* be transferred and Killaloe would suit him and us. . . . Waterford would not suit Healy as well, but it would do."
39. B, 49821.

Ross," he began more stiffly with "My Dear Colonel Ross."[40] He explained, "My letter to you went by mistake to Dublin Castle," adding coldly: "I quite understand the difficulties about Bishop Healy; and, of course, I recognise the frequent impossibility of carrying out any views which we may form on the subject of Ecclesiastical appointments. I merely desired to let you know who seemed to me to be the best man so far as I have material for forming a judgement on the subject."

When Ross did not at once receive a reply from Balfour, because of the mistake in address, Norfolk decided to write Salisbury asking for an explanation of why the Malta mission had not been announced. "I am sorry to trouble you so soon after your leaving London," he explained, coming straight to the point, on September 7, "but having heard nothing of the reason why the Mission to Rome was not announced in Parliament I am anxious to know how we stand in the matter. I should be very much obliged if you could kindly write to me to *Hotel du Parc Vichy France* letting me know when and in what way the announcement is to be made" (SY). Salisbury, who was also on his holidays, replied several days later. "Very many thanks for your letter," Norfolk responded from Vichy on September 13 (SY). "I was only anxious to know whether the change of plan about the announcement points to any further possible change in your intentions. I am very glad to hear that things remain the same as when I last saw you. Of course, in due time I should be glad to know when and how the matter is to be made public." "I also expect," Norfolk then noted, "to get back to England about the middle of October." Why Salisbury did not announce the Malta mission, of course, was that he had shrewdly decided to steal a march on his own ultra-Protestant supporters. If he had announced the mission when Parliament adjourned at the end of August, as a part of the government's proposed program for the autumn session, which would begin in late October, the "no-Popery-die-hards" in his own party would have had the whole recess to fret and fume and perhaps make trouble.

"Will you let me remind you," a chastened and more respectful Ross asked Balfour on September 26, from Rostrevor, "of a conver-

40. B, 49828.

sation I had with you just before you were leaving town about a month ago? But first I may say I have written about Waterford and Killaloe and I trust the proper persons will be appointed."[41] "I saw Turner before coming to Ireland," he explained, naming the special commissioner of the Royal Irish Constabulary in the southwest,

(after I received your two letters) and he gave me what I think ought to prove conclusive against McRedmond, the first on the list for Killaloe, viz. his public approval of Cox M.P. who had urged the Plan of Campaign after the issue of the Decree. Now with respect to the conversation I had with you, I thought it would be a good thing, if it could be managed, to get a short Memorandum prepared, showing what the Clergy (Bishops and Priests) and those associated with them, had been doing with regard to Boycotting and to the Plan, since the appearance of the rescript to the present time. . . . I have already given Cardinal Rampolla many of these details, but I should like to do so again in a more complete and categorical form. . . . I think, as I told you, it would be quite possible for me to draw up such a memorandum; but if you feel you can order it to be done for me, I should prefer it. . . . Moreover, I am sure that a greater effect would be produced, if I were able to vouch for the facts which I bring forward—not as being collected by private efforts, but as being based upon substantial and reliable information. I am certain you will sympathise with me when I say, that if any information is to be given to the authorities of the Catholic Church, it is also necessary to be perfectly certain that the information is quite complete and accurate.

"My dear Ross," Balfour replied from Prestonkirk, more cordially if more briefly, on October 4, "I am trying to do something in the direction you suggest."[42] That same day Balfour wrote his secretary at the Irish Office in London, enclosing Ross's letter. "It would be well I think," he advised, "to have a Report prepared *for our use* of the kind indicated in the enclosed letter. When completed, there will be no harm in sending the writer a copy."[43] Colonel Turner, meanwhile, had also written Balfour about his conversation with Ross in London adding some interesting details about the Killaloe *terna*. "While I was in London," he reported from Ennis on September 22, "I saw Lord Emly and Ross of Bladensburg at the Tower about the question of the Bishop of Killaloe. I may say that I wrote to Lord Edmund Talbot whom I knew, & asked him

41. B, 49821.
42. B, 49828.
43. B, 49821, Balfour to T. Browning.

to get the Duke of Norfolk to move in the matter, & the latter handed it over to Ross."[44] "They both agreed," Turner added, "that McRedmond '*dignissimus*' was totally unfit as shown by his sympathy with Cox M.P. & his collecting subscriptions from the Clergy of Clare for him, after the issue of the Papal Rescript. But McRedmond got 38 votes & the 'dignior' & the 'dignus' who were the President & Vice President of the Ennis Diocesan College about 4 each, the two latter only being put in to form the necessary trio. Nothing is known against them or for them." "As I have written to Ross after careful enquiry today," he further reported, "it is believed they are two moderate men, but Nationalists. By far the best P.P. in the County would be Fr. J. Cahir P.P. of Mullough, but he got no votes, & being a very staunch Loyalist would not of course get any in this County. The only other good man I know is F<sup>r.</sup> Fogarty who got one or two votes; he is loyal & thoroughly well meaning, but was weak as Administrator to the late Bishop."

"I return Turner's letter," Ridgeway reported to Balfour from Dublin a week later, on September 29.[45] He incorrectly informed Balfour, "Dr. Casey a good man has been appointed Bishop of Waterford over the head of the selected firebrand. Turner's nominee for Killaloe is I fear an impossibility. He is wasting strength which would have been better concentrated on Bishop Healy." Some ten days later, Turner again wrote Balfour, enclosing a letter written by McRedmond in support of Cox. "Of Cox I need only say," Turner explained in this letter of October 9, "that he has been the worker of the Plan of Campaign in Clare—the great apostle of Boycotting, & has been three times convicted for inciting to illegal practices."[46] "A number of Clare Priests," he reported, "are going on as usual, & McRedmond who is 'locum tenens,' does nothing to check them, & did nothing while Vicar General with a senile old Bishop. . . . When I went to see him about the conduct of some of the curates, in keeping up the League, Boycotting, &c, he would not listen to me. He is a regular Croke-ite, an intense Nationalist, and all the Clare priests are longing for his appointment. I need not say more to show, what a dangerous appointment his would be."

44. B, 49820.
45. B, 49810.
46. Ibid.

Both the appointment of McRedmond and the pope's taking the Waterford appointment into his own hands had been announced by Simeoni in his letter of September 27 to Croke. Not only was the government's intelligence, as conveyed by Ridgeway to Balfour on September 29, incorrect, but the information gap, at least as far as Killaloe was concerned, had not been bridged by October 9, when Turner wrote Balfour. Rome had obviously paid little attention to the efforts of Ross to block McRedmond's appointment and had not even bothered, apparently, to keep him or Norfolk informed. "We were startled on October 3," an incredulous Errington wrote Smith, who was still holidaying in Paris, "by the statement in the Freeman's Journal that the See of Waterford had been filled by the appointment of Father Casey!! Can this be true?" (S). "I can hardly believe it," he noted significantly, "for business is seldom done at this time in Rome, and you also were of opinion that the Election would not take place till Nov." "Pray let me know when you leave Paris," he then concluded anxiously, "and whether I can get you any information &c: I should like also to hear about Waterford." When the appointment was finally announced in mid-October, however, the choice of an outsider demonstrated that the pope was not disposed to satisfy the government and its Catholic friends by translating Healy from Clonfert. "It is now said," Errington glumly informed Smith on November 4, "Dr. Egan is named Bishop of Waterford; I do not know him, but I am told he is 'amiable & well meaning, but not strong'" (S). Errington was too experienced a Roman hand not to know that business was being done in Rome at a most unusual season of the year, but what was even more important, Smith was not being kept informed about Irish episcopal appointments. Because Errington's own usefulness at Rome now depended entirely on Smith's star, which appeared to be in eclipse, he was understandably depressed; he was all the more upset because he had been so recently exhilarated at being once again at the apparent center of things in the matter of the Kerry appointment.[47]

47. That Errington felt his exclusion from the company of the great and from the associated sense of power is obvious from another portion of his letter of November 4, 1889, to Smith: "I have to attend a large Unionist Meeting this month in Lincolnshire in the very town where in 1886 I stood as a Gladstonian. It is a difficult position, but I think we are all bound to do what we can, even at inconvenience to

From Rome's point of view, the appointments to Killaloe and Waterford were very difficult. The authorities could hardly have been reassured by the reports they received from Ross about McRedmond, and if an outsider had to be chosen for Waterford, why did the pope select Egan rather than Healy or even Fitzgerald? Furthermore, how was Rome able to act decisively and relatively quickly at so unsuitable a season of the year? Though the evidence is largely circumstantial, the answer to these questions appears to be that Monsignor Persico's influence in the making of Irish episcopal appointments had become crucial. McRedmond, for example, was a good friend of the bishop of Limerick, whom Persico liked and respected, and Persico knew he was a friend; O'Dwyer had undoubtedly voted for his friend in the report the bishops of the province had forwarded to Propaganda, making that report unanimous; and finally, Persico had most likely met McRedmond, who was then vicar general, in his visit to the diocese of Killaloe in 1887. It was for these reasons, apparently, that the appointment went to McRedmond in spite of Ross's injunctions and suggestions. Why either Healy or Fitzgerald was not translated to Waterford is easier to explain than how Egan came to be appointed: Persico, it appears, disliked Healy, and that would be reason enough to exclude him, whereas Fitzgerald was obviously made too much in the image and likeness of Croke. There is no evidence, however, that Persico even knew Egan, though the probability that he had met him in Dublin is very high: Egan was not only known to O'Dwyer but was a lifelong friend of McRedmond.[48]

In any case, in whatever way Egan came under the notice of the pope, the Killaloe and Waterford appointments could only have increased the government's anxiety to have Ross on the spot in Rome. "Very many thanks," Norfolk wrote Salisbury on Tuesday, October 29, "for your appointment for Friday afternoon at the F.O. You do not name an hour so we"—meaning Ross and himself—

---

help the cause; besides, even on lower grounds, it is fatal for a public man to efface himself & stand aside, especially when he ought to come forward. I shall be glad when it is all over."

48. For the O'Dwyer-McRedmond friendship, see Persico to Walsh, December 25, 1887, Patrick J. Walsh, *William J. Walsh, Archbishop of Dublin* (Dublin, 1928), p. 307 (cited hereafter as *Walsh*); for Persico's dislike of Healy, see W, Croke to Walsh, January 12, 1888; for the McRedmond-Egan friendship, see K, McRedmond to Kirby, October 21, 1889.

"shall come at 4 o'clock and wait your convenience. I hope much you will put Ross in as high a position on this mission as you can. It may greatly increase his chances of success in the special object we wish him to work for" (SY). Salisbury, in fact, did handsomely by Ross in appointing him secretary to the head of the mission, especially as Ross's qualifications regarding Malta were hardly existent.

"You will remember that at our interview you gave me in July," Norfolk reminded Salisbury on November 1, shortly after he and Ross had seen the prime minister, "I pointed out to you the wish expressed by Cardinal Rampolla in his letter that he might be allowed to have confidentially some indication of the special points connected with *Malta* with which the Mission would deal. At the time you remember you said it was better to defer answering this point until the Mission was about to start. Do you think I might now furnish Cardinal Rampolla confidentially with such points as you think well and if so will you let me have them. I am of course anxious to do what would be civil to the Cardinal and not to leave his request unattended to" (SY). "Many thanks," Norfolk noted briefly two days later, on November 3, "for your cheque for £ 100 —which shall be paid in to my personal account" (SY). "The payment I have to make," he added mysteriously, undoubtedly referring to Ross, "shall be made in bank notes." "Many thanks also," he concluded, with a reference to the official instructions issued to Sir John Lintorn Simmons as head of the mission, "for the copy of the instructions which I will deal with in the manner you desire."

The mission then set out for Rome, arriving some time after the middle of November. "I saw Card. Rampolla yesterday evening," Ross reported to Balfour from Rome on Sunday, November 24, "& had a long talk with him. We had an audience of the Pope in the morning, & I could not see H. E."—Rampolla—"before. I did not go into the important matter connected with the action of the clergy in Ireland, confining myself to the more pressing question of Education."[49] After a long account of his interview with Rampolla on educational matters, Ross continued:

49. B, 49821.

I find there is the greatest anxiety to appoint the best men as Bishops. Card. Rampolla showed me clearly that this was uppermost in his mind; and further I should tell you (most confidentially) that Mgr. Persico is here, & takes the most vivid interest in the matter; having sufficient knowledge & position he can press his point perhaps in a stronger manner than anyone else. The question now concerns the Diocese of Derry. The choice lies between the first & the second upon the list, Drs. O'Doherty & McLaughlin, who have only one vote between them. I got a confidential report from Sir W. Ridgeway, written by Foley a Dist. Insp$^r$, by which it appears that O'Doherty ought to be the best candidate, as it is stated in the report that he & two brothers take no part in politics whereas it is stated that Dr. McLaughlin takes prominent part in them. Now it appears that McLaughlin has the reputation of being the most learned, & consequently the appt inclines to him. As however it is a fact that learning is not everything that is required in a Bishop, but also some backbone to be able to govern properly . . . would it be possible to give me some further information with regard to the character & previous actions of these two Priests?

Because the congregation of Propaganda that would make the final recommendation to the Pope would meet in the second week of December, Ross concluded, "if this is possible, it would be well that I should get it before the end of next week (first week in Dec.)."

In a long reply on November 30, mainly concerning educational matters, Balfour assured Ross that the information he desired would be sent on as soon as possible.[50] Ross responded on December 10, explaining that the Irish situation was not really understood in Rome.[51] "In fact," he pointed out, "since we left Rome last year, we have so to speak lost headway. The impression seems to be here that things are improving in Ireland, that the Bishops have generally done their best to enforce the Decree; in fact that moral teaching has had its effect, & that political excitement more or less is all that remains. I need not say I am busily engaged in giving the Cardinal as accurate account as possible, and in correcting the false impressions which seem to prevail. I am also showing how isolated Dr. O'Dwyer is, how improper this is, & how he ought to be supported." "Having got this done," he then reported, "I feel Educ$^n$ will then be more easily discussed here."

"I am careful," Ross reported again to Balfour nearly two weeks

50. B, 49828.
51. B, 49821.

later, on December 23, "how I deal with Irish matters here, confining my representations to Rampolla & to Persico. The latter takes an active interest in Ireland, and has a good deal to say, to the appointment of Bishops. But he is anxious to keep himself in the background, & does not wish it to be known that he has anything to say to these questions."[52] "I know no one," he assured Balfour, and obviously Persico was still in very good form, "who so thoroughly understands the true state of things, as he. Owing to the fact that I cannot discuss Irish matters with more than these two officials (& I think you will approve of the precaution), I am not of course able to reveal the true state of things to as many persons as formerly was the case, when I was here two years ago. But at the same time Cardinal Rampolla always receives me most cordially, & has told me repeatedly that everything I put before him will receive the greatest attention."

"I have already," Ross then pointed out, "given the Cardinal a long Memorandum, based to a great extent, upon the report with which you furnished me, relating to the conduct of the Clergy since the issue of the Decree. This Memorandum, besides giving information upon the revolt against the Decree, showed the present isolation of Dr. O'Dwyer, and explained how considerately offending Priests were treated by the Law (a matter I found the Cardinal had entirely misunderstood)." "I have also," Ross then noted, with reference to a quarrel in Derry that had broken out between the vicar capitular, who had been elected to govern the diocese during the episcopal interregnum, and the local prison's board, over the rights and duties of the prison chaplain, "fully explained the Derry Gaol case." "I told the Cardinal," he then added, "that I thought it would be a misfortune if the new Bishop (who is to be appointed) were to have this disagreeable legacy thrust upon him, upon his assuming his episcopal duties, & I pressed upon the Cardinal the necessity of dealing with the matter at once. He promised to speak to the Prefect of Propaganda—(Cardinal Simeoni) immediately on it & he appeared to realise the importance of settling it without delay."

"I imagine," Ross then continued, apparently unaware that Rampolla was indeed politely receiving information as mere information,

52. Ibid.

"that one of the best means of effecting a change in Ireland, is by getting better men as Bishops." "This is a thing," he added, somewhat naively, "they do not see here, but it will require careful attention, because not only active agitators are to be avoided, but also those good priests who have little or no backbone & who therefore fall ready victims to the strength of the present majority. Card. Rampolla has spoken to me several times about Arch. Walsh." "He seems to feel," Ross noted most significantly, "that he is an obstacle to pacification, in fact an agent of the agitators; Persico *knows* this thoroughly. There is however the difference (outwardly at least) between Walsh & Croke, the former is very wary and keeps himself officially within bounds, while the latter is far more impetuous & does not mind doing officially what is entirely reprehensible. . . . I personally feel that Walsh is the most dangerous of the two."

"With regard to Dr. Healy," he informed Balfour, "I think it would be useful if he got the administration of the Diocese of Clonfert. I am attending to this. I was able to show that Dr. O'Dwyer has been left entirely isolated by his brother-Bishops, & to this matter I am also devoting myself. I told the Cardinal that if the other Bishops had followed the example of Dr. O'Dwyer, Ireland would not have been in a very different position, & I added that their now having done so was all the more extraordinary since there were many Bishops in quieter Sees than Limerick. Hence there is no possible excuse for these Bishops." "However," Ross observed considerately, "I need not trouble you with too much detail, I fear I have already wearied you with it. On the whole, I think I am progressing, & that they are beginning to realise here that things in Ireland are not as they were represented to them, & I have no doubt that before long they will see this all the clearer. As now even, you may imagine, it takes time to bring these matters home to them, & I hope I may have this necessary time to do so." "I must ask you to pardon me," Ross then apologized in conclusion, "for so very long a letter, & with my best wishes for Xmas & the New Year. . . ."

The next day, however, Ross was more alarmed, and wrote the duke of Norfolk a letter marked "*Private & pressing.*" "I have heard a rumour," he informed Norfolk on December 24, "that the Maltese Government are *pressing* for the immediate return of Dr. Carbone" (SY). (Carbone was the Maltese attorney general and one of the secretaries to the mission.) "The absence of Dr. Carbone w$^d$ be a serious blow to the mission." "Its character," he warned, meaning the Irish, rather than the Maltese, purpose of the mission, "w$^d$ be altered, in the eyes of the public, if it were to remain here without him. He may be wanted in Malta, but he is urgently wanted here, & if anything is to be done here, it is necessary that the Mission should not be dissolved too soon." "All I can say is," Ross then pointed out in conclusion, "that *time* is required here, & it would not be easy to get on without Carbone from every point of view." On receiving this letter from Ross, Norfolk decided to forward it to Salisbury. "I have received the enclosed private note," he explained apologetically to Salisbury on December 28, "and I think it better to let you see it. I do not feel clear that I ought to do so, but it would be very unfortunate if anything were to happen to spoil a mission which appears to be working so smoothly and so gaining in confidence here that I hope I may let you know privately the fear that has gotten into Ross's head" (SY).

The mission, however, survived the "Carbone" crisis, and, meanwhile, John Keys O'Doherty, the *dignissimus* on the *terna*, was appointed bishop of Derry. William McFeely, a Derry priest and an alumnus of the Irish College in Rome, wrote Kirby on January 13, 1890, from Coleraine, "Bishops of wisdom, and holiness, having a sincere love for the Holy See, are just now required in Ireland" (K). "Of late," he reported ingenuously, "there has been a good deal of friction between the Irish people, and the authorities in Rome. It seems unfortunate that these things should take place, but let us hope, they will lead to no evil consequences. I am sorry to find an idea firmly established in the minds of the priests, that Rome must not be trusted. Every rumour circulated about the Pope's intentions, and inclinations being hostile to the wishes of the Irish people, is at once seized upon as another proof of the truth of the assumption. Father O'Doherty has always been moderate in his ideas, but he has at the same time given general satisfaction." "He is," McFeely concluded more ambiguously, "a gentleman of great piety, of refined manners, endowed, I understand, with prudence, and ability."

In attempting to reconstruct her power and influence in the Irish Church, Rome had given due notice, in the appointments to Killaloe and Derry, that only men of moderate views were acceptable and, in the cases of Kerry and Waterford, that men of conservative views were actually preferred. The lesson could hardly have been lost on the Irish clergy, high and low, and the result, even if deeply resented, must certainly have been sobering. Because the Irish people, furthermore, had been all but hopelessly alienated by the Decree, Rome was at least secure in the knowledge that, as long as she confined her action to her admitted prerogatives in the Irish Church, things could not get much worse this side of schism. Then, too, Rome had also learned in recent years, and in Ireland as much as anywhere, that the vagaries of public opinion were unpredictable. Because public opinion, from Rome's point of view, depended neither on an informed intelligence nor on the ability to sustain memory, but rather on the pabulum of the press and the direction of an interested leadership, the result was a predictable tendency to sacrifice principle to sentiment in the name of the democracy and in the interests of power. The correct policy for Rome to pursue, therefore, was one with which she had a long experience—watchful waiting. Moreover, by quietly pursuing her own interest in Ireland, Rome was able to keep alive the pope's deep desire—diplomatic relations with England—without giving the British government any real advantage, while acquiring a good deal of useful and valuable information about the situation in the Irish Church.

# 3

# HIGHER EDUCATION
## January–December 1889

The agrarian agitation and the supposed Roman-British alliance, however, were not the only serious embarrassments the Irish Church faced in its efforts to preserve the Clerical-Nationalist alliance. For nearly two years, hardly anything had been done in any way or on any level concerning education in Ireland. For mainly diplomatic and tactical reasons, apparently in order to keep Rome on hand, Balfour had explored the possibilities of Irish Catholic higher education in the summer and autumn of 1888, but his efforts through Father Klein and the earl of Denbigh were not sustained beyond the new year. Balfour did promise an irate duke of Norfolk, in early December 1888, that as soon as the government's proposals were "in shape," he would be the first to see them. Given the Irish administration's preoccupations with the landlord syndicate, evictions, and the Pigott exposé, little progress was made in the matter of higher education during the winter and spring of 1889. Balfour had, however, early in 1889, asked Thomas Arnold, a fellow of the Royal University of Ireland and an English Catholic convert, to inquire into Catholic education on the Continent, particularly at Freiburg in Baden and Louvain in Belgium. "The enclosed memo," Arnold informed Balfour on January 25, "contains what I have been able to make out on the points you desired me to inquire into."[1] "Thinking over what passed at the interview with which you favoured me last Monday," Arnold noted further, adding a refer-

---

1. B, 49842.

ence to the Catholic University of Ireland, which was then under the management of the Society of Jesus, "I have come to the conclusion that I rated the University property in Stephen's Green much too highly. Not £40,000, but from £20,000 to £25,000, must be more like its real value;—and that sum would include the premises of the Cath. Univ. Medical School in Cecilia Street."

"When I said that there were no Theological lectures in the strict sense given at the College in Stephen's Green," Arnold observed, "I should perhaps have added that religious instruction *is* regularly given to all the students, all those who at least are Catholics. A Wesleyan was attending some of our lectures two or three years ago; he was, I need scarcely say, *not* required to attend the religious instruction. It occurs to me, with reference to the doubt which you seemed to feel in regard to the *reality* of the interest taken by the bishops in University education, that perhaps their inactivity, and failure to take any initiative for several years past, partly led you to think so." "But," Arnold asked, "is not that inactivity due to the understanding which, if I remember right, they came to three or four years ago with the Irish parliamentary party, to employ that party as their organ in any further applications to the Government or the legislature on educational questions?" "For this and other reasons," Arnold added discreetly, "the Bishops will take no initiative. But what I hear,—and I think on good authority—leads me to believe that even the most anti-English of them would not venture to *refuse* any reasonable offer made by the Government, in order to settle the University question."

Why the Irish bishops did not take the initiative in educational matters, however, had perhaps as much to do with their inefficiency as a body as with the terms of the Clerical-Nationalist alliance. Some ten days later, on February 4, Walsh wrote Gillooly that, as far as university education was concerned, things looked very dim (G). He supposed that Gillooly had seen Mr. Arnold's very "insolent" article in the current *Dublin Review*.[2] "Dr. Woodlock," Walsh added, naming the bishop of Ardagh, who was also a secretary to the episcopal standing committee, "who had not seen it, or

2. Thomas Arnold, "Louvain and the Dublin Universities," *Dublin Review*, January 1889.

heard of it (!), has just been here apparently quite delighted at the idea of getting a number of Fellows—including this Mr. Arnold—reappointed tomorrow for another term of 7 years. The whole is discreditable to us all." "I have written to the Primate," Walsh then explained, referring to Logue, who, as primate, had the right of convening the standing committee, "asking him is there no way of having our position recognized in this University Question. I see quite plainly that as long as the initiative is left to him nothing will be done, and we shall be simply effaced. I suggested to him the idea of *fixed* meetings, say quarterly, of the Episcopal Committee. I thought it well your Lordship should know of this at once. I give up the good Bishop of Ardagh in despair."

Finally, in the following month, a meeting of the standing committee of the episcopal body was called; it met on March 21, and a comprehensive series of resolutions, inspired and drafted mainly by Walsh, covering all aspects and levels of the Irish education question, were duly considered.[3] Provision was also apparently made for the standing committee to give further consideration to these proposed resolutions before the usual general meeting of the Irish Bishops at Maynooth in late June; and a meeting of the committee, therefore, was scheduled for shortly after Easter. "The meeting," Walsh informed Gillooly in despair on April 26, "will not be held. Dr. Woodlock remembered only the day, forgetting the hour and the place, and sent his circular forms up here to be filled up and sent out! Then I had to write the Primate. He had forgotten all about it, and had made other arrangements." "In the meantime," Walsh then noted, "great mischief has been done. But I have exhausted every possible means of bringing about a meeting."

At their general meeting at Maynooth on June 27, in any case, the Irish Bishops adopted the resolutions and instructed Archbishop Walsh to bring the particular question of university education for Catholics in Ireland to the attention of the Irish Parliamentary Party. "I have been deputed," Walsh explained to Parnell on July 8, "to communicate with you upon the subject, requesting you at your earliest convenience to put a question in reference to it to the repre-

3. Patrick J. Walsh, *William J. Walsh, Archbishop of Dublin* (Dublin, 1928), p. 490.

sentative of the ministry in the House of Commons. The resolutions, as you are aware, were forwarded some time ago to the leaders of the ministry, and to those of the opposition as well, in both Houses of Parliament.''[4] ''I would ask you then,'' he requested formally, ''on the part of the bishops, kindly to ask in the House of Commons whether the attention of the Prime Minister has been directed to the claim in the *matter of University Education* put forward in these resolutions, and whether it is the intention of the Ministry to adopt the necessary measures for the removal of the grievances complained of. I am also deputed to convey to you the request of the bishops that, in the event of the reply not being satisfactory, you would press this matter on the attention of the ministry, and of the House of Commons by every means at the disposal of the Irish Parliamentary Party.''

Herbert Vaughan, the bishop of Salford and editor of the *Dublin Review*, as well as owner of the *Tablet*, which had taken up a strong anti-Nationalist line in recent years, meanwhile continued to interest himself both publicly and privately in the question of Irish university education for Catholics. ''I know,'' Vaughan wrote Balfour, in a letter marked *''Private & Confidential,''* on June 17, ''you will allow me to throw out a suggestion, which may not have presented itself to you in the midst of other matters. It is conveyed more in detail in the article headed *the Gov$^t$ & Higher Education in Ireland*, which appears in the current *Dublin Review*. I send a copy of it, but the gist of it is to pass a short Bill *this* session to right the Higher Education Question in Ireland. Reasons not mentioned in the above article, for doing so are:—that you would thus revive & strengthen the confidence which has been somewhat shaken in Rome by a Parnell Commission.''[5] ''In Rome there is a feeling,'' he then pointed out to Balfour, referring to the dropping of the Maltese negotiations at the end of February, ''that they have been played with, used & thrown over; and of course there are not wanting those who preach that the Conservative Gov$^t$ is utterly selfish, ungenerous & untrustworthy. Now the passing of an Education Bill would explode this argument & would go far to conciliate the Holy See.''

4. Ibid. For the resolutions see the *Irish Catholic*, July 6, 1889.
5. B, 49845.

"But it could have another effect," Vaughan argued; "it would conciliate & strengthen English & Irish Catholic supporters of the Gov^t, it would shut the mouths of many of the Irish Bishops & Priests. You may raise this objection:

(1) The time is too short. To this a reply is given, & a good one, in the article in the Dublin.
(2) The Irish Bishops, & Irish Members would oppose it. The article shows they could not.

"And I know from Archbishop Walsh," he assured Balfour, "that he is commissioned by the Bishops to accept such a Bill. If you have not their Resolutions on this subject & would like to have them, I think I could procure them for you. I need not point out how desirable it would be for the Gov^t. to bring in such a Bill of their own accord, & let this be an act of Justice freely offered. Such men as the Bishop of Limerick ought to get a little encouragement for their support." "Pray forgive these lines," Vaughan concluded, "dictated in the interest of the Government as well as Order & Religion."

After receiving Walsh's letter on behalf of the Bishops, Parnell gave formal notice in the House of Commons of a question embodying the archbishop's request. "No formal decision was come to at the Cabinet," Balfour noted in a short memorandum to Salisbury on July 15, "with regard to the answer to be given to Mr. Parnell's Question today on the subject of Catholic University Education in Ireland. The answer I propose to give is that the matter has long engaged the attention of Her Majesty's Government, and that it is one of the subjects in respect of which we hope to be able to make proposals to the House."[6] Shortly after, Gillooly obviously wrote Walsh asking him what significance should be attached to Balfour's statement, for Walsh replied on July 28 that his information suggested taking Balfour's promise as meaning something substantial (G). Walsh, meanwhile, was characteristically leaving very little to chance. He proceeded to prepare for private printing the "Memorandum on the Irish Education Question" he had written for Monsignor Persico in November and December 1887, in order to distribute it among those members of the Irish Party who, though they might be interested, were not much acquainted with the intri-

6. B, 49828, no date [July 15, 1889].

cacies of the many aspects of the question. On July 2, Walsh had explained to Gillooly that though he had been busy on the Report of the Intermediate Education Commission, he had not neglected the readying of this "Memorandum" for private printing (G).

Higher education for Irish Catholics, however, was raised again in the closing debates of the parliamentary session, when, on August 28, Thomas Sexton made a powerful speech on Irish educational grievances on the primary and intermediate as well as the university level.[7] He was answered by Balfour, who maintained, "I repeat in the House what I have said outside the House, that in my opinion something ought to be done to give higher University education to the Roman Catholics in Ireland."[8] "The experiment of undenominational higher education in Ireland," he then noted, "has now been tried sufficiently long to make it, I am afraid, perfectly clear that nothing Parliament has hitherto done to promote that object will really meet the wants and wishes of the Catholic population of the country. That being so, we have no alternative but to try and devise some new scheme by which the wants of the Catholic population shall be met. This would not be the proper time for me to suggest, even in outline, the main lines of what such a scheme should be, but we ought to make some attempt, if possible, to carry out a scheme of the kind I have indicated." Parnell, in order to pin him down, immediately pressed him to indicate whether he proposed to embody his proposals in a bill the following session. "With regard to the question with which the hon. gentleman concluded," Balfour continued to hedge, "there is now possibility, I believe, of dealing with the question of University education without a Bill."[9] "Of course," he added, avoiding an explicit commitment for the next session, "I cannot give any pledge at the moment as the exact order in which the questions will be brought before the House."

T. D. Sullivan, a member of the Party and editor of the *Nation*, wrote Walsh on August 30: "Allow me to congratulate you on the victorious close of a long struggle for Catholic rights in the matter of higher education in Ireland."[10] "Of course I know," he then noted,

7. *Hansard's Parliamentary Debates*, 3d ser., 340, cols. 743–54.
8. Ibid.
9. Ibid.
10. *Walsh*, p. 541.

"that only the principle has been conceded by the Irish Secretary, and that the details of a measure for the establishment and endowment of an Irish Catholic University have yet to be shaped, considered, and settled; but in this case the principle is almost everything." "Unless I am much mistaken," Sullivan warned Walsh, "this announcement on the part of the Government will bring on a good deal of political trouble. The English Home Rule ranks will be divided over it, and there may be a row in the Tory camp. The English Non conformists and Radicals are almost to a man secularists in educational matters, and after what happened in the Royal Grants question, the arising of a new cause of difference between them and us may, I fear, impair to some degree their sympathy with us on the Home Rule question. We shall soon know more on these points." "Our Lord Mayor's admirable statement of the case in Parliament," Sullivan then concluded, referring to Sexton's speech, "was a thing that every friend of our educational cause may well be proud of; but it is not too much to say that this task was greatly facilitated by the admirable volume of materials which you supplied to him and to other Members of Parliament, and for a copy of which I have to thank you."[11]

When Walsh had first heard the good news that Balfour had conceded the principle of university education to Catholics on terms they could accept, he appeared not to have anticipated the political threat to the Liberal-Nationalist alliance. In writing to Cardinal Manning on August 28, in fact, he had added in a postscript: "Our Lord Mayor telegraphs cheering news on Education Question. On more than one ground, it is satisfactory that the Irish members have moved, & so effectively, in the matter" (M). On Monday, September 2, however, in announcing to the cardinal that he needed a little change and rest and would be passing through London, Walsh explained that he would chance a call on Wednesday at eleven. He had by then received Sullivan's congratulatory letter, and he noted accordingly, "An awkward complication has arisen out of the announcement that the Government intends to deal with the Education Question" (M). Walsh visited the cardinal on his way through

---

11. Ibid., p. 491. This sentence would appear to follow on the others, but there is no way of knowing for certain without examining the original.

London and obviously agreed to keep him informed. "I have just received among my letters from Dublin," Walsh explained on September 8, from Bonn, "one from a Protestant gentleman who kindly volunteers to help keep me supplied with information as to the state of English opinion, and the general drift of English criticism, upon the expected measures of reform in our Irish Education Question. He sends me as a first installment a number of an English paper (apparently a penny weekly)—*The British Weekly* of Friday Sep[t] 6th. It contains a most important interview with Mr. Stead. I will ask your Eminence to secure a copy of the paper, and to read both the interview and a signed article by Mr. Dinchly (whom I take from the editorial comments to be [a] well known *Liberal*)." "Everything looks well," he assured the cardinal; "Mr. Stead definitely takes up the position which as I mentioned to your Eminence on Wednesday evening I inferred from one of his paragraphs he was likely to take up. It is I think quite clear there will not be anything like a United Liberal opposition to the Government proposals."

If Walsh had not anticipated the strain Balfour's education proposals might put on the Liberal-Nationalist alliance, he certainly thought that he had taken adequate precautions against any strain being put on the more fundamental Clerical-Nationalist alliance. He had moved both cautiously and discreetly, and entirely through the Irish Party, in attempting to initiate action on the education question. A number of the members of the Irish Party, however, suspected that the introduction of the question of university education was perhaps the result of a bargain between the government and the Bishops, influenced by orders from Rome; such a bargain would presage, as Michael Davitt, prominent agrarian reformer and land nationalizer, remarked at the time, "the abandonment of the 'single-plank' position of Home Rule for a mess of Catholic University pottage."[12]

Among those most concerned about the new development was John Dillon in far-off Australia. He immediately wrote Dr. Joseph E. Kenny to ask what was really happening. Kenny, who was able to reply only some seven weeks later, when he received Dillon's letter and when the whole crisis was over, responded in a most interesting

12. Ibid., p. 542; quoted, but no source is given.

as well as reassuring letter. "Don't be uneasy about University question," Kenny explained on October 21;

I think it is dead and buried. I was not there when Balfour spoke, but I surmise this is what really happened. I have no doubt Dwyer, Healy (Bishops) etc., were intriguing secretly with Balfour on the question but none of our Bishops were so far as I can learn & Walsh himself told me only a few days before he did not want the question raised. He did however want the question of denominationalism in primary schools raised & asked Sexton to do it. He wanted since the primary schools are in Ireland practically denominational that they should be declared so in fact so that religious instruction might be given in them wherever pupils of one religion are attending whether Protestant or Catholic. He also wanted something said on the unfair way Catholic intermediate schools are handicapped. Now S[exton], having commenced with primary & gone on to secondary, naturally I fancy was led to round off his subject, as you know he is fond of doing. As for P[arnell], I fancy he had no previous chat or consultation with Sexton, or anticipation of what was going to happen, when he heard S. [Parnell] must have thought he had a brief from the Bishops, & then thinking probably . . . it would not be well to thwart their Lordships he chimed in. You know, he doesn't like doing anything that would seem to savour of want of sympathy with Catholic claims.

The Liberal-Nationalist and Clerical-Nationalist alliances were not the only political combinations to be jolted by Balfour's declaration on higher education for Catholics in Ireland. Many, if not most, of the Liberal and Radical Unionists were in educational matters at least as much in the secularist tradition as the great majority of the Liberals who followed Gladstone. Because the Liberal Unionists had also been in large part the "no popery" wing of the Liberal Party before their secession, it becomes obvious that the strain imposed on the Liberal Unionist-Conservative alliance by Balfour's declaration might, if persisted in, prove fatal to the life of the ministry. On September 2, Lord Hartington, one of the Liberal Unionist leaders, wrote G. J. Goschen, chancellor of the exchequer and a former Liberal Unionist, who was not quite yet a Tory: "Since I wrote you last week, another subject has turned up, on which I should have liked to have had a talk with you, I mean Balfour's declaration on the subject of University Education in Ireland."[13] "I think that when we met in Arlington St.," Hartington added,

13. B, 49706.

referring to a recent conference among Salisbury, Balfour, W. H. Smith, Chamberlain, Goschen, and himself, on the legislative program to be pursued in Ireland, "Balfour mentioned this as one of the subjects which he should like to discuss, but said that it was not the most pressing, and so far as I recollect we did not discuss it at all."[14] "His speech, however, will very probably make it the subject of very general discussion during the autumn, and I should be glad to know what yours and Lord Salisbury's ideas on it are. I should have no objection to making an attempt to satisfy the R.C. Bishops and Priests as to University Education; but I am not one of the difficult ones to satisfy." "But," he then warned, "I should think that there would be great danger from some Radical Unionists and also from bigoted Protestants in Scotland & Ulster." "The chance of aggravating the split between the Radicals and the Parnellites," Hartington then admitted in conclusion, making reference to the recent controversy in the House on the question of Royal Grants to denominational education, "is most tempting, but I am rather afraid that it may split us about as much."

Ridgeway reported to Balfour the following day, September 3, from Dublin: "The general feeling"—meaning Irish opinion—"is strongly in favour of a College not a University."[15] "A College," he pointed out, "is what Walsh originally asked for and there would be comparatively little opposition especially *if* something were done for Queen's College Belfast. The Catholic Gentry I understand would far prefer it." Balfour replied the next day from North Berwick, attempting, at least, to set Ridgeway straight. "As regards Catholic Education," he insisted, "I have never contemplated any other move than that of founding a College—(a University is out of the question), and I have always intended to do something material for Queen's College, Belfast, at the same time that we aided higher Catholic teaching in Dublin."[16] "What I should like to do," he explained, "would be, 1. To found a Catholic College say for £ 20,000 a year. 2. To give £ 5,000 a year more to Belfast. 3. To abolish Galway Queen's College. 4. To turn Cork Queen's College

14. B, 49828. For the arranging of this conference, see Balfour to Salisbury, July 2, 1889.
15. B, 49810.
16. B, 49828.

into a Middle Class Catholic School. 5. To Turn the Model Schools outside Ulster into Protestant, and partly into Catholic places of Secondary Education." "This, however," he admitted in conclusion, "is all very vague for the present."

Nearly two weeks later, Salisbury forwarded his nephew a letter from the dean of Norwich in order to apprise him which way the Protestant wind was blowing. "It will be interesting," Balfour replied from North Berwick on September 17, returning the letter, "to watch the movement of public opinion about the proposed Catholic College—not University, as everybody seems to assume."[17] "We shall have trouble," he surmised, "and my impression is that the trouble will come rather from the no-popery middle class of England than from the agitators in Ireland. But I may be wrong:—I have at present little to go upon but the correspondence I receive on the subject. It is curious that the row, if row there is, should have been deferred so long, for I said nothing in the House which I had not before said on more than one occasion on the platform; though for some reason or other Protestant sensibilities have never before taken alarm." "However," he explained, "it is satisfactory that, at a period so long before any Bill could be introduced, we have a means of gauging public opinion on the subject, and of forming some sort of judgement as to what can or cannot be done in the direction of satisfying the demand for higher R. Catholic Education in Ireland." He continued, somewhat cynically: "If, as seems not impossible, the feeling aroused by my proposal is so strong that we have to abandon it, we shall be bound in honour to inform the English Catholics and the Pope of the fact as soon as possible, unless indeed the influence of Rome in enforcing its own Decrees is so feebly exercised as to absolve us entirely from any feeling of obligation towards them. The whole question will have to be discussed at an early Cabinet, and we must endeavour to form some idea of what the value in votes is of the opposition which is being got up." "I should like to see," he concluded with a touch of that detachment for which he was noted, "if putting the case fairly before our people would soothe their outraged feelings—but I will say nothing until we meet."

17. B, 49834.

"I am unwilling," Balfour explained to Ridgeway the next day, September 18, "to enter into any public response now in the newspapers with regard to higher Catholic Education. But that can be no objection whatever to your stating to whomever it may concern that you know as a fact that it has never entered into the mind of the Government to found a Catholic University. I have never said anything in public that I know of which could suggest that idea. I have talked, indeed, of University Education, but this is a phrase quite as applicable to the plan of the Government as it is to the plan which these people say I am going to adopt. Indeed, there is no other phrase which expresses the idea!"[18] "I am getting seriously uneasy," Balfour confessed, with a good deal less detachment than he had expressed in his letter to his uncle the day before, "as to the possibility of our being able to carry through any scheme of the kind. I am not much afraid of Irish opinion, but it is the middle class 'no popery' element which I had hoped was dying out, but which I am bound to say appears to me to be stronger than I had anticipated."

Less than a week later, the "no popery" pressure became so great that Balfour decided to pour some oil on the troubled waters. In a letter, published on September 24, to the secretary of the Scottish Protestant Alliance, Balfour explained ambiguously that he had never suggested that the founding of a university was the proper means of attaining higher university education for Catholics in Ireland.[19] Balfour was immediately criticized for this letter by T. M. Healy, a prominent, and certainly one of the less obtuse members, of the Irish Party. Healy appeared to misunderstand Balfour and accused him of reneging on his promise of university education for Catholics. At the fortnightly meeting of the central branch of the Irish National League in Dublin on September 24, he referred sarcastically, if not to the general body of the Bishops, at least to his namesake of Clonfert and the bishop of Limerick: "I trust those with whom the Government have been bargaining in high places will consider themselves sold."[20] Healy also maintained,

18. B, 49828.
19. *Evening Mail* (Dublin), September 24, 1889; noted in C. C. O'Brien, *Parnell*, p. 237. See also B, 49828, Balfour to John Friens, Secretary of Bayswater Loyal Orange Lodges, marked "Private," September 19, 1889.
20. *Freeman's Journal*, September 25, 1889.

in the course of his very provocative remarks, that "those who imagine at Rome or elsewhere that matters can be concluded with the British Government without a complete debate and discussion in Parliament, and without the complete assent in Parliament of the Irish Representatives, and that the Irish Representatives will not be courageous enough to face any temporary obloquy they may incur by resisting to the utmost of their power every attempt to govern Ireland through Rome, such parties are, in my opinion, very gravely mistaken." Walsh, who was still holidaying in Switzerland, and who was always supersensitive in the face of such innuendo, undoubtedly read Healy's remarks: not only did he rarely miss anything that appeared in the newspapers and especially in the *Freeman's Journal*, but when he returned to Dublin he went out of his way on two occasions to refer to Healy's comments.[21]

Walsh's concern for the well-being of the Clerical-Nationalist alliance was further increased a week later when he read an article by Justin McCarthy, a much more friendly member of the Party, in the October number of the *Contemporary Review*. Walsh reported to Manning in his letter of October 2 from Bâle, referring to his memorandum on the Irish education question, which he had recently distributed to some members of the Party, "What he says about my 'memorandum' may set people talking" (M). "It may even be said," he added fearfully, "that some underhand work had been going on, to which some of the Bishops and some of the Irish party were parties. Would it not be well to silence all this by simply acting on Justin McCarthy's suggestion and publishing the Memorandum?" "If I were to publish it now," he then further suggested, "I might put a short preface, stating all the circumstances of the case." "On all this," Walsh, who planned to be in London the following evening, alerted the cardinal, "I should wish for your Eminence's advice. The Memorandum, if published, should be brought up to date as regards statistics. I wrote the greater part of it (and printed it), for Mgr. Persico's information in 1887. Hence many of the statistics are a little behind time." "P.S.," Walsh then added at the

21. For November 7, 1889, at the opening of Catholic University Medical School's academic session, see *Walsh*, pp. 544–45; and for December 5, 1889, at Blackrock College, see *Freeman's Journal*, December 6, 1889.

end of this letter, on Wednesday afternoon, " 'Charing Cross Hotel' will find me on Thursday evening or Friday *morning*."

"I must ask your Eminence's permission," Walsh requested the cardinal on Saturday, October 6, from Dublin, "to dedicate my little volume (the Memorandum on Education) to you—I have written to Justin McCarthy to tell him that I have decided on publishing it" (M). "There is one other matter which I will venture to add," Walsh then noted, "as regards the few lines which I asked your Eminence to send me in reference to the help given by the Irish Members. I should have explained the state of the case more fully than perhaps I did. From the following, your Eminence will see what it is that I want:—at our last Episcopal meeting, last June, we passed a Resolution that the Irish Members be asked to sustain the efforts of your Eminence in reference to denominational Education. The Standing Committee of the Episcopal body asked me to give effect to this. The only opportunity that has arisen was in reference to the Technical Instruction Bill. Your Eminence knows the rest." "Of course," Walsh assured the cardinal, "I do not ask for a letter of publication." "Publication just now," he observed, in reference to the recent testiness of some of the Irish members, "would, I think, be unwise. But I should like to have a few lines to read at the meeting of the Bishops next week, referring to their action in the matter and to the good services of the members in consequence of it," Walsh shrewdly concluded, meaning of course to use the cardinal's letter to offset the effect of the recent remarks of Davitt and Healy on his more conservative episcopal brethren.

After the Bishops' usual general October meeting was over, Walsh again wrote Manning, explaining that in the midst of all he had not forgotten the education question. "I send your Eminence a copy of today's Freeman's Journal," he wrote on Friday, October 18; "You will see from it that I have opened my campaign on the Education Question. My address is altogether too long, but I had scarcely any time for preparation. The days immediately preceding were all taken up with long meetings of our Bishops about Maynooth and other such business."[22] "We have done nothing on the Educa-

22. M, See *Freeman's Journal*, October 18, 1889, for Walsh's speech at St. Patrick's Training College, Dublin, where he pointed out that, in England, denominational colleges connected to the Church of England were supported out of the

tion Question," he reported, "but pass a vote of thanks to Mr. Sexton for his speech. The vote was moved by me and seconded by Cashel." "I arranged this," he noted pointedly, obviously determined to keep up the episcopal end of Clerical-Nationalist alliance, "with a view to the effect on certain critics on the Nationalist side. If your Eminence can make out the part of my address in which I deal with the plea that Parliament has finally abandoned the policy of endowing denominational Colleges, I would ask you to read it. I do not think it possible to give a satisfactory reply to my argument." "P.S." Walsh then added, naming the former Liberal chief secretary in Gladstone's last Ministry, and a pronounced agnostic, "Jno Morley turned up here quite unexpectedly on Wednesday. I had Cashel and some other Bishops to dine that evening. He came on a very informal invitation, and seemed quite at home among so many Christians!"

The conversation with Morley, however, was obviously more political than religious, for as soon as Walsh had a free moment he also wrote Gladstone concerning the government's promise about university education and the Liberal-Nationalist alliance. "I have just received your letter," Gladstone replied from Hawarden on Saturday, October 19, "and I shall be very happy to make myself acquainted with your argument."[23] "It appears to me plain," he reasoned, "that an anti-Home Rule government *ought* to endeavour to give at Westminster what might be reasonably expected by the

imperial treasury, although the ministry of the day maintained that this support was impossible in Ireland. Walsh demanded "equality" and added that the exchange in the House of Commons between Sexton and Balfour had indeed pledged the ministry to "equality" in university education. The most important remarks, however, were perhaps those made by the archbishop of Tuam, John MacEvilly, in proposing a vote of thanks to Walsh for his very considerable effort that day in behalf of Catholic education. MacEvilly said in part:

Anyone who has watched the career of his Grace since he sat in the chair of St. Laurence O'Toole, anyone who has watched his herculean labours (for I suspect he hardly ever sleeps at all) (laughter), cannot fail to be grateful to Providence for having placed him in the responsible position he now occupies. . . . He has this one great advantage also—although I am not authorized to speak for the Episcopacy of Ireland—that I may say with truth he is backed up by the unanimous feeling of episcopal brethren (applause). I can speak at least for one Province, and I can say that there we have deep veneration for the utterances of his Grace, and that in all substantial points we agree in the measures he has adopted and in the manner in which he expresses his opinions (applause).

23. *Walsh*, pp. 542–43. More than likely Walsh enclosed the *Freeman's Journal* report of his presentation on October 17, 1889, at St. Patrick's Training College.

Roman Catholic body from a Parliament in Dublin. But I think you will feel that another question arises when the Liberals, and especially the Presbyterians and Nonconformists are asked, by their votes, to reverse a policy which, with respect to universities and colleges, they have been pursuing steadily for half a century.'' "It seems to me, however, I frankly own," Gladstone observed shrewdly, "that for practical purposes the question has gone back into the clouds, from whence Mr. Balfour drew, or pretended to draw, it down. I think he launched it to divide the Liberals. The reception of it by some newspapers appeared to give him hopes of success. He seems to have remained in that 'fool's paradise,' until he found that his candidates were inconveniently pressed by the elections. He then produced the explanation which your Grace and your colleagues have doubtless read. I have great doubts whether we shall ever in Parliament have it upon us as a practical proposition."

"My desire has been," he then assured Walsh, "as I have told Mr. Parnell, to do what is fair on the one hand by the British Liberals, and on the other by the Irish, especially by their bishops, who must principally feel the difficulty. Mr. C. Williams''—a prominent member of the Liberation Society and a leading Nonconformist —"came here immediately after the scene in the House of Commons; and I thought him reasonable. I advised him to limit Nonconformist action, if he could, to this, *that they would not vote in the British Parliament for endowing a denominational university or college out of British funds.* My own personal opinion is that a scheme of the kind cannot be carried, and that it is better left to the Dublin Parliament. I have not, however, said this publicly." "I feel pretty confident," he reassured Walsh on the more fundamental question, "that the movement on behalf of Ireland runs no risk of being broken up." "Even if the Government," he concluded shrewdly and practically, "were disposed to make a sacrifice in order to remove this grievance, I doubt whether they would do it in 1890."

In his reply to Gladstone the following day, October 20, Walsh pointed out, "I see a clear gain in having the Education question disposed of by the Tories, to whatever extent they are prepared to legislate on denominational lines."[24] "Until this has been done,

24. *Walsh*, pp. 484–85.

there will always be a set of otherwise well-meaning people," Walsh went on, indicating the English Catholics, "not numerous perhaps, but not without influence, who will lean more or less to the side of keeping the Tories in office, or of bringing them into office, in the hope of getting the Education question settled." "If we had from the Tories," he concluded, somewhat ingenuously, "all that the Tories are inclined to give, there would be an end of this."

The anti-Catholic tide, meanwhile, had finally begun to rise among the Tory back-benchers, who, for Salisbury at least, were the ultimate arbiters of all ministerial proposals. "Dear Lord Salisbury," wrote one of them—Henry John Atkinson, member for Boston—on October 18, in the kind of language that the prime minister understood best, "I write to say I hope you will not allow your nephew to bring forward his R.C. scheme *as he stated in the H. of C.* If I had been there, I would have opposed it *on the spot.* It has cost us two bye-elections already, *and will cost us the entire Ministry if introduced.* And NO ONE *will be conciliated in the least.* They will get all they can, & bite the hand that gives (viper-like). I and many others must vote & speak against it" (SY). Atkinson, who was writing from Algiers, went on with a reference to the Liberal Unionist member for Barrow-on-Furness: "I met *Caine* the other day by accident travelling. He said the same. DO STOP IT." "This *I hope,*" Atkinson then explained more calmly, "is to you & to Mr. Balfour, for I do not trouble him with a note." "It is a pity," Atkinson lamented in conclusion, "such a talented man, & one who has crowned himself with honour by the way in which he has acted for the past year, should be deluded by the R.C. & H.R. Irreconcilables, & bandy compliments *before the nation* with men who would delight to see him dead, or a failure in statesmanship, or a pervert." Salisbury, it appears, forwarded Atkinson's note of warning to Balfour without comment.

When Parliament met in late October for its autumn session, the announcement, finally, of the Maltese mission to Rome only increased the nervousness of the supporters of the government both inside and outside the House; Salisbury's reluctance to announce the mission before the autumn recess was certainly justified. "Our Mission of Sir J. L. Simmons," Salisbury observed wryly to Lord Dufferin, the British ambassador in Rome, on November 15, "has somewhat afflicted the Protestant mind'' (SY). ''They forget,'' he pointed out, laying down his line of argument, ''that though Malta is very defensible with a friendly population, its defence will be both costly and precarious if the population is hostile.'' ''The Pope is therefore,'' the prime minister concluded amusingly, if cynically, ''to be looked upon in the light of a big gun—to be kept in good order, & turned the right way.''

Balfour, meanwhile, depending on the point of view, had either begun to prepare the ground for a very skillful withdrawal on the education question or continued to wrestle bravely with the afflictions of ''the Protestant mind.'' ''It is evident,'' he explained to Lord Emly, a friend of Ross and Norfolk and a leading Irish Liberal Unionist, on November 11, ''that any scheme for Higher Catholic Education is likely to meet with very serious opposition,— opposition so serious that it may be doubtful whether it will prove possible to do anything.''[25] ''It has, however,'' he added, ''to be considered whether my policy could not be made more palatable to our Protestant public if I could lay down a condition accompanying any Grant of Public Money to a Catholic College that none of it would be used to endow Theological Chairs and that students not belonging to the Catholic Faith, if such there were, would be protected by a Conscience Clause, that is would not be compelled to attend either Theological Lectures or Services in the Chapel. I apprehend that neither of these conditions would in any way militate against the efficiency of the College as its acceptableness to Catholics generally.'' ''It is on this latter point,'' Balfour concluded, ''that I should like to have your opinion before I say anything in public.''

Four days earlier, on November 7, in an address at the opening of the academic year at the Catholic University Medical School in Dublin, Walsh had not made Balfour's way any easier. In a two-hour effort exhausting the subject of university education, Walsh concluded by pointing out that, some four years before, Sir Michael Hicks Beach, Balfour's predecessor as chief secretary, had also promised the Catholics of Ireland justice in the House of Commons

25. B, 49828.

with regard to university education. "We are now in 1889," Walsh noted. "Recently some new promise has been made—there is some confusion about the precise terms—as to something that is to be done in 1890, or possibly in some other future year."[26] "I cannot see a lot there is in it," he confessed, "more definite, or more encouraging as to the hopes of its fulfillment, than there was in the promise given in 1885 by Sir Michael Hicks Beach." "But, taking facts as they are," he then added, ironically paraphrasing Balfour, "I find that promise still unfulfilled, confronting me in solemn warning not again to be so easily misled. It is not for me to say whether the new promise that has recently been made is likely to be as lightly treated, or to be as unfruitful in results as the old one has been. It seems to me of much greater moment that I should add some words as to another point."

"Justice," Walsh then declared, "was long denied to us. It has been long delayed. But, take my assurance, it shall never be sold. It takes two to make a bargain. I do not indeed wish to insult the ministry of the day by ascribing to them the foolish project ascribed to them by some. Insinuations have been made on the subject. It is humiliating to have to speak of such things, but as these insinuations have been made—and they have been made from quarters from which such things should not have come—it is forced upon me to notice them." "I do not attribute to the ministry," he protested, coming down heavily on the side of the Clerical-Nationalist alliance, "the folly of supposing that by any concession of justice they could make to us, they could hope to detach the influence and sympathy of the Irish episcopacy from that side of our great public questions, on which that influence and that sympathy have up to this been unitedly and steadfastly exercised." "I do not believe," he protested, with a little overemphasis, "that they can have entertained a thought of it." In conclusion, he assured the political and agrarian wings of the National movement: "But, however this may be—speaking now not only for myself, but, as I know I am justified in speaking, also for my brethren of the episcopacy of Ireland—I give you this assurance, that whilst we claim justice, we shall never stoop to purchase

26. *Walsh*, pp. 544–45.

it, and least of all could we even harbour the thought of purchasing it at the sacrifice, or even at the risk of the rights of the Irish tenants or of the Irish nation.''

The *Freeman's Journal* drew the appropriate moral from the archbishop's lesson for the uninitiated or the doubtful. ''This explicit assurance,'' wrote the *Freeman*, ''gives the quietus, administers the *coup-de-grace*, to the sedulously insinuated story that an arrangement was entered into between the Irish Episcopacy and the British Government.''[27] ''They dare not,'' the *Freeman* boldly declared; ''They would not. The Archbishop of Dublin has dissipated some misty and malicious misstatements; in his day he has burst some bubbles from Pigottism and Balfourism. But never has he done a more splendid service than the . . . settling and securing the national confidence, in his impassioned assurance that himself and the other Prelates of the Irish Bench would cut off their right hands before they would abate one jot of the National claim to National rights for any concession or consideration in the matter of education or any other matter that Minister could proffer or majority ratify. We commend the clear and brave words of the Archbishop of Dublin to both the English political parties.'' ''If the Coercionist party had hopes,'' the article concluded eloquently, ''those hopes are blasted. If the Liberal Party had fears, those fears are banished.''

After Balfour had raised with Lord Emly the questions of a conscience clause and of not endowing theology in the proposed Catholic college, asking him further, in effect, whether these conditions would be acceptable to that portion of the Irish laity that he at least informally represented, the chief secretary proceeded to brief Ross before he left for Rome on the Malta mission. When Ross arrived in Rome, he immediately initiated a discussion with Cardinal Rampolla on the ''pressing'' matter of education, rather than on the ''important'' question of the conduct of the Irish clergy. In his interview with the cardinal on the evening of November 23, Ross explained the conditions laid down by Balfour as necessary to the introduction of any proposed measure in the House of Commons for higher Catholic education in Ireland. ''The Conscience Clause,'' Ross reported to Balfour on November 24, ''as defined by you, does

27. *Freeman's Journal*, November 9, 1889.

not seem to disturb the Cardinal."[28] "I put it to him in this way," Ross explained:

A Conscience Clause, that is to say, it would be enacted that no student who presents himself to the College would be obliged to attend Lectures, where the teaching is opposed to his Conscience, or to the Conscience of his Father or Guardian. This clause would not interfere with the teaching, & probably it would never be necessary in a Country where non-Catholics have so many establishments proper to themselves; but it is proposed to introduce it, in order to prove that the Irish Cath[c] College, endowed by the State, would be always ready to receive Students of all Denominations, but that none of them belonging to a Protestant Communion would be obliged to receive instruction which might be opposed to his Conscience.

"I trust you will think," Ross observed dutifully, "that I have faithfully interpreted the matter as you represented it to me." "The Cardinal told me he found the Clause really useless, since there would be no desire to force the teaching of a denomination upon unwilling ears." "I explained to him," Ross added dryly, "that it often became necessary in a country like ours to enact these (apparently) useless clauses, to satisfy persons whose views are peculiar."

"With regard to Theology," Ross then explained,

I am bound to say I found the Card. unpropitious. He seemed to attach far greater importance to the matter than I should have supposed he would have done, judging from our conversations with him two years ago. I put the matter thus to him:—

It would be hardly possible to allot a public endowment, to found a Theological Faculty in the new College. This Science can of course be taught by the energy or charity of private individuals, & there will be every facility to promote this Study; but for reasons which I think are sufficiently clear, there would be great difficulty to grant funds from the State Treasury in order to establish a Chair of Theology.

The Cardinal seemed disappointed. He said, that meant to take away from the proposed College one of the most important branches of learning, & hence to lessen its importance. He continued:—

"Your Gov[t] intend to have nothing to say to Theology; they would leave it to private individuals, to the efforts of the Bishops. Your Gov[t] cannot wish to exclude the Catechism, and yet Theology, although it requires trained Professors & therefore Funds to teach it properly, is nothing more than an extended Catechism. In fact, Theology is the Catechism worked

28. B, 49821.

out & developed, upon scientific principles, or in other words the Catechism is Theology reduced to the appreciation of the most ignorant. I do not therefore think that the proposal to exclude Theology is a logical one.''

"I explained that it was not always very easy to be logical in England,'' Ross reported, ''& told him freely and forcibly what the difficulties were, under which any scheme for Cath$^c$ Education must labour, owing to the opposition of well meaning but somewhat bigoted Protestants who are Unionists, & owing also to the attitude of the Parnellites as well as the Gladstonian Party, who have in the past unfortunately introduced a tradition (now very difficult to eradicate), that no direct endowment for the future should be given to the teaching of the tenets of any Religion. I further suggested that whereas every Cath$^c$ was bound to know the Catechism, only Priests must necessarily go through the more extended Science of Theology.''

"But the Card. did not endorse this view,'' Ross went on, ''for he said that in many Universities lay men were taught Theology, & he also mentioned that in Germany the State did assign public Funds to found Chairs of Theology. He then continued:—'Even from a political point of view, I think the proposal to exclude this branch of learning is undesirable. You are always arguing out against the ignorance of the Clergy. You say that they involve themselves in politics & neglect study; surely then Funds are required.' '' "He then asked,'' Ross noted, ''if there were no special funds which might be alloted to this Faculty; but I told him I thought not, since every penny I knew of,—& I did not believe I was mistaken—was administered by Parliament, without whose consent nothing could be granted. The Cardinal then asked me how it was proposed to exclude Theology.'' "I told him I could not be sure,'' Ross confessed, ''but I imagined the exclusion would be provided for in the Charter of Corporation which would create the College & that this Charter would be submitted to & examined by Parliament before legal sanction to it was obtained.'' Ross continued, indicating how little the cardinal understood either the temper of, or the way business was done in the English Parliament, and reflecting also perhaps some of the naivetés of the Jesuit father, Baynard Klein, "He then thought it might be possible to let the question relating to Theology slide, as it were, that is, better to say nothing about it so that it might

slip in as a matter of course, & that it might be retained if possible.''
"Of course I do not in the least know how far it may be necessary to
give some public and prompt guarantee upon the subject, to allay
prejudices,'' Ross informed Balfour, alluding here to the rising anti-
Catholic tide and to the difficulty a public pronouncement against
endowing theology would add to the "important" part of his task in
Rome, ''but I confess I should be glad if it were possible that for the
present at least, a pledge need not be given.''

Balfour assured Ross some six days later, on November 30:

You have most accurately represented to the Authorities the views which I
hold with respect to the constitution and endowment of the proposed Roman
Catholic College on the two questions of a Conscience Clause and the
endowment of Theological Chairs. I do not deny that I am much concerned
at the views on the second of these points by Cardinal Rampolla. What I
was anxious to do, had it been possible to carry the feeling in England &
Scotland with us was, as you know, to provide out of Public Funds for the
cost of building and endowing a College, the discipline of which should be
conducted on principles agreeable to Catholics in Ireland, and which the
whole cost of secular branches of learning should be borne by the State.
The difficulties of carrying out such a scheme would, as you know, have
proved in any case enormous, possibly insuperable; but there is no use in
proposing it even as a matter for discussion under the condition which
Cardinal Rampolla has imposed; and I shall be compelled to say at Glasgow
on Monday that where as our plans could only be carried into effect if these
conditons were fulfilled (i.e.—that they could be made generally acceptable
to English public opinion, that their proposal in the House of Commons
would not be perverted by Irish representatives into an occasion for attempting to inflict some political blow upon the Government; and that they
were generally acceptable to those for whose benefit they were designed)
but such evidence as I have been able to collect upon the subject does not
appear to point to the conclusion that any one of these conditions is at
present fulfilled.[29]

"Under these circumstances, of course,'' Balfour placidly pointed
out to Ross, obviously aware that the conditions imposed were
certainly impossible taken together, and apparently unaware that, so
taken, they were patently unconstitutional, ''further progress with
the measure must for the present be deferred. I must say, I am considerably puzzled at the Cardinal's attitude. I suppose that nineteen-
twentieths of the whole cost of the College would be borne under

29. B, 49828.

my plan by the State." "In the face of so great a relief to the pecuniary resources of the Roman Catholic population in Ireland," Balfour maintained, revealing a failure to understand that the question was really one of equality and not money, "there should be no difficulty in finding the remaining twentieth; more especially as I suppose that their Professors of Theology would probably be vowed to celibacy and not impossibly to poverty also. I almost gather from your letter that Cardinal Rampolla was under the impression that we desired to interfere with or at all events to discourage the teaching of Catholic doctrines in the new Catholic College." "I need not say," Balfour concluded, finally taking the high ground of equality, "that this was never my intention, and that I merely declined to do for the Catholic what is not done for, so far as I know for [sic] any religious denomination in England or Ireland, namely providing out of the Taxes for professional teaching in dogmatic Theology."

Balfour now began the difficult but necessary task of effecting a strategic withdrawal on the education question without absolutely extinguishing Catholic hopes, while at the same time assuring his "no popery" critics that all such hopes were virtually dead. He began the more delicate side of the operation—keeping the Catholics' hopes alive—with a short note to the duke of Norfolk, written the same day as his reply to Ross; he obviously intended that the duke should also write Cardinal Rampolla explaining the complications, in order to conserve to Ross what was left, if anything, of his bargaining power in Rome. "I enclose," Balfour informed the duke on Saturday, November 30, "a letter from Ross, and my answer. I am much grieved at Rampolla's view."[30] "It makes (*for the present at least*)," he noted in conclusion, with a skillful shifting of responsibility, "*failure certain*, when it was very probable before."

The public announcement of the general withdrawal, however, had yet to be made, and the occasion, as Balfour had mentioned to Ross, was to be a Unionist banquet on Monday evening, December 2, in the Glasgow suburb of Partick, where the "Protestant mind" seemed to be most affected. Just before the Partick meeting, Balfour, it appears, was made acutely aware of the state of Conservative feeling in Glasgow by a letter forwarded to him by Sir William Thompson,

30. Ibid.

celebrated scientist, inventor, and ardent Unionist. "Now," Peter S. Hutchison had informed Thompson on Saturday, November 30, "as I represent to some extent the strong Protestant element of the Conservatives of these two Divisions I am repeatedly asked the question 'Is the Government going to aid in any way the Higher Education of Catholics in Ireland out of the Imperial Funds?' "[31] "The evident tendency of trafficking with Rome is seen in the sending of Sir John Lintorn Simmons as Envoy," Hutchison warned, adding ominously, "and these circumstances are having a depressing effect on the minds of a large number of Conservatives not only here but elsewhere and it is a pity that the Government who have been doing so well in the government of Ireland should not have left this alone as I feel and I say it with regret, that unless this proposal, to give funds from the Imperial Exchequer for the Higher Education of Catholics in Ireland is abandoned it will be of fatal consequences to the present Government."

Balfour's Partick speech was admitted by one and all to be a very able one. In effect, he posed his set of impossible conditions, which assured the "no popery" element that the question of higher education for Catholics in Ireland was dead and buried, and then outlined safeguards, which were really irrelevant given the antecedent conditions, to encourage the Catholics in their hopes of a resurrection of the question. "I am clearly of opinion," he explained,

that upon this question of higher Catholic education in Ireland, it is absolutely impossible that anything could be done except by general consent. There are three conditions which I lay down as being absolutely necessary to be fulfilled before anything effective can be done in the direction which my predecessors indicated, and in which I have attempted to follow them.

The first condition is, that what we propose to those desiring higher education in Ireland should be cordially accepted by them as a solution of their difficulties. The second condition is, that the proposal of measures of that description in Parliament should not be used by any Party in Parliament as a means of inflicting a political blow upon their adversaries. And the third condition is, that the general opinion of Englishmen, of Scotchmen, and of Irishmen, should all concur in desiring that this particular boon should be granted to the Roman Catholic population of Ireland.[32]

31. B, 49845.
32. *Times* (London), December 9, 1889; quoted in *Walsh*, p. 547.

"And unless these conditions are fulfilled," Balfour warned, "I, for one, would never counsel my colleagues to embark in so difficult and so arduous an enterprise as that of dealing with the education question."

Balfour then skillfully turned to his safeguards, adroitly playing thereby on Catholic hopes by intimating that there was really still something left to discuss. "It is not our business," he argued encouragingly in Protestant Partick,

to inquire how far the undoubtedly conscientious objections of the Roman Catholic population to use the means of education at their disposal are wise or unwise. That is not our business. What we have to do is to consider what we can do consistently with our conscience to meet their wants.

My own view is that we cannot with public advantage found a Roman Catholic University, and I think so because I am of opinion it would be fatal to the course of higher education in Ireland, if the Catholics and Protestants were not brought into competition in obtaining the degrees and honors of university training. If you do not bring them into competition, you might find that either the Protestant or Catholic standard was lowered to meet the temporary interests of their clients, and the cause of good education would suffer.

The second thing, I think, we cannot give, is any State endowment of theological teaching.

The third condition which I think ought to be laid down before any college of the kind I suggest is founded, is that there should be what I believe is called in other departments a conscience clause, or, at all events, some provision by which any man attending the college, who did not share the religious tenets of the governing body, should not be compelled to attend either theological lectures or theological services.

"But subject to these three conditions," Balfour concluded bravely, if irrelevantly, "my opinion is that we ought to give them a well-equipped college—a college well equipped for all modern purposes of higher education."

Three days later, on December 5, at Blackrock College near Dublin, Walsh replied to Balfour's Partick speech. The safeguards demanded by Balfour appear to have troubled Walsh not at all. He had always preferred a college to a university, and like Cardinal Rampolla he did not think the required conscience clause involved any matter of fundamental principle. Unlike the cardinal, however, Walsh seems not to have been overly concerned about the refusal to endow the study of theology. Walsh certainly understood that Irish theological needs were being amply met in the national seminary at Maynooth as well as in the network of numerous diocesan seminaries throughout Ireland. What Walsh really objected to was the imposing of what to him was the one condition—requiring a consensus of English, Scottish and Irish opinion—that made all the rest mere words signifying nothing. "The fulfilment of the condition here stated," Walsh declared, "is manifestly a matter of absolute impossibility. I say nothing of its obvious unreasonableness."[33] "I do not even care to raise the question," he noted, raising the question, "whether any such extraordinary condition was ever before attached to an official announcement of an important measure of reform." Walsh continued with the fundamental argument of the party of the constitution in Ireland for Home Rule: "I make but this one comment upon it, that since the veteran leader of the English Liberal party first put his hand to the work of setting our local concerns in Ireland free from the vexatious trammels imposed upon them by the need of looking to an Imperial Parliament for every measure of reform, I have met with no statement more clearly conclusive than that which I have now quoted in demonstration of the hopeless folly of those who even still believe that such a Parliament can be regarded as an effective machine for working out and administering a system of good government for Ireland."

"Last Thursday," Walsh explained privately to Manning on Saturday, December 7, "I had an opportunity of speaking at one of our Colleges on Mr. Balfour's speech on the University Education question" (M). "That speech was," Walsh acknowledged, "in my opinion a singularly able one. So I determined to go as far as I could to meet the speaker. I had to do it rather delicately, speaking, as I did, in the presence of over 200 schoolboys and University students. I send your Eminence a copy of the *Freeman's Journal* that you may have it by you for reference if any occasion for referring to it should arise. But do not read it otherwise, as I shall have it reprinted in pamphlet form. The report, however, as it stands, is quite accurate. I always see a 'proof' of such things of mine before they are printed in the newspaper." "The Tablet article on Mr. Balfour's speech," Walsh noted approvingly, "is good." "Our Protestant

33. *Freeman's Journal*, December 6, 1889.

papers here," by which he meant particularly the Dublin *Evening Mail*, "are fairly friendly. They have practically given up the argument of the case. Now they seem to aim only at putting off all action."

"P.S.," he continued, making reference to an influential member of the Roman Curia who had just returned from an American mission, "Mgr. Satolli came to Ireland mainly on my invitation, for a friendly visit of a few days. When the mischievous reports of a 'mission' were circulated, I wrote to Dr. Howlett (his travelling companion and Secretary) sending the letter to Dr. Howlett's father's place in Co. Kilkenny, where they were to stay for a day on their way to Dublin, saying that I feared I was bound in my duty towards the Holy See to seem to violate my duty of hospitality."[34] "I explained in a very long letter," he reported, "the present state of feeling here in reference to the political action of the Holy See— English influence—the evil results of the Persico mission—the awkward position in which we should all be placed if it could be said that my attitude towards the Ministry in their Education proposals was not spontaneous, but was the result of a communication from the Holy See etc. etc." "I spoke strongly on the whole question," Walsh assured the cardinal, and again referred to Abbot Smith: "—also on the fact that the person who supplies the information to the *Daily Chronicle* is still kept in the position which gives him such facility for communicating with high personages about the Vatican, although the Holy Father and the Card. Secretary of State are fully aware of his proceedings. Mgr. Satolli & Dr. Howlett have, of course, passed through without making a stop in Dublin. The Monsignore may be relied upon to speak very plainly (as I have asked him to do) to the Holy Father. He also means to communicate much that he picked up in America."

The duke of Norfolk was more pleased than Walsh with Balfour's Partick speech. "I am much ashamed," he finally replied on De-

34. B, 49810. On November 5, 1889, Ridgeway informed Balfour, incorrectly, "Persico is here and there is an evident attempt being made by Archbishop Walsh and the Higher Clericals to moderate the zeal of the more violent Nationalists. There can be no better sign that we are winning." A month later, Errington wrote Smith (S, December 4, 1889): "I am glad to hear that the ridiculous rumour in the Weekly Register, about Mgr. Satolli having a Mission to Ireland is not true."

cember 13 to Balfour's note of November 30, "I have not sent you back sooner the two enclosures with many thanks to you for having let me see them. I am sorry and surprised at Rampolla's line, and am puzzled as to what is in his mind."[35] "I need not say," Norfolk noted, turning to the more congenial subject of Partick, "with what interest I read your speech." "If I may say so," wrote the Duke, who seems to have been almost as optimistic as he was ingenuous in politics, "I think you put the matter admirably for the ultimate success of the whole question." He went on admiringly, if even more ingenuously, to refer to the "no popery" wing: "It must have needed a lot of pluck to offer such a defeat to such a party. I am half sorry you put your third condition quite as strongly as you did. It may encourage the hostile party"—the "no popery" wing—"to keep up an agitation which without being really general or important may make it difficult for you to do anything without apparently breaking your pledge." "But I have no doubt," Norfolk concluded, confident that the man who had constructed the labyrinth could certainly find his way out of it, "you have foreseen and guarded against these dangers."

Ross, meanwhile, had also written Balfour complimenting him on his Partick speech. "I cannot tell you yet," he explained on December 10, "what impression exactly your Speech of the 2nd has produced here. But two things seem to have been made clearer to the authorities by it—clearer than any words of mine could have done. (1) That you got no support from the Bishops, who ought to have supported you & (2) That there must be some give & take in non-essentials, if any business is to be done here."[36] "I have little doubt," Ross assured Balfour, "the Cardinal will see upon reflection that the scheme is one he can endorse even without State aid to a Theological Chair. I must however say, there was scarcely sufficient time to go properly into the matter—I had to report before the 2nd—especially as the situation in Ireland is not understood. In fact, since we left Rome last year, we have so to speak lost headway." "Had I gathered from the conversation I had in London with you," he observed pointedly, "that there was an immediate idea of postponing the Educn scheme, I should I think have told you that it

35. B, 49821.
36. Ibid.

would be better to have a little longer time here in Rome, before I could report." "I would say in conclusion," he then reassured Balfour, echoing the duke of Norfolk, "that I trust sincerely that what you said so well upon Denominat[l] Educ[n] in Ireland, will impress Protestants, & facilitate the Educ[n] Scheme, as I am sure it will, even should it have to be delayed for a short time." "On the whole," Balfour noted on the face of this letter when he read it on December 14, "more satisfactory than I hoped."

"Upon the first occasion I saw Card. Rampolla," Ross reported nearly two weeks later, on December 23, "after my last letter to you, I read & gave him a Memorandum, which I had prepared, upon your speech of the 2nd inst. & upon Arch[bp] Walsh's reply thereto. I reminded the Card[l] that the scheme was deferred for the present, & told him the best way of raising it soon, was for those to whose advantage it was intended to accept it, & to press for it."[37] "I thought it advisable," he noted further, "to let the matter rest there for the present, & that it w[d] be more satisfactory if the H. See were of its own motion to take the necessary steps to cause the Hierarchy to accept the scheme. Whether the Cardinal thinks he can do so will shortly appear, but I had to unfold a sad tale of Irish revolt against the Papal Decree—and have more to give him after the Xmas holidays—he *may* think that it will take him all his time to subdue this revolt." "When alluding to Arch[bp] Walsh's speech," Ross further reported,

I drew attention to the following three points:—

1. I explained that the non-endowment by the State of the Theological Faculty was a final decision, notwithstanding what Walsh might say, & I hoped that there would be no difficulty raised in Rome—showing how any such difficulty would be detrimental to the interests which the scheme proposes to serve. . . .

2. I told the Cardinal that the contention & reiteration that your third condition (consent of the United Kingdom) *could not* be fulfilled, was not the way for any Catholic to hasten the realization of the scheme; & I further drew his attention to the fact that your other two conditions were not alluded to, by the Arch[bp], in his speech.

3. It appeared to me that the main point in Walsh's speech, was contained in that portion which he devoted to the Dublin University. I gave the Cardinal some information upon the matter, in order to warn him of the

37. Ibid.

difficulties the scheme would encounter if this element of discord were to be introduced. I told him it would not be possible to interfere with Dublin University, that Training Institutions could not be destroyed, & that there was no need of doing anything of the sort, since Gov$^t$ could not confer prestige &c &c. I thought it well to say something upon this point, so that they should not have got hold of false ideas with regard to it that might later on be difficult to eradicate.

"In reply to my Memorandum," Ross pointed out to Balfour, "the Cardinal, among other things, said he would be glad to read the full text of the Archb$^{p's}$ speech, & I gave it to him, begging him however to examine carefully (at the same time) the various points which I had brought to his notice. This he promised to do."

For all practical purposes, higher education for Catholics in Ireland was thus buried for nearly a generation. Balfour's tactic of raising Catholic hopes in the closing days of the parliamentary session in August was certainly a very astute political move. First of all, he put both the Clerical-Nationalist and the Liberal-Nationalist alliances under considerable strain. Secondly, he strengthened the government's bargaining position in Rome and at the same time increased the Irish Church's suspicions about Rome's intentions, which certainly did nothing to improve Irish-Roman relations. Thirdly, he introduced this element of discord at the end of the session and thereby minimized the effect such an announcement would have on the Liberal Unionist-Conservative alliance, by giving himself time before Parliament met again, in late October, to see how the "no popery" wind would take his political kite.

As a situation over which he had less and less control developed, Walsh reacted quickly and ably to contain the worst effects of Balfour's clever gambit and thereby to reduce the pressure on the two alliances he had sacrificed so much in recent years to sustain. What actually wrecked Balfour's intentions, however, was the strain his proposals put on the Liberal Unionist-Conservative alliance, especially after the government announced its special mission to Rome. The mission to Rome, moreover, as far as Ireland was concerned, was a complete failure. The pope, who had now been twice bitterly disappointed in his efforts to persuade the British government to enter into diplomatic relations with the Holy See, had finally learned his lesson. That Rome should have further jeopardized her already delicate position in Ireland by entering into a discussion about the *mere basis* for negotiations for a *proposed* Catholic College was ludicrous. This was really what was on Cardinal Rampolla's mind when he chose to break off conversations on the education matter over the really unimportant question of endowing the study of theology in the proposed college. Rome and Leo XIII had, in fact, gone as far as they would go toward diplomatic relations with Britain if the quid pro quo involved Rome's action in Ireland in any but her own interest.

# 4

# IRISH NATIONALISM
## November 1889–September 1890

Irish suspicions of the Simmons mission to Rome were, if anything, deeper than the fears of the "no popery" section of British public opinion. Walsh's chaplain, Denis Pettit, was a good example of what had happened to a pious, Roman-trained student in an Irish atmosphere in recent years. In writing to Kirby early in the new year, explaining that the winter was mild and that the poor in consequence had suffered a good deal less than usual, Pettit soon passed on to what was troubling him. "There is a good deal of uneasiness," he confessed to his old mentor on January 8, "as to the presence of General Simmons in Rome, as it is believed that there is question of establishing diplomatic relations between the Pope & England. The whole hierarchy here appears to be against it & so is Cardinal Manning"(K). "I hope at all events," he added innocently, "nothing will be done without consulting Cardinal Manning & the Bishops here." Pettit went on to mention Walsh's address at the Catholic University Medical School of November 7 and his reply to Balfour of December 5: "I hope to send you in a few days the Archbishop's addresses of Cecilia Street School & at Blackrock. They are being published in pamphlet form & will be ready very soon." "The Government," he concluded ingenuously, "can scarcely evade dealing with the University question this coming session."

What the Irish clergy, high and low, did not appear to realize was that the government's recent withdrawal of the proposal for higher education for Catholics in Ireland was also hope deferred for any official British diplomatic relations with the Vatican. If the government did not dare the lesser in the face of the "no popery" threat, how could it have braved the greater? Though the Irish do not appear to have understood this difficulty, Rome certainly did; Rampolla's coolness to the nonendowment of theology in the proposed college was a very useful tactical ploy, in that he could conscientiously avoid bringing any pressure to bear on the Irish Bishops concerning Balfour's education proposal.

Rome, however, did have a very great interest in reasserting her authority in the Irish Church, and Rome's real difficulty was that she had no really reliable source of information now that the great majority of the Irish bishops and clergy had rallied to Walsh and Croke. This was the reason, of course, why Monsignor Persico had been appointed secretary for the affairs of the oriental rite at Propaganda, in March 1889, and had assumed so important and influential a part in Irish episcopal appointments. In Rome, his knowledge of Irish affairs was certainly unrivaled, for on his recent mission he had not only met but had undoubtedly taken the measure of nearly every important ecclesiastic in Ireland. Still, if Croke had been correct in complaining to Kirby that the Irish bishops had a limited ability to pronounce on the fitness of the various candidates for episcopal office, because for the most part they had never heard of them before, then Rome certainly needed more particular information than even the memory of Monsignor Persico could provide—hence Rampolla's pointing out to Norfolk in July 1889 that Rome would, of course, have no objection to receiving information, if it was understood that it was "mere information" and that Rome was under no obligation to act on it. Rome, therefore, encouraged Ross's memoranda and reports on the "important matter" of the right conduct of the Irish clergy. This information was undoubtedly collated with what other reports Rome might receive through Smith, Kirby and those others who thought to write Rome direct, and was finally refined and evaluated by Monsignor Persico. Rome could in this way form some intelligent opinion about what was really happening in Ireland and proceed to make those decisions so necessary and vital to a reconstructing of her power and influence there.

In his first letter to Balfour after his arrival in Rome, Ross, after explaining Rampolla's reaction on the "more pressing question" of education and asking for more particular information about the candidates for Derry, also pressed Balfour for intelligence that would, in effect, enable him to persuade the authorities in Rome that the new Tenants' Defence Association was in violation of the papal decree and should therefore be condemned. "The last matter," he had explained to Balfour on November 24, "relates to the Smith-Barry struggle. It appears to me to be so important & a thorough test case, that I should like to give it *in extenso*."[1] "Croke committed himself last summer," Ross reminded Balfour, with a reference to Croke's latest letter forwarding fifty pounds to the T.D.A., "& now he recommits himself by his recent letter."[2]

Most of Ross's time until Christmas was taken up with the preparation of a memorandum for Cardinal Rampolla on the Balfour-Walsh exchange on the education question. "I hope soon," he promised Balfour in the course of his long letter of December 23, "to give full details upon the Smith-Barry case, & this taken by itself & in conjunction with the new Tenants League, seems to me to be perhaps the most important case that has yet appeared."[3] "I have now (some days ago)," Ross finally reported to Balfour on January 7, "put into Card. Rampolla's hands a full account of the new Tenants' Defence League. The first part of my Memorandum was based upon that very useful paper you sent me. I then proceeded to show that the recrudescence of the Plan of Campaign under Archb[p] Croke's patronage & guidance, has been taken up all through Ireland, & in view of this, I gave ample quotations (1) from the Bishop'[s] letters to the Conventions & (2) from the speeches of M.P.'[s] thereat. I pointed out how the pretence of legality was a hollow show. I finally examined Dr. O'Dwyer's position, & gave an account of what he did & tried to do."[4]

"In presenting this paper to Card. Rampolla," Ross further noted, "I gave him verbally an outline of the factors, & he promised to consider attentively the whole document; in a short time I ought to know the effect. In conversation he assured me that the H. See had

1. B, 49821.
2. Ross was referring to a letter written by Croke in early July 1889, which called Smith-Barry, among other things, "an aggressive busybody and a virulent partisan" for his interference in the Ponsonby quarrel. See the *Irish Catholic*, July 6, 1889.
3. B, 49821.
4. Ibid.

frequently & forcibly—(energiquement) called the Bishops to account for the reported neglect to which the Decree is subjected, & he told me that they either denied point blank the accusation that disobedience to it existed, or else they admitted that a few infractions still prevailed which they were endeavouring to correct & hoped soon to suppress!!'' "The Bishops rely,'' Ross pointed out, "upon the admitted diminution of Boycotting &c, since the Decree was issued; & I fancy in some cases at least, they deny the existence of the P. of C., alleging that when the Landlord has evicted, he has obtained his legal remedy & that no plan (properly so called) can exist upon a vacant farm as upon a farm where other tenants have got possession instead of the Campaigners.'' "I do not like to give you so much trouble as I repeat I have already done,'' Ross then apologised,

but as I think it well to go somewhat into detail, I thought if a table could be prepared, somewhat upon the lines I have enclosed, regarding the different Plans that exist & that have existed (or at least some of the principle ones, if all cannot be given), the information would be very useful here. This table will show such cases as the two successive Plans upon the De Freyne Estate (the second *after* the Decree) in both of which I believe the Landlord yielded. It would also show the Plan upon the Kenmare Estate where the Landlord has won without the introduction of new tenants; & in respect of this case, it would be satisfactory to learn whether the Bishop & Clergy had anything to say to the cessation of the Plan there. Boycotting also seems to be on the increase, if not in Ireland generally, at least there where the Tenant League is at work. I have put a note also on the enclosed page with regard to this, as information upon this point would also be material.

"It appears Dr. Carbone (the Maltese Attorney General, who is a Secretary to our Mission),'' Ross then pointed out to Balfour, as he had already written Norfolk, "is urgently wanted in Malta, & must return there soon. This may put an end to the Mission. If this is so I shall be sorry for it, because it is not easy to get Irish matters done in a short time.'' "However,'' he assured Balfour in conclusion, "you may rely upon it, I will leave no stone unturned to do all I can.''

"I am much obliged for your letter,'' Balfour replied on January 22, "which has much interested me, and I send you the information which you require on certain points connected with the Plan of Campaign and Boycotting. There can, I think, be no doubt whatever, in the first place, that the action of some of the Bishops, though it may not technically violate the Papal Rescript gives the impression, and is intended to give the impression, that they are favourable to the policy pursued by Wm O'Brien and his followers which is avowedly based upon Boycotting and the Plan of Campaign."[5] "And secondly," he maintained, "that in every case where the Plan of Campaign has assumed formidable proportions a Local Priest has been more or less encouraging it. At this moment, the central point of the Irish controversy is the Tipperary and Ponsonby contest. I think myself that Smith-Barry must win. Various indications lead me to believe that Croke and the Priests are frightened at the storm they themselves have raised; but they do not know how to get out of the position into which they have blundered, and the local Tipperary Priest (Father Humphreys) is unmanageable even by his Bishop." "I hope," he assured Ross in conclusion, "there is no chance of the Malta Mission coming to an untimely end—I should profoundly regret it."

"*P.S.*," Balfour added in a long postscript, "with regard to the Tenants Defence Fund, so far as I can discover there have not been many cases brought to the notice of the Police in which direct intimidation has been used although some specific examples of this have occurred; and a very bad speech of a priest urging Subscriptions has just been brought to my notice. It is possible that in this latter case, we may prosecute." "It has also to be recollected," he explained, "that the subscriptions in a very large proportion of cases have been taken at the Chapel doors, often with the Priest himself standing by under circumstances which made it extremely difficult for any member of the congregation to refuse his contribution. In many instances every gate into the Chapel except the one where the collection is being held was closed." "Quite apart, however, from the method in which the money has been collected," he observed finally, returning to higher ground, "it must not be forgotten that the avowed object of it is to support the illegal conspiracy which now rules in the Ponsonby Estate and in Tipperary and therefore from the point of view both of the Government and of the Church the whole proceeding is tainted from the very inception."

5. B, 49828.

Ross replied to Balfour on February 6, thanking the chief secretary for his letter of January 22 and its enclosures, and continuing: "Having had a slight attack of influenza, I was unable to see Card. Rampolla till yesterday. I last saw him upon the 20th Ult. but as he had not then read my Memorandum upon the Smith-Barry case, I did not write to you by the last Messenger. On the 17th Ult., I had a private audience of H.H."[6] "The Pope seemed disinclined," he noted significantly, "to talk to me on Ireland, although he entered very fully upon Indian matters; I have already written about this to Norfolk by the last mail. With regard to Irish affairs, the Pope, after I made some allusion to them, confined himself to the consideration of concessions, talked of a 'Diet' of 'Agrarian Reform' & of 'higher Education.'" "In reply," Ross pointed out to Balfour, "I told the Pope that any idea of a 'Diet' was an impossibility, that I thought Agrarian Reform would not be neglected in the shape of an extension of the Ashbourne Act, & I reminded him that higher Education had been for the present rendered impossible by the action of Irish Catholics themselves." "Subsequently, when I saw Card. Rampolla," he added, referring to his interview of January 20, "I was able to enforce what I said to H.H. & told him I thought when he had read my paper on the Tipperary Case, his views of Ireland would be altered. I brought forward other facts & arguments to show the real state of things, & how different this was to what perhaps the Bishops might have led the Holy See to suppose."

"Yesterday, upon being able to go out again," Ross continued, "I had the satisfaction to learn that my paper had been read & digested, & that it had produced a strong effect upon the Cardinal; but he said he would first have to consult Propaganda, & that he had not done so before owing to the fact that two Prelates of that Congregation had been unwell, & its Prefect (Card[l] Simeoni) was over-worked in consequence." "He mentioned however," Ross observed, "that in his view the most careful selection of Bishops is imperative; & here I thoroughly agree with him, because if once there were two or three who would openly support the B[p] of Limerick, the Revolutionary Clerical Party headed by Walsh & Croke would infallibly decline & dwindle into impotence—even if these

6. B, 49821.

two latter were not more directly attacked by Rome; it would of course be easier to attack them under these circumstances than it is now." "Card. Rampolla," he maintained interestingly, "sees that Walsh & Croke are both incorrigible, & spoke to me quite openly about them, as the two pillars of much of the evil that prevails in Ireland." "With regard to the appointment of Bishops," he suggested, delicately introducing once again the awkward subject of diplomatic relations, "I could see that the Vatican is anxious to get advice upon their selections, within reasonable limits, but it would be difficult for them to receive their advice unless there were someone here with whom they could confidentially confer. This seems to be the difficulty at present." "I took occasion also yesterday," Ross then remarked, "to say a very few words upon the idea of concession by an 'Irish Diet,' which had been previously alluded to by the Pope, & I told the Card[l] that my honest opinion was that if it were granted the Clergy would be first to suffer, and that would be necessarily so, owing to their own persistent policy of immorality. He seemed to accept my statements more readily than formerly, & I cannot but hope that at least a different feeling is being produced, owing to the Tipperary case, which from a Roman & moral point of view transcends many other cases." "I do though hope," he concluded encouragingly, "that a first step has been taken here, although I admit it is not a big one at present."

Shortly after Balfour received this long letter from Ross, he forwarded him the report of the Parnell Commission, which had just been published. "I am much obliged for the report on the Special Commission," Ross thanked him on February 19, "and for the pamphlet on the Ponsonby Estate, which reached me Monday afternoon. Since I last wrote to you, I have given the Cardinal that portion of the Queen's Speech referring to Ireland. . . . "[7] "With regard to the Gov[t] proposals for Ireland," Ross then explained, "the Cardinal hoped I should be able soon to let him have some detailed idea of what was proposed, & I told him, I thought after I had read your speech (fixed for Monday 17th), I should be in a position to do this, at all events as regards the extension of the Ashbourne Act & something concerning the remedial measures con-

7. Ibid.

templated for the congested & poor districts of Ireland." "It is evident to me," he maintained, "that the H. See wishes to do something concerning Ireland, & owing to the fact that there was no one here after the Decree [was] issued, the Vatican was to a certain extent worsted in the arguments that took place between it and the Bishops after the Decree became to be more thoroughly known. Hence, the H. See could do little, but now it thinks that it can do something in a more effective manner, if an opportunity presents itself." "Measures of Reform," he argued somewhat unconvincingly, "when proposed are considered to afford such an opportunity; & if these measures are contemplated some previous pacificatory action on the part of the Pope could not fail to be of use. I told the Card$^l$ that the Local Gov$^t$ proposal seemed to me to be a great step, and I should like to see a calming policy adopted by the Holy Father. I told him, as far as I could see, that the Irish Nationalists either pretended to disbelieve in your proposals, or else openly asserted that your measures would be utilised as a base from whence to make greater demands."

"Today I brought the Card$^l$," Ross then further informed Balfour, "my first Memorandum upon the Special Commission, which I read to him. In this paper I made a preliminary statement, giving a history of the matter; showed him that the report was a judicial statement, based upon evidence given under oath & subject to cross-examination, and drew a distinction between the three findings,— 'not guilty,' 'guilty,' & 'not proven.' " "With regard to the last," he pointed out, "which is well understood here, I said that in order to ascertain the probability of guilt or innocence, it would be necessary to read the report through, but for the moment I would confine myself to the 'conclusions' of the Report which I gave in detail, including the three charges against Parnell & the two against Davitt." "After I finished my papers upon the Special Commission," Ross then continued, "which I left with him, he told me he had an important communication to make to me, and this was the most interesting part of my interview with him this morning."

"The Holy Father," Ross noted, "had seen my paper on the Tipperary affair, & was going to take some step with regard to Dr. Croke." "He asked me," Ross added, meaning Cardinal Rampolla, "to let him have a short paper of the distinct charges that are made against the Archbishop, and this I will do at once. He further said that this action would be taken entirely of the Pope's own initiative. I can not yet say whether this action will be private or more public. The Cardinal told me that this matter, was for the present a *most secret one*, and it would be highly detrimental to the H. See if any one were to know of it before it came off. I told him that I was quite sure, this secrecy would be respected at home, and that he might rely upon my discretion." "He then said," Ross noted, returning to the theme of diplomatic relations, "that he hoped the fact would be understood that it was only owing to there being some one here, who could give them reliable information, that the H. See had known of the Tipperary case & of Croke's action there in; & he thought, that this was a matter which ought to be appreciated. He alluded to the Pope's previous action (the Decree), which he said was also entirely due to the Pope's own initiative, but that our presence in Rome then had been very useful."

"I am much obliged," Balfour replied to Ross on February 24, "by your letter of the 19th inst. As regards the last part of it, I need not say that absolute discretion will be maintained on this side of the Alps."[8] Balfour turned to the subject of the report of the special commission, ignoring Ross's hints about the need for Roman representation: "I think some of the people here and possibly some of those with whom you have to deal at Rome have not realised how relatively unimportant is the finding of the commission with regard to the forged letter." "Had that letter been really Parnell's," he maintained, laying down the line he had been taking since the *Times*'s case blew up the year before, "the only legitimate interpretation that could have been put upon it, in my opinion, would have been that he was anxious to keep in close touch with and to retain the support of that faction of the Nationalist Party who propose to attain their objects by means of crime." "But this charge is amply proved," he declared, leaning very heavily on the argument of guilt by association, "not indeed with regard to the Invincibles, but with regard to Patrick Ford and the Clan-na-Gael. Even had the letter been shown to be genuine, it would in my judgement, have been utterly absurd to base upon it the theory that Parnell was cognisant

8. B, 49828.

of the designs of the Invincibles before the Phoenix Park Murders.''
''My Land Purchase Bill,'' Balfour then reported, ''will be the first
and the principle measure of the Session; and it will be introduced
by me, in what I fear will prove a very long Speech, as soon as
public business will allow.'' ''But,'' he noted in conclusion, speci-
fying the necessary Parliamentary business to be done, ''we have
still to finish the address; to get some necessary Supply; and to get
through the Debate upon the Commission before we can begin
legislative operations.''

The government, in fact, in spite of Balfour's apparent calm, was
having a very difficult time of it in the House. Shortly before Balfour had written Ross on February 24, the ministry had only just
beaten down what were, in effect, two successive motions of censure by majorities of forty-eight and sixty-seven, and there was still
the very awkward business of the debate on the report of the special
commission to be faced. The debate, which began on March 5, was
both partisan and bitter; on March 10, the government mustered a
sullen majority of sixty-one to defeat the crucial amendment, which
had been moved by Gladstone, to the government's motion accepting the report and thanking the judges who sat on the commission.
The rally was only made because the question at issue for most of
the supporters of the government involved the lesser of two evils
rather than any greater good. The morale of the government's supporters was still further shaken the following evening, when Lord
Randolph Churchill delivered an acrimonious and intemperate indictment of the ministry and its complicity in the making of the
*Times*'s case. ''Late events have,'' Errington sadly summed it all up
for Abbot Smith on March 16, ''weakened our Government, and I
am afraid there is much fear of the dangerous old man coming back
to power if he lives long enough & he seems stronger than ever; the
East Winds do not do their duty'' (S).

On March 5, soon after the debate on the report of the special
commission opened, the government instructed Sir John Lintorn
Simmons to conclude his mission to Rome as soon as possible.
Given the evident weakness of the government, and having Balfour's Irish land purchase bill as the first and chief order of legislative business of the session, Salisbury was obviously determined
that the opposition should not have the added advantage of being

able to raise indelicate questions about the government's relations with Rome, in order to undermine further the confidence of the government's supporters. Balfour's chief difficulty, however, was that the mission had to be concluded just when Ross finally seemed to be gaining ground in Rome and was on the verge of having something material done about Croke's conduct during the Tipperary imbroglio with Smith-Barry. ''Yesterday,'' Ross informed Balfour on March 6, ''I learnt with pleasure that the action I spoke of against Dr. Croke, had been taken. A private letter has been addressed to him, last Monday the 3$^{rd}$ inst., calling him to account & mentioning the great displeasure of the Pope at what he has done. This letter has gone to Croke through Walsh, & in doing so the Holy See has had in view a reprimand to the latter,—or at all events a reminder to him to beware how he acts,—because Walsh is here considered to be a more dangerous offender than Croke.''[9] ''In their view,'' Ross concurred, ''they are right. I understand the letter is a strong one. But it is only the first attack, & when the reply is received in Rome, it would be very useful to see that the proper information is given to the authorities here in order that the action then may be effective.''

''I told the Cardinal,'' Ross further pointed out, ''that if this matter is not seen to thoroughly, the decree is dead in Ireland; that when Croke was last reprimanded by the Pope personally, in 1883, he returned to Ireland & publicly said he came back 'unchanged & unchangeable'; & that what has now to be done is to make Dr. Croke repair the evil he has effected to the serious detriment of his own people.'' ''With regard to the last point,'' he added, ''I mentioned that I thought Smith-Barry w$^{d}$ deal leniently with his former tenants provided they left the conspiracy against him. I dare say, without giving any reason (for the matter is confidential), the course of affairs in Tipperary may be watched by you with the greater interest, in order to see whether the letter produces any result. I told you in my last letter I had given the Cardinal a first Memorandum upon the Special Commission,'' he reminded Balfour.

Besides the official copy you sent me, Norfolk also sent me one, and after marking the important passages in the latter copy, I gave it to the Cardinal on the 27th ult. He was very glad to get it, thanked me, & said he would

9. B, 49821.

have a precis made of it. Knowing however that his precis might take long to draw up, & appreciating the full importance of the matter, I told him I would draw up a translated resume myself, and I should be glad if he would compare it with the one he was to get made. Accordingly I have now got my own precis in French ready from beginning to end, but it is a long document, & being obliged to recopy it, I have up to now only been able to give the Cardinal a portion of it, which I did yesterday.

He was much interested, & promised to read it, & I begged him earnestly to do so, leaving at the same time for his consideration three points which I think it will be useful to develop in the future. (1) the point regarding the "fac-simile" letter, you sent me, & which is unanswerable, (2) that as O'Brien is the intimate friend of Croke, so is Parnell the close ally and friend of Walsh (this the Cardinal appreciated most fully) and (3) that the Cath$^c$ Irish outside Ireland must be in a deplorable state, seeing that the great movement which is held up to their admiration, is under control of an extreme & abominable Secret Society. This last point comes out very clearly under charge number 9. I therefore think that what with Croke's acts in Tipperary, (bad in themselves but worse when his connection with O'Brien is concerned [sic], what with the issue of the Special Commission report, at this time, and joined to the fact that in a short time remedial measures are to be introduced in the House, an opportunity is *now* afforded, (if ever there were one) which the H. See could seize in order to cooperate for the good of Xtianity & for the advantage of public order.

"Perhaps I should tell you," Ross finally explained, "that yesterday afternoon, Sir Lintorn Simmons got a telegram instructing him to arrange to wind up the Mission, & from this I imagine we shall all clear out of Rome before the end of this month (March). I can only hope that before the time comes for going, I shall be able to put before the authorities here the remaining information I have still to submit to them. There will be little time; but I will do all I can." "Up to a short time ago," he again reminded Balfour, "I have had (as you know) a very uphill task of it, in order to have matters made clear to the Papal authorities; I feel now that I have surmounted these difficulties." "I ought however I think," Ross warned in conclusion, "to tell you that my belief is, the moment I leave Rome, other influences which abound here will be brought certainly to bear—as was the case before—, and whether the Holy See will be able, unaided to cope with these influences and to utilise the present opportunity, which seems so favourable, is a matter upon which I could not express myself."

"Do you think it would be possible," Balfour asked the duke of Norfolk on March 17, about a week after he received Ross's letter of March 6, "for our friend to remain in Rome after the Malta Mission was over if his expenses were provided? On the latter point, I think there will be no difficulty if only obstacles connected with leave and so forth could be smoothed away. Will you think the matter over?"[10] What Balfour really meant, of course, was that the duke should sound Rampolla on the question of Ross remaining unofficially in Rome. The question was a very awkward one for Rome, as the accepting of Ross on an unofficial basis, especially after he had been officially accredited to the Vatican, would be a very long step backward in Rome's desire to effect diplomatic relations. The pope had, indeed, astutely attempted to provide the British government with a solution in his audience with Ross on January 17, when he emphasised Indian rather than Irish affairs. Ross relayed the hint to Norfolk, suggesting that the "Radnoads" problem in India might provide a sequel to the Malta mission. "I enclose a Report from Ross," Norfolk had explained to Salisbury on February 13, "on the 'Radnoads' question in India. It is a full and interesting history of the question, with suggestions as to the importance of having communication upon the subject with the Holy See but no other matters are introduced"(SY). Salisbury, however, in the face of his Parliamentary difficulties, had decided on another withdrawal rather than a diplomatic sequel. Because Ross did leave Rome at the official conclusion of the mission, Rome was obviously not disposed to accept a diminution in diplomatic status. Further, what Rome was interested in, besides encouraging diplomatic relations, was Irish information, and Ross could supply his memoranda and reports just as easily from London as from Rome.

"Since I wrote last to you," Ross diligently reported to Balfour from Rome on March 12, "I have given the Cardinal the remainder of the translated Precis of the Report of the Special Commission, I had prepared."[11] "The Plan of Campaign Table," he then noted, "has arrived; I am much obliged for it. I now come to the Tipperary incident. Walsh"—who had apparently answered for Croke, as the reprimand was sent through him—"has answered, in what appears

10. B, 49828.
11. B, 49821.

to me to be a very shuffling manner; I was therefore very glad to be here to give the Cardinal (in a Confidential Memorandum today) materials for further action. I am sorry I shall not be able to see this matter through, owing to our approaching departure; but I am leaving all the information I can, & doing what I can to ensure that the action may be effective." "I have done all I can," he assured Balfour, "to impress upon the Cardinal, the vital necessity of rigid attention to Irish matters. I told him (and as a Catholic rather than anything else do I feel this strongly) that in spite of statistics which certainly show a better state of things, my real view is that the Bishops are under the power of *'la Secte'* (the spirit of Secret Societies, rather than any particular Secret Society, a term thoroughly well understood here)." "I said perhaps there were only two of them," Ross observed, meaning Walsh and Croke, "who supported this spirit of anarchy, but the rest were ruled by it, and had no liberty to govern their Dioceses. I gave him examples, & referred him to the Report, and feel satisfied I produced a very strong impression upon him."

"What do you think," Ridgeway had meanwhile asked Balfour, on March 16, "of publishing this corr^ce? I am personally in favour of open war with Arch^b Walsh."[12] "He would be far less dangerous," Ridgeway asserted, seriously underestimating his man, "as an open enemy and he would I am inclined to think be more inclined to come to terms. If you do not like to publish, I suggest that [a] copy of corr^ce be sent to Ross. Surely this is a clear instance of contempt of the Pope's Rescript." Balfour prudently decided on the second alternative, rather than "open war." "One line," he wrote Ross on March 20, "just to cover a correspondence between Mr. Stokes, Divisional Commissioner, and Archbishop Walsh."[13] "I think the correspondence explains itself," he noted, "and I would only add that neither Stokes' letter nor Walsh's is marked 'Private,' and that the only caution you should observe in using them is that, of course, if Walsh becomes cognisant that the Court of Rome is made acquainted with them he will more than suspect that it must be through the direct action of the Government. I think you will agree with me that nothing could show more clearly how Walsh subor-

12. B, 49810.
13. Ibid.

dinates religion to politics than the course which he has taken in this matter."

"Let me congratulate you," Ross replied to Balfour on March 31, "upon the Purchase Bill, which has been introduced so successfully. The measure is calculated, I believe, to produce a radical change for the better in Ireland, and will I hope raise the influence & power of the Gov$^t$—the only Gov$^t$ in my humble opinion that has grappled thoroughly with the Irish question."[14] "Directly your speech reached Rome (the 27th inst.)," he explained, referring to Balfour's speech introducing the bill on March 24, "I verbally gave Card. Rampolla a short outline of your proposals, and after-wards I drew up a Memorandum on the subject which I handed to him yesterday. I read him the principal portions of the scheme as summarized in the Memorandum and explained them to him." "He expressed his satisfaction," Ross then pointed out, "at the liberality of the measure, and begged me to tell you so; he thought it a large minded & comprehensive scheme, which touched the root of the question, & said he would bring the matter to the attention of the Pope. I then took occasion to remind him what he had mentioned to me at a previous interview, viz:—that where measures of reform are proposed by Gov$^t$ an opportunity for the pacificatory action of the Holy See presents itself—I said that such an opportunity was now at hand." "He appreciated this remark," Ross assured Balfour, "& said that opportunity would be utilised in his action with Walsh."

Parnell had declared against the bill on March 25, and Ross accordingly continued: "In my Memorandum above mentioned, I also gave him all the information I had, with reference to the attitude of the Parnellites towards your Bill, & told him that the explanation of this attitude would be clear to him, on referring to the Report of the Special Commission. The Cardinal had, in a previous interview I had with him, told me that Walsh (when he was in Rome two years ago) had said to him that the Ashbourne Act had his active concurrence, and therefore the Holy See expected little resistance from him." "I replied however," he explained, "that I had no confidence in what this Archbishop might say to his superiors in Rome, and for my part would only judge of his real thoughts &

14. B, 49821.

ideas, by his action in Ireland. This conversation took place upon the 27th, when I gave the Cardinal a verbal outline of your proposals; but the opinion I then expressed upon Walsh was brought home to the Cardinal, because on that day I told him of the Stokes-Walsh correspondence which I had received." "This is perhaps all I need now say," Ross then observed, "except that the answer to Walsh will not go to him until after Easter. I have done my best that this action may be effective: I have certainly given them here the fullest materials so that this matter should not miscarry."

"It is perhaps too soon," Ross then informed Balfour, "to measure the net result which has been produced by my stay here. Nothing striking has occurred, & no public action has been taken as was the case before. In some ways this is not altogether unsatisfactory; but whether this be so or no, I believe that the really effective action which the Holy See can bring into play is a slow action, & that its influence is best felt by steady pressure." "I firmly believe," he affirmed, "this steady pressure has been begun, & that it will be continued as far as the Vatican is capable of keeping it up when unaided. Events have happened which have helped me in my representations, and these have undoubtedly made them see here, that the Bishops have not given a correct version of the moral situation in Ireland." "I think I have left behind me," Ross finally concluded, "materials to ensure that the pressure will be as effectual as possible, even though it be private at present and slow, and I trust it may produce some real advantage to a people who deserve a better fate than be the instruments of the Clan-na-Gael. P.S. I have ascertained our Audience is on Easter Monday [April 7]. I leave Tuesday, arriving in London on Thursday afternoon."

Early in March, Kirby had obviously been persuaded by the Roman authorities to extend an invitation to General Sir John Lintorn Simmons to the annual St. Patrick's day dinner at the Irish College, and Simmons had accepted.[15] After the dinner, Kirby was so uneasy about the effect his invitation would have in Ireland that he wrote at least three of the Irish archbishops, half apologising for

15. K, Simmons to Kirby, March 11, and 18, 1890, respectively accepting the invitation and thanking Kirby for the dinner.

inviting the Queen's envoy. "I had read all about the General's visit to the Irish College," Walsh replied coolly on March 24, "in the *Moniteur de Rome*. I suppose it is useful to keep up a certain show of not regarding all this diplomatic business as disastrous" (K). "But disastrous it certainly is," he declared firmly, "as we see the condition to which the Church is reduced in countries where that system is maintained, as compared with what we see here, and in England, and in America." Not only was the archbishop of Armagh more reassuring in his reply about the Queen's envoy, but his view of the present state of Irish public opinion toward Rome was quite different from that of his brother in Dublin. "The people here," Michael Logue assured Kirby on March 27, "know your Grace too well and your entire devotion to their interests to misconstrue any course you may take" (K). "I trust," he then observed hopefully, "the days of suspicion and want of confidence are gone. The people are now pretty generally convinced that every attempt made at Rome hostile to the interests of the country has been detected and discounted. Hence, there is not the same sensitiveness or fear of misrepresentation that existed some time ago." The following day Kirby's old friend, the archbishop of Tuam, also assured him that he had taken the right course with the Queen's envoy (K). After congratulating Kirby on his speech on the occasion, however, Mac-Evilly turned to a discussion of his own recent temperance efforts.

Shortly after Easter, the effects of Ross's efforts in Rome finally began to be felt and complained of in Ireland. "Mr. Ross's presence in Rome," Denis Pettit confided to Kirby on April 14, after congratulating him on his St. Patrick's Day speech, "does not bode well for Ireland. It is to be feared that he has the ear of the Vatican and is making the most of his opportunities. Statements, at all events have reached Rome, in connection with occurrences in different dioceses in Ireland, which are not only unfriendly but absolutely untrue" (K). Pettit was undoubtedly alluding to the pope's recent letter, received by Walsh, concerning the Smith-Barry affair in Tipperary. The actual letter, however, does not appear to have been nearly as strong as Ross understood, or was given to understand by Rampolla. The pope complained to Walsh about various irregularities in a number of dioceses, and not just Cashel, concerning enforcement of the Decree and further asked Walsh to use his valuable influence in seeing that these irregularities were corrected. Walsh, in the reply described by Ross to Balfour as "shuffling," maintained, it seems, that because the Smith-Barry struggle had nothing whatever to do with either the Plan of Campaign or Boycotting, the question of enforcing the Decree did not arise at all.

When Ross left Rome, therefore, the authorities decided once again, for two main reasons, that the best course in Irish affairs was watchful waiting. In the first place, the weakness of the government was patent to one and all, and every succeeding day was making it even more evident. When, after Easter, the combined opposition, Parnellite and Gladstonian, launched a full-scale parliamentary assault, which by July had forced the ministry to postpone not only Balfour's Irish land purchase bill but several other important pieces of legislation until the autumn session, the talk about a dissolution and a general election before Christmas was quite common. The second reason why Rome decided to bide its time regarding Ireland was that Walsh and Croke's position in the Irish Church, given the confident and rising political temper of Irish political opinion, was almost impregnable. In fact, any public assertion of Rome's authority would tend only to consolidate further the archbishops' very formidable position. How formidable it had become since the issuance of the Decree two years before was further illustrated when Lord Emly decided that the new bishop of Waterford, John Egan, would make an ideal candidate for senator in the Royal University. In promoting Egan's candidature, Emly undoubtedly looked to embarrass Walsh once again, as he had done some three years before when he was instrumental in securing the appointment of O'Dwyer to the senate of the Royal University, over the objections of Walsh and the overwhelming majority of the Irish Bishops.

"I have heard through Lord Emly," Ross reported to Balfour on Thursday, May 29, from Victoria Barracks in Windsor, "that within the last few days (last Tuesday I think) Dr. Egan has said that he sees no reason whatever to prevent him from accepting the 'Senatorship' if it is offered to him. He has said this to Father Carbery," Ross added interestingly, naming Croke's Jesuit cousin, the president of University College, Dublin.[16] "I was sorry to hear," he noted

16. B, 49821.

further, "that Dr. Molloy had recently been put upon the Standing
Committee of the Senate. I wish it had been Dr. Egan." "Would
there be any inconvenience," he asked Balfour in conclusion, "in
letting me know privately, exactly what part the Priests of the Cashel
Diocese took to countenance the recent illegal meetings in Tipperary,
& which of them thereby still aided the Plan of Campaign Conspiracy upon Smith-Barry's Estate?" Indeed, the appointment of
Egan to the Royal University at this moment was the very least
among Balfour's Irish preoccupations. Dillon, who had finally returned from Australia, had in concert with O'Brien held a large
meeting on Sunday, May 25, in New Tipperary, and there had been
a riot with a number of people injured.[17] In Cashel, two days later,
they held another meeting, which had been forbidden by the government, and in the consequent baton charges by the police some
twenty-five people were injured.[18] A measure of the seriousness
with which Balfour viewed the developing situation in Ireland was
the "Confidential" note he wrote S. K. McDonnell, one of the
permanent officials in the Foreign Office. "Major Ross of Bladensburg," Balfour informed McDonnell on Friday, May 30, "who
was attached to Lintorn Simmons' Maltese Mission, would, I think,
find time to go to Rome again for a few weeks immediately. Would
it be possible to find any diplomatic excuse for such a journey
in the shape of winding up any unsettled questions that may still
remain over in Malta or otherwise?"[19] "I am afraid," he explained
in conclusion, "that if he goes merely as a tourist his position at the
Vatican would be an awkward one."

Several days later, when the pressure had eased a little, Balfour
found time to attend to the matter of promoting Egan's appointment.
"I enclose a letter," he informed Ridgeway on June 5, "just received from Ross of Bladensburg. It will be an excellent idea, I
think, to appoint Egan to the Catholic Vacancy in the Royal University. I do not know what Ross alludes to in the second paragraph. I
suppose that Molloy's appointment to the Standing Committee of
the Senate had nothing to do with any Government action. I hear
very bad accounts of Molloy, who appears to be a mere tool of

17. *Irish Catholic*, May 31, 1890.
18. Ibid.
19. B, 49828.

Walsh."[20] "As regards the last paragraph in Ross's letter," Balfour advised Ridgeway in conclusion, referring to the information about the Cashel clergy, "I shall be glad if you will supply me with the information. I will then forward it to him." The government then proceeded to go through the formal motions of appointing Egan to the senate, but at the end of June, just before the appointment was officially made, he suddenly informed the government he could not accept the honor. Lord Emly immediately wrote Father Carbery asking for an explanation of the bishop of Waterford's strange conduct.

"Your letter has just now reached me here," Carbery explained from Saint Coleman's College in Fermoy on July 1, "where I am engaged in conducting the Diocesan retreat. The day after the meeting of the Bishops"—the annual June meeting at Maynooth—"poor Dr. Egan called on me to explain the very awkward position in which he found himself by the resolution passed at that meeting calling on Dr. Woodlock as '*their*' representative to resign his seat on the Senate. He had received a few days before the usual letter expressing His Excellency's intention of recommending him for the Senatorship, and replied immediately that he would gratefully accept the honor."[21] "Had the appointment been made," he assured Emly, "there would have been no difficulty.—But, being unable to avert the resolution, and feeling that, as this was the first occasion when he took part in a general meeting of the Bishops, it would seem strange and in fact give scandal to outsiders if, immediately after a resolution which excited so much attention, his name were to be announced as a New Senator, he at once on leaving the Meeting wired the 'Irish Office' not to take any step until they should have heard from him—and wrote by that days post an explanation of his change of position." "As these circumstances could not have been foreseen," Carbery noted, attempting to soften the disappointment, "and as he really expressed his wish to be honored by the office, the unpleasantness of the position, which I fully understand, has been, as far as possible minimised. He asked me to express to your Lordship his gratitude for your kind interest & his regret for the inconvenience."

20. B, 49811.
21. B, 49821.

"Lord Emly," Ross informed Balfour dryly on July 7, from Windsor, "has asked me to send you the enclosed which is Dr. Egan's explanation of his recent exploit with reference to the Senate of the Royal University. I need not say that Lord Emly is very much vexed as I am too. I have no doubt Dr. Egan was placed in an uncomfortable position; but he had accepted the part. The incident shows what exceedingly strong influences are brought to bear upon the wrong side, & how weak are those who would gladly support the cause of order."[22] The significance of Egan's inability to rise to the occasion provided by Lord Emly, as O'Dwyer had done in similar circumstances some three years before, was not only a measure of Walsh's real influence, but also in this case a most likely example of his foresight. If he had learned that Egan's appointment was in the making, and it would have been difficult to keep it a secret, having Woodlock resign was as astute a move as it was effective. In any case, both Healy and O'Dwyer, who were still senators, were still further embarrassed by their episcopal colleagues' manifest disapproval, and because Egan refused to defy the episcopal body, Healy and O'Dwyer were even more isolated than they had been before.

What was even more significant about this meeting at Maynooth than the checking of Egan's appointment, however, was what the Bishops chose *not* to say in the issuing of the crucial resolutions after their meeting. They confined themselves to a series of six resolutions on the education question and left issues that were troubling them even more at the moment discreetly alone.[23] They accepted in silence, for example, the Irish Party's decision to oppose Balfour's land purchase bill, though most of them probably supported the measure.[24] The Party's decision was politically under-

22. Ibid.
23. *Irish Catholic*, July 5, 1890.
24. K, Edward McGennis, bishop of Kilmore, to Kirby, May 1, 1890, perhaps expressed the prevailing feeling:

Ireland is very quiet, there is a prospect of a good Season. The Spring was dry and the Crops were got in under favourable conditions. Cattle are bringing a good price. The Purchase Bill recently introduced into Parliament is likely to pass. Under a Tory Executive it will be worked in the landlord interest but tenants buying under it will get considerable reduction of rent. If the Land question were settled on fair terms Ireland would be peaceful and prosperous. Some form of County Government will be given us very soon and the present Grand Jury System got rid of. We expect the next election will drive the Tories out of office.

standable, in that it wanted to bring down the government, but the Bishops, who were embarrassed both at home and at Rome by the mounting land war, would have been undoubtedly happy to accept a measure that might have gone a long way toward solving the land question: it would have placed some £33 million at the disposal of those tenants who wanted to buy out their landlords, though the terms of purchase, as the Irish Party had pointed out, were certainly in the interest of the landlords rather than the tenants. Even more important, however, and an underlying issue, was what appears to have been a growing awareness among all the Bishops, as well as a rising resentment among some of them, that in the fundamental matter of the Clerical-Nationalist alliance they had become less partners and more auxiliaries. At the Maynooth meeting, in fact, Gillooly drafted a letter addressed to Parnell that, though it was not sent, was an interesting measure of the developing irritation and its causes:

Maynooth<br>June 26/90

Dear Mr. P.

At a General Meeting of the Bishops held here on yesterday some questions of great interest, political as well as religious, were under our consideration; and I have been asked to convey to you the conclusion arrived at by the Meeting. The chief object for which the Resolutions were adopted is to maintain, and if possible to strengthen, the relation which has hitherto existed with such happy results between the Clergy and the National Parliamentary Party; and for that purpose to remove causes of misunderstandings, which would surely be most painful to Clergy & Laity, and which might prove ruinous to our political Prospects.

The bishops have much confidence in your prudence & foresight; and therefore wish to call your attention, and thro' you the attention of the Party, to those disquieting matters before they attract general notice and lead to division in our ranks.

The matters I refer to are:

1. The attempt lately made in Parliament to deal with the Education Question, which we regard as essentially religious, without the knowledge or approval of the Bishops, altho' a formal undertaking was entered into some years ago by yourself and other leading Members of the Party, that no action on Educat$^l$ Subjects should be taken without previous consultation and understanding with the Episcopal Education Committee, representing the Bishops.

Any violation of this Compact the Bishops should feel themselves strictly bound in conscience to at once publicly condemn & oppose.

2. The independent action of individual members of the Party in originating & organising movements involving the gravest consequences, political, social & moral, without the sanction of the Party as such. This sanction should in all acts of importance be sought & obtained, before priests or people are invited to give their cooperation.

In future the Bishops will consider it their duty to refuse their cooperation and that of their Clergy, to proceedings taken under individual responsibility.

3. The adoption and putting forward of Candidates to Parliament without the previous sanction of the Electors, given through their assembled delegates as in past years; and even without the public declaration of their opinion or Pledge as to their future action in Parliament.

The Clergy & other Electors will gladly take advice from the Parliamentary Party as to the choice of new Representatives but the right of selection is theirs and they will not bear to see it ignored or superceded.

4. The discredit cast on the National Party by the foul personal attacks for which United Ireland has become noted. That paper is regarded as the organ of the N[l] Parliamentary Party. The Leaders of the Party and the Clergy who cooperate actively with them are therefore justly held responsible for its opinions and its direction—even for its scurrilous attacks on individuals. The bishops can no longer be silent, if due supervision is not henceforth exercised over the editorial department of that Paper.

The bishops earnestly recommend the above matters to your practical consideration and that of your fellow Members; and will be happy to find, that they will be so dealt with as to preclude the dangers they apprehend from a continuance of the toleration and apparent approval, hitherto given to those abuses.[25]

How many of the bishops were in favor of sending the letter, of course, is a most interesting question. Because it was not sent, and because there is no evidence that it was even formally discussed, it is obvious that a substantial majority were not then inclined to act; but because a modified version of the same letter, omitting points one and three, would be sent to Parnell by Logue in the unanimous name of the Bishops after their next general meeting, in October, it may be surmised that in June the number of those who favored sending it, or some modified version of it, was not entirely negli-

25. G, "Draft of Letter to Mr. Parnell." See also W, Croke to Walsh, January 27, 1891: "But I remember some such Epistle was drawn up by Dr. Gillooly on a former occasion. I looked over it; and having found in it some things that appeared to be objectionable, it was withdrawn."

gible. What the Bishops were really objecting to was that the Party, especially since the issuing of the Decree two years before, had arrogated to itself in various matters a good deal of the initiating power that the Party and the Bishops had formerly shared. The effect of the Decree, in fact, had been to tip the scales slowly in favor of the lay politicians in the Clerical-Nationalist alliance. The Bishops were unable to redress the balance because they were vulnerable, despite their constant assurances to the contrary, to the accusation of a possible betrayal of National aspirations, either by orders from Rome or by those supposed "Castle" bishops, like O'Dwyer and Healy, in their own ranks. The club the lay politicians held over the Bishops' heads, which was much evidenced in Walsh's constant complaints to Kirby that the Irish Church would be reduced to the state of its Continental sisters if Rome did not act more prudently in Irish affairs, was the mounting of an anticlerical public opinion in the name of Irish Nationalism; of this action the politicians had already given the Bishops a rude taste after the issuing of the Decree by Rome. The Bishops held their collective hand in June, however, undoubtedly because of the still very great influence of Walsh and Croke and the argument that to send such a letter on the eve of a dissolution and a general election would be an act of sheer folly.

That the Bishops had held their hand was also undoubtedly owing to the very astute action taken by Walsh about a week before they were scheduled to meet. Though the evidence is still only circumstantial, it appears that Walsh, who was always extremely well informed, had either learned about or sensed the developing uneasiness of his episcopal brethren over the increasingly independent line being pursued by the Party. In any case, on June 19, he wrote a very curious and uncharacteristic letter to the editor of the *Freeman's Journal*:

I have just learned by a telegram from London that in a critical division in the House of Commons this evening the Ministry has been saved from defeat by the narrow majority of four. It would furthermore seem that for its escape the Ministry is indebted to the fact that a considerable number of our Irish representatives were absent from their posts. If all this be true, as I fear it is true, a grave crisis has arisen in the public affairs of our country. The country, I trust will call the absentees, every man of them to account.

The crisis has not come on our representatives without the fullest notice. Last week more than once the Ministry escaped defeat by majorities then regarded as exceedingly narrow—majorities of between 30 and 40 votes. Two or three days ago the majority was brought down to 29. On all these occasions Irish members who ought to have been at their posts were absent from them. It was plain to everyone that some most critical division might take place this evening, the issue of which might depend upon the presence or absence of our representatives. Notwithstanding all this it would now seem that a number of these representatives were absent from their posts, and that by their absence they saved the ministry from a crushing defeat.[26]

He concluded with a very grim warning: "For my part, I feel bound to lose not a moment in stating that if a satisfactory explanation be not forthcoming for what has occurred—I do not care who the absentees may be—I shall find it hard to place any further trust in the action of the present Irish Parliamentary Party."

At first glance, this was indeed a most curious and uncharacteristic outburst from Walsh, who was always, at least in public, very careful about what he had to say. On examination, however, what appears to be an explicit threat to the Clerical-Nationalist alliance is actually something a good deal less than that. In the first place, Walsh was very careful to point out that he was speaking for himself and not for the Bishops as a body. Secondly, it must also be noted that he was complaining about a question of political conduct or tactics, rather than about any fundamental issue. He was not, therefore, raising a question of principle, and at this stage nothing less than that could really jeopardize the Clerical-Nationalist alliance. Thirdly, what he was asking for was an explanation, and he was careful to reserve to himself the right to judge whether it was satisfactory or not. In a word, Walsh in his letter had cleverly kept the whole game in his own hands. He was really trying, of course, to create the impression among his episcopal colleagues, just prior to their meeting, that he was as much displeased as some of them about the Party's recent tendency to take them for granted. His letter greatly strengthened his capacity to restrain those of his colleagues at the meeting who might be insistent that the Bishops take a more aggressive line toward the Party. Walsh could now argue with great effect not only that he had just taken such a line, but that they must

26. *Times* (London), June 21, 1890.

at least wait upon the explanation before they could take any action as a body. Above all, he had by his letter reminded both the Leader and the Party that the Bishops would no longer allow themselves to be simply taken for granted in their joint enterprise.

A week later, on June 28, at a dinner given him by his parliamentary colleagues to celebrate his forty-fourth birthday, Parnell took occasion during the course of what was a major policy address to make the explanation required by Archbishop Walsh.[27] He began by eulogizing the Liberal-Nationalist alliance and ended by emphasizing to his colleagues that the next general election would finally bring them their hearts' desire in the form of Home Rule. Fundamental in bringing the question to its present happy issue, he maintained, was the Irish component of that alliance—the Party. In fact, not only was the Party in good heart, but its integrity was intact and its devotion to duty unimpaired. Parnell then turned to Walsh's recent criticism. " 'Some of us,' " he admitted good-humoredly, " 'were absent in this critical division. Undoubtedly I believe I was one of the number' (Laughter)." " 'But the party,' " he declared amidst cheers, " 'were there, and they were there in greater strength than any other party.' " " 'Now,' " he then asked, " 'what were the figures? There was a total vote of 456 members, or 68½ percent of the total number of members of the House. There were 53 percent of the Tories in that vote, there were 73½ percent of the Liberals, and there were 78 percent of the Irish Party' (Cheers)." " 'I say that this,' " he maintained, " 'is a very creditable result for the Irish Parliamentary party' (hear, hear), 'many of whom to come to town for the division had to travel 300 miles by sea and land; and, so far as the Irish party as a body goes, it would be most unjust of me if I did not bear my testimony to the fact that they had stood by their posts during the last five years as a body like men' (cheers), 'and that they have done their duty without complaint—a laborious and a fatiguing and a disagreeable duty; that they have fought an uphill battle, and that as a party and as a body our countrymen are proud of them' (Cheers)."

In the course of these remarks Parnell also denied that the members could have anticipated the critical division, because it was

27. Ibid., June 30, 1890.

sprung upon them by the government. Even if they had known about it and had issued a whip, he further maintained, it would have proved self-defeating, because it was notorious that the government opened all their letters. In effect, then, Parnell took the side of the Party, inasmuch as he denied that the assumptions of fact made by Walsh were correct. By also pointing out that, in judging the Party's performance, it was necessary to take the longer and more comprehensive view, and by devoting the rest of his speech to the theme that Home Rule was now within Ireland's grasp, Parnell was also implying that any rocking of the constitutional boat at this critical juncture was neither safe nor sensible. Walsh did not rejoin, if indeed he had ever any intention of rejoining, for by his letter not only had he gained the tactical point of preventing any overt criticism of the Party by the Bishops at their meeting, but, by eliciting Parnell's prompt reply, he had secured a responsible indication that the Bishops were not being taken for granted.

When some two weeks later, on July 11, John Dillon attacked the bishop of Limerick in the House of Commons in a most intemperate and imprudent outburst, while speaking on the Irish civil service estimates, he precipitated the crisis that both Walsh and Parnell had been trying to avert. The *Freeman* printed a long account of Dillon's statement to the House in general and Balfour in particular: "Speaking then as an Irish Catholic and on behalf of the Catholics of Ireland, he told the right hon gentleman that he and his coreligionists were as independent of Rome and of the agents of his Holiness in all political matters as any Nonconformist on those benches (cheers). They were far more independent in political matters of Rome than the right hon gentleman and his uncle were, who debased the honour of England by crawling to the Court of Rome and offering bribes to his Holiness to aid them in crushing the people of Ireland (loud cheers)."[28] "There was no fouler stain cast on the people of England," continued the report, "and no more intolerable grievance inflicted on the people of Ireland, than when the right hon gentleman succeeded in getting his Holiness to send an agent to trade on the reverence of the Irish people. They would never allow his promises for one single hour to interfere between

28. *Freeman's Journal*, July 13, 1890.

them and the goal on which they had set their hopes (loud cheers), nor would they allow him to use them as a means to sow discord between the Irish members and the Irish people.'' Dillon had gone on to the university question:

They scorned his offers; they had been denied justice in that matter, and now they could afford to wait a little longer. They would have the University in Ireland they desired when they had a home Parliament. The right hon gentleman had succeeded by his promises and schemes in capturing two Irish bishops, one of whom, Dr. O'Dwyer, had written a most violent and dastardly letter.

The CHIEF SECRETARY—I rise to order. I don't think an attack on an Irish bishop can be made on this vote (oh).

The CHAIRMAN—I understand the hon gentleman was referring to the right hon gentleman's action. If he went on to attack the bishop no doubt he would not be in order (Ministerial cheers).

Mr. DILLON—I think the action of the right hon gentleman in springing from his seat to defend the bishop—

The CHIEF SECRETARY—I again rise to order. I sprang from my seat because I thought the hon gentleman went beyond the vote. I shall not attempt to defend the bishop (oh, oh).

Mr. Dillon said he would say no more on that point (hear, hear).[29]

"All he would say," the summary concluded, "was that, as an Irish Catholic, that gentleman [the bishop of Limerick] had done his worst against the Irish Church, and he was exceedingly glad he stood alone among the Episcopacy of Ireland with his scandalous conduct (cheers)."

Parnell, who spoke about an hour after Dillon in this debate, must have realized, especially after his own recent exchange with Walsh, that the Bishops were very uneasy about any further escalation of the land agitation and that Dillon's outburst would only tend to increase their nervousness. When he rose to speak, therefore, Parnell attempted to pour oil on troubled waters. He first of all offered Balfour an olive branch by proposing to terminate the strife on those estates where the Plan of Campaign was still in force. "After the experience of the successful arbitration," he explained, "in reference to one of these estates carried out by the hon. and learned Member for Hackney (Sir C. Russell), it ought not to be difficult to frame a measure which would pass through the House without difficulty or opposition, and which would provide for an inquiry and a

29. Ibid., July 14, 1890.

fair settlement of the dispute on each of these estates."[30] "I have myself little doubt," he then added, after assuring the House that his proposal did not emanate from weakness and that the evicted tenants would be protected to the end, "that my suggestion will have been made in vain, but I shall have the satisfaction of knowing that I have made it, and that the responsibility will not rest on me." Even more surprisingly, he then turned to the recently introduced land purchase bill, which he and his Party had so successfully obstructed and opposed that it had to be withdrawn for that session by the government. He proposed that if the bill were suitably modified when introduced again, it would receive his cordial support. Finally, he recommended that the local authorities in Ireland be given more power in administrating the proposed land bill. Indeed, it is difficult to understand either Parnell's temporizing attitude regarding the Plan of Campaign—on which, he emphasized, he had not consulted his colleagues—or his *volte face* regarding the land bill—also apparently made without consultation—if one does not appreciate that he, as Leader, was undoubtedly once again playing to the episcopal gallery in an effort to stabilize the consensus.

The bishop of Limerick, however, proceeded to make a difficult situation impossible by replying in kind a few days later in a bristling and indignant letter to the press in which he accused Dillon of being, among other things, dishonest, a coward, and disrespectful in his language about the pope. "Sir—" O'Dwyer wrote the editor of the *Freeman's Journal* on Saturday, July 12, "I once heard a beggar woman pouring forth the foulest abuse in the public street on an apparently respectable and inoffensive-looking man."[31] "My curiosity being stimulated," he continued his parable, "I enquired the cause and learned that he had informed some casual passerby who was touched by the number and poverty of the children into giving alms, that these children in reality were not her own, but had been borrowed from a sympathetic neighbour for eleemosynary purposes—*Hinc illae lacryma*." "It is only in the same way," he explained, referring to a Plan estate in his diocese, "that I can account for Mr. Dillon's outburst of outrageous language in denouncing me for the simple and matter-of-fact letter which I gave to

30. *Hansard's Parliamentary Debates*, 3d ser., 346, cols. 1516–23.
31. *Freeman's Journal*, July 14, 1890.

the public on the Glensharrold case." "He has been engaged," the bishop continued, "labouring of late collecting money, ostensibly for the relief of evicted tenants. He and his party are still occupied in the same profitable employment, and just as they hoped to strike another golden vein by the exhibition of death sentences ruthlessly carried out upon the hapless victims of heartless landlordism, it must have been very provoking to have the real facts of the case exposed and the pockets of the sympathisers closed. I am not equal to a contest in Billingsgate with Mr. Dillon, nor do I mean to try it." "But I will tell him this," O'Dwyer added, turning from a discussion of Dillon's honesty to his courage, "that if at any time I should find myself put into prison for a cause that I professed to believe just, I would rot there before I allowed my friends to send up a miserable whine for my release from every end of the country on the plea of health, and that if I sneaked out thus and then went off to the Antipodes on a twelve months' tour until the storm blew over and my vows to defy the Act of Parliament under which I had been imprisoned were forgotten, he might call me a dastard without fear of contradiction."

"But, sir," O'Dwyer went on, "I am almost ashamed of myself to waste so many words on this gentleman's personal offensiveness to myself, when I read the language which he dares to use towards the august and sacred person of the Vicar of Christ. It is no disgrace, but an honour, for a poor, simple bishop to receive a few spatters of the dirt that is flung at the representative of his Divine Master." "If only I could get it all," he continued archly, while cleverly making points, "and be covered with opprobrium while I lived, so as to spare our old Catholic nation the shame before the world that one of the foulest charges ever levelled against the successor of St. Peter was hurled at Leo XIII, amidst the cheers of English Protestants and English unbelievers by one who professes to be a member of the Church. Why, the Giordano Bruno people do not impeach the Pope's personal honour. M. Constans and his colleagues in France believe in no God and attack religion, but they never stoop to charge the Head of the Church with charlatanism." "But," O'Dwyer charged, "here is a Catholic boasting of his Catholicity, the friend of bishops and archbishops, using the privileges of the faith in order to get near the Father of the Faithful and stab him in the back." "This gentleman," he then observed, "has often boasted of his intimacy with bishops and archbishops, and the aid which he got from them at home and abroad." "It will be interesting to observe," the bishop remarked, invoking a variation on the theme of Boycotting, "how many of them now will be anxious to identify themselves with him publicly until this insulting slander is withdrawn."

"The question for the public is," O'Dwyer then asked, indicating that he for one was not satisfied with conditions of the Clerical-Nationalist alliance, "am I or am I not within my rights in thinking as a man, and teaching as a bishop, that the Plan of Campaign and boycotting are against the law of God?" "And this suggests another grave question," he then added, "which I beg to submit to the consideration of thoughtful statesmen such as Mr. Parnell, Mr. Justin McCarthy, Mr. Sexton, and Mr. Arthur O'Connor. If Mr. Dillon, whether he has the right or not, has the power, without check or remonstrance from any one of his party, to denounce an Irish bishop as he has denounced me simply and solely for my action in the exercise of my spiritual jurisdiction, what guarantee is there, should Home Rule come, that all of us bishops shall not find our authority crippled, not by words, but by force?" "Are there not interests enough arrayed to the death against Home Rule," he asked shrewdly, "to make it at least a matter of common tactical prudence not to force the bishops in Ireland to review their position in relation to it?" "I commend that view of things," he then advised, "to the consideration of serious Home Rulers, and beg of them not to drive us to compare the religious liberty we enjoy at present with the prospects of things under Mr. Dillon as Minister of Worship. Again and again, I have said I am a Home Ruler. At home and abroad I have maintained the right of my country to self-government. In so far as the agitation legitimately advances that cause, I am with it. I would join it to-morrow if I had any assurance that the movement was to be purged from sinful methods, but while Mr. Dillon and men like him, in defiance of their own leader, are the practical leaders, I must only stand aloof." O'Dwyer finally closed with another parable: "I may illustrate my position by a humorous incident. Some time ago, great crowds attended the sermons of a revivalist here in Limerick. At the end of a very vehement discourse he called upon all those of his audience who wished to go to Heaven to stand up. All stood up except one Catholic young man, who ought not to have been there at all. 'Young man,' said the preacher solemnly, 'do you not wish to go to Heaven?' 'Oh yes I do,' said the young man, 'but not with that crowd.' '' Dillon immediately denied that he had used, as far as he could remember, the language about the pope attributed to him in the reports of some newspapers.[32]

Croke, who certainly qualified as an expert in the matters of awkward public statements and bristling letters to the press, was asked on July 15, by the editor of *L'Univers*, a French Catholic paper, his opinion on the merits of the case (C). "Both Dillon and Bishop O'Dwyer," Croke replied evenhandedly to M. Godre on July 18, in a letter marked "*Private*," "are to blame for the very unpleasant incident to which you refer" (C). "Dillon's language in the House of Commons," he admitted, "in reference to Dr. O'Dwyer, besides being quite uncalled for, was most offensive and reprehensible. But on the other hand, Dr. O'Dwyer's letter was unjust so far as Dillon was concerned, and most undignified as coming from a Bishop. Dillon denies having used the offensive and highly disrespectful language about the Pope which some papers have attributed to him. That is very good. But the letter in which he denies having employed such unbecoming language toward his Holiness was not all that might reasonably have been expected from him, under the circumstances." "To his refutation of the words imputed to him," Croke maintained, "he should have added that if, in the heat of any debate, he had used language that could be fairly construed into disrespect for the Pope, he was sincerely sorry for it—that would have been satisfactory and creditable. But instead of that, he simply says that so far as his memory goes, he did not use the words concerning the Pope, which have given offense to so many good Catholics." "In short," Croke summed up, "—Dillon erred grievously in attacking the Bishop in the House of Commons, and discussing his conduct in a landlord and tenant dispute as dastardly and scandalous—and the Bishop erred more grievously still by flinging a notoriously false accusation of cowardice against Dillon—and belaboring Home Rulers and politicians generally, whether

32. Ibid., July 15, 1890.

clerical or lay, in a flippant, sneering and undignified manner." "I have not time," he finally apologised in conclusion, "to write any more just now as I wish to catch the evng's post."

"The Protestant papers of to-day," Walsh reported to Kirby some ten days later, on July 30, "announced with great prominence that Dr. O'Dwyer of Limerick has received a letter of approval from the Holy See in reference to his attack on John Dillon" (K). "If this be true," Walsh warned once again, "it represents the biggest advance that has as yet been made towards driving our people into the attitude into which the Catholic populations of so many countries on the Continent have long since been driven." "The letter of Dr. O'D." he declared, "was a grossly offensive one to all the Archbishops and Bishops of Ireland. In opposition to the most notorious facts, he equivalently asserts in it that the only reason why the Nationalist leaders attack him is that *he* is maintaining in Ireland the authority of the Holy See, meaning, of course, that he alone is doing it. Now it seems the Holy See has endorsed this infamous accusation!" "Dr. O'Dwyer, in reality," Walsh explained to Kirby, "was attacked by John Dillon for a most shameful proceeding of his towards a number of poor tenants in his diocese who were evicted for inability to pay a most excessive rent. The Bishop wrote to prevent funds being raised for their relief. John Dillon attacked him for this in very intemperate language, and the Bishop then represents the attack made on him as having been made because he, unlike the rest of us, is upholding the authority of the Holy See! I thought it well Y.G. should understand all this." "P.S.," Walsh added with obvious pleasure, "there is great trouble over the *Malta* affair. Plainly the H.F. did not count on the publication by Lord Salisbury of so much of what occurred. Everyone sees that in all the negotiation about the appointment of Bishops, the case really in view was Ireland!"

Several days later Croke also wrote Kirby a brief note commenting on the latest crisis. "The Dillon O'Dwyer episode," he confessed sadly on August 3, "is in various ways, the most regrettable incident connected with the Irish Agitation. Both parties were in fault: but the Bishop erred ever so much more grievously than did the layman" (K). What Walsh and Croke did not know, however, was that Kirby had already committed himself to the other side in this quarrel. Though the pope, as had been reported in the press, had not sent the bishop of Limerick a letter, he had asked Kirby to deliver a consoling message in his name. "I cannot tell your Grace," O'Dwyer explained to Kirby on August 5, "what a comfort this has been to me, in the midst of much obloquy. I thank your Grace most heartily for the wise and holy suggestions of your letter just received" (K). "If some one else, the Primate, or one of the Archbishops," he countered cleverly in conclusion, "would speak out, it would be much better; but if I have to write again I shall take care that no provocation induces me to go beyond the high and strong ground of principle."

The bishop of Elphin was also deeply disturbed by the recent turn of events and wrote to Walsh to complain of them and their significance. "All that your Lordship says," Walsh agreed on August 17, in a letter to Gillooly marked "*Confidential*," "about the disastrous tendency of the present course of affairs is obviously true. But the practical question is, what is the remedy? The time when individual action could have been of use has long since disappeared. I was in Rome at the time. But even at a distance it was plain to see that the practical inaction of the Bishops in the crisis that arose on the appearance of the Decree of the Holy Office meant the extinction of useful Episcopal influence except in so far as the Bishops could again be pulled together to act with unanimity in public affairs" (G). "I took it for granted," he confided, "after the criticism so freely expressed on the occasion of our last meeting in Maynooth that more energy would be shown in future in calling together our Standing Committee. But seeing that even the crisis that grew out of the Limerick-Dillon incident has not led to anything like an awakening of energy I have given up all hope of united action being taken in our present practically headless condition. Dillon's language was, of course, indefensible. So was Dr. O'Dwyer's. We cannot take action against one without taking action against the other." "The sooner action is taken against both," he declared firmly, "the better it will be for the interests of both Church and State in Ireland."

"It is a monstrous thing," Walsh continued bitterly, "that any Bishop pursuing a crochety line of his own as Dr. O'Dwyer is, can be allowed, when attacked for his individual proceedings, to say that he is singled out for attack because he (meaning he alone) is duly discharging the duty of a Bishop in regard to the acts of the Holy See in Ireland. He alleges this publicly. The Episcopacy of Ireland lies down under his slanderous statement and allows itself to be walked over by him. We certainly shall have no reason to complain if the Holy See, from our silence, assumes the charge made against us by our colleague to be true." "In reference to the Decree," he observed, "the Bishops came to a unanimous decision (on lines suggested by me) at our meeting in June 1888. If any Bishop has failed to carry out in his diocese the practical programme then agreed upon, let Dr. O'Dwyer attack him as violently as he may feel called upon to do. But, he has no right to assail our whole body as he is doing." "All this, however," Walsh argued further, "is a question for the body and not for individuals, except in so far as we may hope to bring about some corporate action. I am tired [of] writing to the Primate." "He will do nothing," Walsh concluded wearily, "but write long letters of lamentation that nothing is being done!"

Dillon, meanwhile, was in anxious consultation with O'Brien, who was on his honeymoon in Switzerland, about a meeting scheduled for Limerick on Sunday, August 24, which, it appears, had been arranged before his exchange with O'Dwyer had taken place. "It is evident," O'Brien noted on August 11, from Interlaken, in reply to a letter of Dillon's, "the clerical feeling is deep and general. You ought to summon Dowd to Dublin & ascertain how Limerick feeling goes" (D). "It seems to me," O'Brien then observed, "there is absolutely no alternative except to go ahead & make the demonstration as overwhelming as it is possible to make it. I think Joe Cox ought to go down to bring in the Co. Clare. The Emly priests also ought to be urged to put in an appearance. A visit to Fr. Michael Ryan at Murroe, Fr. O'Dwyer of Goda, Fr. Power of Kilterby would be well worth the trouble. Harrington's presence I regard as indispensable. If Healy can be got to come so much the better." Dillon replied that Harrington had agreed that there was no alternative except to go ahead with the Limerick meeting. "No defeat," O'Brien responded on August 16, "could be comparable to the effect of an abandonment" (D). "If the thing is properly organized," he assured Dillon, "I believe the feeling against O'D. will sweep all before it."

"You will be in Limerick next Sunday," Father M. B. Kennedy, curate of Meelin in County Cork and an intrepid Campaigner, wrote Dillon on Wednesday, August 20, "and will there have to meet several of the local Nationalists. Will you permit me to say that the *utmost discretion* ought to be exercised by those in charge of *the selection of speakers.* One gentleman, named *Moran*, is reported as having said, 'I am a *Nationalist first*, and a *Catholic* AFTER' " (D). "I have the best grounds for saying," Kennedy assured Dillon, "that foolish expression was reported to Rome as representative of 'the kind of fellows those Nationalists are at heart.' I need not point out how injurious are wild utterances for this sort, and what a handle they give to those on the alert for such extravagances." "I *can't* go to Limerick," he then explained, adding, in a reference to Meelin, "there is not in Ireland a district so cruelly harrassed. We have now 47 PEELERS IN CHARGE of this parish, which till '81 *had not a single constable.* The people have been, & are being literally danced upon. *A famine* will crush the poor in early Spring. The Potato crop is an *utter failure* in *all this district.*" "Don't you think," he asked in conclusion, "it would be well to advise the farmers to refuse paying *any rent at all* till they have first bought *flour* for the sustenance of their little ones?"

Father David Humphreys, curate in Tipperary town and a leading spirit in the Smith-Barry struggle, reported to Dillon the next day, Thursday, August 21: "The priests of Cashel can not attend the meeting on Sunday" (D). "In the time of Cardinal McCabe," Humphrys then explained, "a law was made prohibiting priests from attending public meetings without the permission of the parish priest in whose parish the meeting is held. I believe the Bishop of Limerick is parish priest of the place where the meeting will be held on Sunday. So we will not ask permission." What would have happened if the Cashel clergy had asked for permission to attend was made evident in a short note of apology from Father Bernard E. O'Mahoney to the secretary of the "Dillon Demonstration." "I would attend your meeting to-day," O'Mahoney explained on August 24, "as an adopted American priest, but my late Bishop, Most Rev. Dr. O'Dwyer, sent me a message that he would suspend me if I did" (D). "The old '*ipso facto*' suspension could not meet my case,'' O'Mahoney noted humorously, ''so a special thunderbolt has to be forged.''

The meeting in Limerick on Sunday, August 24, was attended by some thirty thousand representatives from all parts of Munster. The main burden of the speakers' remarks, especially Dillon's and O'Brien's, from the platform in the afternoon and at the banquet in the evening was emphasis on the indissoluble bond that existed between an Irishman's religion and his nationality. '' 'I tell you from my heart,' '' Dillon declared, '' 'and I tell you the simple truth, that if it were merely a question of my private character you would not see me here today.' ''[33] '' 'I came here,' '' he then explained, '' 'to ask the people of Munster whether in politics—I speak not of religion—but whether in politics they are prepared to follow our leadership' (cheers and cries of 'We are'), 'or the leadership of the Bishop of Limerick' (no, and cheers). 'If the result of this meeting left the slightest doubt upon my mind as to the feelings of the people of Munster on this issue—that is, the political issue—you would hear of me no more in Irish politics.' '' '' 'I say, then,' '' he insisted, '' 'that the great significance of this meeting is this, that you are here in your tens of thousands' (cheers) 'to tell the Irish nation and the scattered Irish race in millions all over the world who will read of this meeting tomorrow, that your confidence in the Irish Party is unshaken' (loud cheers).''

'' 'I see around me to-day,' '' Dillon then continued, '' 'tens of thousands of people who are as devoted to the Catholic Church as any in the world, or as their fathers, who had shed their blood and parted with every bit of property rather than forsake their religion' (cheers). 'I see men around me who know what devotion means and who are ready to-morrow if the occasion demanded to make the same sacrifices' (loud cheers) 'which their fathers did for religion' (cheers).'' '' 'But while they are as devoted to the Catholic Church as any in the world' ('and more so'),'' Dillon observed, '' 'they are as free in politics as any in the world' (cheers), 'and they have proved on more than one occasion how well they know to draw the line between politics and religion' (cheers). 'Well, I say, you know how

33. Ibid., August 25, 1890.

to draw the line between politics and religion; let me say this also, that I scorn the man who talks of opposition between Irishmen's religion and Irishmen's politics' (loud cheers)." " 'There is no opposition,' " he declared, " 'between them, and the man who is a good Catholic is a good Nationalist' (cheers), 'and the best Nationalists are to my own knowledge very frequently the best Catholics, too' (cheers)." " 'The day is gone by,' " Dillon then assured his audience, " 'and I thank God for it, when anyone can sow dissension between the religion of the Irish people and the nationality of the Irish people, which it has always been our proudest boast have been kept in harmony, bound together by links which no Government and no coercion can tear asunder' (cheers). 'The religion and nationality of the Irish people are bound to-day by stronger bonds than ever, which no power, whether it be a Catholic bishop or a Coercion Government, will ever sunder' (cheers)."

" 'I wish to say a few words now,' " Dillon boldly noted, putting that indissoluble bond to the supreme test, " 'in reference to another matter, and a matter in my judgment more important than that about which I have been speaking to you; that is, about a practice which I think is pretty well known to you, and which I may characterise as an old friend in this country, and that is the practice of boycotting.' " Someone in the crowd voiced agreement, and Dillon continued:

'I hear a voice in the crowd say that boycotting is a good friend. It is a good friend' (cheers). 'It has been a good friend to many a man going out of his home in Ireland' (renewed cheering).

'Boycotting has been condemned in this district in exceedingly strong language, and I think it is only fair for me, who have always advocated that practice and defended it, to say a word or two on the subject of this good old friend of the Irish people' (laughter). 'The practice of boycotting is one which, of course, can be grossly abused, and no doubt it has often been grossly abused, but that is no argument against its use for just ends, and to defend the rights of the people' (hear, hear). ''War itself is often abused for the base purposes of human greed and oppression, but that does not detract an iota from the glory of those immortal struggles made for justice and human liberty, when some great cause has been sanctified by human blood shed in its defence. So it is exactly with the practice of boycotting. Boycotting is the war of unarmed people, and while nothing can be more mean and contemptible than boycotting used for private spite or base or mean ends, boycotting wisely used and wisely controlled, used for the vindication of right and the enforcement of justice, has proved a most effective weapon in the service of the Irish people' (cheers). 'It has enabled a people crushed to the earth by an unexampled and complicated machinery of tyranny to rise to their feet and advance rapidly along the upward path of social and political progress' (loud cheers). 'Looking back over the past ten years of the struggle in Ireland, ten years so rich in advance for the national cause of Ireland, and the social emancipation of our people, I say deliberately and with the full knowledge which comes from intimate acquaintance with the facts, that but for the weapon of boycotting no single step could have been taken that has been taken in the cause of the people, and nothing could have been achieved of the vast advances which have been made since the year 1880' (cheers). 'But for boycotting we would never have had the Act of 1881. There would never have been an Arrears Act, and the Land Commissioners, when they were appointed, would never, but for the fear of boycotting, have given you one shilling of reduction on your rents' (cheers). 'But for that mighty weapon farms would be letting at the old very high rents, and the landgrabber would be in as good health as he used to be, and as plentiful' (groans). 'Do you suppose that without boycotting the land courts would have given you reductions? Nothing of the sort' (loud cheers). 'And but for boycotting what would be the course of the administration of the Purchase Act? People are now beginning to forget WHAT THE PRACTICE OF BOYCOTTING has done for them. When we commenced boycotting in Ireland every vacant farm had half a dozen men looking after it, bidding against the old owner, and if you had a Purchase Act to-morrow in Ireland without boy-cotting, and with the land-grabber in abundance, what price I would like to know would you have to pay for your farms? Why, what is the salvation of Irish people to-day?' (A voice, 'Boycotting.') 'The salvation of the Irish people is this, that there is only the one buyer for each farm, and that when the man who is in the farm does not like the price, then he can wait until the price comes down' (cheers). 'And I say that if boycotting was stopped to-morrow, and land-grabbing allowed again, that the Purchase Act would be the curse of the people. Well now, if it be true that boycotting has done all this for the people of Ireland, and that it is perfectly free from all association with crime, then I ask the people of Ireland are they going to part with this good and old tried weapon' (cries of 'No' and cheers). 'Let them judge for themselves.'

" 'But this I will say in conclusion,' " Dillon finally summed up, " 'for there are others to come after me you will be anxious to hear, that for my part I confess that it fills me with disgust and contempt that men who have never made one sacrifice for the National cause, who have never raised a finger to save the roof tree over one Irish tenant, and who stayed at their fires while we were facing the elements and the batons of Balfour's policemen, should find nothing better to do than criticise and abuse us.' " " 'If they find fault with our motives,' " Dillon challenged, " 'let them come down and propose something better.' "

At a gala banquet that same evening, O'Brien responded to the first toast of "Ireland a nation." As reported in the *Freeman*, he said that "it had been his pleasure and privilege to make many hundred responses to this toast, but he had often thought that the most eloquent speech he had ever heard on the theme of Ireland a nation was a cry of Mr. Parnell's, their great leader, one night during the discussion of Mr. Gladstone's Home Rule Bill. One of the Tory orators was arguing that the Bill would make Ireland a nation, and Mr. Parnell shouted across the floor of the House of Commons, 'She is a nation' (cheers). That was the whole Irish question in a nutshell."[34] " 'Ireland a nation,' " the report then continued, "was no longer a question of mere wild speculation." "It was," O'Brien had assured those present, "a matter of utmost mathematical certainty and absolute certainty that the day was coming when that toast and that principle of Ireland a nation would be recognised and welcomed just as warmly by the working millions of Great Britain as it was by that audience, and when the only wonder of Englishmen, Scotchmen, and Welshmen in future would be that it had taken seven centuries to discover the justice, the safety, and the indestructibility of the principle of Irish nationality, for which Sarsfield once filled the breach at Limerick, and for which Robert Emmet died on the scaffold (cheers)." In then taking to task those who had stood silently by while the bishop of Limerick had traduced the character of John Dillon, O'Brien had charged "that they defended themselves upon the whimpering plea that they were Catholics first and Irishmen afterwards ('oh')." "That plea," O'Brien had said, "was a fraudulent and dishonest cry (loud cheers). They might as well talk of being men of flesh first and men of blood afterwards, or men with a right leg first and a left leg afterwards. The men who would defend themselves for being bad Irishmen on the score of being good Catholics were simply men who were cowardly trimmers first (loud cheers) and slaves and hypocrites and renegades after (cheers)."

34. Ibid.

The bishop of Limerick was not slow to reply. "Notwithstanding the criticism of your article of to-day," he wrote the editor of the *Freeman* on August 25, "I venture to think that a good body of Catholic opinion in Ireland will not endorse your judgment on yesterday's meeting or regard it in any other light than as an attempt by popular intimidation to silence everyone who presumes to disobey the present leaders of politics in Ireland. Whatever be the merits of the controversy between Mr. Dillon and myself, I should like to know how far does the shouting of a multitude go to settle them."[35] "Whether I am a dastard," O'Dwyer argued, "and an unfaithful bishop to the people, or whether Mr. Dillon has acted ignobly in presence of the Coercion Act, I maintain it is an improper thing to come into a bishop's cathedral city and there by denunciation of him to rouse the passions of his people against him as a mercenary and a traitor, and that if it is allowed to go without protest it will become a fatal precedent." "But what particularly I object to," he maintained, "in yesterday's proceedings and in your article of to-day, is the utterly unfair misrepresentation which precludes from the consideration of the public, the great, solemn, and supreme issues that were raised by Mr. Dillon's memorable speech in Parliament by the clever plan of concentrating attention on the merest fringe of the whole controversy." "But I take it," he then further observed, "that whatever explanation may be forthcoming consistent with Mr. Dillon's veracity we may assume now, after yesterday's silence, that the line is drawn at Rome, and for the future the sacred person of the Vicar of Christ will be held above all attacks. That alone is something gained, and although you may think very lowly of me as a bishop, I assure you in all honesty that I regard it as a result worth all the annoyance of achieving it."

"Towards the end of your article," he continued,

you invite me if I have a plan for the regeneration of my country to propound it. I discuss this, not for the purpose of scoring any point against you, but because it is a matter of very grave importance. I am not a politician. I have another profession. My mission is to teach to the people of the Christian religion the duties that it imparts, and my interference, such as it has been, in public affairs, has been only in discharge of it. Now, soon after my consecration I was confronted with the practices of boycot-

35. Ibid., August 26, 1890.

ting and the Plan of Campaign, and after the best consideration which I could give them I became convinced of their utterly sinful character. Soon a judgment followed exempt from the uncertainty with which I should necessarily regard my own. The Pope spoke. A decree sanctioned by him personally, and promulgated by the Holy Office by his command, was published absolutely condemning them. I have studied that condemnation to the best of my ability, and affirm on my responsibility that there is not in canon law or theology a shadow of a shade of grounds for doubting its binding force upon our consciences. Nay more, I am convinced it is my duty as a bishop by every legitimate means in my power to give effect to that teaching of the Head of the Church. I am within my rights in so doing. Not only that, but is it not my clear duty when the Pope has spoken on the question of the moral law to enforce respect and obedience to his word? With me, then, it is not a question whether the Plan of Campaign and boycotting are effectual means for any end, but whether they are lawful means; and I tell you plainly that if the use of them freed Ireland from political thraldom to-morrow, and established a Parliament in Dublin, and diffused wealth and prosperity throughout the length and breadth of the land, I should say—I should have to say as a Catholic—we must not do evil that good may come. It is not a question that admits of compromise. It is one of right or wrong, and therefore it is altogether beside the issue to ask me to propound an alternative.

"You simply ask me," O'Dwyer charged, "to acquiesce in sin if I cannot find a more effectual way to success. That I will not do. If I were a simple priest in a parish I would stand aside and rigorously abstain from all interference in the politics of men who persist in defying the Head of the Church and bringing his authority into contempt, but being a bishop, I cannot without cowardice shirk the obligation of teaching my clergy and my people the course which they are bound to follow." "Furthermore," he added, "to be very frank, I am distinctly of opinion that the persistence of the Irish people in disobedience to the Holy See, and worse, in the impugning of its authority, will, like a canker, eat into the heart of their faith, and leave it without vitality for the hour of trial that may come. Loyalty to Rome is the foundation of the Catholic system, and whoever impairs that is undermining the people's faith." "I hold my authority," O'Dwyer then finally concluded his very long letter, "not from politicians, not from the people, and while God spares me to govern this diocese I shall maintain to the best of my poor ability, my own personal independence and the rights and prerogatives of the Vicar of Christ."

Because the bishop of Limerick had referred to him by name in his most recent letter to the *Freeman*, as had indeed Dillon and O'Brien in their speeches in Limerick, Archbishop Walsh wrote the editor of the *Freeman* to protest the use to which his good name was being put. "I feel that the good sense of the Catholics of Ireland," he wrote on August 27, "whether laymen or ecclesiastics, will bear me out in my view that I am called upon to make a very earnest protest against the use that has been made of my name in the course of the angry dispute now raging in the South of Ireland. The matter of which I have to complain being of the most public occurrence, I feel that my protest should also be publicly made."[36] "I shall probably be absent from Ireland," he explained, "for the next few weeks. In my absence I shall not have a fair chance of speaking out for myself, as I should undoubtedly feel called upon to do, if this novel species of public controversy, involving the use of my name as a weapon whether of attack or defense, were to go on much longer." "I trust, then," Walsh concluded, "that if this unhappy wrangle is to be continued, those directly concerned in it will see the propriety of paying what respect they can to my now publicly expressed protest against the dragging of my name into a dispute with which, in any of its aspects—political, personal, or otherwise controversial—I have nothing whatever to do."

Croke, however, was prepared to go further than his archepiscopal brother in Dublin. After the Limerick meeting on Sunday, Dillon and O'Brien proceeded to Clonmel, where Dillon received on Tuesday the freedom of the city. "John & myself were rejoiced," O'Brien wrote Croke on Thursday, August 28, "with your Grace's happy thought of going to the train to meet him. It is a thousand pities that he did not come by that train. The bare announcement of your Grace paying him that compliment would have been worth a dozen Limerick meetings" (C). O'Brien observed, referring to Walsh's letter, which had appeared that day, "If not a single word was spoken, it would be the end of the controversy, & would form a memorable contrast with to-day's dubious declaration. It is one of those cases in which the right word rightly spoken would complete the chastening effect visible in every line of His Lordship of Limerick's letter." "It is his impression that the Bishops dread him," O'Brien maintained

36. Ibid., August 28, 1890.

of O'Dwyer, "that alone emboldens him. He is a most dangerous man to run away from. I don't think one word more is necessary on our side." "It seems a pity," he lamented again, reverting to Walsh's letter, "that if there was to be any voice from the Episcopacy it should have so uncertain a sound as today's." "Action such as Your Grace's, even without a word spoken," O'Brien added, reiterating his and Dillon's main theme in Limerick, "would have sent a thrill of comfort through the Irish race as an assurance that there is not the smallest risk of collision between Faith & Nationalism—that the people are Catholic to the core & that the Bishops (or at least their leaders) are no less Nationalist to the core." "Your Grace, after all," he declared, "is the one man who typifies that union in all its intensity. I tremble to think what we should do without you in critical hours. I find we will not be able to go to Mallow for Sunday, so that we are at your Grace's disposal altogether as to day & hour of our arrival. I fancy if John Dillon was included in the invitation he would be heartily glad to accept, & in view of our American mission the conjunction would be of enormous importance."

Shortly before the Limerick meeting, Kirby had occasion to write the new bishop of Kerry on ecclesiastical business, and he alluded, of course, to the recent controversy. "It is most deplorable, as your Grace justly observes," John Coffey replied on August 30, "to see men calling themselves the Leaders of our people, and calling themselves Catholic, making use of language—in and out of Parliament—which is naturally calculated to subvert ecclesiastical authority and bring it into disrepute" (K). "It is asserted with persistent effrontery," Coffey continued indignantly, "that the condemnation of the 'Plan of Campaign and Boycotting,' was obtained through *English intrigue* at Rome—and the latest interpretation put upon it, is by Mr. Gladstone, who in an address to the Wesleyan Assembly (in which by the way, he speaks of His Holiness as 'the gentleman in Rome'), says that the condemnation alluded to, was in return for some concessions received through the diplomatic mission of Sir Lintorn Simmons in reference to the recent arrangements in Malta." "While you have orators who command the sympathy and ear of our people," he pointed out to Kirby, "giving expression to calumnies like these with the persistent assurance that they speak with authority and knowledge, and who also boast of the friendship and hospitality extended to them by dignitaries of the Church, it is no wonder that the deplorable state of things to which your Grace alludes, should exist in our unhappy country.''

"Last Sunday, there was a gigantic meeting in Limerick," Coffey reported, "which was wholly taken up with the abuse of the Bishop, Dr. O'Dwyer, and with an expression of determination to preach and uphold the 'Plan of Campaign and Boycotting,' more vigorously than ever—the orators at the same time appealing that their action and all their views, have received the sympathy and practical approval of nine-tenths of the Bishops and priests of Ireland, especially making allusion to the venerated names of the Archbishops of Dublin and Cashel, saying that they can afford to despise and hold at naught the Bishop's attitude and pronouncements, while they have such illustrious names at their side." "There was indeed," Coffey then explained, "the day before yesterday, a letter in the Freeman's Journal from the Archbishop of Dublin, deprecating that his name should be introduced into what he calls 'this unhappy wrangle raging in the south of Ireland'—but unhappily the view to which he gives expression, is by no means of a decisive character—as a proof of which, one of your own students—a Father Fuller who is Parish Priest in this neighbourhood,—who had [an] interview with me yesterday and in conversation, he said he took the Archbishop's letter especially reprehensive of Dr. O'Dwyer, who happened in some way to introduce into [sic] (the Archbishop's) name." "I believe," Coffey added, "this view is entertained by many both of the clergy and laity and so the letter of Dr. Walsh will not bear much fruit in the way of settling this unhappy state of things." "In all my life," the bishop of Kerry then confessed, "I have never taken any part in politics. I believe there is a great deal too much of it in our unhappy country. I believe that much of it is devoted to the nurture of a false and dangerous sentiment, which we must only hope and pray may not result to the detriment of the interest of the Church and religion in this country.''

"I got [a] letter," Coffey informed Kirby, turning to a no more congenial subject, "from the Cardinal Prefect of Propaganda calling my attention to the fact that my diocese has not yet made any contribution in aid of the proposed Church of St. Patrick at Rome, and expressing a wish the same should be made in the coming month of October.'' ''In my reply,'' he explained, ''I have to observe to his Eminence that I am not at all forgetful of the claims of this church upon the diocese, but since my consecration, the calls on my people who are poor, for diocesan and local objects, have been many, and an addition to them just now and especially for a purpose that can well wait, would be most unwise and inopportune. It will be impossible therefore to meet his Eminence's wishes at the time indicated in his letter and for two very grave reasons.'' ''First,'' he noted, ''because I have arranged in Synod that the Peter's Pence collection will be made on the Feast of the Dolours (Sep. 28): and secondly, the gloomy prospect of the harvest, owing to the extensive spread of the potato blight, will make this one collection alone a more than sufficient call on the resources of my poor people.'' ''Much then as I would wish to meet and cooperate with the slightest wish of his Eminence,'' Coffey pointed out politely but firmly, ''I am reluctantly obliged to defer the collection to a more favourable and opportune time.''

In fact, one of those ''dignitaries of the Church'' of whom Coffey obliquely complained to Kirby for extending ''friendship and hospitality'' had only the day before invited Dillon to pay him a visit. ''My dear John,'' Croke explained on Friday, August 29, acting on O'Brien's suggestion in his letter of August 28, ''William O'Brien and Mrs. O'Brien are coming to me, on Monday next, for a couple of days. You may as well 'join the sport' and come with them. We will have a nice quiet time of it, and can talk over recent and future events'' (D). ''I send this to you,'' Croke concluded, in a playful reference to O'Brien, ''through the 'Rev$^d$ William.' '' Croke undoubtedly hoped to persuade Dillon and O'Brien that the controversy with the bishop of Limerick should be allowed to drop. With the general meeting of the bishops only some six weeks away, it would not be prudent—especially given the temper of a good many of the bishops at the general meeting in June—to have that controversy still a burning issue when they met. While Dillon was visiting Croke, Father Kennedy of Meelin wrote to him also advising that the matter should be allowed to drop, so that the Bishops could better deal with O'Dwyer at their next meeting. ''For,'' Kennedy explained to Dillon on September 1, ''he is worsted'' (D). ''A sentence in his last letter," he explained shrewdly, "where he says that 'being a Bishop he could not *without cowardice* but speak out,' is certain to bring down on him the censure of the other Bishops at their next meeting." "At a recent conference of the Limerick priests," Kennedy then confided, "he urged them to exhort their parishioners to subscribe *generously* to the *Peter's Pence* Collection as his reception at Rome (whither he is about going) would largely depend on the amount of that Collection. On every account, I would let a Dignitary, so envenomed and *minded*, drop entirely out of view; as his presence in the arena of Irish politics is a positive detriment to religion, whilst no hope whatever can be entertained of his conversion to sound political opinions." "His *power* to *do hurt to us*," Kennedy assured Dillon in conclusion, "is now *nil*."

If report serves, however, the bishop of Limerick was throughout the controversy not only confident and in good heart but far from thinking at any time that he had been reduced to naught. "It may interest you to know that Lord Emly (who is now in Ireland) recently saw the Bishop of Limerick," Ross had informed Balfour on July 29, from Windsor, "& to hear what the latter's opinions are upon Parnell's late moderate speech."[37] What Ross was referring to, of course, was Parnell's speech in the House of Commons on July 11, the day after the government announced that it was postponing the land bill, in which he said that an improved measure would have his support and that he would welcome any suggestions (arbitration) that would end the turmoil on the Plan estates. "The Bishop hopes," Ross continued, "this speech will not deceive any one, & told Emly that 'it would be madness' to accept the offer of settling the Plan of Campaign difficulties by arbitration, that in his opinion were this done, the Govt. 'would only be dodged & thrown over,' but that if the Campaigners are left 'to stew in their own juice' the enemy would soon be in great straits for money." "Lord Emly adds," Ross noted further, "that the agitation against Dr. O'Dwyer on account of his letter, is very fierce, but that he does not mind it. I thought you might like to hear how the Bishop expressed himself, & how diametrically opposed his views are to those of Dr. Walsh, who now rules the Irish Hierarchy. Whether O'Dwyer has always said quite

37. B, 49821.

the right thing upon every occasion, I do not stop to enquire, but undoubtedly he is as true as steel in his loyalty to the Holy See & in his endeavours to have the Decree obeyed in Ireland.''

Some six weeks later, and three weeks after the Limerick meeting, one of Balfour's more disinterested if no less partisan correspondents wrote to report a recent interview with O'Dwyer. "I had a long conversation on Sunday," J. Parker Smith informed Balfour on Tuesday, September 16, from Clonmel, "with the Bishop of Limerick to whom I was introduced by Lord Emly. He made one or two suggestions on politics of which I think it may be worthwhile to let you have a note. I asked him in regard to one of his remarks whether he had let his views be known at Headquarters & his reply was, 'oh no I regard politics as a game of chess which I look on at from outside. I have talked these matters over with many of my priests but I take no direct part in their solution.' ''[38] "In case therefore a statement of the views of so strong a man may be of use to you," Smith noted helpfully, "I send a note of them of which I wrote down the substance on leaving him. If not of use they will in any case do no harm. I found him very firm & confident in his power of maintaining his ground against Dillon & O'Brien." '' 'I have spoken,' '' Smith quoted him for Balfour. '' 'My strength is to sit still. They come & hold a meeting & then they go. I stay here & in a month or two the effect of the meeting is over & then I can move.' '' "He was a good deal annoyed," Smith explained, "by the letter of 'Vatican' which appeared in Saturday's Times. While it is true that he has received a letter of thanks from the Holy See, it was not true that he had received a letter of approval from Dr. Logue. The statement was the more annoying because he knew that Dr. Logue had had such a letter written for a week past & was just waiting and hesitating whether to send it. It is also true that the Bishop is forthwith going to Rome." "I am just coming to the end of a fortnight's tour in Mayo, Galway, Limerick & Tipperary," Smith blandly assured Balfour in conclusion, "& have been much gratified by the prosperity of the Country & its general tranquility."

Parker Smith's notes of his conversation with the bishop of Lim-

38. B, 49847.

erick provide an interesting insight into the character and ideas of this verbally pugnacious and very clever ecclesiastic:

Every sensible man in Ireland feels that a land bill ought to come before Home Rule. We bishops & priests most strongly. If H.R. came before the land question was settled we s$^h$ have robbery & spoilation at once. It w$^d$ bring us into direct conflict with the people—& that is a most serious position for a church not endowed in any way but depending wholly on the people. They all feel this but they will not speak out.

As to the Parnellites on the land bill they will bark but not bite. You will have to shove y$^r$ 33 millions down the throat of the poorest nation in Europe like a horseball. It is very absurd but they will not decline to swallow it.

Only they will do their best to knock the gilt off y$^r$ gingerbread & not allow you to get any credit with the English constituencies.

But y$^r$ safe rule is to go for whatever they oppose. They oppose because they know it would be fatal to them. To settle the land question w$^d$ be to take away the mainspring from Home Rule.

Everything depends on the next election. If that goes against them the whole thing will go flat to the ground.

As to the Land Bill—they will attack you for not putting any of the power in the hands of the local bodies you are going to create. They will say you don't trust the Irish people. You should meet that—you sh$^d$ take the option—you should give the local body the power if it wishes to take the administration of the act & to give its security—as an intermediate security between the British Gov$^t$ & the farmer—and you sh$^d$ give it a commission in return for its security—and you should also keep in your own hands the option of dealing direct with the tenant individually.

On *University Education* the Bishop said why do you not give us proper University Education. We have nothing to complain of the National Schools—the point about not putting up images is a trifle (but I must not be quoted as saying so).

But we want a College endowed with £ 10,000 or £ 20,000 a year—as Mr. Balfour pointed out in his speech of Partick. The fight is not between Catholic & Protestant—it is between the churches & infidelity—we think the open colleges not sufficient protection for our young men.

Let Gov$^t$ keep the degree in their own hands & let them impose any tests in regard to secular subjects they please, but let us have the teaching in our own hands.

The Parnellite members w$^d$ bark & howl but they w$^d$ not dare to oppose.

Let the Gov$^t$ make the offer—not pledge themselves to it—as a stand or fall question but offer it to the Irish to take or leave—(I suggested this course w$^d$ greatly encourage Protestant opposition & the B$^p$ acknowledged the force of this objection [)]. The Bishops & priests w$^d$ be more influenced by this than by anything. It is our only real educational grievance in everything else in education we are freer than in any country in Europe. (I suggested this was just carrying into Higher Education the principle of the National Schools)—to which the Bishop assented.[39]

"I am very much obliged to you for your letter of the 16th," Balfour replied to Parker Smith on September 20, from North Berwick, "and for the accompanying notes of your conversation with Bishop O'Dwyer."[40] "I have read them with very great interest," he confided, "and very general agreement. His statement that if the next General Election goes against the Parnellites 'the whole thing will go flat to the ground,' I concur in absolutely." "Unfortunately," he noted more realistically, "the Parnellites have allies in this country influenced by motives wholly unconnected with Ireland, and who seem perfectly prepared to sacrifice any and every Irish interest for the purpose of securing a temporary Party victory. As regards English politics, the effect of the next General Election must be transitory, whoever is the victor; as regards Ireland, the consequences will no doubt be of a permanent character if we are successful, but I fear that in the opposite event we cannot look forward to their being easily effaced."

"I observe that the Bishop's view," Balfour further noted, "as to the vexed question of giving the Local Authorities a veto under the Land Bill inclines in the direction of Chamberlain and Parnell, though I gather, that he would, if possible, put as an alternative in the hands of the Government the power of dealing directly with tenants if the Local Authority shows symptoms of obstructing the Bill for party purposes." "This is a compromise between the two opposing views," Balfour admitted, "which if it could be carried out would have much to recommend it, but it is not easy to conceive the precise means by which the Executive would determine when the Local Authority might legitimately be deprived of the powers given them by the Bill and when they might be allowed to exercise them." "I am very desirous for many reasons," he further explained, "of introducing the Local Authorities as parties to any transaction between the Government and the tenants, but I have never been able to see my way clearly to accepting a policy which would practically

39. Ibid.
40. B, 49829.

hand over the full control of a great remedial measure to those who least deserve to see the remedy applied.'' ''With what the Bishop says about Catholic Education,'' Balfour finally concluded, ''I am in entire agreement, and few things have caused me more vexation during my tenure of office than the impossibility of convincing Protestants, either in England, Scotland, or Ireland that our religion is not endangered by teaching Roman Catholics Classics, Mathematics, Philosophy, and Medicine.''

In his comments to Parker Smith on the opinions of the bishop of Limerick, Balfour unerringly put his finger on what was politically at the heart of the matter. The real question at issue, of course, was who should govern in Ireland, and to place the administration of the proposed land purchase bill into the hands of local bodies would, in effect, be turning it over to Parnell and his Party. For more than three years, Balfour had been struggling to break de facto Parnellite power in the country by coercion, and for him to capitulate now in the administration of the land bill would be tantamount to admitting not only that he had not broken Parnellite power in the country but, worse, that he did not think he could. In fact, law and order in Ireland, after three years of coercion, was still much more dependent on Parnell and his Party and the clergy than on Dublin Castle and its constabulary. Indeed, what the public manifestation at Limerick revealed was that Balfour's efforts to undermine what was basic to Parnellite de facto power in Ireland, the Clerical-Nationalist alliance, had had no real effect, for even those bishops who were most disturbed about the way in which their brother of Limerick was treated in his cathedral city dared not come publicly to his defense.

The Limerick affair, however, could not have failed to reveal even to those bishops who detested O'Dwyer that the balance in the Clerical-Nationalist alliance had been seriously upset. What Dillon and O'Brien were asserting at Limerick was not simply that Nationalism and Catholicism were at one in Ireland, but that in any conflict that might arise between them the interests of Nationalism were paramount. Moreover, they arrogated to themselves the power not only of defining but of enforcing that paramountcy by invoking the will, if not indeed the wrath, of the people. They had invoked it against Rome when it issued the Decree, and they now invoked it against the bishop of Limerick. The Bishops as a body might well have wondered what indeed the limits of such a unilateral arrogation of power were, and what it boded for the future. In any case, after Limerick, there was a hardening of episcopal opinion concerning the agrarian wing of the Party, as represented by Dillon and O'Brien, and an attempt by the Bishops to turn the National movement in a political and constitutional rather than a social and agrarian direction. In their attempt to achieve their more conservative position, moreover, and restore thereby the balance in the Clerical-Nationalist alliance, the Bishops also began to move in the direction of a rapprochement with Rome.

# II

# THE FALL OF PARNELL

Charles Stewart Parnell
*Photograph by William Lawrence, Dublin*
*Reprinted by permission of the National Library of Ireland*

# 5

# THE FALL OF PARNELL

## September–December 1890

Shortly after the Limerick meeting, the bishop of Elphin was so concerned about the deteriorating political-religious situation in Ireland that he took the unusual course of writing directly to the cardinal prefect of Propaganda, suggesting that something must be done. Gillooly began by explaining to Cardinal Simeoni that, because the center of political-religious power in Ireland was in Dublin, the archbishop of Dublin was the key man in any course of action that might be decided on. "Since the death of Cardinal McCabe," Gillooly pointed out in his letter of September 1, "important interests, above all in educational affairs, have been neglected: There have also been grave omissions in political affairs—and these, I am convinced, would not have taken place if the Archbishop of Dublin had had the right and the responsibility of convoking the Standing Committee of the Bishops, who represent the body."[1] "The Primate," Gillooly complained, referring to Logue, "is slow and indecisive—he is not conscious of the importance of events because he does not understand them, or only partially understands them, and then the Archbishop of Dublin throws the responsibility on him and does not interfere. On several occasions, I have pressed the Archbishop of Dublin to enter into an understanding with the Primate for convoking the Standing Committee, but without result." "All would welcome it," he assured the cardinal, "in order to prevent scandalous Meetings like that which took place in Limerick.

1. G, draft of letter in French (my translation).

We have tried, myself and several other Bishops to make the Arch-bishop of Dublin intervene but the latter does not want to interfere individually."

"The Archbishop of Dublin," Gillooly then maintained, "has a great capacity for business—he well knows how to preside at episcopal meetings—he has a clear and attentive eye for all that occurs —he knows how to anticipate and choose the appropriate means to attain his ends—he has an uncommon industry and perse-verance." "But," Gillooly added, turning to the debit side, "he knows better how to lead than to follow, and he is not disposed to help shoulder the responsibilities of those who follow, and does not seem to bother himself very much about their inabilities in carrying the issue. In spite of this character trait, I am convinced that he would make every effort to meet the confidence that the Holy See might repose and carry out the decisions of the Holy See and the *Episcopal Body.*" "Besides," he noted, "the assembled Bishops, and the Standing Committee of the bishops exercise an independent judgement & to which the Archbishop would know well how to accommodate himself. The essential thing would be to thrust on him the obligation of summoning the Standing Committee, and if neces-sary, all the Bishops after having taken counsel with the other Arch-bishops, every time that the interests of religion and Society, would seem to them to demand common counsel and decisions, or when the meeting would be demanded by a certain number of Bishops, let us say 10 or 12." "One can, I know," he admitted, "advance very serious objections to the arrangement I dare propose, but on weighing the gravity of the reasons for and against, it seems to me the reasons against what I propose are very much less serious—and I am led to this judgement more by experience than by calculating the probabilities." "Having discharged my conscience in this let-ter," Gillooly concluded, "I leave the result to that good Provi-dence which has always watched with so much mercy over the Church of St. Patrick." Cardinal Simeoni obviously took the bishop of Elphin's letter seriously, for some time early in October he wrote the Irish Bishops collectively through the primate, the archbishop of Armagh.[2] In his letter to Logue, the occasion for which was the

2. W, Walsh to Manning, October 15, 1890.

annual general meeting of the Bishops scheduled for October 15, the cardinal recommended to the Bishops that they work out some effective way of acting uniformly on political-religious affairs.

While the bishop of Elphin was thus recommending to Rome a course of action that would make for a more formal and effective leadership in the Irish Church, at the same time lessening Croke's influence and increasing the Bishops' influence generally with Walsh, Ross was also attempting to turn his "mere information" to account through Abbot Smith. "It may interest you to know," Ross reported to Balfour from the Guards Club in London, on September 10, "that I sent without any delay, full details of the recent scandalous proceedings at Limerick & elsewhere. I think the Roman Authorities have now pretty well everything before them."[3] "In my first letter," he explained, "I said that there were four points of importance, exclusive of those which were suggested by the insults that have been heaped upon the Pope & the B<sup>p</sup> of L. viz. (1) public glorification of Condemned methods; (2) gross interference with a B<sup>p</sup>'s pastoral liberty; (3) doctrine that Irish religion & Irish politics are indissoluble, & that where they clashed the former must yield to the latter; & (4) open announcement that Irish Episcopacy espoused the side of men who promoted these things." "It so happened I saw Dr. Healy," Ross noted, naming the coadjutor of Clonfert, "(who was passing through town, a few days ago,—he is going to Rome) & I put these four points before him; he took a note of them & told me he would develop them in Rome.

"In my last letter to Rome," Ross further informed Balfour, "I said that the situation was becoming daily more threatening in Ireland; that the B<sup>p</sup>s were intimidated & that nothing was to be expected from them." "I said moreover," he noted, "that of the two clerical leaders of the Nationalists, one had pronounced himself in favour of the Revolutionists, while the other after having done as much damage as he could to Dr. O'Dwyer had disappeared from the scene, just when he was about to be appealed to by the B<sup>p</sup>s for support & counsel in the emergency. I look upon Walsh's flight as being quite as bad as Croke's hospitality; Walsh is the leader of the B<sup>p</sup>s, without him they appear to be quite unable to act; his flight has

3. B, 49821.

effectively silenced them & prevented any action on their part." "I have since learnt," he confided, "that Walsh has within the last few days been closeted with Card. Manning. Where he means to go I know not; no one seems to know. Dr. Healy seems to think that he means to go to Ober Ammergau & thence to Rome. I somewhat doubt this; he may suspect that once there, it will not be easy for him to leave the Papal City."

"Added to my letters to Rome," Ross continued, "I sent very full translations & extracts of the letters, speeches, articles (in the Revolutionary & non-revolutionary press) & acts relating to the Limerick scandal." "I did not confine myself to this phase of the agitation," he assured Balfour, "but gave further information of the apprehended partial potato blight, pointing out that the Light Railways Act was only passed in the teeth of the most active opposition by Healy, & that the clauses of the Purchase Bill relating to congested districts were lost by reason of Gladstonian-Parnellite obstruction." "I also showed," he further pointed out, "that if unfortunately there were to be some distress, how the Nationalists hope to profit by it, by a still further endeavour to prevent the payment of rents & by an effort to get that rent into their own hands. I hope I have not omitted anything. I feel that unless Rome is well posted up in everything, it will be difficult for them to come to a right decision on the matter." "I have some suspicion that the Nationalist papers have been purposely omitting to record Humphreys' recent action in Tipperary," Ross admitted, referring to the curate prominent in the Smith-Barry affair in Tipperary town.

I am aware that as he evades the police there is a difficulty for officials to report his doings. I feel sure that Croke has been called to order with regard to him. Lately I have observed United Ireland has been very silent concerning this curate, & I hoped he was being reduced to some degree of order; but just before the Limerick demonstration a short paragraph made me think that this was not so, & suspect that United Ireland had rather some object in not parading his National virtues too ostentatiously. I wonder how far there may be any truth in this, & whether there is any record of the recent proceedings of this eminently Christian Priest. I know his efforts pretty well, up to the middle of July, & I am constantly writing about him.

"I observe," Ross noted, turning to another Christian priest, "F$^r$ Kennedy of Meelin & O'Brien have been lately demonstrating together in favour of the P. of C. In fact, there appears to me to be a strong effort made to rejuvenate Boycotting & the P. of C. everywhere, so as to intimidate Rome. In other words, to establish more thoroughly the National position, while other people are considering what they ought to do. I put this danger for consideration in Rome." "The action of Dillon & Co.," he pointed out shrewdly, "is useful in so far as it has brought things to a crisis, & we must now expect some action." "I wish some one were in Rome," he suggested, somewhat more indiscreetly than usual, "but failing this, the best must be done from a distance." "I have observed with interest," Ross then noted for Balfour, and really dredging for his "information," "the laudation bestowed upon John Boyle O'Reilly, the Fenian whose career in this country was so specially treacherous. It is another indication, if one were needed, to show how the Nationalist movement is essentially a conspiracy of Secret Societies, which are in deadly enmity to the Church. I suppose the potato blight is by no means so serious as it was at first reported in the Nationalist Papers & that this fine weather will check distress if it cannot put an end to it everywhere." "I got the B$^p$ of L'$^s$ first letter (July 13)," he assured Balfour in conclusion, "in a French paper; it is being circulated; a pamphlet in French dealing with the whole matter will follow shortly."

"I am very much obliged to you," Balfour replied to Ross from North Berwick on September 12, "for your letter of the 10th which I have read with the very greatest interest. You have done a very great service to the cause of public morality by keeping your friends in Italy acquainted with what is really going on, and most assuredly nothing is more likely to open their eyes to the realities of contemporary Irish history than the O'Dwyer-Dillon episode. You seem to have taken up every point and to have put it very effectively before the authorities."[4] "I think even those who most obstinately shut their eyes to the governing tendencies which are shaping the future Irish history," he noted, taking refuge in the generalities of Ross's letter rather than the particulars, "must have realised that no more dangerous ally for religion could exist than the so-called 'Constitutional Revolutionists.' I do not think I need say anything more now. I will keep you informed of anything of interest that occurs, and you

4. B, 49829.

will not hesitate, I know, to ask me for more detailed explanations upon any subject which you think requires it [sic]."

Within a month of his writing so superciliously to Ross, however, Balfour had lost a good deal of his aplomb. He was obviously very annoyed when he found that the Irish party had by resolution approved the reopening of the Tenants' Defense Association fund, which had been closed the previous May at a figure of £61,000. This action meant that the Association would be financially ready to meet his syndicate during the coming winter and spring. Dillon and O'Brien were in fact planning to leave for a tour of the United States to collect funds, and they did so at the end of October in company with four parliamentary colleagues, though both had been sentenced to six-month jail terms for their recent activities on behalf of Smith-Barry's tenants in Tipperary. "I wish," Balfour requested Ross on October 10, from Prestwick, "you would look at the article in the 'Freeman's Journal' of Wednesday the 8th. You will see that they are driven to make a new collection from the Irish tenants (whom by the way they profess to be serving). This is from many points of view very interesting, but I want you specially to notice that there is now no concealment that the call is to support the Plan of Campaign, and therefore that any Priest who takes part in it is deliberately violating the Rescript."[5]

Walsh had, as usual, taken his annual month's holiday in early September, and both going and coming from the Continent he had conversations with Cardinal Manning in London. "After I saw your Eminence on Sunday," Walsh reported from Dublin on Wednesday, October 8, "I ascertained there was no post from London on Sunday, so that I had no means of sending my 'interview' to the printers here. The delay may be of use. On reflection, I have thought it wiser now to do *nothing* until I have had an opportunity of consulting with some of the other Bishops next week. On my return here, I find a general belief that I have been 'summoned' to Rome. The authority alleged is a statement of Cashel's that he had been summoned, that he thought it a little hard but that he was in good company as I had been summoned also" (M). "I have no information of any kind,"

5. Ibid.

Walsh assured the cardinal, "but there *may* be some element of truth in what is said." "It is earnestly to be hoped that there is," he concluded, appearing almost as anxious to go to Rome as Ross. "I will write again in a few days."

"Our general meeting," Walsh reported to the cardinal a week later, on October 15, "will be held to-day" (M). "Trusting that I may be able during the meeting, or at its close," He explained "[to],

add a few words to this to let your Eminence know the final result. I think it well beforehand to give you a short statement of the progress that has been made, so far. First I should say that the singularly definite and detailed statement so prominently set forth in the last Sunday's Tablet led us all to believe that the news was authentic. The statement was that the Holy Father had summoned *for the 1st of Nov* the 4 Archbishops and the Senior Suffragan of each Province—the next Senior to take the place if the Senior were unable to go.

Now it would appear that there is no truth whatever in the statement. The Primate, in fact, has received *within the last two or three days* a *private* letter from Propaganda which is quite inconsistent with the supposition that any summoning is to take place.

The project, however, has made good way. We had a meeting of the Episcopal Visitors of Maynooth on Monday—there were present the Primate and Tuam, Elphin, Galway, Kildare, and Clogher—the College business was got through quickly, and I then put my views on the question of a deputation to Rome, before them. The only hesitation was on the part of Tuam and Elphin, in both cases on the score only of advanced age and shaken health.

"I am to propose, then, today," Walsh informed the cardinal, "that we apply to the Holy Father to receive the deputation for the purposes of Conference etc. as in 1885, with such modifications as the present state of affairs may render advisable. I cannot of course as yet say how my proposal will be received by the general body. I am now going to the meeting, and I hope before post time to be able to add a few words giving Yr. Eminence, of course in strictest confidence, the latest news." "P.S." he noted, "Deo Gratis, the proposal to request the Holy Father to receive a deputation has passed, practically unanimously." "Also," he added significantly, "we have arranged to address a Pastoral Letter to our people dealing with the distress, the unprotected tenants, and the Decree of the Holy Office, confining ourselves *absolutely* to quotations from the Episcopal Resolutions, and my 'Interview' of June 1888." "All this of course," Walsh cautioned the cardinal in conclusion, "is *most strictly confidential.*"

What Walsh did not tell Manning, however, was that the Bishops at their meeting had resolved to take some very significant private as well as public action. Besides approving what was virtually the same proposal the cardinal had made to the pope some seven years before, about an Irish episcopal delegation to Rome, and addressing a pastoral letter to their flocks, which was to be read in all their churches on Sunday, October 26, the Bishops also addressed a letter to Parnell and passed a number of important resolutions governing the activities of their clergy in collecting for the Tenants' Defence Association fund, reopened on October 6 by resolution of the Party. The letter to Parnell, sent by Logue in the name of the Bishops and dated October 15, was a considerably modified version of the original composed by Gillooly the previous June. The letter of October 15 also appears to have been drafted by Gillooly, but the modifications and corrections in the rough draft are an interesting indication of the Bishops' fundamental anxiety not to endanger the Clerical-Nationalist alliance:

Dublin, Oct.
Dear Mr. P.

At a Gen$^l$ Meeting of the Bishops held here on the 14th Inst. some questions of great interest political as well as religious were under consider$^n$ and I (have been) was asked to convey to you the conclusions unanimously arrived at by the Meeting.

Let me premise as requested to do—that the chief object for which the Resol$^n$ were adopted is to maintain, and if possible to strengthen the relations which have hitherto generally existed with such happy results, between the Clergy and the *National* Parliam$^n$ Party [corrected "Irish *National* parl$^y$ Party"] and to remove causes of misunderstanding which would surely be most painful to Clergy & Laity which *might* [corrected *"could not but"*] prove ruinous to our political prospects. I have also to observe that on the two questions to which we now call your attention, the disapproval of the Bishops should have been long since notified to their flocks, were it not for their anxiety to preserve the unity & strength of the National movement and their expectation that the proceedings ["evils" crossed out] they condemned would shortly cease without their interference.

The Bishops have much confidence in your prudence & foresight, and hope ["as well" crossed out] that the influence & authority you exercise in [word or words illegible crossed out] the Party will remove the disquieting abuses they refer to before they further attract public attention and perhaps lead to [word illegible] disastrous open opposition & division in our ranks.

The matters to which the Bishops presently request your attention are:

1. The independent action of individual members of the Party in originating & sustaining movements involving the gravest consequences political, social and moral, without the sanction of the Party as such.

Manifestly this sanction ["this sanction" (*sic*) crossed out] should in all acts of importance be sought & obtained before priests and people are invited to give their cooperation.

The Bishops feel the time has come to declare that they cannot in future sanction ["in future the Bishops will not sanction" crossed out] the cooperation of the clergy in proceedings taken under individual responsibility.

2. The want of supervision, even in matters of gravest importance, over United Ireland. This Paper is regarded as the Organ of the Nat[l] Party and for that reason the Clergy who cooperate actively with the Party, are by many held responsible for its editorial comments, even the [*sic*] its vituperative attacks on individuals.[6]

The resolutions that concerned collecting for the reopened Tenants' Defense Association fund were spelled out for his clergy by Gillooly in a letter to one of his parish priests. "I am this day forwarding to the Clergy of the Diocese," he explained to Father Patrick Hanly on Thursday, October 23, "the Pastoral address of the Bishops which is to be read for the people on Sunday next" (G). "At their late Genl. Meeting, the Bishops unanimously decided," Gillooly noted,

1—That the intended collections for the Tenants' Defense Fund should not be made at the doors or gates of our churches or chapels.

2—That the Clergy might contribute to the fund individually—intimating that they do so, in so far as it is to be employed for the relief of evicted and distressed tenants *generally*, (and not *exclusively* for those evicted under the Plan of Campaign).

"In our Diocese," he instructed, "the Clergy bearing in mind the above restrictions, may contribute and recommend their flocks to contribute, but they will not act as organisers or collectors. Kindly communicate with the priests of your Deanery on this subject as

6. G, draft, "Letter to Mr. Parnell," original dated October 15, 1890; printed in T. M. Healy, *Letters and Leaders of My Day* (London, 1929), 1:353–54.

speedily as you can, that those instructions may reach them before the collections.''

The pastoral approved by the Bishops at their general meeting, which was to be read in all their churches on October 26, was obviously drawn up by Walsh. It began with a long denunciation of the government for being remiss in the face of the recent failure of the potato harvest in many parts of the country and then reminded the people briefly that, as the visitation they were threatened with was Providential, recourse should be had above all to Him—''Our God is our refuge and strength, a helper in troubles which have found us exceedingly (Psalm xiv. 1).''[7] The pastoral then turned to the more delicate task of asserting the pope's right in matters of faith and morals. ''From some recent events, as well as from the comments of certain newspapers no less hostile to the faith than to the national aspirations of the Irish people,'' the bishops noted cautiously, ''we find with regret that the attitude of the Bishops of Ireland on some important questions has been misrepresented and misunderstood. Moreover, certain undoubted principles of Catholic doctrine have frequently been called in question.'' ''We deem it our imperative duty, then,'' they maintained more boldly,

to reiterate the instructions already publicly given by us to our flocks with reference to these questions and these points of doctrine.

In that instruction, issued two years ago from a general meeting of the Archbishops and Bishops of Ireland assembled in Dublin, we warned our people, as it was our duty to warn them, ''against the use of any hasty or irreverent language with reference to the Sovereign Pontiff, or to any of the Sacred Congregations through which he usually issues his Decrees to the faithful.'' Furthermore, in obedience to the comments of the Holy See, and in willing discharge of the duty thus placed upon us, we put it on public record that the Decree of the Holy Office which had then recently been issued to the Irish Hierarchy had been issued in reference to the domain, not of politics, as such, but of morals alone. And we emphatically reminded our flocks that ''in all questions appertaining to morals,'' as on those that appertain to faith, the Sovereign Pontiff, the Vicar of Christ on earth, has ''an inalienable and divine right to speak with authority.'' This instruction of the assembled Bishops of Ireland was followed up by a statement from the Archbishop of Dublin, in which the scope and binding force of the Decree were most fully and most lucidly explained.

In that statement it was pointed out, first of all, that the Decree was ''a

7. *Freeman's Journal*, October 27, 1890.

decision strictly and exclusively on a question of morals''; that the point
dealt with in it was as to the lawfulness, "the moral lawfulness," of
employing, in the agrarian struggle described in the question, the methods
of action known as the Plan of Campaign and Boycotting; and that the
decision was in the negative, that is to say, "that in the struggle in question
those methods of action could not lawfully be employed."
It was also pointed out by the Archbishop that, whilst the matter so dealt
with by the Sacred Congregation had, no doubt, a most important political
aspect, "this aspect does not, and cannot, alter the essential character of
the question itself."

"Similar expositions, of the scope and authority of this Decree,"
the Bishops then closed this portion of their pastoral, "were given by
other Bishops, as occasion required, in their respective dioceses."

"In conclusion," the Bishops added, turning to the burning and
more popular question, "we deem it our duty to express our deep
sympathy with those unhappy tenants who, from various causes,
have been evicted from their farms and their homes, and have been
thus deprived of the means of procuring subsistence for themselves
and their families. Proposals designed to procure the restoration of
these poor people to their homes have already been made in Parliament, and appear to have been favorably received in the most influential quarters. We earnestly hope that the wisdom of Parliament
may be able to devise some means of effecting this most desirable
object." "It is indispensable," they warned, "for securing the peace
of the country. For there can be no hope of peace or harmony in
Ireland so long as those unhappy families are left thus homeless,
and depending for their daily bread on the generosity of their fellow-
countrymen. Neither can we deem it consistent with justice or
humanity that evictions should now be carried out, especially in the
distressed districts, where by a visitation of Providence, the poor
tenants have become unable not only to pay any rents but even to
procure from the soil the absolute necessities of life."

"From the enclosed," Walsh explained to Manning on October
24, meaning the pastoral, "Your Eminence will see that my project
of united action on the lines laid down two years ago has had a good
success" (M). "It is hard to conceive," Walsh then emphasized,
"a more distinct enunciation of the authority of the Holy See in the
matter. The letter is a quiet rebuke to those who have been so ready
to proclaim that we had ignored the Decree. It gives a sore blow to

those who thought to force us on to some action which they could then represent as inspired by them." "I do not wonder at Your Eminence thinking," he conceded, "the Tipperary case might be an instance of the adoption of the Plan of Campaign since the issuing of the Decree. But you need have no anxiety on the point. In Tipperary there is no question of the Plan of Campaign at all! The London *Times* keeps audaciously speaking of the Plan of Campaign there. This naturally enough has misled many people." "There is not," he insisted, "a particle of foundation for the statement. In its article on the first appearance of Dillon & O'Brien before the Magistrates, the Times said they were being prosecuted for their work in furthering the Plan of Campaign in Tipperary. It referred to the warrants which were set out in full in its Dublin Correspondence. Now in these there is no reference whatever to the Plan of Campaign." "In fact," he reassured the cardinal again in conclusion, "there could be none, as the combination there was of a totally different kind."

"P.S.," Walsh added in a postscript as long as his letter, "As to the Roman project, I took the somewhat audacious course of writing a full statement of the case to the Holy Father himself." "As he had sent me a commission some time ago," Walsh explained, referring undoubtedly to the pope's letter of the previous March, "to use my 'valevole influenza' to check certain irregularities that had been reported as taking place in a number of dioceses, I felt free to write strongly. I stated that in my clear opinion there is only one way of setting things right. I mentioned the great favour with which my suggestion had been received by the Bishops at their meeting in Dublin. I explained that their formal request for its adoption by the Holy Father would be officially forwarded by the Primate through Propaganda." "I added," he pointed out, "that in my anxiety to secure the great advantage for it of a full consideration by H. H. himself, I ventured on the unusual course of writing direct. I sent the letter to Card. Simeoni, mentioning that it was on an important Irish affair, and begging to be excused for asking his Eminence to give it to the Pope direct." "Liberavi animam meam," Walsh concluded characteristically. "If the suggestion be not adopted, I can at all events have the satisfaction of feeling that the responsibility for anything that may go wrong lies elsewhere than here."

That same day, Errington, who had only just returned from Ireland, wrote Smith about the Bishops' meeting. "Dr. O'Dwyer," he reported on October 24, from Chippenham in Wiltshire, "hurried back for the Meeting you allude to, the results of which have so far been kept secret, but I am told that there was a very *considerable* minority in favour of Order & of the Papal decrees, siding with Dr. O'Dwyer in fact; among the names I heard were Dr. McRedmond (Wexford I think), Dr. Donnelly, in all I heard 6 or 7 names & others alluded to. This if true is very important & consoling" (S). "All we foresaw as to the disastrous effects of the Irish Bishops during these years is being verified," he added gloomily, drifting from hard information to soft; "in trying to go with the revolution at all risks the Irish Church has lost enormously even with the people, & those who are the cause of that conduct have a terrible responsibility. I doubt that Religion will ever recover from the blow in Ireland, & if Home Rule comes the Clergy will realise that they have, so far from averting, only hastened their doom." "The political aspect is more unsettled than ever," he complained further, obviously depressed; "everything depends on Gladstone's life: if he lives till next election I fear he will have a majority & may then inflict the most serious blow the English Empire has ever had. Socialism too in England is making alarming though quiet strides, & Card. Manning is the great Christian Socialist." "I wrote to Msgr Jacobini," he explained finally, concluding with a pathetic example of that political inconsequence he had desperately sought to avoid, "sending an interesting document about S. African Company & the Jesuit Missionaries, which ought to please him: ask him to show it to you."

How soft even Errington's hard information was becoming was made evident in Gillooly's report of the Bishops' meeting to Cardinal Simeoni several days later. "I profit from this occasion," Gillooly noted politely, in forwarding some two hundred pounds in Peter's Pence, on October 28, "to tell your Eminence about our last episcopal meeting and of the letter that you addressed to it through the Primate—that this letter was very well received—that it will serve greatly to establish among the Bishops a uniform manner in acting on political-religious affairs, which the Bishops have already responded to by two important letters—the first a pastoral letter— addressed to their flocks signed by the 25 Bishops, who were present

and which was read last Sunday in all the churches of Ireland—
except those Bishops absent in Rome.''[8] ''The second letter,'' he
added, ''addressed *privately* to Mr. Parnell in the name of the
Bishops on the isolated conduct and irregular proceedings of some
Members of his party (Messrs Dillon and O'Brien) and they notified
him that the clergy would refuse their cooperation in all political
measures which should not have the approval of the entire party. In
this letter, the newspaper 'United Ireland,' organ of the party was
also censured.''

''It was happy,'' Gillooly then observed, after assuring the cardinal that all went well and that everyone agreed to the letter, ''that
the Archbishop of Cashel was not there. He would have strongly
resisted, as he has unfortunately done on other occasions, and possibly the others would not want to involve themselves in a quarrel
with him. In speaking of him, I am obliged to say in confidence to
your Eminence that he has been the principal cause, I might say the
only cause, of the imprudent and dangerous connections that the
Clergy in the majority of the dioceses have formed with the National
political party.'' ''He is hasty and reckless in politics,'' Gillooly
reported, ''—and the Nationalist party uses his example to declare
themselves just and moral and to condemn whomever it was that
opposed them. His great mistake was to act and decide by himself
without consulting the other Bishops, in matters which affected the
religious interests of all the dioceses of Ireland.'' ''He is not a
man,'' Gillooly summed up Croke shrewdly, ''to foresee the results
of his acts—he loves popularity too much.''

''The Archbishop of Dublin,'' he assured the cardinal, ''has not
encouraged or joined in this recklessness—he weighs his acts and
can foresee the consequences, but he has appeared to be too much at
one with Cashel to think of consulting you in discussing these
matters at this time.'' ''When the Archbishop of Dublin is at Rome,''
he suggested delicately, ''is when your Eminence will have the
opportunity of giving him useful counsel. He means well and would
appreciate your Eminence's kindness. He has need above all, it
seems to me, to be warned and cautioned against isolated action—
the effect of leading—in the affairs which concern the general

8. G, draft of letter in French (my translation).

interests of the dioceses. In important affairs needing action, all the Bishops can take counsel, without having a General Meeting of the Bishops, at least through the Standing Committee, which represents them and which can be easily convened." "This is a necessary means," he argued further, "for uniform and prudent conduct, and it would be a powerful guarantee for whatever rules of conduct your Eminence should decide to make in the future. I beg your Eminence to pardon these suggestions from the *doyen of the Irish Bishops* who will soon surrender his privilege to another." "I keenly feel our deficiencies," he concluded gracefully, "and I would wish, having soon to be on my way, to see effective remedies applied to them."

Thomas Eyre, one of Abbot Smith's more loyal if intermittent correspondents, wrote on November 3, from London, of that bishop who loved popularity too much: "You have I believe Dr. Croke, Archbishop of Cashel, in Rome" (S). "He will have some difficulty I imagine," Eyre observed of Croke, who was making the *ad limina* visit, required at least once every five years, "in explaining his extraordinary conduct in so ostentatious [a way] by extending his hospitality to Messrs. O'Brien and Dillon immediately after the Meeting at which they so shamefully attacked Dr. O'Dwyer, the Bishop of the Diocese, in his Cathedral Town—and in the tale of their landing in America in this day's Papers it is mentioned that a Flag was unfurled before them sent over to represent Tipperary by Dr. Croke!" "Have you noticed," Eyre pointed out in conclusion, inadvertently paying tribute to Parnellite de facto control, "that Mr. Balfour the base—the bloody—the brutal &c &c has been driving about the West of Ireland without any escort, and has been received everywhere with the greatest civility and respect!"

"I had a letter to-day from Cashel," Walsh informed Manning on November 3 (M). "He wrote when he was about to leave Rome." "He seems highly pleased," Walsh noted significantly, "with everything connected with his interview with the Holy Father. My project was brought in by the Pope. Dr. Croke, as it happened, had not yet received a letter that I had sent him telling him of it. The Holy Father gave him the letter I had written, telling him, as he knew Italian, to read it, and to read it aloud for him! At the end, he asked Cashel's opinion, which was favourable to the project only in a qualified way. The Pope, however, seemed to him to be quite in favour of it. I thought it well your Eminence should know all this. But you will regard it as strictly confidential." "Cashel," he concluded, "will be home next week."

Walsh reported again to the cardinal nearly a week later, on November 9: "The Archbishop of Brisbane, formerly a priest of this diocese, has come to Dublin after his visit *ad limina*. The Holy Father spoke to him not much about his own diocese, and a great deal about Ireland. H. H. was most sympathetic throughout. The audience was immediately after that of Cashel. The Pope spoke to Brisbane about the letter he had from me. He then said it was near at hand, and turning round he gave it to Brisbane to read" (M). "After getting an expression of opinion in favour of the project," he added, "he said there are some here who are not in favour of it, but I do not take their view. I think it would be most useful to have a number of the Irish Bishops here. Not only in reference to the Decree, but also in other matters, there are many things that could be arranged very easily in conversation. There the matter ended. I do not at all wonder that 'there are some there who oppose the project.' The carrying out of it would, I am satisfied, let in a good deal of light in some dark places."

"Yʳ Eⁿᶜᵉ will not be very much displeased to hear," Walsh further observed, continuing the tale of the flowing Roman tide, "that a strong letter of remonstrance, if not of reprimand, has been sent by Card. Simeoni to the Bishop of Salford in reference to the Tablet. The audacious paragraph inserted a few weeks ago about the Irish Bishops being summoned to Rome for the 1st of November has caused great annoyance at Propaganda." "Having mentioned this," Walsh noted evenhandedly, "I ought to add that there is really a good article on the Irish University question in the weekly Tablet. It does not spare the Tories, quite the contrary." "I had occasion to speak at the opening of our Catholic University Medical School last Wednesday," he noted, and enclosed a copy of his remarks. "I dealt especially," he pointed out in conclusion, discreetly reinforcing the Clerical-Nationalist alliance, "with the ridiculous fiction of the Tories being supporters of denominational education in Ireland."

Meanwhile, one of the inhabitants of those "dark places" Walsh had referred to earlier in this letter to Manning had been desperately trying to find out what had really happened at the Bishops' meeting.

Abbot Smith's source of information on Irish affairs had been very significantly reduced, it appears, from Propaganda to Errington, as Rome began once again to give unmistakable signs of a change in her policy in Ireland. Errington explained to Smith on November 9, from Wiltshire, that he was very pleased to receive Smith's letter and hastened to write a few lines, "though I have not yet any news (which I expect soon) about the Irish Bishops. I agree with you that anything more shifty & less honest & straightforward than the recent Episcopal address could not be. How discreditable to such a body of men, no straightness or courage" (S). "But it seems to me," he observed, referring to Simeoni's letter to Logue for the Bishops' meeting, "*very important* that Rome should have desired them to take action."

What Errington seems to have forgotten, however, was that he had included in his general indictment of those who had "no straightness or courage" the bishop of Limerick, who had not only hurried back for the general meeting but had signed, along with his twenty-four brethren, the "discreditable" joint pastoral. Furthermore, O'Dwyer characteristically had no reservations about what he had done. "So far your Grace will be pleased to learn," he explained to Kirby on November 10, "that the recent result of the united action of the Bishops has been most satisfactory. If we had done two years ago what we did last month, we should have saved our poor country a great deal of sin" (K). "When the Holy Father raised his voice in condemnation of the Plan of Campaign and Boycotting," O'Dwyer declared, with somewhat faulty hindsight, "the Irish people, who are faithful to their heart's core, would have obeyed if their duty had been put before them plainly. Now that we have spoken out, I trust that the trouble is over." "There is nothing to divide the episcopacy," he concluded, at his ultramontane best, "as long as the teaching of the Holy See is loyally maintained."

"I know your Eminence will be delighted," Walsh reported ecstatically to Manning two days later, on November 12, "to hear that our Roman policy is a splendid success" (M). "I have this morning," he explained, unable to contain himself, "received a letter *from the Pope*—'singolare consolazione,' 'piena approvazione,' etc. etc. He is naming a special Commission. He has notified this to the Propaganda, and arrangements will at once be made for the coming

of representatives of the various provinces. I will send on the letter
in a day or two." "I cannot send it to-day," he noted apologetically,
"as I think Cashel is likely to be here to-day or to-morrow, and of
course I must have it to show to him. Without sending the letter,
Y. E. could not appreciate the paternal and affectionate love in
which it is written. For this conclusive evidence of a change so long
looked for and prayed for, I know how much we have to thank the
unwearied kindness of Yr. Eminence." "I am sorry to say," Walsh
then confided to the cardinal, "that I have found out that Card.
Simeoni was strongly *contra*. So, it is said, was Dr. Kirby, who,
however, in matters of policy, outside the beaten track, does not
count for much."

Walsh, however, had also written Kirby that same day. "I acknowledge without delay," he reported on November 12, "the letter
which the Holy Father has been so graciously pleased to write to
me. I need not say that this is an honour which I never expected to
receive" (K). "I knew that I took a very great as well as a very
unusual liberty," he noted, alluding discreetly both to a privilege
accorded only to cardinals and to his by-passing of Kirby, "in
writing at all to the Holy Father. Nothing but my extreme anxiety
for the acceptance of the proposal which I made to the Bishops,
and which was with practical unanimity approved by them, would
have induced me to write to his Holiness." "I assumed on many
grounds," he explained, somewhat ironically, "that the project
would not be favourably received by some who naturally have influence with the Holy Father. Hence I saw that it was of especial
importance that I should write to H. H. direct. We must now do our
part for the success of this project for the reestablishment of unity as
the only solid basis of unity among the Bishops of any part of the
Church—that of a thorough understanding and union with the Holy
See."

"A great deal," Walsh pointed out, "has already been done. In
addition to the Pastoral, which was drafted by a Committee named
by me, and representative of *all* shades of opinion, and was then
*unanimously* amended in some verbal points, and finally *unanimously* adopted, we have come to a most salutary agreement in
regard to future proceedings." "It has been *unanimously* agreed,"
he informed Kirby, indicating that Gillooly had had his way, "that

when in future any matter of wider than diocesan scope arises, in which a Bishop finds himself in any way embarrassed as to the action he should take, he is to communicate with me." "I am then authorised," he added, coming to the heart of the matter, "to call a meeting of our Episcopal Standing Committee, and if the Bishop in question does not happen to be a member of it for the year, he will be invited by me to be present at the meeting so that the matter may be fully discussed. I think it might be well if H. H. knew of this. It has pleased him to say that my letter announcing our action on the project of the Roman visit is for him '*un motivo di singolare consolazione.*' I think H. H. will take the same view of the other matter which I have now explained to Y. G." "I am now in a grand new house," he added happily in a postscript, "where I have, *for the first time since I left Maynooth*, the advantage and comfort of a Library. This facilitates my work enormously."

Archbishop Walsh had, indeed, every reason to be satisfied with the recent turn of events and especially his own part in them. After nearly three years of intense effort and strain, all that he had worked so hard for was now apparently secured—the Clerical-Nationalist alliance was not only preserved in its integrity, but it had once again received Rome's tacit approval. This formidable consolidation of Catholic power, furthermore, was achieved at a moment when the Conservative government appeared to be tottering toward its end, and the return of Gladstone and the passage of Home Rule were virtually assured. Walsh, moreover, had emerged as the undisputed leader of the Irish Church, as the various factions in the episcopal body represented by Gillooly, O'Dwyer, and Croke all made their submission. The price paid for Rome's favor and for unity in the episcopal body was, of course, the condemnation of the Plan of Campaign in the joint pastoral issued by the Bishops. Because there had been no new instance of the Plan being started after the Decree from Rome some two years before, the price paid was more formal than real, especially as the Bishops were virtually unanimous in their support of the Tenants' Defense Association. The troublesome agrarian agitation was thereby effectively contained without impairing the Clerical-Nationalist alliance, and the National movement in general was turned in a conservative and political rather than in a radical and agrarian direction. In summary, Walsh and his episcopal brethren had finally and effectively thrown their weight toward Parnell and away from Dillon and O'Brien. In doing so they had judiciously and prudently secured their own unity and Rome's blessing on the eve of the most hopeful and promising general election in the history of their country.

At this optimum and most critical moment, the Clerical-Nationalist alliance was suddenly shaken to its foundation. The story of how Captain O'Shea in his suit for a divorce named Parnell as corespondent, and how the verdict on November 17 went against Mrs. O'Shea and Parnell, neither of whom entered a defense, is well known. Although O'Shea had filed his petition for a divorce nearly a year before trial, and the depositions of his witnesses had been available for some months, when the news of the revelations in the divorce court were published in the press, the Bishops and nearly everyone else in Ireland were surprised and stunned.[9] When the petition had been originally filed, Michael Davitt had personally asked Parnell about the truth of the alleged charges. According to Davitt, Parnell, in effect, denied his complicity and asked him to reassure their friends in Ireland.[10] Davitt then informed Walsh what he had been authorized to say by Parnell, and the archbishop was not only delighted but "intensely relieved."[11] The willingness of Davitt and Walsh to take Parnell's word alone might appear a little naive had Parnell not been vindicated the year before, after being even more grossly libeled in the publication of Pigott's forgeries in the *Times*. He had emerged from that ordeal unscathed, having pledged no more than his word, and there was no good reason to suppose that he would not also surmount his new difficulties. The depth of this faith in Parnell's integrity was well illustrated by a comment in a letter of the bishop of Ardagh to Walsh shortly after the scandal broke.[12] "The very last day I had the pleasure of seeing Your Grace," Bartholomew Woodlock wrote Walsh on November 25,

9. See the *Irish Catholic*, January 4, 1890.
10. Michael Davitt, *The Fall of Feudalism in Ireland* (New York, 1904), p. 637.
11. *Walsh*, p. 406.
12. See also K, John Egan, bishop of Waterford, to Kirby, November 30, 1890: "Nothing in my time has more deeply affected the clergy. They are stunned by the blow. No one or at least very few believed that the charges would be proved, hence the event had the effect of a sudden and unforeseen calamity."

"I was on the point of turning back after leaving your house to ask you: What about the approaching trial—but I did not as I felt convinced the accusations were like the forged letters" (C). On the day of the verdict, Croke, who had only just returned from Rome, was so disturbed that he could only manage a few lines to Walsh regarding the pope's recent letter. "I return his Holiness," Croke noted on November 17 (W). "Will reserve further commentary until we meet. Parnell's business has completely upset me. The enemy will make the most of it against us."

After the initial moment of stunned surprise, Walsh was immediately beseeched from all sides to take action. "Clearly," Gillooly pressed him on November 19, "our position has been made by this scandal very delicate & difficult—and I think it is an emergency that calls for a meeting of the Standing Committee. Our silence will be sure to be interpreted & quoted by the Party Leaders as an approval of the policy they have adopted. And should Parnell marry the adulteress, as is not unlikely, can we still condone the outrage to Catholic doctrine & morality, by our silence?" (W). That same day, Manning wrote Walsh twice from London. In the first letter he pointed out that the "O'Shea case is a supreme disaster" and then circumspectly recommended it as his "hope" that Parnell would retire in favor of a committee of the Irish party.[13] In his second letter of November 19, Manning warned Walsh that English feeling, especially among the Nonconformists, was rising rapidly against Parnell. "What I wrote this morning," he added more explicitly, "I most strongly repeat as my conviction and hope."[14] "And," he concluded, referring principally to Davitt, "I know that it is the mind of some of the most forward of the Irish politicians here."

Davitt, in fact, wrote Walsh the following day, eloquently confirming all that Manning had written. "The cause of Home Rule," he warned on November 20, "stands face to face with the deadliest peril. If Parnell persists in placing his own personality before and above the cause of Ireland and insists upon remaining in his position, there is no more hope of Home Rule being won at the General Election than there is of the Queen sending for me to form a Cabinet. You would I know be convinced of this if your Grace was here and

13. *Walsh*, p. 408.
14. Ibid., p. 409.

knew as well as I do the current of feeling now running through the length and breadth of the Liberal movement." (W). "Although I know what it will cost me," he added, "both in abuse and other ways, I am speaking out in today's Labour World what in my heart I believe every right-minded man in the Irish National Movement would say if, knowing what I know, he obeyed the dictates of his honest convictions. I ask Parnell to note the tone of the British Home Rule press, and by studying the terrible import of neglecting British Nonconformist opinion, to decide at once to efface himself for a few months." "The language of the *Methodist Reformer* of today—the organ of the Rev. Hugh Price Hughes—" Davitt reported by way of example, "voices the determination of those who are Gladstone's backbone in the Liberal & Home Rule Party. 'If Parnell remains as leader of the Irish people, then we tell Mr. Gladstone that he does not get our votes at the General Election.'" *"Four days only remain,"* he then further warned Walsh, "for us to make the choice between Parnell and Ireland. If he appears next Tuesday at the opening of Parliament as the *newly elected* leader of the Irish people, goodby for *this* generation to Home Rule, and God help Ireland."

"The case as it stands," Walsh admitted to Davitt the following day in his *"Confidential"* reply, "is deplorable. The crisis, as you say, is beyond question the gravest that has yet arisen. The case seemed one for grave deliberate action. Yet, we find a particular course publicly urged on the country with the greatest vehemence, so that all those who differ from the view so taken, have to choose between effacing themselves and running the risk of causing a split. I can, I think, see a way in which perfect political loyalty to Parnell could have been reconciled with the other requirements of the case" (W). "But," he added sadly, "that way has not been taken. Perhaps indeed I ought to be glad that the whole affair has been so managed as to leave me and the Episcopal body as a whole, no voice in the consideration of it in principle or in detail. We stand clear of the responsibility that has been so rashly undertaken by others." "But," he added, even more sadly, "I cannot think that the proceeding is very encouraging to those who had grown hopeful of seeing built up a united Irish Nation. As the result of it all, I see nothing before me personally but to stand by. Of course if I have to do that, I will do it simply *by abstention* for the future."

Why the archbishop chose not to interfere publicly was immediately surmised by the politically astute Gladstone. "I own to some surprise," he wrote on November 18, the day after the verdict, to John Morley, his chief adviser on Irish affairs, "at the apparent facility with which the R.C. bishops and clergy appear to take the continued leadership, but they may have tried the ground and found it would not *bear*."[15] Indeed, Walsh was only too well aware of the boggy nature of the terrain. Before the divorce court disclosures, he had been in close communication with Dr. Joseph E. Kenny, a prominent member of the Party and later one of the staunchest of Parnell's supporters. They had been discussing the details of a huge meeting to be held in Dublin's Leinster Hall to launch a new fund-raising campaign for the Tenants' Defense Association. "Owing to the turn events have taken," Kenny explained to Walsh on Tuesday, November 18, "since our conversation on Sunday, our meeting will not now be one to forward movement for relief of evicted tenants at all, but one of a strictly political character, viz. to proclaim undying confidence in our leader. We are not therefore sending Your Grace an invitation, which would of course require an answer, as we desire above all things not in any way to embarrass you or any member of the Episcopate" (W). This decision to change the nature of the Leinster Hall meeting had been made at the fortnightly meeting of the Central Branch of the National League, the nerve center of the Irish Party's political machine. The Central Branch meeting had, in fact, been turned into a Parnellite rally, and Dr. Kenny had obviously been excited by his experience there. "Today," he then continued his letter to Walsh, "we had the largest & most enthusiastic meeting of the League I ever remember. Speaker after speaker announced unswerving fidelity to Parnell amidst thunders of applause. Nothing could be better than the tone of the meeting."

When Gillooly read the reports of the same meeting the next morning in the *Freeman's Journal*, he too was impressed, but for different reasons. "Is not this Parnell business," he asked Walsh in

15. John Morley, *The Life of William Ewart Gladstone* (London, 1906), 2:670.

his letter of November 19, "very sad and shameful and discon-
certing? In the Freeman's defence of the man, and in the speeches
delivered yesterday at the Meeting of the League in O'Connell
Street, all is unqualified eulogium, not a word even of regret—
moral turpitude is not to be noticed in a leader—only his political
capacity to lead" (W). "This is false & dangerous doctrine—" he
declared flatly, "and in the mouths of Catholics it cannot be justified
by the example of Protestants. The speakers yesterday threatened in
the clearest terms all who might dare to differ with them in opinion
respecting P.'s leadership, no matter who they might be. I presume
this note of warning is intended for the clergy." "The view taken by
the Freeman," he then warned Walsh in conclusion, "will be generally supposed by its readers—and by the public in England &
Scotland to have the sanction of the C. Clergy of Ireland."

In an interview with Walsh that same morning, Kenny opened the
question of sending to the Parnellite meeting scheduled for the next
evening in Leinster Hall the customary greetings the archbishop had
been wont to send to significant Nationalist demonstrations in his
archdiocese in the past. In a memorable letter to Walsh later the
same day, Kenny actually asked him formally to endorse the meeting
to be held in support of Parnell's leadership. "Since I had the
pleasure of seeing you this morning," Kenny wrote, "the importance has become fixed in my mind of Your Grace making in your
letter, some expression of approval of the attitude of the Irish people
at this crisis, thereby displaying the gratitude they ought to feel
towards one who has rendered them services so extraordinary &
unparalleled, & their intelligence in so fully recognizing how essential he is to the success of their cause. If Your Grace could do this, it
would be of immense service, and we wd. be very grateful" (W).
"I fear I am troubling you a great deal," he then concluded, in a
masterpiece of understatement, "but I know Your Grace's interest
in the question is equal to my own. P.S. I should mention I received
today from John Redmond from Limerick Junction a wire asking me
to see Your Grace & ask you for a letter & secure attendance of as
many of City Clergy as possible."

Needless to say, Walsh did not send any communication, and
though he held his tongue he rankled at the arrogance of the Party
in taking upon itself the sole direction of what had long been a

common effort. His feelings may be easily gauged from a letter Croke sent in reply to one of his, which had enclosed Manning's earliest comments on the crisis. "And as for the 'Party' generally," Croke agreed, "I go with you entirely in thinking that they make small or no account of the bishops and priests now, as independent agents, and only value them as money gatherers and useful auxiliaries in the agitation."[16] "This I have noticed for a considerable time past," he concluded grimly, "and I believe we shall have to let them see and feel, unmistakably, that without us, they would be simply nowhere and nobodies."

That instinctive connoisseur of power, Cardinal Manning, had also been among the first to notice and to remind Walsh of the all-too-apparent ascendency of the Party. "Apart from all this," Manning had written to Walsh on November 19, "if ten years ago the bishops and priests had spoken and acted together, the movement would not have fallen into the hands of laymen. There is now both in Ireland and in Rome the opportunity of your regaining the lead and direction."[17] The Irish Bishops were only too well aware of the ascendency of the Party, and they were even more distressed about it because the burden of responsibility in what was becoming a very ugly situation would soon be theirs. "Indeed," the popular and influential "advanced" Nationalist bishop of Galway, F. J. MacCormack, wrote Walsh considerately on November 28, "I often thought of writing to Your Grace for the last week—but was loath to trouble you with a letter" (W). "The conduct of the Irish Party," he complained, "seems to me most intolerable. The members that attended the Galway Convention last week had a Res$^n$ of Confidence suddenly sprung upon the priests. Some of the clergy ventured to express their views upon the delicate affair—but Mr. Sheehy gave them to understand that it was a *political* affair—in which priests had no special part." "They won't stop," he noted angrily, "until they reduce the whole Decalogue to politics."

The supreme question, however, as Davitt had pointed out, was what Parnell would do on Tuesday, November 25, the day the House of Commons opened and the Irish Party customarily elected its

16. *Walsh*, p. 409.
17. Ibid.

chairman for the session. The hope of Walsh, as well as of Manning and Davitt, was that Parnell would voluntarily retire and an honorable way out of the embarrassment would thus be found for all concerned. The consensus at the time seemed to be that the retirement need not be permanent. Croke, for example, though he feared it was already too late, thought that "something might have been done to facilitate or bring about a reasonable compromise, such as abstention from the House of Parnell for a month or so, or for all the present session."[18] Walsh, in fact, privately did everything in his power to persuade Parnell to retire. In an interview with Kenny the Sunday before, Walsh strongly urged this view. After the interview, Kenny wrote the archbishop explaining that the Party was determined to apply no pressure and that the decision was all in Parnell's hands: "I cross over tomorrow night for meeting of Party, for no matter what course he himself may determine to adopt for a time we are determined to reelect as our chairman unanimously" (W).

Considering the enormous provocation, Walsh responded in a very temperate and reasonable way. In a long letter, obviously intended to be shown to Parnell, Walsh tactfully posed the alternatives and only implied the inevitable. "The question now," he pointed out to Kenny on Monday, November 24, "really is this, whether we are to have things go on unchanged, or to have Home Rule in our time. Both cannot be combined."[19] "All that has been done by the members up to this," he added, going out of his way to be conciliatory, "is excellent. It puts an end forever to the stories of disunion. But *above all*, it makes it easy now for him to do the right thing." Earlier in this letter, the archbishop constructively attempted to pose a common denominator on which the Party could unanimously focus in the crisis. "But, depend upon it," he advised Kenny, "the necessity of standing by the evicted tenants is your best centre of unity. No matter what may go wrong, the question will always remain, what justification does this give for abandoning those poor people? Even in the most desperate case, the necessity, the public duty, of standing by the tenants will save the movement from absolute wreck—it will keep something afloat for better times. Anything

18. Ibid., pp. 409–10.
19. W, Walsh to Kenny, November 24, 1890 (copy). See also *Walsh*, p. 410.

beyond this, it is, I am satisfied, hopeless to look for unless the leader by a bold manly act now adds one more to the many claims he has established upon the country." "I don't think," he then explained, "it is at all good policy to allow the Tenants' Defence Conventions to be turned into the political channel or to allow them to get mixed up with the grave personal question in its present aspect. Still no doubt what has occurred in this matter also may be of use in helping in a useful practical solution of that question. "Everything will depend," he summed up for Kenny, "on what to-morrow may bring. I wish some of you would see Cardinal Manning as soon as possible."

The cardinal, meanwhile, having received no reply from Walsh to his two letters of November 19, tried another tack. He wrote Gladstone on November 21 that the issue "rests more with you than any man" and urged him to recommend to Parnell that he retire for the sake of Home Rule. "I have not spoken publicly," he informed Gladstone, "for fear of clashing with the Irish Bishops—but I have let them know my mind."[20] The next day Manning was still urging Gladstone on: "To this end you must let the weight of your words be felt. Do not efface yourself."[21] Several of the Irish bishops were also hopeful that both the meeting of the Party and the efforts of Gladstone would result in resolving the crisis. The bishop of Ardagh lunched on November 24 with the bishop of Elphin and reported to Walsh the next day, the day of the meeting in London. "He told me," Woodlock reported of Gillooly, "he had written to Your Grace as soon as this last unhappy business was published—and suggested the desirability of calling together our Standing Committee. But now, both he & I think, the time is past" (W). "However," Woodlock explained to Walsh, "we hope that to-day's proceedings in London may get us, at least in some measure, out of the slough, into which the cause of Holy Ireland seemed to be drifting, or rather to be driven madly. His Lordship & I hope, that Gladstone will avert the sad catastrophe. For my part, I can but look forward with dismay to our interests, religious as well as civil, being placed under the guidance of a convicted adulterer. A man false to God & to friend-

20. Gladstone Papers, British Museum, Add. MS, 44250.
21. Ibid.

ship cannot be expected to be true to his country—and especially that country being Catholic Ireland.''

On Monday afternoon, November 24, the day before the House was to open and the Irish Party was to elect its sessional chairman, Gladstone decided to act. Making a momentous decision, he wrote John Morley that in view of the state of Liberal opinion in the country, he would have to give up the leadership of the Liberal Party if Parnell did not retire. He asked Morley to communicate this decision personally to Parnell. Gladstone had also asked Justin McCarthy, an influential Irish member, to inform Parnell of his decision, and he further asked McCarthy, if Parnell gave no indication that he would retire, to inform his colleagues as well. Parnell opportunely arrived just a few minutes before the scheduled meeting, and McCarthy hurriedly delivered Gladstone's message. Though Parnell gave no indication that he would retire, McCarthy kept his peace as the Party unanimously reelected Parnell chairman for the session. Shortly afterwards, Morley finally contacted Parnell and read him Gladstone's letter, but Parnell was unimpressed and remained determined not to retire. That same evening, Tuesday, November 25, Gladstone released his letter to the press.[22]

When the news of Parnell's unanimous reelection, accompanied by the fateful text of Gladstone's letter, reached Ireland the next morning, the bishop of Ardagh was terribly upset. "How is the unhappy complication and disgraceful exhibition of Ireland," Woodlock asked Walsh on November 26, "which took place in Westminster yesterday, to end? Is it not the duty of us, Bishops, to speak for our people, and to tell the 'Freeman' and our M.P.'s that God's commandments must be respected, and that HE cannot be ignored." (W). "What a grand Old Man Gladstone is," Woodlock exclaimed; but a second thought prevailed: "and are we to allow him and a lot of nondescript Ministers to proclaim the laws of Christian morality, while we are *canes muti non valentes latrare*. Excuse me, my dear Lord Archbishop, if I write so strongly—But I feel the position intensely, and I believe, my poor people here feel it intensely also. What would your Grace think of summoning a special meeting of our Standing Committee for some day next week!'' ''For my part,''

22. Morley, *Gladstone*, 2:679–81.

he confessed, "I feel powerless for good, and fear I would do more harm than good, were I to speak. Only your Grace or Dr. Croke can raise your voice with any effect—and I hope you will do so before it is too late." Walsh immediately telegraphed and wrote Woodlock in an attempt both to calm and to instruct him. As is evident from Ardagh's reply, Walsh was determined to prevent any precipitate public interference by the Bishops. "Thank God," Woodlock replied on November 27, somewhat reassured, "your telegram and second letter came to show that the atmosphere is clearing after the hurricane. God grant us to come safely to the end. I quite agree with your Grace that if we can get our M.P.'s to do their duty, it is better for us not to intervene—at least publicly—and I would hope that the Standing Committee's intervention would be sufficient, if any be necessary, and it need not be public, at least for the moment. I agree with you also that in all probability, a great many of the Bishops would not come to a general meeting just now, and a non-representative meeting might do more harm than good." "As Justin McCarthy & I," he suggested in conclusion, "are on very good terms, since he was M.P. for Longford, let me know if I can do anything in that quarter."

Meanwhile, when the contents of Gladstone's letter reached the Irish members that fateful Tuesday evening, thirty-one of them, over Parnell's objections, "requisitioned" a meeting to reconsider the question of leadership; and on the next day it was decided to convene a full meeting of the Party for the following Monday. Both sides were anxious for the adjournment, which they hoped to put to good use in strengthening their respective positions. Those who supported Parnell insisted on the delay because they wanted to know the opinions of John Dillon and William O'Brien, who were in America leading a delegation of the Party in an attempt to raise funds for the evicted tenants. Those opposed to Parnell, though they were in the majority, also welcomed a postponement because they were still without any effective leadership. "It almost looks," Walsh finally summed up for Manning on Wednesday, November 26, "as if we had reached the end of the Home Rule movement. But I trust that a way of safety may yet be found. For some days past, my view has been known to an M.P., who is in pretty close relations with Mr. Parnell. But as yet I cannot say that Parnell himself has

come to know it." "I telegraphed today to the M.P. (Dr. Kenny),"
he further explained, enclosing a copy for Manning of his letter to
Kenny, "saying 'I hope you have shown *him* my letter.' "[23] "To-
day," Walsh then continued, with a reference to William Martin
Murphy, a wealthy but junior member of the Party, "another M.P.
telegraphed to me that there was no one on the spot 'strong enough
to insist upon the only course that could avert a catastrophe,' and
asking me to say something. I have replied just now, referring to my
letter to Dr. Kenny, saying that my view is unchangeable, suggesting that the M.P.'s should 'take time,' and pointing out to them
that they have 'no mandate from the country that would authorise
them to wreck the movement.' I also urge the necessity of 'calm,
full, deliberation.' " "I assume," Walsh assured the cardinal, "that
if all representations fail, we shall have a meeting of our Standing
Committee. In this grave crisis, the M.P.'s whose policy we have so
loyally supported, are surely bound to consult us. Whether they do
or not, it will be our duty to speak out." "But in every interest,"
Walsh concluded, firmly, "it will be better if we can discharge our
duty by speaking with them in quiet conference, without being
forced to speak out to the world outside."

When Walsh received a long letter from Murphy the next morning,
following up his telegram of Wednesday, and informing the archbishop of the adjournment, Walsh decided finally it was time for the
Bishops to make their move.[24] "Under a resolution providentially
come to at our October Meeting," Walsh reminded the cardinal on
Friday, November 28, "I am authorised in such cases to call a
special Meeting of our Epl. Standing Committee." The time for this
will be after the M.P.'s have acted. I have called it for next Wednesday. It will be made known tomorrow I have done so. This will
exercise a strong influence on Monday's proceedings, and in a form
that no politician can object to" (M). "We cause no embarrassment
by pressure," Walsh concluded generously, "but we make it known
that after their decisive act, we meet to see how it affects us and
our priests and our people." Earlier in this same letter, in asking
Manning to write Gladstone again, the archbishop made it quite

23. Kenny later, in fact, replied, "Have not yet done so but shall do so this evening" (W, November 26, 1890, 4:26 P.M.).
24. For Murphy's letter, see W, November 26, 1890.

clear, in a polite but firm way, who was in control and directing the campaign. "As Yr. Eminence has kindly written on the subject of *our* position in the matter," he explained, "I would venture to ask you to send on a supplementary line to say that you have since ascertained I am in communication with several members and influencing them strongly."

As he had reported to the cardinal, Walsh chose to break his silence that same Friday morning by answering a letter from the editor of the Dublin *Irish Catholic*, who had been pressing him for advice. In a very guarded reply that appeared in that paper on Saturday, November 29, Walsh noted that in view of the gravity of the situation he was reluctant to come to any decision without first having consulted his episcopal brethren. He then pointed out that because the Party was to meet on Monday, December 1, the Bishops then would have to decide how much confidence could be placed by them in the Party in the future. Walsh wound up his letter with a reminder that Parnell's side of the case had not yet been heard and that a "final judgement," therefore, could not be formed. "In this way," he reasoned in conclusion, "I may be illogical, but it is better to be illogical than to run the risk of being uncharitable or unjust."

Parnell's first public pronouncement appeared the same morning as Walsh's letter to the *Irish Catholic*. In a long "manifesto" in the *Freeman's Journal*, purporting to be an answer to Gladstone's letter, Parnell decided to appeal over the heads of the majority of his Party to the Irish people. He accused his opponents in the Party of having been seduced by machinations of the Liberal party in the persons of Gladstone and Morley and stirred up once again those anti-English passions and prejudices that he, more than any man, had done so much to allay in recent years. He then charged Gladstone with having revealed to him in private conversation at Hawarden the previous December the details of the next Liberal Home Rule measure for Ireland.[25] In breaking this confidence, Parnell claimed that the Irish membership at Westminster was to be reduced from 103 to

25. Gladstone immediately denied the allegations, and all the available evidence—his own memorandum made at the time of his interview with Parnell at his home in Hawarden (Morley, *Gladstone*, 2:660) and Parnell's own statement, in which he eulogized Gladstone, the day after the interview (Morley, *Gladstone*, 2:686, no. 1)—supports him.

32, the "land question" and the constabulary to be indefinitely reserved for ten or twelve years. He also claimed that, only a few days before, John Morley had tried to bribe him with the offer, either for himself or for a member of his Party, of the chief secretaryship of Ireland during the next Liberal administration. In his "manifesto," Parnell argued that he alone stood between the Irish people and this spurious Liberal offer of Home Rule. Judged in the light of Parnell's own purposes, the manifesto was a Machiavellian masterpiece. The issue was no longer in the divorce courts and moral, but in the halls of the House of Commons and political. The Irish people were, in effect, asked if they were willing to throw over their leader at the bidding of an English politician for a mess of Liberal pottage. In all his nobility, Parnell did not object to being sold, but the least his betrayers could get as a price for him, he maintained, was a decent Home Rule bill.

The "manifesto" only increased the pressure on the Bishops to speak. "Severe pressure from many quarters," Croke wrote Walsh hurriedly that same Saturday afternoon, "has been put on me to say what I and my clergy think on the present crisis; and after much consideration, I have just sent the following telegram to Justin McCarthy:

All sorry for Parnell; but still, in God's name, let him retire quietly and with good grace from the leadership.

If he does so the Irish Party will be kept together, our honourable alliance with Gladstonian Liberals maintained, success at general election assured, Home Rule certain.

But if he does not retire, alliance will be dissolved, election lost, Irish Party seriously damaged, if not wholly broken up, Home Rule indefinitely postponed, coercion perpetuated, evicted tenants hopelessly crushed, and the public conscience outraged. Manifesto flat and otherwise discreditable.[26]

"I do not think the above can do any harm," Croke argued; "anyhow—Something was called for—especially by the clergy." "Mr. Parnell's manifesto," Manning wrote Walsh as soon as he read it, "makes it more advisable and even necessary that you

26. *Walsh*, p. 416. The sentence following this quotation is not included in *Walsh* and is quoted instead from the original letter.

should speak.''[27] "And if the bishops and clergy speak," he argued characteristically, "the guidance of everything in principle will return to your hands." "The late leadership," he noted in conclusion, "had become a domination." "I expected something from the Parnell Manifesto," the archbishop of Tuam wrote Walsh the next day, November 30 (W). "Why not a word of defence? It is evidently meant to wreck Gladstone & Co. & break faith with them all. All *extra rem.*" "Home Rule with such men," MacEvilly further argued, "What would it be but the crippling of the Irish Church, and relegating the clergy to the Sacristies as long as they would be allowed even there!" He concluded with a woefully accurate prophecy: "Great harm I anticipate will come of the breaking up of the party, which I regard as inevitable, be the result of Monday what it may."

The day after the "manifesto," Walsh granted an "interview" to the representative of the Central News Agency in Dublin. The "interview," which was published on Monday, December 1, was accompanied by the text of Croke's telegram to McCarthy. "If the Irish leader," Walsh finally declared unequivocally, "would not or could not, give a public assurance that his honour was unsullied, the Party that takes him as its leader can no longer count on the support of the Bishops of Ireland."[28] As for the "manifesto," Walsh maintained that it was strictly a political matter, but that in his opinion it was nothing less than "an act of political suicide." On the face of it, the reasons why Walsh hesitated to speak for nearly two weeks are obvious. In the first week of the verdict, the apparent determination of the Party to maintain Parnell as Leader in spite of everything and anyone resulted in Walsh's choosing a private rather than a public course of action. When Gladstone's letter posing the alternatives—Home Rule or Parnell—split the Party, Walsh continued to pursue a private course in an attempt to save the Clerical-Nationalist alliance from being completely destroyed. The difficulties of lay politics, however, were further complicated by the delicacies of ecclesiastical politics, for Walsh was obviously concerned that precipitate action

27. *Walsh*, p. 424.
28. *Freeman's Journal*, December 1, 1890.

on his part might once again result in open controversy among the bishops. "Your Eminence will see," he pointed out to Manning on Monday, December 1, when forwarding a copy of his "interview" with the Central News Agency, "what I have said on the subject of *unity of action* in our body. I am convinced it is better to run the risk of seeming a little remiss, than to have any risk of a renewal of the recent disturbing individual action" (M).

Not only, however, did Walsh have to be responsive to the wishes of his episcopal brethren, but his difficulties were compounded by his obvious and ultimate responsibility to Rome. What effect the news of the Parnell affair had on the pope may be easily surmised from Croke's remarks to Walsh in one of his earliest letters on the crisis. "It is fortunate for me," Croke had remarked on November 22, "that I had left Rome before this sad catastrophe had occurred. The Pope would surely 'have at me' about it; for he had a personal dislike somehow, to Parnell, and was not pleased with me for having constantly defended him" (W). Walsh, however, had already anticipated the worst and had written Kirby the day before in an attempt to cover the Roman flank. "By this time," he had explained on Friday, November 21, "Y. G. has heard, of course, of the disgraceful revelations in the O'Shea case" (K). "They cannot but be disastrous in their consequences," he admitted, "but we must await a few days more before forming a final judgement." "P.S.," he added shrewdly, noting that two briefed and reliable sources of information were on their way to Rome, in the persons of Logue and O'Donnell, "The Primate was here on Wednesday evening, and left Ireland yesterday morning *ad limina*. The Bishop of Raphoe was here yesterday evening, and left this morning." Kirby's reply would, in fact, have been amusing if the situation had not been so serious. "The account of the conviction of the accused in the Divorce case," he reported to Walsh on November 27, "has just arrived. The fact is a grave one all things considered, & suggests serious reflections which it would be premature at present to discuss" (W).

Two days later, Kirby wrote Walsh again. "I see," he observed on November 29, "that a great discussion is going on about the P. case. Let us trust & pray that God who disposes all for the best will turn in the end these discussions to his glory & the good of his faithful people. The policy of our Irishead [*sic*] politicians, their principle for adhering to Mr. P. (that of *expediency* for their cause), I look upon as not only injurious to religion, but as most ruinous to the true final interests of the country, as that principle sacrifices the eternal to the temporal which cannot be blessed by God'' (W). Kirby's piety, however, was exceeded only by his apparent penchant for intrigue, for he appears to have written the bishop of Limerick suggesting that perhaps Roman action might be required in the Parnell case. O'Dwyer, however, was too shrewd an ecclesiastical politician to be taken in by Kirby's gambit and replied on November 28, "I think the attitude of those who are responsible for the spiritual interests of our people should be caution" (K). "For myself," he advised Kirby, endorsing, in effect, Walsh's current policy, "I should regret very much to see any move made by the Holy See beyond whatever suggestions it may find it necessary to make confidentially through individual bishops. Men are so excited now that in their anger they will turn fiercely on anyone who may be suspected of interfering with their projects. Of course Yr. Grace will understand that I write thus freely in confidence to yourself only." Why Kirby initiated this apparent intrigue was, of course, that Walsh in recent months had virtually ceased to rely on him for important ecclesiastical business. Moreover, Walsh had once again raised the question of a permanent Irish representative at Rome, responsible to the Bishops; and if this project were effected, Kirby would be reduced to a cipher, after having been at the center of Irish ecclesiastical business for more than fifty years.[29]

Kirby, in fact, had had an audience with the pope before he wrote his two rather innocuous letters to Walsh, and he had reported the result to Croke rather than Walsh. "I have just got your letter," Croke replied on November 30, undoubtedly realizing its significance, "giving me an account of the interview with the Holy Father, in reference to the Parnell scandal. I lose not a moment in sending you a line in reply. Parnell will never again be the leader of the Irish party. Bishops and priests will unanimously repudiate him. I respect and am touched by the Holy Father's grief over this great scandal" (K). "We are all," he noted sadly, "humbled by it to the dust, and

29. See W, Gillooly to Walsh, November 19, 1890, explaining that he thought the suggestion of a permanent representative in Rome a very good one.

our long cherished hopes seem for the present to be blighted. But
God is good, and our cause is just, and truth triumphs at last. Kindly
convey from me to the H. Father, at first opportunity, the solemn
assurance, that I will use whatever influence I possess in driving the
wicked and deceitful man from public life, and position in Ireland.''
"Yesterday," he further explained, enclosing a copy of his telegram, "I forwarded to Mr. Justin McCarthy, M. P. for publication in
the London papers, and to be read for Irish members at their next
meeting tomorrow, a strongly worded telegram expressing my views
and those of the Cashel clergy on the present crisis." "I can say no
more just now," Croke then concluded; "I am writing to Mr. Gladstone on the situation." "Read telegram," he added in a postscript,
"for H. Father."

The Roman situation was made even more delicate for Walsh, if
possible, by the fact that Manning was so full of advice. In early
urging on Walsh the view that the Irish bishops must speak, the
cardinal solemnly added, "Moreover, I am sure of the judgement
and feeling of Rome."[30] Though Walsh was much too experienced
a churchman to believe that Manning intuitively knew the mind of
Rome,[31] no one was more aware than he how influential the cardinal
was in helping shape that mind on Irish affairs. Walsh, therefore,
had to depend greatly on Manning's good will in this all-important
Roman area. In urging him to speak out after Parnell issued his
"manifesto," Manning reminded Walsh indirectly, and perhaps
inadvertently, just how precarious his position was in Rome. "This
is a supreme moment," he had advised Walsh on November 29,
"to convince Rome that you do not put politics before faith and
morals."[32] When Walsh finally did speak out in his "interview"
with the Central News Agency, Manning was overjoyed. "Catholic
Ireland will now speak with one voice," he trumpeted, "and I hope
(as I wrote yesterday to the Pope) 'il resultato della presente crise
[sic] deplorabile sara la subordinazione della politica alla fede ed
alla morale.' "[33]

30. *Walsh*, p. 409.
31. See W, O'Donnell to Walsh, December 5, 1890, for an interesting comment
by Monsignor Jacobini, secretary of Propaganda, to O'Donnell: Msgr. Jacobini
"did not conceal his regret that it should be necessary to part with our Parnell."
32. *Walsh*, p. 424.
33. Ibid., pp. 424–25.

The government, meanwhile, was naturally very pleased by the incredible turn of events. "I think," Balfour wrote Ridgeway from London on November 27, "you would like to hear a little gossip from here as a change from your labours in connexion with the relief of distress."[34] "I have very little to say," he admitted, "which has not already appeared in the papers. Gladstone's action in pronouncing against Parnell was, I am told, prompted by the report of the feeling at the Sheffield Conference brought home by Morley and Harcourt. He thereupon against his better judgement wrote a letter which appeared in the papers next day. He is naturally furious at the Irish Parliamentary Party having been asked to give an opinion on Parnell in ignorance of the said letter. It serves him perfectly right— he should have recollected Lord Carnarvon and have formed a more accurate estimate of our friend." "The division last night," he pointed out, "was a most curious and significant one. Parnell ostentatiously voted for the Government, and carried with him some four and twenty of his own followers (mostly extremists) and was deserted by the rest of his Party. My own private belief is that Parnell's back is now up, that he will stick to his guns as long as he can, and that nothing but *force majeur* will turn him out. I do not see where this *force majeur* is to come from unless he has lost far more influence in Ireland than I believe to be the case." "How all this is to end," Balfour confessed candidly, "I do not know, and I do not much care. It is extraordinarily amusing while it lasts, and at all events, it enables us to get through our business in a reasonable time—*Now* the rapidity with which Parliament does its work is almost embarrassing, and we do not know how to spend our evenings after 8 o'clock!!" "Loving deputations of priests," he observed more significantly, "come to me every day, and altogether the situation is so novel that I feel quite out of my element. Unless the Gladstonian Parnellite Party shows powers of reorganization of a remarkable kind the Session will be over far sooner than we anticipated, and I shall turn up in Ireland before the 20th Dec[r]"

"Many thanks," Ridgeway responded from Dublin Castle on November 29, "for your private letter of yesterday."[35] "How could the G. O. M." he exclaimed, meaning Gladstone, "have been

34. B, 49829.
35. B, 49811.

such a fool! It seems grotesque that a great policy should be thrown away because Parnell had carnal connection with Mrs. O'Shea. And what fools the Parnellite majority has been!'' ''If they had only stood by Parnell,'' he argued naively, ''the storm of cant would have passed over and the G. O. M. would have had him again at Hawarden. One thing is clear—namely, that there is not—bar Parnell or Davitt —a man of prescience among them. Only a few days ago, they were here shouting increased confidence in Parnell, instead of waiting to see how the Nationalist cat jumped. It is impossible to say what Archbp Walsh means. I believe that he means to stick to Parnell.'' ''If he does,'' Ridgeway continued, ''it is because he knows that the people will follow Parnell and not the Priests and this would be a fatal blow to the R. C. Church. *That*, I think, explains the silence of the Bishops. They would like to go against Parnell but dare not do so. O'Brien and Dillon will be in a fearful fix. If they go against Parnell they will lose the support and money of the Extremists and may as well come back to prison. Parnell will keep the money bag—Kenny and all the Fenians cling to him.'' ''It is a great joy,'' he then concluded happily, ''to see the other side making such fools of themselves.''

All eyes now turned to the meeting of the Party in Committee Room 15 in the House of Commons. The evening before the meeting, William Martin Murphy wrote Walsh, astutely labeling as ''insidious'' Parnell's demands for guarantees from the Liberals before he retired. ''This is of course,'' Murphy explained, ''intended to embarrass the Liberal Party & to insult us by implying that we are not fit to be trusted to make terms when he retires'' (W). Murphy went on to make the inaccurate prophecy that, after the public pronouncements by Walsh and Croke and the telegram just received from Dillon and O'Brien in America refusing to support Parnell's leadership, the Irish Leader would not get five members to follow him the next day. ''Some of his stalwarts,'' Murphy reported to Walsh in conclusion, ''have since the telegram from the American delegates shown signs of ratting.'' At the meeting the next day, December 1, however, Parnell mustered over twenty-five supporters among the seventy-odd members present. The prospects for a short and merciful end, therefore, were not bright, especially with Parnell in the chair arbitrarily accepting and rejecting what motions he pleased. "In my life," Murphy wrote Walsh during the course of the meeting, "I never spent so awful a time & am harassed body and soul. I do pray that all may turn out best for Ireland" (W). "We are still," Walsh reported to Manning the next day, December 2, "in a state of suspense here. Of course, Parnell's opponents will stand firm. Equally, of course, he will refuse to go. He will then be power- less for good, but his holding on can hardly fail to ruin the Irish Party and the Irish cause" (M). "Parnell," Walsh then confessed in conclusion, "seems to me to have lost his head."

The following day, Wednesday, December 3, the episcopal stand- ing committee met and drew up its considered opinion on the fitness of Parnell for leadership. Walsh immediately sent a telegram to Jus- tin McCarthy, leader of the anti-Parnellite majority, which summed up the "Address" later released to the press: "Important you should know bishops issue unqualified pronouncement. Mr. Parnell unfit for leadership, first of all on moral grounds, social and personal discredit as a result of divorce court proceedings, also in view of inevitable disruption, with defeat at elections, wreck of Home Rule hopes, and sacrifice of tenants' interests."[36] "Of course," Walsh wrote Manning the next day, "your Eminence has seen our address. I am quite sure that it has given you satisfaction. We were all in earnest and determined at all events to do our duty towards safe- guarding the interests of religion and the cause of Ireland" (M). "The meeting," he reported, "was an unusually full one. The Com- mittee consists of 10: all were present, except the Primate, who is in Rome. We were in every respect absolutely unanimous." "It is plain," he then observed, "that Parnell can do great mischief. I see no prospect of our escaping a disruption of the party and the conse- quent wreck of everything that was of promise."

The Party's deliberations, meanwhile, dragged into the fourth day, and despite the pronouncement of the Bishops, Parnell was no nearer to being deposed on Thursday than he had been on Monday. Walsh was obviously becoming worried that Parnell might yet effect some sort of compromise that would allow him to retain the leader- ship. He wrote Murphy on Friday, December 5, reassuring him that

36. *Walsh*, p. 418.

the country was rising rapidly against Parnell. "All this," Walsh admitted, "may not represent a majority, or anything like a majority, but it undoubtedly represents an enormous voting power hopelessly or all but hopelessly, alienated, if Mr. Parnell succeeds in forcing the continuance of his leadership on the Party" (W). The archbishop was, however, much more disturbed than he let on in his letter to Murphy, for he gave open vent to his feelings in a long letter to Manning the following day:

It will take time for our Address to work its effect. This is the result of the wretched proceedings in which the Irish Party has become entangled. To my mind the one straight course for the members was, and is, to say "This protracted proceeding is simply playing into the hands of the enemy: from all we now see, Mr. Parnell is a man absolutely unworthy of trust in public or in private affairs: The Westminster Palace Hotel Speech of June 30, six months after the Hawarden interview, now put side by side with his recent "manifesto," takes away his last vestige of standing ground—we have nothing to do with what Mr. Gladstone, or any one else, may or may not have to say about the police force in Ireland—the one question is whether Mr. Parnell is fit to be our leader—we now see clearly, beyond all question, that he is not—the "Irish People" may have him if they like—*we* will not have him—we hereby declare the chairmanship vacant—we shall answer to our constituents at the general elections, which now, as the result of his treason to Ireland will in all probability, end in disaster.

But they will not do this. They will be led on from point to point, their position gradually becoming weaker and weaker, and their majority probably dwindling away, at each successive demonstration of their miserable inability to hold their own.

I have written strongly to Mr. Murphy, one of our City M.P.'s, and I have authorised him to show my letter to Healy, Sexton, and to "one or two others," if he thinks advisable. [M]

In concluding this letter, Walsh also asked Manning to notice that not all the Irish bishops had signed the Address drawn up by the standing committee. "Yr. Eminence will see," he pointed out, "that 3 have not signed: (CONFIDENTIAL) They have refused to sign! This throws a strong light on some previous acts of dissent from the body." "I hope Yr. Eminence," Walsh suggested in conclusion, in an obvious hint about the Roman flank, "will not forget this when next *writing*." Two of those who refused to sign were Walsh's long-standing ecclesiastical enemies, the bishop of Limerick and the

coadjutor to the bishop of Clonfert.[37] The third was the bishop of
Kerry, John Coffey, who in explaining to Walsh why he refused to
sign complained that the last paragraph in the address was political
in nature and that he therefore could have nothing to do with it. In
justifying his refusal, Coffey maintained that it was not really a
question of the greater good, but one of the lesser of two evils. "It is
an abomination," he declared on December 5, "to see the destinies
of this Catholic country confided to the arrangements of one who
has made such a figure in the way of base domestic intrigue and immorality—but the alternative consisting of men like Healy, O'Brien
& Dillon, is fraught with equal and to my mind greater danger"
(W). "These men," he pointed out, "have denounced and calum-
niated Bishops. They have gone over the length and breadth of
Ireland preaching disobedience to the Holy See—two things to be
sure to result in the demoralization of our people and the destruction
of the Church in this country."[38]

Meanwhile, the meeting stretched into its sixth day, Saturday,
December 6, and the Party was still no closer to a deposition of
Parnell. "You have no conception," Murphy reported to Walsh
at 4:30 that afternoon, "of the indecent and unscrupulous tactics
adopted by Parnell" (W). "If we can succeed in getting rid of this
man," he then explained, "and reconstructing the Party—Ireland
will have escaped from one of the greatest dangers with which she
was ever threatened. While acknowledging his enormous services in
bringing the question to its present position, if we got Home Rule

37. O'Dwyer, however, had shrewdly forestalled any such move by Walsh at
Rome by writing Kirby on December 6, in part, "With the Bishops' Manifesto I en-
tirely agree, but I have not signed it as I have never been either a follower or ally of
Mr. Parnell, whom the true instinct of our Holy Father condemned years ago" (K).
38. Coffey was not the only Irish bishop who felt this way. See K, Nicholas
Donnelly, bishop of Canea and Walsh's auxiliary, to Kirby, December 10:

I cannot help looking on the whole state of confusion into which we have been plunged as a
hand of retribution for the hostility in some quarters, & indifference in others, with which the
Holy Father's injunctions were met, for the conduct employed by some of our political men
towards the Bishop of Limerick for daring to enforce those injunctions, & for the general disregard of both the 7th & 8th Commandments which was allowed to pass unchallenged during
the whole course of the ten years' agitation. For my part *politically*, I have no more regard for
Dillon & O'Brien than I have for Parnell, & feel that we are sadly punished by both. God send
us safe!

with his power unimpaired we should be only exchanging British Parliamentary Rule for the autocracy of a man who has proved himself to be filled with some of the worst passions of Human Nature.'' An hour and a half later, Murphy reported to Walsh that it was all over. Some forty-five members finally withdrew, leaving Parnell in the chair commanding a rump of twenty-eight. ''Parnell,'' Murphy prophesied, ''will 'cut up' very badly I feel sure. [He] Will hold on to the funds and otherwise endeavour to destroy the Irish Cause to revenge his defeat; for he knows well he can no longer serve it.'' Three days later, Parnell returned to Ireland to continue the struggle for power by appealing over the heads of the majority of the Party and the Bishops to the Irish people.

# 6

# CATHOLIC POWER
### December 1890–December 1891

When Parnell was deposed by the majority of his Party in London on December 6, 1890, both he and they knew the question of his leadership was still very far from settled. Parnell maintained that he held his mandate as Leader directly from the Irish people, and not because he had been elected chairman of the Irish Party in the British House of Commons. Three days after he was deposed, therefore, he returned to Ireland to prepare for the submission of the leadership question to the Irish people. Though the majority of the Party were as determined to repudiate his leadership in the country as in the Party, whether they could prevail upon the Irish people to reject him was another matter. Indeed, the advantage seemed to be all on Parnell's side. Not only did he have control of the Party's machinery and its funds, but the largest and most influential Nationalist daily in Ireland, the Dublin *Freeman's Journal*, had unequivocally declared for his leadership. Further, he had carried with him a very strong and able minority of the Party. Then, too, there was his undisputed political genius and the fact that he was still the Leader. But more than all this, perhaps, was the magic in the name of Parnell—that strange quality which could evoke the passionate loyalty of the Irish peasant for his "chief" and which has often exasperated reason and defied ruination.[1]

1. See the *Irish Catholic*, December 27, 1890: "Well did Mr. Parnell know when he took the field the enormous disadvantage at which the Patriot Party was placed, and the powerful influences to be arranged in his own favour. There was his own high position, the unquestioned leader of a week ago. There was the charm of his

Those opposed to Parnell were not without resources, but they were utterly disorganized and were obliged, therefore, to lean heavily on that section of their forces who were best organized, the Bishops and priests. The clergy not only fought a very successful holding action but, in the further effort to mount a counterattack on Parnell, acquired a greater than usual political influence. They were largely responsible for raising funds, founding a new daily paper, and building a new political machine, which enabled the majority of the Party by early March 1891 to meet Parnell and his supporters on more than equal terms. Given Parnell's unequalled political genius, however, mounting a counterattack on him was no simple task. His strategy was to give his enemies enough time to fall to quarreling among themselves, and his tactic was, therefore, to play for time by entering into negotiations, while attempting to drive wedges between the factions that made up the opposition. Still, when all is said and done, it was the Bishops and their clergy who did most to depose him as the Leader of the Irish people and to contain the power of those who laid claim to his political legacy.

When Parnell returned to Ireland to continue the struggle for power by appealing over the heads of the Party and the Bishops to the people, he gave immediate and forceful evidence of how and why he had emerged among so many talented men as Leader. Gone was the aloof, cool, reserved, and thoughtful "uncrowned King." Revealed instead was a rhetorically passionate man of action, who had come to crush rebellion or be crushed by it. Fundamental to an understanding of Parnell's greatness is an appreciation of those qualities which transcended his mask or mood and which he exhibited whether he was in power or fighting for it—an uncanny and effective judgment in the moment of crisis, a subtle sense of touch for the levers of power, and the utter unscrupulousness of a man convinced of his "mission."

The morning of the day he returned to Dublin, he and his followers "seized" the offices of the influential Nationalist weekly *United Ireland*, and that same evening he launched his campaign for supreme political power with a remarkable meeting at the Rotunda.

---

*prestige* and name. There was the magnetic spell of his personality. There was the passionate loyalty with which the Celtic peasant clings to the fate and fortunes of their leaders, even when ruined and overthrown.''

His speech to an enthusiastic, handpicked audience revealed in a telling way a side of this unusual man that he had seldom allowed to be seen. "What is the depth, length, height, and breadth of their outcry," he asked and, in the same instant, answered "—that if Ireland is false to herself and to me she will lose the progress of the last sixteen years."[2] And what kind of a movement was it, he asked again, that maintained that the cause of Ireland was not wrapped up in the personality of Parnell? "My God!" he exclaimed, in answer again, "if it was only an honest movement of hypocrisy [cheers] from top to bottom. It is a movement which, while professing anxiety for the success of Home Rule, is undertaken and forwarded by men whose Home Rule is skin deep [cheers], but whose hatred of Ireland is not skin deep [cheers]. It is a movement which depends in some of its main features upon what we will call for the sake of politeness a temporary aberration of judgement." "It is a movement," he continued, referring for the first time publicly to the divorce action that originally precipitated the crisis, "which depends upon testimony of which only one side has been heard; and you do not think there is no other side? [cries of 'We do']." "I need not dwell," he said, trading now heavily on his honor, "on this portion of my defence. I need not [cries of 'No necessity' and cheers]. My defence will be known some day [loud and continued cheers] and I could not come amongst you and look you in the face tonight, did I not know there is another side to this question, as to every other question, and if you wait to hear that other side [cheers] before you decide that, unworthy as I am [cries of 'No'], I am not too unworthy to walk with you within the sight of this promised land which, please God, I will enter with you [loud cheers]."

Parnell lost no time in securing to himself as many of the remaining levers of power as he could. When he learned the morning after his Rotunda speech that his opponents had reoccupied the offices of *United Ireland*, he did not hesitate for a moment. Crowbar in hand and leading a large group of his most militant supporters, he personally battered down the door, scattered his enemies, garrisoned the premises, and permanently annexed the paper to his own interest. Within two weeks, in a further consolidation of his power, he

2. *Freeman's Journal*, December 10, 1890.

had captured and purged the National League, the Irish Party's political machine. Two of the essential levers of power, however, were already in hand when he returned to Ireland—the Party's funds and the all-important Nationalist daily, the *Freeman's Journal*. The control of the funds was assured to Parnell because he and his warmest supporter, Dr. J. E. Kenny, were two of the three trustees of the fifty thousand pounds on deposit with an American banking firm in Paris. The *Freeman* had declared for him at the very beginning of the crisis and had never wavered. Indeed, the support of the *Freeman* proved to be the strongest card in Parnell's very strong hand.

No one was more aware in the early days of the crisis than Archbishop Walsh of the real precariousness of the situation. "Popular feeling," he had explained to Manning on December 4, the day after the Bishops met in Dublin and two days before Parnell was deposed, "runs very high just now in Dublin and Cork. We are sure to have many noisy manifestations. It may be of use to some of us to find ourselves, for once, on a really unpopular side!" (M). What Walsh had learned from the assembled Bishops the day before may be easily surmised from a letter to Kirby by the bishop of Cork. "I got your kind letter," T. A. O'Callaghan noted on December 6, "on my return to Cork after attending the Meeting of the Bishops in Dublin and I am very grateful" (K). "We all feel intensely and are alarmed," he then explained, "at the dangers that have been revealed to us. The state of the country is something indescribable. The people seem to have gone mad and lost their reason. What is most singular is that even good pius [*sic*] people who frequent the sacraments are in some instances carried away by the fury. A few priests have made fools of themselves, but they are very few. I hope when they have had time to think they will return to a better state of mind."[3] The news that Walsh was receiving from the country was

3. When O'Callaghan wrote Kirby again three weeks later, the situation had hardly improved: "In Cork there is much division. The mob is for Parnell and the priests were insulted and hooted lately in the streets. . . . You will have heard before this reaches you that a shot was fired at Dr. Healy of Clonfert, from which you may imagine what we are to expect. An attack was made on me some time ago in Cork. Fortunately the man in rushing at me slipped and fell at my feet, receiving a wound on his forehead" (K, December 27, 1890).

no more heartening. The bishop of Kilmore, Edward McGennis, reported from Cavan on December 5 as though he were writing a hurried dispatch in the midst of preparations for a military campaign:

The priests' reports of the state of opinion in their parishes point to a hard fight and a doubtful issue.
The Freeman has done almost irreparable harm. The people are bewildered by the contradictory attitude of the Irish Members.
A pronouncement from Cardinal Manning would have great weight in England.
The Irish Members should come to a vote at once and elect a leader. Money should be collected in Ireland and if possible in America.
Would it be practical to start a daily paper in Dublin? Even the threat would have an effect on the *Freeman*. *United Ireland* will have great influence in many parts of the country. Even a just acknowledgement of Parnell's services is now dangerous. [W]

The greatest cause for concern among the Bishops during the whole of the struggle for power was the attitude of the *Freeman's Journal*. "Is there no way to stop the 'Freeman'?" asked Bartholomew Woodlock, bishop of Ardagh, of Walsh on December 6 (W). "It is doing incredible harm. Who is responsible for it?" "I thought it might be well," wrote the bishop of Kildare and Leighlin, James Lynch, to Walsh that same day, "to ask your Grace, if possible, to set the Freeman right" (W). He referred to Edmund Dwyer Gray, the twenty-two-year-old owner and editor of the paper: "He is doing great damage to the cause of Ireland. He was always under your wise control. How has he gone wild against your Grace & the country." Worse than all this, Woodlock had reported in his letter of December 6 to Walsh that the evils of the press not only were pernicious but were proving contagious and even blasphemous: "The local paper here—the W. Meath Independent—has an abominably blasphemous leading article today—I think it will be my duty to denounce it tomorrow. It says of this wretched adulterer: 'Who two days before was lauded to the skies,' is now 'tortured and spat upon, until the recollection of the entry into Jerusalem and the Crown of Thorns forced itself vividly before our minds.' Is it not abominable?" (W).

Archbishop Walsh hoped, but in vain, that the tone of the *Free-*

*man* would change after Parnell was deposed on December 6, 1890.[4] "The *Freeman's Journal* here," Walsh explained to Manning on December 14, "has gone unreservedly with him [Parnell] in everything. This has been an enormous loss to the right side. We are left without a daily paper. Fortunately, the Provincial papers, with few exceptions, are equally strong against him" (M). The damage entailed by the defection of the *Freeman*, Walsh added, was being repaired, to some extent, by a small, half-penny daily, the *Insuppressible*, and by an attempt "to work up the *Irish Catholic* into a good Catholic weekly." More important, however, was the news: "A company is being formed to start an independent first class paper in the Nationalist interest, so as to crush the monopoly of the *Freeman*." "The prospectus," Croke wrote Walsh two days later, "has not yet appeared in these parts" (W). "The shares in the new paper," he then assured Walsh, "will be taken up freely, I think— Well to have them £1—I could not go so far as £1,000. In fact at this moment I could hardly command £100. Calls on me are dreadful. Still I mean to do fairly when I see the prospectus."

Though Walsh was doing all he could to mobilize opposition to Parnell, he had to admit in his letter of December 14 to Manning that, in addition to everything else, Parnell had also achieved a considerable tactical success by shifting the issue in the public mind from the moral stigma involved in the divorce case to the specious political question whether Gladstone or the Irish people were to choose the Irish Leader. This early success enabled Parnell and his followers to argue later, with many refinements, that clerical interference was unwarranted, as the question of leadership was undoubtedly a political and not a moral one. In the same letter to Manning, however, Walsh shrewdly put his finger on the flaw that, in the end, would prove fatal to the Parnellite cause. "Your Eminence may not be aware," he observed to that sublime connoisseur of power, "that he did not venture to hold an *open* meeting in Dublin. Admission was carefully controlled by ticket. In Cork, he

---

4. See W, Woodlock to Walsh, December 9, 1890: "I am sorry your Grace's hopes—*in re* the tone of the Freeman—were not realized yesterday. You have no idea of the mischief it is doing here in the country. I believe the mass of our people is sound and will stand with the Priests and the Bishops; but their views will not be published, or will be misrepresented."

did not venture to hold a meeting of his constituents at all! Everything is so grossly perverted by the *Freeman* that almost everyone is misled. The whole proceeding is about the most disreputable that could be conceived" (M).

Though the reason why Parnell chose not to hold an "open" meeting had probably less to do with the suspicion that he would find a majority against him than with the fact that a rowdy minority could make a shambles of any public meeting, an at least partial test of his strength could not be long delayed. A by-election was scheduled for North Kilkenny on Monday, December 22, 1890. The candidate, Sir John Pope-Hennessy, had been selected before the crisis broke and in the ordinary course of things would have been elected unopposed. On December 9, however, Sir John informed Parnell by telegram that, in view of the Bishops' address declaring against his leadership, he could not as an Irish Catholic stand by him.[5] "The main declarations," Sir John privately wrote John Redmond, a staunch Parnellite and chairman of the convention that had selected him as candidate, "that I then made and which govern my position now were independence of English Parties, working with the Irish members and acting on the advice of the Irish Prelates."[6] "Whatever you might, personally," he continued, "have thought of the latter declaration, the delegates accepted it; &, as far as I am concerned, it cannot be overlooked now." Because Sir John was immediately endorsed by the majority, Parnell decided to enter his own candidate in North Kilkenny.

"All interest," Walsh had written Manning on December 14, "is now centered in Kilkenny. The Bishop writes that, so far, everything is going well. But money and drink are going freely at Parnell's side, so there are large crowds at his disposal in the more populous places" (M). Croke also reported to Walsh two days later: "Kilkenny is doing well. Parnell, they say, will be well beaten there" (W). Three days before polling day, December 19, Croke continued confident and calculated a majority of "about *1,000*" against Parnell (W). "Big meeting to be in Cashel on Sunday," he added in hurried phrases, "If disturbed by roughs, the blackthorn will be

5. *Times* (London), December 9, 1890.
6. Pope-Hennessy to Redmond, December 9, 1890, Redmond Papers, National Library of Ireland, pc 262 (xiv).

mercilessly applied. Ossory very nervous,'' concluded Croke, referring to Abraham Brownrigg, the local bishop, ''Day of battle at hand.
I wish it were nearer. Steam great.'' The following day, however,
Croke wrote Walsh explaining that Brownrigg had just written him
''a most dispiriting letter. He seems to think our success is very
doubtful'' (W). ''All other accounts . . . opposite,'' Croke added
reassuringly, yet, ''Defeat would be dreadful.''

The election proved instead a dreadful defeat for Parnell, as his
candidate, Vincent Scully, lost by 1,162 votes in a poll of nearly
3,900.[7] The campaign, however viewed, was vicious on both sides,
with each side giving no quarter, while claiming that every inde-
cency was exercised by its opponents. The *Irish Catholic*, however,
easily took the laurels for unbridled abuse in simplifying matters for
its readers: ''The fight which we have now to fight is a good, a holy,
and a glorious one. It is a conflict into which, we believe, men
might go as Christian soldiers did of yore, crucifix on breast and
shield, into which our priests might well descend crucifix in hand;
for it is a struggle in which are ranked powers of light and darkness,
of Heaven and Hell, of Virtue and adultery!''[8] This license in
language and lack of charity was manifested to the very end of the
bitter struggle by a noisy section of those opposed to Parnell. And
one or two of the earliest examples will serve to illustrate that it
would be indeed difficult to intensify these moments of rhetorical
passion. In a very curious appeal ''to the Christian sentiments of the
people of Ireland,'' Father Joseph D. Sexton, curate in Mitchelstown, asked them

not to allow the councils of the people to be presided over by a man reeking
with the filth and corruption of a London divorce court. Parnell stood a
withered and blasted thing before the eyes of the world—a man who had
entered into the house of his friend under the specious guise of friendship
to debauch and corrupt his wife under circumstances the most atrocious
that ever appeared in a loathsome divorce report. Parnell was now unworthy of the association of honest and good men, and he believed that the
Irish people would write him down as politically dead.[9]

7. *Irish Catholic*, December 27, 1890.
8. Ibid., December 13, 1890.
9. Ibid.

"Were Irish Catholics," a Father O'Callaghan had asked from his altar at first mass, "to set up an avowed and unblushing adulterer as if he were a kind of god?"[10] "They knew," he had continued, "that some of Mr. Parnell's more ardent and indiscreet followers had already compared him to our Lord before Pilate, and in the presence of the clamourous Jews. Was ever greater outrage offered to Christian sentiments than the utterance of these blasphemous words?"

During the Kilkenny election, Parnell was obviously stung by some of the gross references to himself and Mrs. O'Shea, for he made another of his rare public references to the relationship that had led the Bishops to declare him morally unfit for the office of Leader. "The issue is," said Parnell, shifting his ground,

whether we are to give in to all the old women and humbugs in England who are taking this opportunity of airing their virtue all over the country— they need not talk to Ireland about virtue. Irishmen and Irishwomen know how to guard their own virtue without any advice or dictation from England, and when the time comes my countrymen will know that they have not trusted me in vain, and that I have been a faithful and brave leader of the destinies of my country during these sixteen years, so you will find some day that I am not the disreputable man that my cowardly opponents would like to persuade you.[11]

"Kilkenny," wrote the staunchest of Parnellites, summing it all up for a doubtful colleague in Paris, "was the saddest sight I ever witnessed in Ireland. In every polling-booth in the division a priest sat at the table as personation agent. The people were instructed to declare they could not read and the voters came in bodies with the priests [at?] their heads declaring they were Catholics and would vote with their clergy."[12] Another staunch Parnellite and former Fenian, J. J. O'Kelly, was reported as "pretty certain that P[arnell] will be beaten at the general elections, just as badly as he was at Kilkenny. The priests have preached a regular crusade against them."[13]

10. Ibid.

11. *Freeman's Journal*, December 20, 1890.

12. Timothy Harrington to William O'Brien, December 27, 1890, Gill Papers, National Library of Ireland, Dublin; quoted in F. S. L. Lyons, *The Fall of Parnell, 1890–91* (London, 1960), p. 173.

13. William O'Brien and Desmond Ryan, eds., *Devoy's Post-Bag* (Dublin, 1953), 2:317–18; quoted in Lyons, *The Fall*, p. 173. n. 1.

The intemperate language, especially from the clergy, whatever its immediate tactical advantage, was to result in some very bitter political consequences.

While preparing for the result in North Kilkenny, the Bishops gradually became aware that there was, perhaps, a more critical power factor hanging in the balance than even the crucial by-election. Before the divorce crisis broke, six of the most important members of the Party had left for America on a tour to raise funds for the Tenants' Defense Association and the unfortunate victims of the recent land war in Ireland. The American delegation, with the exception of Timothy Harrington, agreed with the majority of the Party that Parnell would have to retire, at least temporarily, from the leadership. Two of the delegates, Dillon and O'Brien, however, maintained that Parnell's retirement should be secured through negotiation and that every effort should be made to reunite the Party and save the cause of Home Rule. O'Brien sailed for France on December 13, because both he and Dillon were liable to arrest for former political activities the moment they set foot in Britain or Ireland. He carried with him a "Memorandum for Paris negotiations," agreed on with Dillon and two other members of the American delegation, which offered Parnell very generous terms if he would temporarily retire.

Croke, however, did not appreciate O'Brien's conciliatory communiqués from America. "I do not like," he had written Walsh on December 16, "O'Brien's attitude, at all, for some days past, in reference to the fallen chief. He desires to patch up some sort of compromise with Parnell. He is dead and buried so far as leadership in Ireland is concerned. I would not touch any party or support any agitation with which he was connected as *Head*" (W). When Croke wrote O'Brien several days later, however, he considerably modified his tone. "Parnell has hopelessly fallen," he patiently explained on December 19. "The Bishops and priests and all good men are determinedly *against* him, and his future leadership under any conditions is absolutely impossible so far as they are concerned. So for God's sake, and country's sake, and conscience's sake, be staunch and steady and no surrender.''[14] That same day, Croke informed Walsh that little was being left to chance: ''McCarthy, Sexton, Condon, and Fr. Humphreys leave tonight for Paris to meet O'Brien. It would be terrible if *he* were captured'' (W).

Soon after his arrival in Paris, O'Brien wrote Croke in order to reassure him. ''No use telling you,'' O'Brien explained, on December 27, ''what our feelings are, or how sadly I looked back upon our *last Christmas* under your dear roof. It is the darkest Christmas time in our generation. I know your Grace's mind. I have only to ask you to trust me to do my honest best after the most racking and soul-searching deliberation'' (C). ''We are perfectly in accord,'' he agreed, ''that P's withdrawal from the leadership is the first condition of any settlement [?] of any sort or kind. If that is once consented to, I believe we ought to go as far as it is possible for men of self-respect to go to smooth his way & assuage his feelings.'' ''A couple of days,'' he then pointed out, ''must decide finally whether P. can be brought to consent. I have only a very slender hope that he can; but it is to my mind as clear as day light that in that hope, slight as it is, lies the only possible chance of winning the General Election.'' ''There are many things I should love to say to your Grace,'' he then reassured Croke again in conclusion, ''but in a letter I find it impossible to do more than entreat you to believe that I understand fully your views and your position and the dearest wish of my heart will always be to return your Grace's affection.''

By the time O'Brien had arrived in Paris on Christmas day, however, it was apparent that two factions had already emerged in the majority opposed to Parnell. One, led by Justin McCarthy and Thomas Sexton, was willing to negotiate Parnell's retirement; the other, led by Timothy Healy, declared for no compromise. Healy's adherents, though backed by the Bishops, were hamstrung, for if they refused O'Brien's good offices as mediator they were afraid it would throw him into the arms of Parnell. The negotiations, which finally began when Parnell met O'Brien in Boulogne on December

14. William O'Brien, *Evening Memories* (London, 1907), pp. 478–79; quoted in Lyons, *The Fall*, p. 194.

30, 1890, continued intermittently until Parnell broke them off in
the middle of February. Because the negotiations were early conducted on a confidential basis, at the beginning the Bishops could
learn only indirectly what was going on. When Healy met O'Brien
in Paris a few days after Parnell had returned to London, he wrote
Walsh a "*Very Private*," "hurried line to catch the post" (W). "As
to the alleged settlement," he reported on January 5, "P.'s first
condition is that McCarthy must go, but what the remaining cove-
nants are we did not hear as we bluntly told Wm it was all tricking,
to gain further leverage. Underlying McCarthy's deposition, we
inferred the truth of the rumour that Wm was to replace him, but this
was not mentioned." He complained to Walsh of O'Brien:

Indeed, altho' we spent some hours with him last night, we were not
entrusted with the condition about McCarthy until today! Nothing cd be
plainer than our talk, & the only reply was that we might not be true
prophets. I fear that everything that has been done in the absence of the
Envoys has been ill done & that there are now 3 parties amongst the 86.
Apparently those who were away disincline to accept solidarity & Wm
seems equally disinclined to fight P. or to do anything but go to jail which
he proposes to do within next fortnight. We cannot look for any help from
him in a *struggle*, altho' he insists on helping to prevent one, in spite of our
declarations that his supposed help will be purely mischievous to those
who are prepared to fight.

"He declares emphatically however against P.'s leadership," concluded Healy with a touch of his sardonic humor, "& if platonic
views on the point are helpful no doubt they will be forthcoming
intersprinkled and begemmed with tears."

In an interview with Walsh in Dublin three days later, Healy and
his colleagues apparently recommended that the Bishops take "determined action," for Walsh immediately wrote Croke, who replied
with no less haste in a long, interesting, and altogether characteristic
letter. "If O'Brien," Croke began gruffly on January 9, "does not
actively oppose Parnell, he is in reality for him, and should be reck-
oned with as such" (W). "The strangest part of the whole proceedings," he then lamented, taking another tack, "is that O'Brien &
Co. have not communicated to either you or me the details, or even
the basis, of the Boulogne negotiations. This leaves us in the dark,
and being in the dark, we should be slow to take any important steps

while we continue so, or indeed, any step whatsoever." "From what I have written up to this," he then finally came to the point, "you may infer that I do not wish to issue any *manifesto* just now." From Croke's letter it was also obvious that Walsh was very angry, especially at the *Freeman's Journal*, for Croke cautioned him: "And talking of manifestoes, I am of the opinion that any Episcopal pronouncement against the Freeman at present would give rise to a great deal of unfriendly, if not injurious comment, and fail to produce the desired effect." Croke concluded by advising that they should wait until after Parnell's meeting in Limerick on Sunday, January 11, to see what he would say about the Boulogne negotiations.

When they read the reports of Parnell's Limerick speech and that of his chief lieutenant, Timothy Harrington, they were aghast. Parnell had maintained that the question at issue was purely political and not moral, for if it was a moral issue, the Bishops should have intervened immediately when the news of the divorce action became public, and not more than two weeks later. Archbishop Walsh, though undoubtedly provoked to exasperation, replied in a restrained and studiously phrased letter to the press.[15] He pointed out that he had intervened privately in a letter to one of Parnell's supporters, Dr. J. E. Kenny, soon after the crisis erupted. Walsh cleverly avoided what amounted to calling Parnell a liar by tactfully supposing that his letter to Dr. Kenny had never been shown to him. Parnell simply ignored the archbishop's reply.

In another letter to the press the same day, Archbishop Croke took Harrington to task for his remarks at the Limerick meeting. Harrington had asked "whether the opposition to Mr. Parnell's leadership sprang not from a love of morality but from an innate love of Whiggery in the hearts of men who were proclaiming themselves Nationalist today."[16] In a scathing and indignant reply, Croke wrote:

My record as an Irishman is before my country, and until the political purist, Mr. Timothy Harrington, dared to asperse me on a platform, at least by implication, no one, even *amongst my enemies*, had ventured to charge me with an innate love of Whiggery, or to insinuate that I had raised or was

15. *Irish Catholic*, January 17, 1891; quoted in *Walsh*, pp. 422–23.
16. Ibid.; quoted in *Walsh*, p. 423.

a party to a cry, in the justice and propriety of which I did not believe.

No, I have never found it necessary to simulate patriotism, nor have I trafficked in it for emolument. My purse and influence have been always at the public service. I have incurred the displeasure of those for whose good opinion I should, if needed, lay down my life, rather than check the onward career of the man whom I am now reluctantly compelled to denounce, or the progress of the cause with which his name has hitherto been honourably associated.[17]

What this exchange really proved, however, was that Parnell was still master in the game of political maneuver. Once again, he appeared in the role of accuser, and it was his enemies who had to justify themselves. Further, he cleverly attempted to bait that section of his enemies, the Bishops, who, without any information about Boulogne, were most uneasy and the most likely, therefore, by a wrong move to wreck the united front formed against him.

Although Parnell's tactic did force the Bishops to defend themselves, it did not succeed in luring them into a false move. The reason they did not rise to the bait, of course, was that they learned and then approved of what was proposed at Boulogne. "I avail myself of Tom Condon's visit," O'Brien finally wrote Croke on January 12, from Boulogne, "to let you know what is going on" (C). "Parnell so little misunderstands me," he then reassured Croke, "or my position that we never exchanged a single sentence except in the way of his retirement, which he knew was the first condition of any treaty between us." "I am not at all sanguine," he confessed again,

our efforts will be successful—we have to contend with such furious spirit of no-quarter on both sides—but what is certain is that the terms now available offer to my mind the only possible escape from a loathsome civil war, ending in loss at General Election, destruction of evicted tenants & general hell.

First then you & we want Parnell's retirement. That we can have. Second you want that the retirement shall be real not nominal. That is answered for by the fact that he has been brought to accept Dillon as his successor. Will any man living suggest that Dillon is Parnell's creature or even his nominee? It was myself P. desired to have, & I had actually to break off communications before he would consent to Dillon. His doing so is an inestimable gain & a most marvelous conversion. The one piece of

17. Ibid.

personal satisfaction he requires is Justin McCarthy's resignation. . . .
The only other thing he requires are [sic] that of private & confidential
assurances on two points as to which every Irish member agrees it would
be better to have no Home Rule Bill at all than a Bill so mutilated and
unworkable. I mean the Land question & Constabulary. P's demands in
that way are reasonable. It is no longer possible for a Liberal Cabinet to
shirk making up their minds on the subject.

"I am fairly confident," O'Brien then continued more hopefully,
referring to Gladstone, "that if the right spirit is shown on our own
side the G. O. M. will not be intractable. The right spirit, I am sorry
to say is not shown by Tim Healy & his friends." "Their methods,"
he argued, "have revolted Nationalist instinct & made Irish American (the working part) solid against us. Securing Parnell's disappear-
ance is one thing—hacking him to pieces & hunting him down like
a wild beast & pelting him with all sorts of filth is quite another
thing & is an absolutely detestable thought to hundreds of thousands
of Nationalists who are just as convinced as he [Healy] that wisdom
demands Parnell's withdrawal." "Where Tim & his wicked English
meddlers of the Labloy & Stead school," O'Brien shrewdly pointed
out, "made their fatal mistake is in supposing that the battle against
P's over. We are only at the beginning of a conflict which P. calmly
contemplates carrying on over a long series of years if he is driven
to it." "Believe me," O'Brien declared firmly, ". . . when I tell
your Grace it is as certain as anything human can be that, although
he will no doubt be beaten at the polls in a majority of the constituencies, he will not only rally the hot-headed youth, but hundreds of
thousands of the best men in the country if his offer to give way to
John Dillon on making those assurances which everybody admits to
be indispensable is flung back with insult in his face."

"If Parnell is acting in bad faith," O'Brien then assured Croke,
"Redmond, Harrington, Clancy & Kenny have given me a promise
to withdraw from him & so end the conflict. We have everything to
gain & nothing to lose from making every possible honest effort at
peace. I believe we have obtained terms which give us all that
anybody could demand, if McCarthy & Healy are willing to make
the corresponding sacrifice of personal feeling & if the G. O. M. is
willing to risk something to save himself & all of us from utter
shipwreck. Your Grace has it in your power, not now for the first

time, to save the Irish cause by an opportune word in the right
quarters." "Believe me," O'Brien concluded this very impressive
and statesmanlike performance, "there will be no act of your life
that you will afterwards look back upon with as much pride &
thanksgiving." What O'Brien had neglected to mention to Croke in
the course of his long letter, however, was that Parnell had cleverly
insisted on reserving to O'Brien and himself the right to decide
whether the assurances were satisfactory, which in effect gave him
an absolute veto. O'Brien had tried to persuade Parnell to include
McCarthy in the decision on the appropriateness of the assurances,
but Parnell could not be moved.

Though Croke agreed to go along with O'Brien's attempt to
negotiate Parnell's surrender, he certainly was not optimistic. "Parnell is a trickster," he plainly told Kirby on January 21, "and,
greatly, I fear, an overmatch for O'Brien and Dillon" (K). "He appears," Croke observed shrewdly, "to be only gaining time. There
is said to be a truce, and Dr. Walsh has written a letter asking to
have it faithfully observed. But a truce means cessation of hostilities
on *both* sides, whereas, in the present instance, Parnell is blazing
away as fast as he can, inflaming the public mind, and stirring up
everything that is dirty and discreditable in the lowest stratum of
Irish life." "I have had a wire from O'Brien," he reported, "this
morning, from Paris, to the effect that 'the negotiations are still
going on, and that they are likely to end satisfactorily.' But, the
issue to be solved is so simple, that one cannot imagine why there is
such delay about it. The issue is—Parnell, or no Parnell. There can
be no compromise. We can never have *him* for a leader. He must
*retire*." "There is," he added adamantly, "no medium course possible. If negotiations or confidences go on much longer, I will
have to express my views publickly on the matter, a thing which I
am most unwilling to do so long as there is any real prospect of
peace."

Kirby replied immediately, for Croke wrote again on January 29:
"I got your letter of the 25., and it afforded me the greatest possible
pleasure, especially as an indication of the feeling in Rome in reference to the Irish political crisis. I am keeping up the steam as well as
I can, but, indeed, I must say, that, as usual, I am comparatively
alone in the fray. However, on the fight must go" (K). "The Bou-

logne Conferences," he then informed Kirby, "are doing a vast deal of injury. Apart from anything else, they are leaving the field open to Parnell, and, to give him his due, he is traversing it at a rapid pace, and with satisfactory results, so far as he is concerned." "The lower stratum of society in Ireland," he explained again, "is almost entirely for him. Corner boys, blackguards of every hue, discontented labourers, lazy and drunken artisans, aspiring politicians, Fenians, and in a word, all the irreligious and anti-clerical scoundrels in the country are at his back. But on the other hand, every thoughtful, intelligent, industrious, and Christian man is strenuously opposed to him. There are, in fact, two camps now in Ireland, arrayed in hostility against each other. It is dreadful—and it is dispiriting. But *Magna est Veritas.*"

Before Walsh learned what the Boulogne terms were, he had been indirectly attempting to influence O'Brien.[18] When he finally learned through Croke what was actually going on, he was not only heartened but a good deal more optimistic than his brother of Cashel. Walsh wrote Kirby confidentially on January 15, suggesting that Kirby speak to the pope: "I write a few lines to let you know, and to suggest that you should *mention* that the great difficulty is, thank God, nearing a solution" (K). "The A.," he added, meaning Parnell, "practically accepts the situation as decided against him. There will in all probability, be an amicable settlement, the basis of it being his voluntary withdrawal." "This will save us all," he assured Kirby, somewhat sanguinely, "a world of trouble, and will in all probability leave the general position even stronger than before. This should be mentioned, for the present, *only to one person.*" Walsh also wrote O'Brien directly, approving his efforts, as Croke had informed Kirby, for O'Brien telegraphed to Walsh on January

---

18. See W, O'Donnell to Walsh, January 11, 1891:

I was personally acquainted with Madame Raffalovich for nearly a year before Mr. O'Brien's marriage to her daughter. I saw her three or four times while I was in Paris with Dr. Healy on Irish College business. She has been very generous to the evicted tenants. The letter I take the liberty of enclosing is the draft of a better one I am sending her by this post. The only improvement however is in the turn of an occasional clause and a strong wind up about the necessity of Parnell disappearing decisively. . . . I am careful to say nothing about the Conference as one living so far North cannot know and cannot be supposed to know how Irish feeling regards them. Your Grace can burn this enclosure whether you read it or not. . . . P.S. Independently of Your Grace's kind letter, I intended writing to this lady. Your allusion spurred me on.

17: "Private Your Grace Letter Invaluable" (W). Because the Liberals did not make up their minds until January 29, the tension toward the end became unbearable. Walsh was obviously afraid that the negotiations were about to break down and wrote Gladstone on January 28 a long "*Confidential*" letter, in which he attempted to make the way for compromise easy for the Liberals. Though the letter was written too late to have had any effect, it is important, nevertheless, because it demonstrates that no one was more interested or had more good will in attempting to achieve a reasonable settlement than the archbishop of Dublin:

I do not know whether I am acting prudently or not in writing to you as I now do. But the case as I view it, is one in which it is wrong to shrink from running a risk on such a point.

Let me say to you that I write in the most absolute confidence. No one knows that I am writing. Except with your express consent no one will ever know that I have written. I think I ought to say moreover that if you consider no good can come of what I have to suggest it will be quite sufficient intimation to me of this, if I do not hear from you at all in reply. I beg of you to take the matter in this way.

What I wish to say has reference to the "assurances" sought for, first in reference to the Police, secondly as regards the Land.

If I were to write a letter say to *The Times* (or perhaps better to address Mr. John Morley or some other public man, if not yourself, in a pamphlet letter), stating my view of the case on the lines of the enclosed, could you see your way to intimating publicly your acquiescence in my views, and to giving in response to a request from me, a sufficiently open declaration of policy?

I propose to face the matter in this way because I see the enormous difficulties that you have to encounter if you do anything that can by any exercise even of perverse ingenuity be twisted into something like a surrender on your part to Mr. Parnell.

What I should propose to write then, is indicated in the enclosed. I would of course, submit this draft to you for amendment before publishing anything.

I remain, Dear Mr. Gladstone
most faithfully yours,
William J. Walsh
Archbishop of Dublin

P.S. Such a statement made by you in this way, in response to an appeal from me which would embody an open & *final* repudiation of his leadership in any shape or form, would, I think, be in no way open to any misrepresentation that it was granted in deference to him.

I have put the enclosed in typewriting as you may perhaps wish to show it to some one or two friends without giving them any idea of the writer (except insofar as you wish to do so; in that, you can act as you think best). Kindly excuse the workmanship. I am somewhat out of practice and, of course, I had to do this myself.

WJW[19]

The Liberals, for their part, hesitated about the proposed assurances and were reluctant to retreat from the position they had taken at the beginning of the crisis; namely, that any agreement with the Irish Party would be considered only when the question of leadership had been settled. After several weeks of deliberation, the Liberal shadow cabinet decided finally on Wednesday, January 28, to give the required assurances concerning the land and the police clauses in the next Home Rule bill. "The Liberals have given 'assurances,'" Healy reported to Walsh on Saturday, January 31, from London, "which Sexton conveyed on Thursday to Boulogne & returned last night stating they were acceptable [to Dillon and O'Brien]" (W). Healy added pessimistically, obviously laboring under a misapprehension: "I don't believe P. will be content, but the judges of their satisfactoriness include O'Brien & McCarthy so we now have 2 to 1. If he shows bad faith, I understand his followers or some of them will come over to us under a Dillon leadership & of course if they or any responsible section of them quit him & Dillon & O'B issue a strong manifesto he is dished." "I suppose," he conjectured in conclusion, "by Wednesday P. will go to Boulogne & perhaps by Friday matters may be in train for publicity."

The Boulogne negotiations were now launched into their final phase and all was confident expectation and buoyant hope. Even Healy was optimistic. "It seems as if P. were thinking of giving in," he wrote Walsh on Wednesday, February 4, from the House of Commons (W). "He has raised a point on the assurances as to the Police," continued Healy, "which I don't think is insuperable & I imagine public declarations from the Liberals may be looked for about Monday." "Of course he may be only 'foxing,'" Healy then concluded, "but I write assuming the Boulogne expectations." Walsh, meanwhile, had been in close correspondence with Dillon and O'Brien. "We are using every possible exertion," Dillon wrote

19. Gladstone Papers, British Museum, Add. MS, 44512.

the archbishop on February 6, from Boulogne, "to bring the negotiations to some definite conclusion and I feel sure it cannot be now
deferred for more than a few days at farthest" (W).

Not all the bishops, however, were as hopeful as Walsh, for the
archbishop of Armagh, Michael Logue, wrote Walsh on February 9:

I fear we are going to have in the Boulogne negotiations a second edition of
the proceedings in Committee Room No. 15. Parnell seems to be playing
the old game and playing it successfully. I think the country should henceforth ignore the Boulogne proceedings and go on as if it had nothing before
it but to fight Parnell. This it will likely have to do sooner or later; and the
sooner it realizes the fact, the less danger there will be of a march being
stolen on us.

Your Grace must have observed how pointedly Harrington speaks of his
treating for Mr. *Parnell's temporary retirement* (W).

Logue's letter was a bad omen, for the next day both Healy and
O'Brien wrote Walsh to tell him that six weeks of painstaking negotiations were all for naught. "We have obtained," Healy recapitu-
lated the situation for Walsh on February 10, "excellent concessions
from the Liberals which were admitted in Boulogne to be satisfactory but at the same time, D & O'B declared that the measure of
satisfactoriness of the proposals was that P. shd be satisfied with
them"! (W) "Nothing they said," Healy explained, referring to
Dillon and O'Brien, "wd be satisfactory or valuable to them which
did not lead to peace. Accordingly, Mr. P. took a wretched point
about the Police; viz., that whereas the Liberals were ready to enact
that the R. I. C. shd be dissolved whenever the Irish legislature had
provided a force sufficient, in the opinion of the viceroy, to replace
it, P. contended that the viceroy shd be compelled to dissolve the
R. I. C. when the Dublin legislature certified that they had provided
a sufficient force to replace it." "The Liberals," he continued,
"[who] with great difficulty & travail got Granville, Spencer, Harcourt & others to consent to give a handle to the Unionists by
disclosing their plans for Home Rule & thus afford grounds for
avoidable criticism in advance, declined to reconsider their offer &
this is to be the pretext for the break-off, altho' the agrarian pledges
are admittedly unexceptionable."

"I am sorry to say," O'Brien wrote Walsh that same day, explaining the failure, "that no real truce was observed on either side, and

we were hampered at every step by the perfectly appalling spirit of
reckless determination (happily with many splendid exceptions) on
both sides to make it a War *a certiorie* & to resent & thwart every
attempt to put a stop to what to me seems sheer National suicide. I
greatly fear that those who were so eager to destroy all chance of
peace will have their way. God send that they may not have many
a bitter day & month to regret it!'' (W). ''So far as we are concerned,'' he added, meaning Dillon and himself, ''we will not further stand in the way of those who are so eager to fight. Time alone
can now decide whether we were right in our solemn convictions
that a continued conflict can bring nothing but disaster both to the
religious and the National influences which we are all so eager to
keep combined and perpetuated in the Irish nature.'' The next day
Dillon and O'Brien issued a statement repudiating Parnell's leadership. Dillon, in particular, said he would rather retire to private
life than serve under Parnell. He was careful, however, to ''put
this statement upon distinctly public and political grounds.''[20] They
both crossed over to Folkestone and were arrested and shipped to
Galway jail, where they began serving their long-deferred six-month
sentences.

When the Boulogne negotiations finally collapsed, Healy prophesied to Walsh on February 10: ''What D. & O'B. will do I fear is to
do nothing'' (W). ''We shall therefore suffer,'' he then pointed out,
referring to the Smith-Barry struggle in particular and the evicted
tenants in general, ''not only from the delay, & their attitude, but
have a nice dish to wash in Tipperary & elsewhere for some time.''
It was now more than two months since Parnell had been deposed
by the majority of the Party, and the opposition to Parnell was still in
the process of building a local political machine, raising the necessary funds, and launching a daily paper. When the Parnellites captured the National League, the anti-Parnellites formed a National
Committee, which held its first general meeting in Dublin on December 22; William Martin Murphy, perhaps the wealthiest man in
the Party, took the chair.[21] Murphy announced that some three

20. *Irish Catholic*, February 21, 1891.
21. Ibid., December 27, 1890.

thousand prominent citizens had joined the committee and that the prospects for a powerful national organization were excellent. Several days later, however, Walsh wrote Murphy complaining that not enough was being done in building a strong local organization. "I entirely agree," Murphy replied on December 27, "as to the necessity of extending and perfecting the organization of the National Committee" (W). "Our way in Dublin," he pointedly reminded Walsh, "would be very much easier if we had the presence and Countenance of the Clergy, which, except in a few instances, have not been hitherto given to us."[22] "It should not be forgotten," Murphy then added, "that it was barely a fortnight since we got home from London till Christmas day arrived, and that we had to face the situation with the National organisation and the National press in Dublin opposed to us. Since then, we have created a new organisation, started and kept going a daily paper, arranged for the establishment of a new morning paper, nearly all our forces being away during the time fighting the Kilkenny election." "Moreover," he observed even more pointedly, "the work was carried on without subscribed funds. I advanced the whole expenditure so far myself. A Committee for each Parliamentary Division to secure the return of a Nationalist Member is a most practical idea and I shall arrange on Monday to endeavour to establish Irish [sic] Committees. I will suggest that each Member should visit his Constituency and if possible hold a meeting and where the members are Parnellites, that some other plan should be adopted."

A week later, Healy and Murphy, together with some of the more wealthy members of the Party, met with Walsh to discuss the launching of the new paper.[23] The Bishops, in general, were very reluctant to back a new paper without some guarantee that their interests would be respected. As early as December 16, Croke had wanted to know from Walsh: "Who is to be Editor? Who are the Staff to be? Until O'Brien had declared in one way or another, I

22. This remark is interesting in light of the fact that Walsh had left very little to chance, in his usual, thorough way. See K, Nicholas Donnelly, Walsh's auxiliary, to Kirby, Saturday, December 10, 1890: "Next Tuesday which will be the last of our City (theological) Conferences for this year the archbishop purposes to convert it into a kind of clerical Meeting so that all may come to a common understanding & work in the same direction."
23. W, Healy to Walsh, January 2, 1891.

would not care to subscribe at all'' (W). ''If you have a moment,'' wrote the politic bishop of Raphoe, Patrick O'Donnell, on December 26, ''please tell me what you think of 'the Irish National Press' programme. I forgot to tell your Grace that in Rome they were all anxious if possible for a Catholic toned paper'' (W). Several days later, on December 30, the influential bishop of Elphin, Laurence Gillooly, wrote from Sligo wishing the archbishop a ''Happy New Year.''

There is a new circular today, to Bishops, from the Secretary of ''The Irish National Press Co.'' informing us that bishops have so far given very little support to the new Company. I don't think the projectors of the new paper have any right to expect encouragement or pecuniary support from the Bishops & Clergy, as such, unless they give some engagement or guaranty that the principles & feeling of the Catholic Clergy & people of Ireland will be respected in the paper. Unless some pledge or declaration of that kind is given in the Prospectus, I for one will have no connection with it. The staff, so far as we know them, offer no guaranty of respect for papal or episcopal authority. It appears to me that it is in [sic] time for the very start, that we should protect ourselves from attacks such as we have had to bear from the Freeman. [W]

The day of his interview with Healy, Murphy, and their colleagues, Walsh received another letter from the bishop of Raphoe, in which O'Donnell intimated that the moment for exacting their quid pro quo from the lay politicians had arrived. ''It is the general view,'' O'Donnell advised Walsh on January 2, ''that safety for the National cause was and is inseparable from hearty consultation with the leading Ecclesiastics who have done so much for it and that now is the time to make that opinion in a quiet way enter into the new order of things. My object in writing is to say that, in case the N. Press shares have not all been taken up, I could do something by an appeal to the priests to push them here, if your Grace thought that course desirable'' (W). The Bishops, or a large section of them, were obviously unwilling to endorse the new paper without some formal undertaking from the directors that their wishes would be respected.

The result of Walsh's interview with Healy and his colleagues was an agreement that O'Brien should be offered the chairmanship of the new paper. His extraordinary talent and experience as a journalist was certainly one reason, and that the connection would bind him more closely to their side was, of course, another. Parnell, however, with his uncanny instinct, had forestalled them again: one of his first conditions in the negotiations at Boulogne was that O'Brien should refuse the chairmanship if offered. Parnell had his way, for Healy wrote Walsh on Janaury 5 from Paris, a few days after their interview: "Wm is not in love with the paper, & I feel certain he will refuse to act" (W). The result was that when the episcopal standing committee met in Dublin on January 14, its members decided that explicit assurances from the board of directors of the *National Press* were necessary. "The principal business," Archbishop Logue reported to Kirby the next day from Armagh, "was to get guarantees from the new Irish publishing company as to the principles on which they will conduct their Journal. They seem inclined to fully meet the views of the Bishops" (K). How far indeed the directors were willing to go to secure the bishops' support was revealed the following day, when Walsh also wrote Kirby. "The Directors," he assured Kirby in a postscript to a long letter on January 15, "were anxious that I should nominate some priest whom they would 'coopt' on the Directorate. But I thought this not quite prudent. I mention it to show their good dispositions" (K).

By the end of the month, the directors had delivered the required assurances in writing to the secretary to the episcopal standing committee, F. J. MacCormack. "We had a quorum of the Board present on today," William F. Dennehy, secretary to the directorate and editor of the *Irish Catholic*, informed MacCormack on January 27, "and I am instructed to express regret for any delay that has arisen, as well as to say that the Directors are determined that anything opposed to Catholic principles shall be excluded from the 'National Press,' and that they will be glad to Cooperate with the Hierarchy in advocating Catholic interests as defined by the Episcopal body" (C). "As Sec. of the Ep. St. Committee," MacCormack informed his colleagues on February 14, enclosing copies of Dennehy's letter, "I am charged with the duty of handing a Resolution of our Committee to the Directors of the 'National Press.' " "The annexed," he then explained, "is the reply I received. The Res[n] sought for a guarantee that anything contrary to faith and morals should be excluded and a genuine cooperation be given in the promoting of Catholic interests" (C). "The new National Journal," Logue assured Kirby a week later, on February 21, "is to appear on the 7th March. The Bishops have got a written guarantee from its directors which will secure its soundness; but of course this is private, as the knowledge of it might be made a handle to ruin the influence of the new paper" (K).

Meanwhile, in a magnanimous gesture, and one much criticized by the Healyite "war party," O'Brien had withdrawn his support at the end of January from the *Insuppressible*, the half-penny daily produced when Parnell seized *United Ireland*. "O'Brien's conduct regarding the Insuppressible," Croke remarked to Walsh in the course of a long letter on January 27, "is most unexcusable. The Insuppressible itself is universally regretted" (W). "I am tired of politics—and of Ireland—" he then confided in conclusion, obviously depressed, "I wish to goodness I was clean out of both." "No news," he added more characteristically in a postscript, "from Boulogne." Without O'Brien's support, the *Insuppressible* collapsed, and the anti-Parnellites were in a weaker position than ever when the Boulogne negotiations ended a few weeks later. The initiative fell to the "war party" opposed to Parnell; and in Timothy Healy, Parnell was finally to meet his match in unscrupulousness.

Immediately after the collapse of the Boulogne negotiations, Walsh wrote Healy again, complaining that not enough was being done by the Party in the way of organization. "I fully appreciate every word," Healy replied on February 13, "contained in Your Grace's letter & so do we all. The Party had a host of matters to discuss re Liberal assurances, Boulogne Conference, etc. so that it was only today we were able to address ourselves to the really vital question of organisation. What we feel is that P. has the mob & also the absence of Blackguards on our side, so that he is able to sweep the towns apparently & forbid us a hearing" (W). "Now prospective victories in the Ballot boxes," he continued, drawing the moral from the lesson for Walsh, "are of course the end all of our work, but we cannot fight openly unless P. is taught some lessons by counter-action. I am deputed to lay the Party's views before Your Grace & I hope Sexton & M'Carthy may be able to come too." Healy then concluded by informing the archbishop he would be in Dublin the following week, when, presumably, he would further discuss the necessary means to the desirable end.

The struggle really began in earnest at this point, and the Bishops and clergy were in the vanguard in mounting the attack. Walsh had already ordered his priests to withdraw from their National League branch if it had fallen into the hands of Parnellites. "My present concern," he added, indicating that laymen might be next, "is with the clergy only. . . ."[24] In Midleton, County Cork, the parish priest went further and instructed one of his parishioners by letter to withdraw from his league branch on the grounds that it supported Parnell.[25] The bishop of Galway, F. J. MacCormack, condemned the Parnell Reception Committee, which was organizing a meeting for Sunday, February 22, in Galway city.[26] A week later, the bishop of Down and Connor, Patrick McAlister, took a more extreme step:

Rev. Dear Sir—
We have now in Belfast what is called a "Parnell Leadership Committee," the ostensible object of which appears to be to honor a man who, by his persistent and impudent attempts to force himself on the attention of the country, defiled as he is with the leprosy of his loathsome crime, continues to outrage the public sense of morality and decency, and tries to subject to his dictation the independence of our country and Church. The Catholic members of this committee, by enrolling their names, have proclaimed their disregard of Christian decency and their contempt for the instructions which the bishops of Ireland considered their duty to impart to the people.
*They have thus become the propagators of public scandal, and have by their own acts placed themselves in the category of those to whom it is unlawful for priests to administer the Sacraments of the Church.*[27]

"I wish also to remind the priest," added McAlister in conclusion, indicating that some of his clergy might not have been wholly enthusiastic about complying with his directions, "that this is not a matter of politics. It is a matter which concerns the interests of the Divine Saviour of Souls, and for which He will one day call us to account. . . ." While in Dublin, Father John Behan, at an anti-Parnellite meeting, had expressed great satisfaction on seeing "so many young men present, as it was evidently part of Mr. Parnell's Plan of Campaign to gull the young men of Ireland. Perhaps Mr.

24. *Irish Catholic*, February 14, 1891.
25. Ibid., February 21, 1891.
26. Ibid.
27. Ibid., March 7, 1891.

Parnell had a large following in Ireland, but he [Father Behan] did not believe that Mr. Parnell had even one follower who was at the same time true-hearted, honest, and intelligent."[28]

When the anti-Parnellites, or Nationalists, decided to meet force with force, violence was not far behind. At Charleville an effort was made to establish a branch of the new organization, the National Federation, in opposition to the local Parnellite branch of the National League, and an "attempt on the part of a Parnellite mob to break up the meeting was repulsed and several of the disturbers severely beaten."[29] On the same Sunday, March 1, at an anti-Parnellite meeting in Mitchelstown, the "local Parnellites formed themselves into a knot in the centre of the hall . . . and Mr. Skinner, a Parnellite, called for cheers for Parnell, which appeared to have been lustily taken up by the Parnellite body and a few others. A body of twenty or thirty men rushed at the Parnellite knot and sticks were brandished and some blows aimed at Mr. Parnell's supporters. The Parnellites kept their position and order was for a moment restored. Mr. Skinner endeavoured to say something but his party were assaulted and a struggle followed, in which the Parnellites were ejected."[30] The violence took a more ominous turn at a meeting in Carrick-on-Shannon, for the clergy were involved as well as the laity. "Father Hourican, of Gowel," the Roscommon *Herald* reported, "was also set upon and assaulted, and his hat was kicked like a football through the streets, and . . . Father Skelly and Father Donohoe, of Mohill, were violently assaulted later on. Mud was flung at Canon Hoare and his coat attempted to be torn off."[31]

In the face of the violence, the Bishops for a moment seem to have drawn back. A letter from Croke was published on March 14, explaining that what the Bishops questioned was Parnell's leadership and not his right to a seat in Parliament or his share of influence in the councils of the Party.[32] The following week the bishop of Meath, Thomas Nulty, moderately maintained that there had been too much recrimination on both sides and actually named the "Healyite"

28. Ibid.
29. Ibid.
30. Ibid.
31. Ibid.
32. Ibid., March 14, 1891.

faction as a main contributor.[33] The pause was only momentary, however, for the bishop of Cork condemned a Parnellite meeting scheduled for Cork city on St. Patrick's Day, and the struggle was soon as violent and as bitter as before.[34]

By early March, however, the anti-Parnellites were finally able to meet their opponents on something more than equal terms. They launched their long-awaited daily paper, the *National Press*, on Saturday, March 7, "under very great difficulties." "The danger of some attempt," Walsh had confided on March 6 to Cardinal Manning, "to smash up the place by violence is a real one. Confidential men in various parts of the office are privately *armed*. The precaution is known to be necessary. See what times we are living in!" (M). Several days later, the anti-Parnellites crowned their organizational efforts by holding a national convention of the newly founded branches of their federation in Parnell's stronghold, Dublin. "The National Federation meeting," Walsh reported to Manning on March 12, "in Dublin on Tuesday seems to have been a wonderful success. Letters (strong ones) were read from the 4 Archbishops and from 13 other Bishops" (M). "Many others will of course write," he added, obviously concerned about the difficulties he faced in maintaining episcopal unity. "But *the four Archbishops* is the great point." The anti-Parnellites were now able to match daily paper for daily paper and political machine for political machine. With adequate funds available, the bulk of the provincial weeklies on their side, and the powerful clerical phalanx at their back, they were now ready to begin the difficult task of grinding Parnell and his supporters into political dust.

Walsh's confidence in early March was demonstrated by his choosing that moment to make his long-deferred trip to Rome. "As we are passing through a sharp crisis," he had written Manning more than two months before, on December 29, "it seemed plain to me that the Roman visit ought to be postponed. Such a visit just now would necessarily give rise to a good deal of embarrassing talk. Besides it is, on more grounds than one, essential that I should be here for purposes of consultation, etc." (M).

33. Ibid., March 21, 1891.
34. Ibid., March 14, 1891.

"On the other hand," he continued, "the three Bishops who were in Rome found everything there so promising that they were unwilling to let pass the present favourable time for action. They feared especially that postponement would result in abandonment of the project—also that a certain clique, now vexed at the Pope's acceptance of our suggestion, might make mischief against us out of the fact that after finding our proposal accepted, we practically withdrew it." "However," Walsh reported of Logue, "the Primate thought it right to act on my view. He now telegraphs the result of an audience last Saturday. Everything has gone well. The Pope praises highly the action of the Bishops. He postpones the deputation, fixing, however, a time for it—after Easter." "Thus everything is secured," Walsh concluded; "I knew Your Eminence would be glad to know all this."

"I am making some arrangements," Walsh confided to Manning finally on March 9, "to have Catholic interests well looked after. This is now practically settled, so, after all, I may be able to go to Rome for St. Patrick's Day. I am strongly inclined to go. I do not ask your Eminence's advice. I know before hand what it would be" (M). "I have made up my mind," he wrote the cardinal again the next day, "to go to Rome" (M). "Everything in Rome," he then reported, "thank God, looks far brighter for us than when I last saw your Eminence last autumn. This is one of the many advantages of the present otherwise deplorable wreck in our public affairs." Though it would have been difficult for even Walsh to have enumerated "the many advantages," he was undoubtedly alluding to that which was very close to the cardinal's heart, the late apparent increase in clerical power in Ireland.

"My belief," the cardinal had written Gladstone at Christmas, "is that Mr. Parnell will steadily go down in Ireland. For ten years he has raised a spirit which would have ended as it has in France by shutting up religion in the Sacristy. Nothing but a great moral scandal could have deposed him: and even this has hardly done its work a day too soon."[35] At Easter, Manning was still harping on the same string to Gladstone: "Ireland . . . has put off a disease of

35. Manning to Gladstone, Christmas, 1890, Gladstone Papers, British Museum, Add. MS, 44250.

wild and dangerous politics during which the Bishops & clergy of
Ireland were bid to be silent and efface themselves. Nothing I believe would have destroyed this false & pernicious policy but an
enormous moral shock."[36] "Ireland now," continued Manning,
revealing how little he understood the Irish situation, "is in a normal
& healthy state of freedom and its moral life is restored to the
authority which guided it through the dangers of rebellion and continental revolution; and of a political movement fed by American
money and animosity." No one, however, except perhaps Monsignor Persico, still had more real influence at Rome over Irish
affairs than Manning, and Archbishop Walsh's judicious phrasing
was the political preliminary to a strengthening of his own position
at the Vatican.

Parnell was indeed a rare political genius. The quality of that
genius was never more clearly revealed than in those exciting days
after he had been deposed as Leader in the House of Commons by
the majority of his colleagues and had returned to Ireland to appeal
their decision to the Irish people. Within two weeks he had secured
to himself all the effective organs of political power in the country,
and his bewildered opponents found themselves without funds,
newspapers, or Party organization. He then coolly, from a position
of maximum strength, opened negotiations for a surrender he never
intended to honor. His strategy was simply to give the various
factions among his opponents enough time to fall to quarreling
among themselves, and his tactic during the negotiations was to
drive wedges at every opportunity. The success of his plan depended
on the inability of his opponents to sink their differences. Given the
ambitions, needs, and temperaments of his opponents, this wager
on factionalism must have seemed hardly a risk at all. In the last
analysis, however, Parnell did not have much choice. Because the
combination against him was bigger and stronger than he was, if he
could not persuade them to turn on each other, he must in the end be
overwhelmed.

When those opposed to him did sink their differences, his political
destruction was only a matter of time. Three months after he was

36. Ibid., April 9, 1891.

deposed as leader, his opponents had successfully redressed the balance of power and were ready to launch their counterattack. By early March 1891, they had founded a new daily paper, subscribed a fund for the support of the Party, and summoned a national convention of the branches of their newly organized Party machine. Moreover, in spite of all the initial confusion created by Parnell's astute and forceful moves, they had won a most impressive victory at a crucial by-election in North Kilkenny. Mounting this counterattack was only made possible because the Roman Catholic hierarchy and their clergy fought a determined holding action until the Party was able to regroup and organize. The Bishops and priests had also made heavy contributions in manpower and money to help the Party build the machinery necessary to wage aggressive political war. To the more politically astute, therefore, it was obvious by early March that Parnell could not win and that he would not surrender.

A civil war, even if conducted only with ballots, is always an ugly business and never more so than when there are religious overtones. Parnell suffered three major reverses in the six months after the launching of the counterattack against him in March 1891. Early in April he lost his second and even more crucial by-election in North Sligo, and in August he was beset by a double calamity. The *Freeman's Journal*, the largest and most important daily in Ireland, which had been both his staff and his rod, refused to continue to support him; and the two most influential men in the Party and the country, John Dillon and William O'Brien, decided, on their release from Galway jail, to fight him rather than retire from Irish political life. Though the Bishops had little or no direct influence on Dillon's and O'Brien's decision, they were nearly altogether responsible for Parnell's defeat in North Sligo and highly instrumental in effecting the change in policy of the *Freeman*. Parnell's unexpected death in early October 1891 changed nothing except to widen the breach between his followers and the Party. The parliamentary power base of those who continued to uphold Parnell's political legacy had actually been destroyed in that great man's lifetime, and the destruction was finally confirmed in the general election of July 1892. The part played by the Bishops and their clergy in this destruction of Parnellism was more than central—it was decisive.

The counterattack against Parnell was launched when one of the more insignificant members of the Party died in the second week of March 1891. The sitting member for North Sligo was hardly dead, in fact, when the bishop of Elphin, Laurence Gillooly, wrote Thomas Sexton, a leading member of the Party, that it was imperative to fill the vacancy immediately. Sexton agreed on March 13 to apply for the necessary writ and to summon a "Convention representing the clergy and Branches of the division" to select a candidate, subject of course to his lordship's "opinion" (G). Because the division of North Sligo cut across three dioceses besides his own, Gillooly alerted his episcopal brethren. "With God's blessing," reported the bishop of Ardagh, Bartholomew Woodlock, on March 14, "your prompt action will prevent turmoil. *Faxit Deus*" (G). The bishops of Achonry and Killala, John Lyster and Hugh Conway, also promised their cooperation the same day. A troublesome note was sounded, however, in the bishop of Killala's letter. Conway reminded Gillooly that "much will depend on the character of the person put forward by our opponents. If he will be an ardent Fenian, he will have a large following for most of the lower classes sympathise strongly with that organisation" (G). The archbishop of Tuam also complained about Fenian influence, in a consoling note to Gillooly that same day. "Are we not fallen on awful times?" lamented MacEvilly (G). "It will take all the honest and united efforts of the clergy to stop the evil," he then warned Gillooly; "Rely on it, if he & his Hillsiders succeed, Religion will suffer. I was always at our meetings against these Gaels. . . . Some of our more prominent men made nothing of it. The Gaels or rather . . . Fenians are our greatest Cross. This of course *entre nous*."

Some days later, one of those prominent men, the archbishop of Cashel, also wrote Gillooly to wish him well in the approaching contest. Indeed, Croke took it for granted in his letter of March 18 that "the people as a rule will go with their priests and that victory will be ours" (G). "Defeat, anyhow," he gravely concluded, "would be disastrous. God defend the right." By this time, however, Gillooly had good reason to suspect the worst—that some of the priests might go with their people. The very day he received Croke's letter, in fact, Gillooly had to telegraph the bishop of Killala in an almost imperative tone for his assurance of support. "Convention of North Sligo Delegates here tomorrow—at which I will preside. Letter from your Lordship promising support to Candidate selected by Convention will greatly oblige and assist. Union is a sacred duty in this crisis watched anxiously even in Rome as I know. Please wire reply—Elphin'' (G). At the convention the next day, Gillooly was most judicious in admitting that among the Killala priests "there might be a few who had not studied the question who might be of different opinion, but he would venture to say the priest who went against all the Bishops of Ireland, and against the immense mass of the priests of Ireland, was not a priest to be admired, and was not a priest to be quoted as an able supporter of any party.''[37] He then read an assurance from the bishop of Killala that he would use all his influence in support of the candidate selected by the convention. The bishop of Achonry, John Lyster, who followed Gillooly, was reported as saying that the Parnellite candidate "had been selected by the other side because he was a Ballina man and because he was a personal friend of the Bishop of Killala, but the Bishop of Killala recognised this was not a question of personal friendship, but of stern principle.''[38]

The reports in the press, however, did not tell the whole story, for the bishop of Killala was obviously a good deal more uncooperative than his episcopal colleagues were willing to admit in public. After the convention, Gillooly asked Lyster to visit Conway and attempt to persuade him of his obligations in the crisis. In reporting the subsequent interview to Gillooly on March 23, the bishop of Achonry, in an interesting order of ascending importance, explained how he brought to bear all the arguments at his command:

I have been in Ballina to-day and have had a long interview with his Lordship. The result leads me to believe that we shall have no *practical* cooperation from him.

He tells me that he for a long time considered that his position was or should be one of total neutrality, and for this reason he delayed some days before sending his adhesion and signature to the Manifesto from the Bishops, last November. His priests approved of this policy, and so, many of them wish to be neutral in this electoral contest. He cannot and will not force them to actively oppose Parnell: the grounds he assigns being he could not press them to oppose their people. He seemed perfectly incredulous when I told him that the Curate of Skrean and the Parish Priest of

37. *Freeman's Journal*, March 20, 1891.
38. Ibid.

Dromore were openly and ostentatiously using their influence in the adulterer's favour. He has written to the priests living in the district—interested in the election—cautioning them against supporting Parnell,—that is the utmost he is prepared to do.

I begged of him at least, to require of Fr. Cosgrave, and the other priests to *preside* at the meeting of our candidate; no one could construe *that* into forcing the people to vote; it would merely show that they were carrying out his Lordship's wishes as expressed in his letter. His only answer was,—if this were done all the people who promised Fr. Cosgrave Subscriptions for his new Church, would withdraw their names, and refuse assistance.

I impressed upon his Lordship that I was not there in my personal capacity. I came at your earnest request and that I gave him not only your views but those of the Archbishop of Tuam and his twin brother, the Bishop of Galway. (I may say incidentally that I made so bold as to request the Archbishop of Tuam to convey his sentiments to the Bishop of Killala.) His only reply to this was that the town of Tuam was more actively Parnellite than the town of Ballina.

I brought under his notice that his own administrator Father O'Hara and the P. P. of Dromore were opposing his Lordship's wishes—that the priests should not support publicly Mr. Parnell's candidate. I begged of his Lordship to interfere to prevent this: he invited me to dine when I would meet Fr. McHale and argue the point with him. As the point for argument was whether Dr. Conway should have his own directions carried out I had to decline.

I referred to the attitude of the Holy See, and alluded to Dr. Walsh's presence in Rome,—with the result that he promised to repeat his instructions to his clergy when he would meet them on Holy Thursday.

He accompanied me to the train and on our way we had to pass through Parnell's meeting. As we worked our way through the crowd ringing cheers were given for Dr. Conway: it is quite clear the rank and file believe that he is with them.

His sickness has left its traces on his Lordship: he is hazy and stupid; and my belief is—he is not fully aware of what is going on. I left Ballina with the impression that it is not his Lordship who rules the diocese, but the Rev. Anthony McHale—"the voice is the voice of Jacob, but the hands are the hands of Esau." I am sorry my mission has not had a more successful issue (G).

Killala's decision to remain neutral was a serious blow to those who were fighting Parnell. According to Gillooly's own figures, there were 8,476 eligible voters in North Sligo. The breakdown for the dioceses of Elphin, Killala, and Achonry, respectively, were

5,055, 2,828, and 593.[39] If the Tory vote, which numbered about a thousand, was cast for Parnell and the Killala voters followed suit, Parnell might actually win. Parnell was, in fact, very confident. He wrote Mrs. O'Shea on March 24, from his headquarters in Ballina, enthusiastically describing that same meeting which had upset the bishop of Achonry:

> The reception here yesterday was magnificent, and the whole country for twenty-five miles from here to the town of Sligo is solid for us, the priests being in our favor with one exception, and the seceders being unable to hold a meeting anywhere. I am to keep in this friendly district, and to hold meetings there, and shall not go out of it.
> The town of Sligo and the district from there to Cliffony is hostile, the priests being against us, and I shall not go into it, but we have a good friendly minority even in this district, whom our agents' will canvass privately.[40]

Meanwhile, Gillooly received on March 23 another note from Croke, full of very sound, if inhibiting, advice. "Warn your priests," Croke counseled, "against any threat of deprivation of Sacraments, or any other spiritual advantage, in the case of parties who may go for Parnell. One cleric committed himself in that direction during the Kilkenny Contest and he was within *a pipe* of ruining the whole affair" (G). "There is no need of violence," he advised Gillooly, who was well over seventy, "as you have the ball at yr. foot—and kick it bravely." "Orations from the altar," he then added in a postscript, "I do not like. They are dangerous. *Parnellites preparing for a petition.*"

With the approach of election day, the priests on the Parnellite side became more outspoken. The press reports of the remarks made on Easter Sunday by a number of the Killala clerics so infuriated Gillooly, when he read them on Monday morning, that he immediately wrote the bishop of Killala asking for an explanation. In his reply the next day, March 31, Conway was still in an incredulous mood, apprehending that "there must be some mistake about the Rev. Fr. O'Hara. His Mission is about 12 miles from Dromore

39. G, Sligo Electoral List. The breakdown of voters is on the basis of parishes.
40. Parnell to Mrs. O'Shea, March 24, 1891; quoted in Katherine O'Shea, *Charles Stewart Parnell* (London, 1914), 2:260–61.

West, and on Easter Sunday it is not probable that he would be
absent from his own chapel'' (G). ''The P. P. of Dromore West,'' he
then naively continued, ''would scarcely use the language attributed
to him after the resolutions passed at our Meeting.'' ''I will,'' he
concluded, trying to mollify Gillooly somehow, ''prohibit both himself and Father O'Hara from taking any part in the Election on
Thursday.'' The damage had been done, however, and there was
nothing more for Gillooly to do except to await the result of the poll.

Though the margin (768) was narrow, Parnell's candidate was defeated, 3,261 to 2,493. Walsh's secretary, W. H. Murphy, who with
the archbishop absent in Rome, wrote Gillooly on April 3. ''The real
significance of the figures,'' he pointed out shrewdly, ''depends on
the extent the Unionist votes were cast for Parnell. This morning's
Express reported that the Unionists voted in large numbers for him,
yet the Freeman states exactly the contrary'' (G). The truth, however, appeared to be something other than these obvious alternatives. ''From enquiry I have made,'' Ridgeway reported to Balfour
on April 10, ''I find that very few Unionists voted. For instance, in
Sligo town out of 400 only 80 voted. If all had voted, Parnell might
have won and the Priests received a crushing blow. You will note
that they get the credit of having voted so they have gained nothing
by their blind abstinence.''[41] In congratulating Gillooly, the archbishop of Tuam expressed his fury with the bishop of Killala and his
priests. ''Ought not something be done,'' MacEvilly asked on April
8, ''about that Diocese of Kill?'' ''I have the greatest regard for the
Episc (who knows him that has not?) But religion is dearer still''
(G). It was Croke, however, who summed up the Sligo election best
in his congratulatory note to Gillooly. ''Considering all things,''
Croke wrote on April 3, ''though somewhat disappointing, a decided victory has been achieved'' (G). ''You must have had an
anxious time of it,'' he commiserated in conclusion; ''the Ballina
clerics acted badly: and the people appear to be an uncouth and
turbulent lot.''

Not all the Bishops, however, were of Croke's mind. ''You heard
of course,'' John Keys O'Doherty, the bishop of Derry, wrote Kirby
on April 6, ''the result of the Sligo election. The result was very

41. B, 49812.

unsatisfactory though Parnell was beaten. It is sad to see that in spite of the Bishops so large a number of Catholics followed him, and, what was still worse, so large a number of priests. In no other part of Ireland could such a thing have taken place'' (K). The Bishops in other parts of Ireland in any case were certainly put on their guard after the defection of the Killala clerics. ''With God's help,'' the bishop of Cork piously assured Kirby that same day, ''things will be better after a while when the real feelings of the people will reassert themselves'' (K). ''A great deal will depend,'' O'Callaghan added, ''on the exertion of the priests, in fact it is altogether in their hands. At a recent election in the city for the Poor Law Guardians, only one Parnellite was elected and it is accounted for by the indifference of a few priests. This will be efficaciously remedied and it is not likely to occur again.'' ''We have no small difficulties,'' Logue also lamented to Kirby on April 13, ''to contend with at present'' (K). ''If the priests were all faithful,'' he added, going somewhat further than his brethren in Derry and Cork, ''we could manage the people, but unfortunately there are a very few individuals among the clergy who are lukewarm or faithless; and though they dare not declare themselves publicly, at least in this diocese, I fear the mischief they do privately is very great. On this day week in the Conference at Drogheda *the priests brought forward a resolution condemnatory of Parnell.* Seeing signs of want of unanimity, I insisted on a division.'' ''All who were for the resolution,'' Logue reported, ''went to one side, and on the other there remained to my disgust and astonishment, a parish priest, two curates, the *Guardian of the Franciscans*, and the *Prior of the Augustinians.* I gave them fair warning that if they took any public action I would not overlook it.''

During the election, the Very Reverend R. M. McLaughlin, in a sermon at St. Mary's Cathedral in Sligo, denounced ''certain newspapers'' as being dangerous ''to the faith.''[42] He further maintained, in what was a veiled but obvious attack on the *Freeman's Journal*, that the opinions put forward day after day were ''anti-Catholic'' and ''anti-Christian.'' Indeed, from the very beginning of the struggle, the greatest cause for concern among the Irish Bishops was the attitude of the *Freeman.* In January, Walsh had been so incensed by

42. *Irish Catholic*, March 28, 1891.

the reporting in the *Freeman* that he went so far as to propose to
Croke that an episcopal pronouncement be issued against the paper.
Croke wisely vetoed the suggestion on January 9, on the grounds
that it was both untimely and useless (W). Walsh, however, was not
so easily contained. "I have had to come out against the *Freeman's
Journal* at last," he reported to Kirby on January 23 (K). "It has
taken the chastisement, of course, very badly. But the feeling of the
country is strongly against it. This will make the feeling stronger
than ever." In his attack on the *Freeman*, which appeared in the
*Irish Catholic* the next day, January 24, Walsh maintained that it
was becoming more and more like the "atheistic Freemasonry
organs on the Continent." Walsh, however, was careful to note in
his attack that for the present he merely wanted "to put the Catholics
of Dublin upon their guard against its poisonous teachings." The
narrowness of the Sligo victory and especially the nationwide publicity given the defection of the Killala clerics by the *Freeman*
did nothing to lessen episcopal anxiety. Shortly after the election,
the archbishop of Armagh continued the oblique attack when he
denounced the "Evils of the Anti-Catholic Press."[43] "They are
weakening the faith," declared Logue, "weakening the respect for
the authority of the Church, and by degrees they will corrupt us
altogether." He then went on to make a rather naive admission and
advance some startling claims: "That is true not only in regard to
uneducated people, for I firmly believe that if I were reading bad
books and bad newspapers—I believe if I were reading these works
for a time that my faith would get weak. Hence it is that the Church
prohibits the reading of bad works, except by those who read them
to refute them, and hence it is that I would be quite within my right,
and acting in accordance with ecclesiastical law, in forbidding the
reading of those newspapers in the diocese which has been entrusted
to my care." "But I know," concluded Logue confidently, "it is
only necessary to warn you against them—to tell you to keep them
away from you."

The main reason, of course, why the Bishops did not formally
pronounce against the *Freeman* was that there was no way in which
they could make their prohibition effective. Further, by any such

43. Ibid., April 11, 1891.

pronouncement, they would be merely giving their enemies another handy stick to beat them with, for the cry of 'freedom of the press' would be even more effective, and especially in England, than that of "clerical intimidation." But if the *Freeman* could not be overwhelmed by assault, could it not be taken from within? The editorial policy of the paper was determined by a board of directors who had declared for Parnell from the very beginning and who showed no sign of wavering. The directors, however, were responsible to the shareholders, and chief among the shareholders was Edmund Dwyer Gray, who, with his mother, controlled twelve thousand of the twenty-five thousand shares outstanding. In a word, as the twenty-two-year-old Gray went, so did the *Freeman*.

When the split occurred, Gray had been on tour in Australia. On his return he had accepted the decision of the directors to support Parnell. The young man, who by all accounts was neither stable nor bright, soon began to waver. After the Sligo election, he put out peace-feelers and interviewed Thomas Sexton and Justin McCarthy, the more moderate men among those who opposed Parnell.[44] These interviews were reported to Manning, and His Eminence immediately reported them to Walsh, who was still in Rome. "What your Eminence tells me about young Gray," wrote Walsh in reply from Rome on April 27, "is very important. But it is important mainly as showing the collapse of Parnellism as a national force" (M). Walsh then went on to give the cardinal a very sharp pen portrait of Gray:

The young man is very vain. He is without education, yet he looks on himself as the one man capable of directing the newspaper, of managing the affairs of the Irish Parliamentary Party, and of "leading" the Irish race. All this was made painfully manifest two or three years ago, when he returned from Australia where he had been at the time of his father's death. In a few months he made himself so ridiculous by his foolish talk that his friends saw the only chance of his righting himself lay in his making another tour in Australia. He came back, I understand, worse than ever.

"I had always been most friendly to him," Walsh continued; "Yet he did not condescend to call to see me on his return! No compromise of any kind will be made with the *Freeman's Journal*," he then declared firmly. "But of course we shall be glad to see it

44. Lyons, *The Fall*, p. 279.

repentant and bringing forth fruit worthy of penance." From Walsh's letter it is obvious that both Cardinal Manning and Gray, for different reasons, were worried about a Roman condemnation of the *Freeman*. "Of course there is no fear of any Roman action," the archbishop concluded reassuringly. "But *young Gray should be left altogether in the dark as to this*."

Several days later, Walsh again wrote Manning to warn him of the apparent change in Parnell's tactics and the effect it might have on the *Freeman*. "From Parnell's speech at Clonmel," Walsh pointed out on April 30, "I infer that he has come to see the harm done to his cause politically by the attacks of the *Freeman's Journal* and his principal supporters on the Bishops and priests. Now it may be that merely the *tone* of the *Freeman* is to be changed, that is, that the attacks on the Bishops and priests are to be given up, whilst the Parnell leadership, against which we have so strongly protested, is to be advocated as before" (M). "The real harm done by the *Freeman's Journal*," the archbishop then argued, "is its advocacy of the Parnell leadership. As to its attack on us, *that* does Parnell far more harm than good." "Hence, it will be well for yr. Eminence," Walsh then concluded, "if you have an opportunity, to make it clearly understood [to Gray] that nothing in the way of a change is worth talking about unless it is proposed to abandon the advocacy of Parnell's leadership."

Gray, meanwhile, had complicated matters still further by writing directly to the pope to ask him for his blessing. "Mgr. Kirby," Walsh reported to Manning on May 7, Ascension Thursday, "was at the Vatican to-night, and has just come here with our young friend's letter. H.H. tells me to go to him on Saturday that we may see what is to be done. As I read the document, I must say the case is a most delicate one" (M). "H. H. at present," Walsh then confided, "thinks that what he ought to do is (1) to express approval of the Catholic sentiments of the writer, and (2) to say that his views are known to the Archbishop of the writer, who will give all the necessary advice and instruction. This seems to cover everything. The blessing sought for, if granted, would be made the subject of a flaring coloured 'cartoon,' for posting up in the cabins of Mayo and Kerry, testifying to the triumph of the paper in question over the *local* authority." The next day, Walsh had a long audience with the pope "about the

Gray case" (M). "The letter proves on examination," he wrote Manning, "to be *most disingenuous*. At a speech made in Cork, the young man not only endorsed the action of the Editorial Committee, but declared it was their stand for 'independence' that made it possible for him to take up with honour the charge of the newspaper!" Indeed, when Gray was reported a week later in the company of Parnell in the House of Commons, the archbishop must have felt his suspicions about the young man's sincerity confirmed.[45] Walsh would have been even more convinced if he knew what Gray had told John Morley only a week after he had been seen with Parnell: Morley informed Gladstone that the young man was only waiting for Dillon's and O'Brien's release from jail to change the policy of the *Freeman*. "This I cannot believe," commented Morley; "what possible good can come to Dillon and his aims from giving Parnell the *Freeman's* support for three months longer?"[46]

The reason for Gray's strange conduct was that the *Freeman* was losing a great deal of money in its support of Parnell. Gray had somehow concluded that Walsh's visit to Rome was concerned with securing a condemnation of the *Freeman*, which, given the already difficult financial situation, might prove ruinous to the paper. He tried, therefore, to take the wind out of any proposed ecclesiastical censure by writing the pope and asking for his blessing. At the same time, Gray realized that this was only a temporary expedient and that, to save his property, he must in the end desert Parnell. Because he did not want to look like a deserter, however, he had to bide his time and wait for what was to his mind a proper excuse. When Gray spoke to Morley toward the end of May, the most promising excuse appeared to be the attitude Dillon and O'Brien would take when they were released from Galway jail in August. Then, instead of actually changing sides, Gray could, perhaps, simply shift his allegiance and thereby desert with honor. What made all this so difficult for Morley to understand was that he had been schooled in a society that subscribed to a different set of first principles. Among the Irish, loyalty is the first principle.

While awaiting Dillon's and O'Brien's release from Galway jail,

45. *National Press* (Dublin), May 13, 1891; quoted in Lyons, *The Fall*, p. 279.
46. Morley to Gladstone, May 23, 1891; quoted in Lyons, *The Fall*, p. 280 n.

Gray, who was still obviously worried about the possibility of a clerical condemnation of the *Freeman*, decided to visit Rome and make a personal appeal to the pope. "Cardinal Rampolla informed me," Gray wrote Walsh some time after the event, "that it was the Holy Father's desire that I should receive your Grace's advice on the matter, and be guided by it."[47] He then went on to explain to Walsh in a chaotic, half-literate, seventeen-page narrative that he had returned from Rome about the time of the release of Dillon and O'Brien and that they refused to take up his proposal for reconciliation. The day they were released, he continued, they pronounced against Parnell; and on that same day, the board of the *Freeman* refused to summon a meeting of the shareholders to elect him a director. "One idea of reconciliation was what held me back all along," he added, in a revealing non sequitur; "that was the desire to obtain control of the *Freeman* without a fight." "I decide consequently," he announced bravely, "that the time has come for repudiation and the fight must be fought." "I act without hesitation," he continued less bravely but still in the present tense, "and the next morning there appears a strong unequivocal letter from me repudiating Mr. Parnell on the ground of his marriage—a good *Catholic* reason for abandoning him."

Actual control of the *Freeman* would not pass to Gray until the meeting of the shareholders, scheduled for late August, elected a new board of directors. "Mr. Parnell," Gray also informed Walsh in his long letter, "has paid up the money due on his shares and will attend the meeting. I believe, if Your Grace were to attend we would pulverize him, and what may take a week would be done in a day, and a *possibility* of defeat averted." Walsh, however, proceeded to write a letter on August 21 to the *National Press*, in which he pointed out that but for the "lamented apostasy" of the *Freeman*,

47. W, no date. See K, Walsh to Kirby, July 19, 1891: "I am glad Y. G. was so careful with E. D. G. It was a piece of sharp practice on his part to go to Rome. When he came to me on my return—as he was directed to do by Mgr. Jacobini in reply to his letter to the Holy Father—he merely told me he was going to the Continent for a holiday and to keep out of the way till Dillon and O'Brien are out of prison at the end of this month. He evidently thought he could succeed in Rome in getting an audience, and so undoing the effect of the letter which merely referred him to his Bishop for advice."

the struggle would have been over long before.[48] He announced also that he felt it his duty to aid in the efforts of the shareholders to wrest control of the *Freeman* from those who directed it. "You certainly have defined your responsibility as regards the Freeman," Croke wrote Walsh on the day his letter appeared, "very clearly. . . . I know nothing whatever about the future directorate. Gray wrote to me yesterday to ask me what I thought of the new Board (to be) and I replied in one line, that 'I thought nothing of them, as I knew nothing of them'" (W). "I wonder," he asked Walsh, "who is Gray's adviser—or has he any? 'Tis to be feared he will fall between two stools. He wishes to conciliate all parties, and like the man and his Ass in the fable, will hardly please anybody."

When Dillon and O'Brien entered Galway jail in February to serve their long-deferred six-month sentences, which they had avoided the previous year only by escaping to America, the question of the course they would pursue on their release was still very much in doubt. Though they had, after the failure of their Boulogne negotiations with Parnell in early February, jointly declared against his leadership, the more fundamental question remained: would they fight him or retire from politics when released at the end of July? In the months just prior to their release they painstakingly explored the possibilities in letters smuggled to each other through the kind offices of the priest who was, presumably, attending to their spiritual needs as well. "I have of course," Dillon wrote O'Brien in early June, "been thinking of our miserable situation wh[ich] does not improve from day to day."[49] "I cannot doubt that this last outburst of filth," he continued, referring to T. M. Healy's most recent editorials in the newly founded *National Press*, "has been a plot of Healy's with the view of getting things into what he considers a wholesome condition for our release—which of course he looks forward to with considerable uneasiness." Healy had, in fact, actually gone so far as to accuse Parnell of stealing the funds entrusted to his

48. *National Press*, August 22, 1891.
49. O'Brien Papers, National Library of Ireland, Dublin (cited hereafter as O'B), Dillon to O'Brien, no date, Tuesday [June 9, 1891?].

care for Party purposes.[50] Further, that the Irish Bishops and a large and influential section of the Party seemed to endorse Healy's policy of war to the knife, and the knife to the hilt, caused Healy to emerge, especially after the failure of the Boulogne negotiations and Dillon's and O'Brien's incarceration, as the "strong man" among those who opposed Parnell. "The articles in the Press," Dillon continued, "are beastly—And it [is] atrocious that H. should have succeeded in getting Dr. Croke to lend himself to such a business."[51] Dillon then promised to send O'Brien, in about three weeks, a memo outlining the conclusions he had reached concerning their future course of action.

"I think," he wrote O'Brien some weeks later,

it would be posssible to carry on the movement successfully in the face of Mr. Parnell's hostility given the following—1st that you had control of a paper. 2nd that the Freeman was neutralized or brought over and I believe that can be done if you were to use your influence with Gray. 3rd that we find ourselves able to control Healy or to isolate him with a small following and finally last—if we could secure O'Connor-Sexton and the majority on our side I should not object to come to an open rupture with Healy—it might be the occasion of a junction with some of the other side.[52]

"Given these conditions," Dillon concluded, coming around again to his starting point, "I believe it would be possible to face Parnell and carry on in spite of him." One might well ask, on reading Dillon's program, who was the real enemy—Parnell or Healy? In his analysis, however, Dillon assumed Parnell was politically dead and the funeral was only a matter of time. His real political astuteness was demonstrated by his assertion that, in the end, Healy must occupy the political grave immediately next to Parnell's. O'Brien agreed that Healy must be buried, but he was much more sanguine than Dillon about the prospects of persuading a large section of Parnell's more reasonable followers to join them in reconstituting the Party.

Dillon replied that he was certainly willing to offer the Parnellites terms, the core of which would be maintenance of the Liberal-Nationalist alliance; but if they refused, and he did not see how they

50. *National Press*, June 1, 1891.
51. O'B, Dillon to O'Brien, no date, Tuesday [June 9, 1891?].
52. O'B, Dillon to O'Brien, no date.

could do otherwise, as they were so deeply committed to Parnell, he thought there were really only two alternatives open to O'Brien and himself—to join those who opposed Parnell or retire from politics. "But I confess," Dillon explained, "that I have always felt that in public life—if one agrees with the principle of a party and objects to its methods—the proper course is to join the party and try to alter it from within."[53] As the date of their release drew near, Dillon's conviction deepened that the only possible course was to join the Party and fight both Parnell and Healy. Every day, he emphasized to O'Brien, "during which we hold aloof from them after our release will increase Healy's power with the party and with the Bishops— and lesseñ the chance of our being able to induce the majority to adopt a conciliatory attitude."[54] On the morning of their release, therefore, they unequivocally declared against Parnell, while holding out the olive branch to all men of good will who would join them in reconstituting the Party. "I say deliberately," Dillon announced that morning in Galway, "that my voice shall always be given in favor of welcoming any rational, patriotic and reasonable offer which comes from any quarter—I care not where—and which points towards a reunion of the national ranks in this country and the banishment of the demon of discord from the people of Ireland."[55]

Dillon's and O'Brien's intention was obvious. They planned to reduce the Parnell and Healy factions to political inconsequence by driving wedges where they thought the factions were weakest. By a policy of moderation and decency, they hoped to separate Parnell from his more "reasonable" followers and deprive Healy of his clerical support. Though O'Brien was optimistic, as usual, and Dillon pessimistic about being able to bring over Parnell's more rational supporters, they were at one on the need to break up the developing clerical foundations of Healy's power. Dillon had argued, in early July, that the result of not joining the Party on their release "would be to increase Healy's power with the priests and with the

53. O'B, Dillon to O'Brien, no date, Sunday [July 5, 1891?].
54. O'B, Dillon to O'Brien, no date, Monday [July 20, 1891?]. See also, for O'Brien's opinion, C, O'Brien to Croke, no date, Tuesday [July 28, 1891?]. In this very long letter, O'Brien discreetly confined himself to his and Dillon's position on the Parnellites and left the Healyites severely alone.
55. *National Press*, July 31, 1891; quoted in Lyons, *The Fall*, p. 293.

party.''[56] He had also pointed out that the ''foolish'' and ''most unwise'' attacks of the more outspoken anticlerical Parnellites had thrown the priests and Bishops into Healy's hands. ''And,'' continued Dillon, ''it is just because I think Healy and the spirit which he is gathering round him so dangerous that I consider it essential, if we are to remain in public life at all, that we should without delay get into the Party and try it out with H. and his gang.'' ''If Parnell,'' Dillon wrote O'Brien some weeks later, contemplating the worst that could happen, ''were to succeed in consolidating and holding together a considerable party, and carrying on an aggressive fight— it is quite possible that in spite of all we could do the majority party would gradually became a Healy-Bishops party—and if I found that the forces were too strong for us—I would then with good conscience retire and have done with Irish politics.''[57] In brief, Dillon and O'Brien were determined that their policy of moderation and decency would not be ground down between a clerical right and an anticlerical left without at least a fight.

While the imprisoned Dillon and O'Brien were discussing the pros and cons of fighting or retiring, the work of destroying Parnell's power steadily went on. The Parnellite defeat in North Sligo in early April had hardly been announced when the ultra-Nationalist bishop of Meath, Thomas Nulty, denounced the local Parnellites in Navan for contesting the election of Poor Law Guardians. Preaching in Navan Cathedral on Sunday, April 5, Nulty maintained he did not understand ''how any Catholic could now follow Mr. Parnell, a man who had shown such an utter disregard of the law of God and the principles of morality.''[58] ''These Parnellites,'' he continued, referring to the local variety, ''had been making it their boast that they did not care about the priests, that they could do without them; but they would find the priests could also do without them.'' ''His Lordship's remarks,'' the *Irish Catholic* noted rather naively, ''made a profound impression on the large congregation present.''[59] Indeed, since the beginning of the struggle, the Parnellites, and more especially those who were Catholics, had not been very tame in the

56. O'B, Dillon to O'Brien, no date, Sunday [July 5, 1891?].
57. O'B, Dillon to O'Brien, no date, Monday [July 20, 1891?].
58. *Irish Catholic*, April 11, 1891.
59. Ibid.

face of clerical denunciation. John Redmond, one of those reasonable Parnellites Dillon and O'Brien hoped to influence, stated the Parnellite case for Catholics best: "I am entitled," he maintained without equivocation, "when the Bishops in a political question advocating a course which my intelligence and my conscience tell me is a wrong one, to perfect freedom to dissent from them, and to recall how, time and time again, in the history of our country, the prelates took action which has since proved to be short-sighted and unpatriotic."[60]

A few weeks later, in early March, when the Party and the Bishops were preparing to launch their counterattack, one of the less rational and certainly less scrupulous Parnellites, Timothy Harrington, published the private letter from the archbishop of Armagh, Michael Logue, written some five months before, in October 1890, and sent to Parnell in the name of the Episcopal Body.[61] The letter, if taken in its proper time context (that is, *before* the attempt to depose Parnell as Leader), proved to be no more than a reasonable protest against irresponsibility. Introduced, however, in the heat of a bitter power struggle, it raised rather sinister, if not ugly, questions about the motives of the Bishops in their combined effort to destroy Parnell's political power. The New York *Catholic Review* noticed that Harrington "is now eating bishop without sauce, and will certainly die of it. He has distinguished himself from the beginning by his violence towards the clergy."[62] "For this," commented the *Review*, unconsciously paying a compliment to Parnell's astuteness, "he has not even the excuse of imitating his leader, whose language in regard to priests and bishops has been studiously respectful." Within a month, however, Harrington again had the Bishops in the dock and was pointing the accusing finger. He now charged the bishop of Kilmore, Edward McGennis, with bigotry for objecting to E. F. Vesey Knox as a candidate for West Cavan in 1890 because Knox was a Protestant.[63] McGennis explained that he had not objected to Knox on religious grounds but on the political principle

60. *Freeman's Journal*, February 25, 1891; quoted in Lyons, *The Fall*, p. 267.
61. Original dated October 15, 1890; printed in Healy, *Letters and Leaders*, 1:353–54.
62. Quoted in the *Irish Catholic*, April 4, 1891.
63. Ibid., April 18, 1891.

that the right of the Leader to recommend and the convention to select candidates was, in the instance of West Cavan, being subverted by the Party, who were simply imposing Knox on the constituency. This systematic raising of "red herrings" by Harrington, unfortunately, finally resulted in retaliation in kind.

The occasion was the annual diocesan visitation conducted by Croke about the middle of May. What usually began as an inquiry into the state of religion generally ended as a political processional. After two weeks of visitations, the archbishop climaxed his denunciations of Parnellism at Kilteely by asking how it was financially possible for Parnell to go through Ireland every week by special train "to knock the bottom out of the priests."[64] "I do not for a moment," Croke emphasized, "wish to insinuate that there was any embezzlement going on or any misapplication of the funds, but I simply express my opinion that a public audit of all national financial transactions is absolutely necessary." Parnell, who usually ignored this kind of innuendo, was obviously badly stung, because the day after Croke's remarks were published he replied to them in detail at a public meeting in Wicklow. The very next morning, however, T. M. Healy, in an editorial in the *National Press* headed "Stop Thief," found fault with Parnell's accounting. Healy, who was never loath to fight fire with fire, actually maintained Parnell had for years "*been stealing the money entrusted to his charge.*"[65] The next day, Healy added fuel to his fire by remarking in another editorial that the *National Press* had been waiting for a writ for libel, but none had as yet arrived. "We called Mr. Parnell a thief," concluded Healy; "we repeat that epithet."[66] That same day, Croke explained that all he had asked for was the right for the public to know how the funds contributed to the national movement were spent. "His Grace," wrote Healy several days later, "nowhere suggested that Mr. Parnell pocketed the money. We did. His Grace did not say he was in possession of knowledge as to the disposition of the moneys. We are. He never suggested Mr. Parnell was a thief. We say so."[67] When Parnell offered some days later to submit a

64. *National Press*, May 30, 1891; quoted in Lyons, *The Fall*, p. 271.
65. *National Press*, June 1, 1891; quoted in Lyons, *The Fall*, p. 273.
66. *National Press*, June 2, 1891; quoted in Lyons, *The Fall*, p. 273.
67. *National Press*, June 5, 1891; quoted in Lyons, *The Fall*, p. 274.

balance sheet to O'Brien on his release from Galway jail, his offer was ridiculed by Healy in the *Press*. The whole distasteful subject was allowed to drop, except for a sarcastic reference to the unproduced balance sheet when O'Brien was released. Dillon immediately remonstrated with the editors and prevented any more publicity.[68] With Healy in the vanguard, the anti-Parnellites easily had the best of it in the charges and countercharges. They also had the advantage of being able to focus their abuse on Parnell, whereas their opponents were obliged to spread their slander thin.

The battles, however, were not all fought with words. Slowly but surely the task of breaking up Parnell's political machine, the National League, was carried out by setting up branches of the rival National Federation throughout the country. Early in April, for example, Ballinasloe reported, "almost all the country members of the National League were in favour of the National Federation."[69] The transfer from the league to the federation, however, did not always proceed so smoothly. In Macroom a "body of Parnellites marched into the meeting in military order with a banner, on which was the inscription, 'God Save Parnell.' The Nationalists tore their banner from them, made cudgels of the poles, and hunted the Parnellite 'hillsiders,' who fled anywhere and everywhere."[70] By the end of June, Parnell's power outside Dublin and Cork, and a few of the larger towns, was broken. For example, when The O'Gorman Mahon's death resulted in a by-election for Carlow in early July, the question was not so much would Parnell lose as how much he would lose by. When his candidate lost by over 2,200 votes in a total poll of nearly 5,300, it was apparent to even the uninitiated that Parnell would be overwhelmed in the next general election.[71] Parnell's countermove, though forceful and made without hesitation, only

68. Lyons, *The Fall*, pp. 275–76.
69. *Irish Catholic*, April 4, 1891.
70. Ibid., April 18, 1891.
71. Lyons, *The Fall*, p. 278. See also B, 49812, Ridgeway to Balfour, July 9, 1891: "The Carlow election has been a crusher for Parnell. So large a majority was entirely unexpected by either side. Our information is that many Unionists voted for the anti-Parnellites. They are quite fools enough and really deserve any fate that may befall them." See also B, 49830, Balfour to Ridgeway, July 13, 1891: "It will amuse you to hear that my cousin, Edward Cecil, came over from Dublin after the Carlow Election with Parnell, and that the latter appeared to be in the highest possible good humour and good spirits."

revealed how weak his position really was. To rally his disheartened supporters, he called for a national convention of all the league branches to meet in Dublin in two week's time. The convention was well attended—over sixteen hundred delegates—but the *National Press* did not let it escape notice that over half the delegates were from the Dublin area and over one-third were from Dublin City and County itself, whereas only fifty-two delegates attended from all of Ulster.[72]

Meanwhile, as Parnell's political machine crumbled in the country, the Bishops did everything they could to increase the pressure. In late June, at Maynooth, on the occasion of their first full meeting since the crisis broke, they passed a resolution calling upon all Catholics to repudiate Parnell's leadership.[73] Walsh had gone to very great lengths to secure unanimity in the episcopal body for the resolution, especially with regard to the three bishops who had refused to sign the resolution of the standing committee the previous December. Walsh had written Kirby, in fact, on June 25, asking him to explain to the pope, in reference particularly to the coadjutor to the bishop of Clonfert, John Healy, that "I have devised a form of protest against Parnell which *one* of the three recalcitrants CORDIALLY accepts, and says that he takes it for granted that the other two (who were *absent* from our meeting) CANNOT REFUSE TO SIGN" (K). "We send it," Walsh explained, "to them [the bishops of Limerick and Kerry] tomorrow. So please God we shall have a demonstration of *absolute unity*. This will gratify H. H., I know."

"Our Episcopal Declaration," Walsh reported to Kirby again on July 1, "goes to the press this evening, to be published tomorrow. It will give great help to the bishop and coadjutor bishop of Kildare, who have on hands a severe election contest in Carlow. There seems to be only one priest there on the wrong side. Fortunately, too, the dissentient minority among the Bishops is now reduced to one" (K). "Of course," Walsh then observed, "I mean the bishop of Limerick," "I know," he assured Kirby, "that the strongest possible pressure has been put upon him by his friend and political ally the coadjutor bishop of Clonfert, Dr. Healy, but all to no purpose.

72. *National Press*, July 25, 1891; quoted in Lyons, *The Fall*, p. 278.
73. *Irish Catholic*, July 11, 1891.

Dr. Healy has even written him to say that he knows from me what importance the Holy Father attaches to united action, and that as this declaration of the Bishops omits all the political references to Home Rule, the tenants, &c, that were objected to in the former one, there could be no reason why any Bishop should separate himself from the body and refuse to sign it.''

"My worst anticipations," Walsh informed Kirby the next day, July 2, "are realised. The Bishop of Limerick has separated himself from the otherwise unanimous body of the Episcopacy. To-day we have the open scandal of a prominent parish priest in Carlow openly nominating a Parnellite candidate, in opposition to the candidate supported by the bishop and the coadjutor bishop of the Diocese. Ecclesiastical authority is simply paralysed'' (K). After the crushing defeat of their candidate in Carlow, the Parnellites, in desperation it seems, actually maintained that the dissent of the bishop of Limerick, who was anathema to every shade of Nationalist opinion in Ireland, indicated a lack of unanimity among the Bishops on the moral issues involved. Needless to say, the bishop of Limerick soon disabused them of the notion that they had his covert blessing, and they were left higher and drier than before.[74] A week after the Parnellite defeat in Carlow, Walsh rocked the teetering Gray in an "interview" with an American journalist, when he laid the blame for Parnell's continued strength in Dublin directly at the door of the *Freeman's Journal*.[75] Gray was finally intimidated by the force of clerical pressure at the end of July; and when, in early August, Dillon and O'Brien decided to fight rather than retire, Parnell's troubles were coming no longer in single numbers but in battalions.

Parnell, however, presented "an iron front to disaster."[76] With a sublime self-confidence and a political resourcefulness that was almost beyond belief, he resolutely continued to make his countermoves. While his supporters fought a stubborn holding action at the various meetings of the stockholders of the *Freeman's Journal*, Parnell was making every effort to launch a new daily paper.[77] Moreover, every weekend in August and September he crossed over

74. Ibid., July 25, 1891. See the Appendix.
75. *Irish Catholic*, July 18, 1891.
76. Lyons, *The Fall*, p. 278.
77. R. B. O'Brien, *The Life of Charles Stewart Parnell* (London, 1910), p. 550.

from London to speak on Sunday in some remote part of Ireland. At these meetings he struck skillfully at the psaltery in every Irish heart by reminding them in military metaphors that the hereditary enemy could never be made to listen to reason. "If I were dead and gone tomorrow," he emphasized at a small meeting in Listowel on September 13, "the men who are fighting against English influence in Irish public life would fight on still. And they would still protest that it was not by taking orders from an English minister that Ireland's future could be saved, protected or secured."[78] Two weeks later, bareheaded in the rain at Creggs, he maintained: "We fight not for faction but for freedom. I know that you look to Ireland's future as a nation if we can gain it. We may not be able to gain it, but if not it will be left for those who come after us to win; but we will do our best."[79] He returned to Dublin where he remained through Wednesday, September 30, attempting to settle the details of launching his new paper, the *Irish Daily Independent*. That evening he left for London, assuring his colleagues he would return on Saturday week. He did not return alive, however, for he died of an attack of rheumatic fever shortly before midnight on Tuesday, October 6, 1891.

"The death of Mr. Parnell," wrote the editor of the *Irish Catholic*, "is one of those events which remind the world of God."[80] "By the grave which is now open," he reminded his Christian readers,

Charity can scarcely find a place. Such tears as may be shed will be those of Memory. Death has come upon him in a home of sin; he has died, and his last glimpse of the world has been unhallowed by the consolations of Religion; his memory is linked forever with that of her whose presence seems to forbid all thought of his repentance; and we know that he has passed into eternity with never a sign of sorrow for the insult he had offered to morality, for his offense against the laws of society, for the revolt which he has sought to create in his native land against the anointed prelates and ministers of God's Church. In these recollections, there is a world of sadness which is all the more drear that its silence is broken by the echo of a wailing whose sounds have not the cadence of a prayer.

"The darkness is pierced indeed," he concluded, "by the cry of sorrow, let the light of Hope shine not, and there is naught but

78. *Freeman's Journal*, September 14, 1891; quoted in Lyons, *The Fall*, p. 304.
79. *Freeman's Journal*, September 28, 1891; quoted in Lyons, *The Fall*, p. 305.
80. *Irish Catholic*, October 10, 1891.

darkness drear and horrid, Charles Stewart Parnell is dead!'' This piece of smug viciousness, which appeared the day before Parnell's funeral, had the effect of making all existing divisions unbridgeable. That same day, the Parnellite opposite number, *United Ireland*, set up a keening that was simply ferocious: ''They have killed him,'' it wailed bitterly; ''under God we do solemnly believe they have killed him. Murdered he has been, as certainly as if the gang of conspirators had surrounded him and hacked him to pieces.''[81]

Parnell's body arrived in Dublin early on Sunday morning, October 11, and was taken to the City Hall. There he lay in state until midafternoon. Those who came to take their last leave of him read the inscription on the magnificent floral cross at the head of his sealed coffin: ''With loving memory to the man, and as a token of loyalty to his political principles from his parliamentary colleagues.''[82] The coffin itself was strewn with wreaths. The excommunicated Belfast Parnell Leadership Committee contributed one on which the words ''Murder'' and ''Revenge'' were worked chiefly in violets.[83] The Gaelic Athletic Association responded with an apt, if somewhat untraditional, resort to Scripture, with ''An eye for an eye, and a tooth for a tooth.''[84] Shortly before two in the afternoon the funeral procession formed and, to the somber strains of the ''Dead March'' from *Saul*, slowly wound its way from City Hall to the cemetery at Glasnevin. Even by Irish standards, the funeral cortege was huge: some one hundred thousand marched and watched as all that was mortal in Parnell was being laid to rest.

''Parnell's funeral,'' Ridgeway reported to Balfour from Dublin Castle the following day, ''passed off quietly. It was a most imposing affair—unique. There must have been nearly 100,000 people out. They were out in defiance of the Priests, who at the Chapels dissuaded the people from attending. I saw the procession,'' he continued, ''at different times & places during the 4 hours they were passing through the City. There was always the same sad stern look on the faces. I had expected nothing so dignified or genuine.''[85] ''In

---

81. *United Irishman*, October 10, 1891.
82. *Irish Catholic*, October 17, 1891.
83. Ibid.
84. Ibid.
85. B, 49812. See also B, 49830, Balfour to Ridgeway, October 14, 1891:

short," he then pointed out to Balfour, "Parnell dead has done what
Parnell living could not do—he has struck a staggering blow at
Priestly domination. The Parnellites have plucked up courage in
consequence and they will fight on. The new newspaper will be
probably persevered [in]." "The contest," he prophesied shrewdly,

will I believe be one against the priests, who will no longer be able to make
Parnell's immorality an excuse for their interference.

Thanks to the Priests the McCarthyites have made a fatal mistake. Had
they shown a little tact and generosity, they might have brought about
re-union, but the priests were too spiteful. And they (the Priests) have lost
their heads—they are now prepared to lead the movement and to recognize
no leader who is not avowedly their servant.

We have now reached an interesting point, and I hope that the result will
be the ultimate defection of the R. C. Church from Home Rule. But it is
not wise to prophesy in Irish Politics. The Fenians are triumphant. The
organisation of the mob yesterday was theirs and it was most creditable to
them.

"There was no disorder whatever," he then added. "The Publicans
themselves closed their houses and there was no drunkenness. The
most striking feature of the demonstration to my mind was the fact
that it was so entirely composed and controlled by the lower classes.
Special trains ran from all parts of the Country and yet there were
few if any farmers present. Townspeople and laborers—and Fenians
—composed the multitude." "Not a single priest was to be seen,"
Ridgeway finally concluded, "but the two Protestant clergymen who
officiated at Glasnevin followed in their robes."

The following day, as Ridgeway had prophesied, Parnell's parliamentary colleagues, after a grim meeting, issued a manifesto affirm-
ing those principles that they claimed as the legacy of their dead
leader. "They would still," they declared defiantly, "be independent
nationalists, they would still believe in the future of Ireland as a
nation; and they would still protest that it was not by taking orders
from an English minister that Ireland's future could be saved, protected, or secured."[86] When they proceeded to elect John Redmond
leader, and he announced that he would stand for Parnell's vacant

---

"Thanks for your most interesting letters on the subject of Parnell's funeral and the
incidents connected therewith. I have sent them on to Lord Salisbury."

86. *Freeman's Journal*, October 13, 1891.

seat in Cork, it was evident that the Parnellites were determined on a fight to a finish. The Cork contest was nothing less than fierce, therefore, as the anti-Parnellites and their clerical allies campaigned vigorously to elect a local butter merchant. When Redmond lost by over fifteen hundred votes in a three-cornered poll of nearly seven thousand,[87] he and his supporters had no doubt why they had been defeated. "They were beaten," William Redmond maintained in the presence of his brother after the result had been announced, "by clerical intimidation, they were beaten because their priests left their churches and their own business to enter into politics and bulldoze the electors of Cork."[88] "The situation is unchanged," *United Ireland* reaffirmed, "for the clerical power remains as it was at Carlow, at Sligo, at Kilkenny—it remains triumphant. And *the clerical power must be fought; it must be fought and conquered. It must be fought and conquered should we not have a single seat within the four seas*."[89]

The opportunity to continue the fight was not long delayed. Late in November, some three weeks after the Cork election, the Parnellite member for Waterford city died, and John Redmond announced his intention of contesting the seat. Despite appeals for a truce from the archbishop of Dublin and Michael Davitt, the Parnellites were determined on a policy of no compromise. To the surprise of nearly everyone, Davitt consented to stand, though reluctantly, as the anti-Parnellite candidate against Redmond.[90] The

87. M. Flavin, 3,669; J. Redmond 2,157; Capt. P. Sarsfield (Unionist) 1, 161; F. S. L. Lyons, *The Irish Parliamentary Party, 1890–1910* (London, 1950), p. 32, n. 3. See also K, T. A. O'Callaghan to Kirby, November 9: "You have heard of the result of the recent election in Cork. Mr. Flavin is a good Catholic well known in the City. He is Vice President of the Confraternity of the Sacred Heart and during the week before his selection as candidate he was not present at the political meetings but was in attendance at the retreat of the Society of St. Vincent's Church. This I think will satisfy you as to the character of our new Member." On December 7, O'Callaghan reported to Kirby that he had given Flavin the picture of the Sacred Heart sent by Kirby and that Flavin was pleased.

88. *Irish Catholic*, November 14, 1891.

89. Quoted in the November 14, 1891, *Irish Catholic*, with the comment: "Here is the naked truth, open and avowed at last. The watchword of these Irish Marats is, 'Away with the Priests!' "

90. Davitt's reluctance is indicated by his comments to Archbishop Walsh only a few days before he consented to stand: "I have been urged by the Federation to stand for Waterford but I have given an emphatic refusal. The fight of the past year

contest was more than fierce; it was ferocious, as the contending parties fought each other with sticks and stones in the streets of Waterford until the result was announced the day after Christmas. Redmond put new heart into the Parnellite cause by winning a narrow victory over Davitt by 1,775 to 1,229 votes.[91] The defeats in Kilkenny, Sligo, Carlow, and Cork were redeemed for a time by the Waterford victory, because the full extent of the undermining of Parnellite political power would not be finally evident until the general election some six months later, in early July 1892, when the Parnellites would be reduced from thirty to nine members in Parliament, and their opponents would be returned seventy-one strong.

To all appearances, the destruction of Parnellism on a parliamentary level was complete by Christmas of 1891. The Parnellites had lost four of five by-elections, and, indeed, in six months they would count for only one in nine of the Irish Nationalist members in the new House of Commons. But to what extent was Parnellite strength in Ireland really reflected in the number of parliamentary seats held or lost? The Parnellite vote, in the four by-elections that were lost, for example, was far from negligible. If the figures for these contests are totaled, the Parnellites actually polled one-third of the Nationalist votes cast. The Party and the Bishops together had been able to swallow the Parnellites, but that was quite a different thing from digesting them. In fact, the Parnellites proved to be indigestible. What had really been created during these contests was a political focus for a very sizable, hard-core, anticlerical minority, which would continue to exist whether it could find adequate expression in Parliament or not. Indeed, the consolidation of this anticlerical base was the price the Bishops and priests and the majority of the Party had to pay for destroying Parnellite power on the parliamentary level and containing it in the country.

---

has broken down my health and left me, financially, all but ruined. It is in these circumstances I am asked to take a step which would be calculated to send me either to Glasnevin or the poor house before another Christmas comes round'' (W, December 8, 1891).

91. Lyons, *Irish Parliamentary Party*, p. 34.

# EPILOGUE

Parnell is the great mythological figure in modern Irish history. In the popular imagination, he still remains Ireland's "uncrowned King." The myth holds that he brought his people to the edge of their earthly kingdom, only to find that he was betrayed in the great moment of promise by "the priests and the priests' pawns," who cruelly broke his heart and hounded him into his grave. The drama inherent in the story of the fall and death of Parnell, however, has certainly obscured the very real political achievement of that great man. In summary, between 1878 and 1891, Parnell both created and consolidated the modern Irish state. In the creating of that state between 1879 and 1886, he structured an effective governing consensus of Leader, Party, and Bishops, which acquired a formidable de facto control in maintaining law and order in the country. This effective control was then consolidated in two distinct phases. In the first phase, between 1886 and 1888, the governing consensus was transformed from an informal, working political arrangement into a constitutional system. In the second phase, between 1888 and 1891, that constitutional system was so strengthened and hardened that it survived the supreme political crisis in modern Irish history, the fall and death of Parnell. This crystallization of a political system, then, which found its focus in Parnell and which has survived virtually intact almost down to the present day, was the real achievement of the second phase of the consolidation of the modern Irish state.

An understanding of the period between the collective letter of the

Irish bishops to the pope in early December 1888, explaining why they could not enforce his Decree, and the beginning of the Parnell crisis nearly two years later, in mid-November 1890, is necessary, therefore, not only to any real appreciation of that crisis itself but also to a perception of what was, in effect, the consolidation of a unique political system. What provided this period with its real political dynamic, was, of course, the continued efforts of the Conservative government, in the person of Arthur Balfour as Her Majesty's chief secretary in Ireland, to break Parnellite de facto power in the country. In this struggle, Balfour not only applied all the legal means at his disposal by enforcing the rigors of the Crimes Act but also resorted to such questionable and extralegal measures as secretly continuing to encourage the pope and his advisers to take action in Ireland, as well as promoting the formation of a landlord syndicate that had the government's covert blessing and support. Although Balfour's efforts to smash Parnellite power by coercion, as well as his attempts to impair, if not to wreck, the Clerical-Nationalist alliance by driving a wedge at Rome, were essentially unsuccessful, he certainly did increase government pressure on the alliance by encouraging and sustaining the landlord syndicate. The syndicate put heart and money into a landlords' cause that was in a state of virtual collapse, and the leaders of the agrarian agitation found both that the Plan was more expensive and that their clerical allies were a good deal less enthusiastic about the agitation than formerly. The result was that the initiative in the agitation fell to the agrarian wing in the Party, led by Dillon and O'Brien, and though neither the Leader, nor the Bishops, nor the majority of the Party was eager to extend the struggle, the agrarian wing continued to force the pace.

Parnell patently dragged his feet on the agrarian agitation from beginning to end. The Bishops were also only reluctantly brought to acquiesce by the fear that their overt refusal to participate might place their own power and influence in an even worse predicament if the agitation should collapse. The situation in the Party was more complex, especially because the agrarian wing comprised so large and active a group. Still, though some forty members of the Party were prosecuted at one time or another for their efforts in behalf of the agitation, the agrarian wing was never able to muster anything like a clear majority in the Party. This is not to say, of course, that the Leader, the Bishops, or the Party was unaware of the importance of the agrarian agitation to the continuing vitality of the Nationalist movement. They all realized that, if the government were allowed to crush the agitation, their de facto control in the country, which in the last analysis depended on the confidence of the tenantry, would be considerably impaired, if not indeed broken. That was why Parnell at critical moments, however reluctantly, moved in the direction of supporting the agitation. His spirited speech in late May 1889 in the House of Commons, when the landlord syndicate was obviously gaining ground, in which he supported William O'Brien in defense of the tenants, was certainly a gesture in this direction. His agreeing to the creation of the Tenants' Defense Association by Party resolution in July, yet refusing to breathe life into it as Leader until October, and then only under his own close supervision, was yet another very clever effort to play for time.

Parnell was obviously attempting to contain the agrarian agitation and was determined that it should not trench on what he thought was the real issue—the ratification of his de facto state by a British Parliament in a measure of Home Rule. The extraordinary success of the Tenants' Defense Association in the winter of 1889–90, however, in putting new life into the National movement and in raising a very considerable defense fund for the tenants, was probably unexpected by Parnell. Yet when he was able, in concert with Gladstone, to mount a substantial political assault on the government in early 1890 in the House of Commons, he undoubtedly understood that whatever its success, the new Association was no longer likely to steal much thunder from the political side of the National movement. Indeed, the reopening of the association's subscription list by Party resolution in early October 1890, and the departure of a strong Party delegation later in the month for the United States to raise more funds, only provided, in the new parliamentary context, more grist for Parnell's revitalized political mill. Parnell's ability to contain in the long run such formidable political personalities as Dillon and O'Brien was not simply a function of his own very great political gifts, for his own stature as Leader of the Irish nation at home and abroad had been considerably enhanced between 1888 and 1890. His vindication before the world, in the collapse of the *Times*'s case against him, with the confession and suicide of Pigott, had so exalted him in the popular estimation that his political ascendancy in Ireland appeared to be unquestionable. In any dealing with the agrarian wing of the Party, therefore, Parnell was always very much the Leader in this period, and he could afford to be brutally frank when necessary because he and the agrarian wing were well aware that he was always negotiating from a position of very real strength.

The Bishops were not nearly so fortunate as the Leader during this period, in their attempts to maintain their position in the governing consensus. In the months succeeding on the issuing of the Decree in April 1888, they had been made painfully aware that they were in great danger of being reduced from equals to auxiliaries, especially on the agrarian side of the National movement. When the Bishops decided not to enforce the Decree, they managed, in effect, to stabilize their position in relation to the agrarian wing in the Party. Like the Leader, the Bishops preferred to see any further agitation channeled in a political and constitutional, rather than in a social and agrarian, direction. The launching of the landlord syndicate in early 1889 upset this delicate balance, however, by forcing the agrarian leadership to take further measures in order to protect the tenants. The Bishops and their clergy, with several notable exceptions among the younger priests, were generally reluctant to intensify the agitation. The lay leadership resented the clergy's more moderate attitude and began to assume more responsibility for the accelerating agitation. The Bishops and their clergy, therefore, steadily lost ground on the agrarian side of the Nationalist movement and were, in effect, reduced to the role of auxiliaries in the founding of the Tenants' Defense Association.

The rising resentment among the Bishops over their deteriorating position in the governing consensus was certainly well articulated in the draft letter addressed but never sent to Parnell, which was drawn up for the Bishops' general meeting in late June 1890 by Laurence Gillooly, the bishop of Elphin. The letter, it will be recalled, noted that there were four problems that, if not corrected, were likely to lead to misunderstandings potentially ruinous to the political prospects of the consensus. In brief, the four problems were: (1) the recent attempt of members of the Party to deal with the education question in Parliament without any previous consultation or understanding with the Episcopal Education Committee, representing the Bishops; (2) the action of individual members of the Party in initiating movements involving the most serious consequences for all without the sanction of the Party; (3) the nomination of members for Parliament without the sanction of convention or even the taking of the Party pledge; and (4) the lack of supervision over the Nationalist weekly, *United Ireland*. The grievances listed by Gilloo1y were revealing in two ways. First of all, they represented what at least one influential member of the hierarchy thought was at stake in the Clerical-Nationalist alliance; and secondly, they reflected an arrangement of priorities, in that complaints were listed in a descending order of importance. Above all, therefore, the alliance was comprehensive, and because the Bishops effectively shared, with the Leader and the Party, joint responsibility for all, they expected their views to be respected and to receive due consideration from all. In the arrangement of priorities, however, the letter correctly put the education question first, for under the terms of the Clerical-Nationalist alliance, that question in all its aspects was the prerogative of the Bishops. The other grievances in the letter were really in a second priority class, and their ranking depended on their given relevance at any special moment. Because the Bishops realized that, in the last analysis, they were also responsible for actions taken in the name of the consensus, they wanted the procedures for sharing responsibility in that alliance that had been worked out, since its inauguration in 1884, to be duly observed.

Although most of the Bishops would certainly have subscribed in principle to Gillooly's understanding of the terms of the alliance as outlined in the draft of his letter, and would have been prepared to take action to defend those terms, many of them would not necessarily have agreed that all his assertions, as in the first point about the lay politicians having seized the initiative in educational matters, were grounded in fact, or that even if some of the assertions were true, as in the third point about the bypassing of conventions and pledges, it was expedient or prudent at the moment to complain about them. What caused the Bishops to take action finally was, of course, John Dillon's imprudent attack on the bishop of Limerick, for in the aftermath of that exchange, the Bishops were given another example of that rough handling they had been collectively subjected to some two years earlier, after the issuing of the Roman Decree. Though the more Nationalist of the bishops, such as Walsh and Croke, were undoubtedly pleased to see the bishop of Limerick publicly chastened, the more conservative, such as Gillooly and Coffey, were aghast at the lengths the lay politicians were obviously prepared to go. If they could publicly single out an individual bishop, and even pursue him into his cathedral city, it was clear that in the long run, none among the bishops might be free to speak out unless they toed the Party line or, what might be even worse, the line of a minority in the Party always prepared to use public opinion as a political club.

When the Bishops assembled for their general meeting in October 1890, therefore, they were more ready to redress the balance of power in the governing consensus than they had been at their previous meeting in June. Archbishop Walsh, who had arrived home only a week before the meeting, must have quickly realized, after his conversations with the other episcopal visitors at Maynooth, that the mood among the Bishops had changed considerably. In any case, when the Bishops did meet, they effected a number of important changes in their own future procedure and policy. First of all, they radically reorganized the way in which they functioned as a body. Acting on Cardinal Simeoni's instructions, which had actually been prompted by Gillooly's suggestions to him in early September, the Bishops approved the setting up of an executive, or standing committee, that could be convened at any time on Walsh's initiative. The existence of such a committee not only made the will of the Bishops as a body more continuous and therefore effective but made Walsh, with Rome's express approval, the real leader of the Irish Church. In the future, therefore, the Bishops would be able, as they had not been able in the Limerick imbroglio, to respond efficiently and effectively to any challenge from whatever quarter. Secondly, a policy of rapprochement with Rome was initiated. Walsh's proposal of a deputation of Irish bishops to Rome to settle all outstanding difficulties was approved, as the Bishops, for their part, agreed to publish a joint pastoral endorsing finally the Roman Decree condemning the Plan and Boycotting. Finally, the Bishops took effective action to check any further erosion of their power and influence in the governing consensus. By privately warning Parnell of the dangers they foresaw in the initiating of unauthorized movements and the lack of control over *United Ireland*, they gave formal notice to both the Leader and the Party that they would no longer be taken for granted. They then proceeded to put some teeth in their private remonstrance by the resolutions they published governing their clergy's role in participating in the recently reopened Tenants' Defense fund. Indeed, the Bishops' achievement at their October meeting was very impressive, for they emerged more efficiently organized as a body for effective action than ever before. They had also secured the critical and vulnerable Roman flank, and they exhibited an invigorated and determined confidence in dealing with the Leader and the Party.

The ebb and flow of episcopal power within the consensus, however, should not be allowed to obscure the fact that the overall power of the consensus increased rather than diminished between late 1888 and November 1890. Though the legal and extralegal pressures brought to bear by Arthur Balfour certainly resulted in a temporary redistribution of power within the consensus, the ultimate effect of Balfour's efforts was to strengthen and harden, rather than weaken, the consensus. The redistribution of power within the consensus was not all to the government's advantage, moreover, in that it weakened temporarily a moderating element, though it certainly provoked tensions and misunderstandings. In a word, the governing consensus was a more serious threat to British power in Ireland immediately before the Parnell crisis broke than it had ever been. The prestige of both the Leader and the Party had never been greater and their grip on the country never more absolute. Once the Bishops had put their own house in order and accommodated Rome, that combination which had brought down the Conservative caretaker ministry in early 1886 and produced the first Home Rule bill was once again fully operative and promising to be even more effective than it had been in the past. A unique political system had emerged, and the constitutional arrangement that had become focused in the aftermath of the crisis precipitated by the Roman Decree had clearly emerged. By November 1890, therefore, the Parnellite de facto state had been consolidated, and there remained only the task of making that state as legal as it was real.

The most convincing proof, of course, that a de facto state had been consolidated, and that a constitutional arrangement had finally crystallized, was the failure of Parnell's challenge to the system he had done more than anyone else to create and consolidate. That, in fact, was the real meaning and significance of the fall of Parnell. The system had worked not only because no member of the governing consensus could impose its will on the other two, but also because any two could exert enormous pressure on the other one. In the crisis that had been precipitated some two years earlier by the Roman Decree, for example, the Leader and the Party had confronted the Bishops, and the Bishops had the prudence and good sense to give way. When Parnell refused to submit, however, he threw the whole system, de facto and constitutional, into a crisis that threatened its destruction. Parnell impugned the probity of the Party by charging that its integrity and independence had been sapped by Liberal intrigue and intimidation, and he also claimed that the Bishops had forfeited their right to pronounce on his moral fitness as Leader by not having spoken out immediately. On his own authority, therefore, he denied to either the Party or the Bishops any special competence to deal with the question whether he was to continue as Leader, and, again on his own authority, he then further reserved to the Irish people alone the right to decide that question. Parnell was unable, of course, to secure the necessary mandate from the people to sustain his authority, and the constitutional arrangement, though severely shaken, survived the ensuing struggle for power in the country. That struggle, however, both weakened the collective power of the consensus (though the Bishops had certainly strengthened their own position in the crisis) and shook the consolidated de facto Irish state. The iron grip on the country that had characterized Parnellite control at its height was seriously impaired by the struggle, and though that control was eventually restored, the governing consensus never again really acquired that pristine authority in the country which had been its hallmark before the fall and death of Parnell.

The most significant fact of all, however, was that the Irish political system survived. Neither British pressure from without, nor the Parnellite challenge from within, had succeeded in bringing it down. Indeed, the power of the British to coerce the Irish was ended with the final consolidation of the de facto Irish state. Coercion would not be tried again by a British government, in fact, for a generation, and when it was tried, after 1916, it only signified the last gasp of de jure British power in Ireland. Actually, the twenty-five years after the fall and death of Parnell constituted a period of significant British concessions to Ireland, which only further enhanced the control of the governing consensus over the whole Irish infrastructure, whether the rationale was Conservative—attempting to kill Home Rule with kindness—or Liberal—preparing the Irish people for self-government. In a word, the reality of British power in Ireland had been rendered marginal by 1890, and it became increasingly marginal until 1921, when it was finally liquidated.

Meanwhile, the Parnellite challenge to the Irish political system actually resulted in some positive gain for the system, as well as loss. The challenge contributed to the system in two unanticipated and fundamental ways. Firstly, because the governing consensus had been able only to contain the Parnellites, and not to destroy them, provision had in fact to be made for the problem of political dissent. In what was essentially a one-party system, therefore, the consensus had to learn early to live with and tolerate dissent. This lesson, needless to say, had important implications for the development of a genuinely representative and democratic tradition. Secondly, the Parnellites, in making an effective appeal to the physical-force party for support, actually helped to draw the teeth of the party of the revolution for a generation. The effect was a further sublimating in constitutional politics of a long tradition of violence, a sublimation that in turn eventually contributed significantly to both the stability and the sanity of the Irish political system.

In the Parnellite crisis and its aftermath, however, a basic readjustment took place in the distribution of power within the governing consensus, which proved to be permanent and which also contributed to the fundamental stability and representativeness of the political system. Because the main burden of resistance to the Parnellites fell initially to the Bishops and the clergy, it would have been indeed surprising, if not unnatural, had the Bishops not been concerned at that critical moment to augment their own power and influence. They had, after all, joined the National movement as the peers of the Party and had been reduced in recent years to the role of auxiliaries, especially on the agrarian side of the movement. They had, moreover, made the crucial decision to redress the balance of power within the governing consensus before the scandal broke, and the ensuing crisis was to them at least an occasion for, rather than a cause of, their new-found determination. Because they did not, however, actually gain more than they had lost after the Irish state had finally been created at the end of 1886, the appearance of a considerable increase in their power during the destruction of Parnellism was greater than the reality. The most responsible of the Bishops, including Archbishops Walsh and Croke, really wanted no more than what had been worked out initially between the inaugurating of the Clerical-Nationalist alliance in October 1884 and the launching of the Plan of Campaign some two years later. They were fully determined, however, not to accept less in the necessary redistribution of power within the consensus that was consequent on the fall and death of Parnell. The Bishops, in fact, would never again be taken for granted by their lay allies and would, therefore, continue to be an integral part of the Irish political system almost down to the present day.

# APPENDIX
# BIBLIOGRAPHICAL NOTE
# INDEX

# APPENDIX

An interesting insight into the bishop of Limerick's refusal to sign the Bishops' declaration in early July 1891 is given in a series of letters exchanged in late February and March among Walsh, Kirby, and O'Dwyer. Walsh had written Kirby, on February 22, 1891, in the course of a long letter:

In the meantime, with or without help from Rome, we are doing our best to fight the enemy. The Catholic spirit of our people was, of course, a good deal shaken by the proceedings between the Duke of Norfolk and the Cardinal Secretary of State, followed up as these were by the famous Decree of the H. O. But, please God, every thing will turn out well.

One or two communities of friars in Dublin are openly Parnellite. But here again we are powerless. They know they have a solid support in their Cardinal Protectors &c &c. [K]

Kirby obviously replied by asking for more information, for Walsh explained, on March 5:

As for the communities concerned, there would be no possibility of doing anything. Y. G. can understand how much can go on in the way of conversation &c., making a general impression and completely undermining the acts of authority, without there being anything on which any one could lay a finger as a basis for a serious accusation.

But the serious danger is the old one, of want of solid unity among the Bishops. The experience of the last few years has shown how much harm is done by the ostentatious taking of of an independent attitude even by a miserably small minority.

It is now openly stated among the Parnellites that the Bishop of Limerick —who, as Y. G. knows, refused to sign our joint Episcopal document—is keeping studiously aloof from his brethren, and this on the ground that it is all nonsense for the Bishops to say that a question of morality is involved —the only question being one of ''good taste'' (!) in the party retaining a leader who has been publicly discredited.

I assume that the fact of three Bishops not having signed the protest has not escaped notice? It is well to have it distinctly understood that the opposition so persistently maintained by that section to the action of the Episcopal body is the direct result of the encouragement given to them on more than one occasion. Ridiculous as it seems, they now habitually take up, at our meetings, the attitude and tone of people fighting for the authority of the Holy See in the face of an all but schismatical episcopacy of the country. [K]

Kirby was obviously impressed by Walsh's arguments, and also by a letter he received from Croke dated March 6 (K), for he took it upon himself to write the bishop of Limerick, setting out Walsh's views as his own. O'Dwyer replied on March 18 with what was really one of his most clever and devastating efforts:

And now having disposed of these matters of business, allow me to thank Yr. Grace most heartily for the frank and even paternal manner in which you have given me your views upon my action or rather inaction in the present political crisis. It is of great importance for one placed so near events as I am to learn the impartial and deliberate judgment of one whose very remoteness from the scene of action enables him to study it with more calmness and accuracy: and I am sure that I need not say that I shall study Yr. Grace's views with the utmost care and give them the full consideration which on every ground they deserve.

As to Mr. Parnell there can be no doubt or room for hesitation as to his utter unfitness for the position of leader of a Catholic Nation, and you need not have the least apprehension that at any time one word will be spoken in his favour by any priest in Limerick or any countenance given to his supporters. But there are circumstances of a total character in which perhaps Yr. Grace may be able to give us some assistance that would simplify matters.

The anti-Parnellite Member for this City transgressed all bounds of decency last year in his attacks upon Mgr. Persico, and the Holy See, and in his personal insults to me. So bad was his conduct that we never can support him unless he withdraws those outrages and apologises for them.

One of our County Members—Mr. William Abraham—is even worse. He is one of the worst libertines whom I have ever known, and it is a matter of common rumour, and I believe true, that he returned himself an Atheist in the last census paper. Surely such a man is not the fit representative for so Catholic a Constituency as ours, and it is a rather excessive demand on the cooperation of a bishop and his priests to ask them in the name of morality to take an active part in supporting such a fellow. Yet that is the position in which I am placed; and if unsatisfactory consequences follow Mr. McCarthy and his friends have only themselves to blame. It is not too much to require as the condition of our support that we get as our Candidates men of good moral character whom Catholics may trust.

It is very painful to find also in the *National Press* and other anti-Parnellite organs constant reference to the Plan of Campaign as if the Pope had never condemned it. Parnell's crime is bad enough; but in my opinion this continuous sapping of the people's faith in the Holy See is worse, and the present resistance to authority of the Bishops is the first fruit that it is bearing already.

If Yr. Grace could bring your great personal influence to bear on those who have the direction of Irish affairs so as to have these things remedied, you would I presume to think render a great service to our Country and its people. [K]

# BIBLIOGRAPHICAL NOTE

The sources for this study were mainly archival, and the printed materials used were few in number. I have not listed the books, articles, and newspapers in a formal bibliography because the reader will easily find what is pertinent in the footnotes. Two works that have been liberally used in the writing of this volume, however, deserve especial mention: Conor Cruise O'Brien's *Parnell and His Party, 1880–1890* (Oxford, 1957), and Patrick J. Walsh's *William J. Walsh, Archbishop of Dublin* (Dublin, 1928). The first is what may be termed a basic book, which no scholar or student of the period can do without, whereas the second contains a considerable amount of original material (sometimes unfortunately inaccurately quoted), some of which has either been lost or is now unavailable to scholars. The archival materials consulted are to be found mainly in Ireland, England, and Rome.

Listed here are the main bodies of material consulted.

IRELAND

The Papers of William J. Walsh, Dublin Diocesan Archives.

The Papers of Thomas William Croke, Cashel Diocesan Archives, Thurles, County Tipperary. Microfilmed and on deposit in the National Library of Ireland, Dublin.

The Papers of Laurence Gillooly, C. M. Elphin Diocesan Archives, Sligo, on microfilm.

The Papers of John Dillon, Trinity College, Dublin.

The Papers of William O'Brien, National Library of Ireland, Dublin.

### ENGLAND

Foreign Office Papers for Italy and Rome, Public Record Office, Chancery Lane, London.

The Papers of Arthur Balfour, British Museum, London.

The Papers of the Marquess of Salisbury, Hatfield House, Hatfield, Herts.

The Papers of Henry Edward Cardinal Manning, Archives of the Church of St. Mary of the Angels, Bayswater, London.

### ROME

The Papers of Tobias Kirby, Archives of the Irish College.

The Papers of Bernard Smith, O.S.B., Archives of St. Paul's Basilica outside the Walls.

# INDEX

## THE AUTHOR

Emmet Larkin, professor of history at The University of Chicago, is the author of *The Roman Catholic Church and the Creation of the Modern Irish State, 1878–1886* (1975) and *The Roman Catholic Church in Ireland and the Plan of Campaign, 1886–1888* (1978).

## THE BOOK

Typeface
Mergenthaler V-I-P Times Roman

Design and composition
The University of North Carolina Press

Paper
60 pound Olde Style by S. D. Warren Company

Binding cloth
Roxite B 53575 by Holliston Mills, Incorporated

Printer and binder
Edwards Brothers

Published by The University of North Carolina Press